Mati Laur, Tõnis Lukas, Ain Mäesalu,
Ago Pajur, Tõnu Tannberg

HISTORY OF ESTONIA

Mati Laur, Tõnis Lukas, Ain Mäesalu,
Ago Pajur, Tõnu Tannberg

HISTORY OF ESTONIA

Original version
Ain Mäesalu, Tõnis Lukas, Mati Laur,
Tõnu Tannberg, Ago Pajur
Eesti ajalugu I-II. Tallinn, 1997
© Avita 1997

Mati Laur, Tõnis Lukas, Ain Mäesalu, Ago Pajur, Tõnu Tannberg
History of Estonia
2nd edition

Translators: Anu Õunapuu (part I and IV-V), Leelo Linask (part II),
 Kristjan Teder (part III), Ester Roosmaa (part VI-X)
Editor (English-language edition): Mel Huang
Layout: Heiki Savitsch, Terje Hütt
Cover: Terje Hütt

© AS BIT, 2000, 2002
 No part of this work may be reproduced or transmitted in any form or by any means, electronic or mechanical, including photocopying and recording, or by any information storage or retrieval system without the prior written permission of A/S BIT unless such copying is expressly permitted by Estonian legislation.
 Address inquiries to A/S BIT, Pikk 68, Tallinn 10133, Estonia.

ISBN 9985-2-0606-1

On the cover: Günther Reindorff. The Oak of Tamme-Lauri.

Contents

I The Ancient Times
1. The Beginning of Estonian History: Origins of the Ancient Times 9
2. Stone Age 13
3. Early Metal Age and Roman Iron Age 18
4. Troubled Centuries 23
5. Estonians in the Late Ancient Times 28
6. Ancient Estonian Religion 33
7. First Period of the Ancient Fight for Freedom (1208-1212) 38
8. The Struggle in the Years 1215-1221 43
9. Final Stage of the Fight for Freedom (1222-1227) 48

II Middle Ages
10. The Lands and Peoples of Old Livonia 55
11. Relations between Foreign Rulers. Cities, Churches and Fortresses 59
12. The St George's Day Uprising: 1343-1345 65
13. Peasantry in the Fourteenth to Sixteenth Centuries 71
14. Domestic and Foreign Relations.
    From the St George's Day Uprising to the Reformation 75
15. Cities and Trade 80
16. The Catholic Church and Reformation 86
17. Education and Culture 92

III The Period of Warfare
18. The Livonian War 99
19. Estonia under the Three Kings 106

IV Swedish Rule
20. The Establishment of Swedish Rule over All of Estonian Territory 113
21. The Strengthening of Royal Power. Everyday Life under Swedish Rule 117
22. Spiritual Life in the Period of Swedish Rule 123
23. The Great Northern War (1700-1721) 131

V Under Russian Rule
24. Estonia after the Great Northern War 139
25. Estonia in the Second Half of the Eighteenth Century 143
26. Spiritual Culture in the Eighteenth Century 147

27. The Abolition of Serfdom in Estonia 151
28. The First Decades after the Emancipation from Serfdom 155
29. Developments in Estonian Society in the Middle of the Nineteenth Century 159
30. Spiritual Life in Estonia in the First Half of the Nineteenth Century 164

VI The Era of National Awakening

31. The National Movement 171
32. The Period of Russification 180
33. Economic Development from 1870 to 1914 184
34. Political Development in Estonia at the Turn of the Century. The 1905 Revolution . . . 188
35. The First World War 194
36. Cultural Development at the End of the Nineteenth and
    Beginning of the Twentieth Centuries 197

VII The Coming of Statehood (1917-1920)

37. An Autonomous Part of Democratic Russia 203
38. Independence 207
39. The War of Independence 212

VIII The Estonian Republic (1920-1940)

40. The Economy in the 1920s 223
41. Development of Domestic Policy in the 1920s 228
42. The Years of Depression 233
43. The Period of Silence 238
44. Foreign Policy 243
45. Cultural Life 248

IX Estonia in World War II

46. The Period of Soviet Bases 259
47. The First Soviet Year 264
48. The Theatre of War 268

X The Soviet Period. Restoration of the Estonian Republic

49. The Post-war Years of the Estonian SSR: Political Conditions and Mass Repression . 279
50. The Post-war Years of the Estonian SSR: Enforced Industrialisation and Collectivisation . . . 285
51. The Estonian SSR as an Exemplary Union Republic 291
52. The Estonian SSR in the New Era of Russification 298
53. Basic Features of Cultural Life in the Estonian SSR 302
54. Restoration of the Independent Estonian Republic 307
55. The Estonian Republic in the years 1991 to 1997 316
56. Estonians in the World 320

Chronology

I The Ancient Times

1. The Beginning of Estonian History: Origins of the Ancient Times

It is estimated that humans have lived in Estonia for nine and a half thousand years.

Considering the history of mankind (which spans roughly 2.5 million years), it is a relatively short period of time. Why then did the very first settlers arrive so late in Estonia? The reason for this was that this country was a part of northern Europe hit by the Ice Age.

The Ice Age. The Ice Age was caused by global climate changes. The universal cooling can be explained by various reasons: the weakening of the sun's radiation, changes in the location of the Earth's magnetic poles, cosmic dust, atmospheric changes and other natural phenomena.

As the climate became cooler, huge layers of ice and snow accumulated on the mountains. As it gradually thickened, the layers started to slide down to the surrounding plains. The ice that accumulated on Estonian territory came from mountains in Scandinavia. From here the glaciers moved even further inland and during the most severe period the seemingly endless sheet of ice reached central Germany and even to areas near Kiev.

The first accumulation of ice began over a million years ago and the retreat of ice from Estonian territory happened as late as 11,000-13,000 years ago. However, the Ice Age should not be regarded as a uniform period. There were four or five cold periods or onsets of ice that alternated with warmer intermediate periods. Some geologists believe that at the present we are also living in an ice-free interval, and the return of the ice could start in perhaps ten thousand years.

However, during the ice retreats, human could have also arrived in Estonian territory. This is quite probable since in the last ice-free interval, about 120,000-130,000 years ago, the climate here was warmer than now and favourable for human habitation in every way. However, no traces have been preserved from these people or their activities, as the return of the ice removed all traces of their existence.

Development of the Estonian landscape. The Ice Age shaped the Estonian landscape to a considerable extent. Glacier sheets one to two kilometres thick carried masses of sand, gravel and clay in them, uncovered the limestone banks in northern and western Estonia, polished the rocks they had taken with them from the mountains and deposited them later as boulders. As the ice melted, lakes and deep river valleys, south-eastern Estonian hills and central Estonian drumlins developed.

One can feel the indirect influence of the ice age even today. Under the weight of the heavy ice load the surface of the earth sunk and, after the ice receded, the surface gradually began rising once again. In north-west Estonia the ground has risen by already some ten metres and the process continues even today – by a few millimetres each year. Because of the rise, Estonian territory has gradually increased at the expense of the Baltic Sea.

The level of the Baltic Sea has also shifted several times within the last ten thousand years; at times it rose and flooded huge territories, while later the level ebbed again. All this occurred due to the rise of the earth's crust in Scandinavia and the sinking on the southern coast of the Baltic Sea and its connection with the ocean.

As the ice retreated, **the Estonian mainland** was considerably smaller than today. The enormous Baltic ice sheet covered a great part of western Estonia and the islands, while Võrtsjärv and Lake Peipsi formed one large body of water. The climate was severe, too. Reindeer, arctic foxes and rabbits wandered around in the plain landscape where vegetation characteristic of the

The retreat of ice from Estonia began: a) about 13,000-11,000 BC; b) about 8500 BC.

tundra started to grow. Encounters with a mammoth or a woolly rhinoceros were also possible. From time to time groups of hunters could have come here by chance in pursuit of reindeer, but no firm traces of them have been found. However, such stopping places are known in neighbouring regions – in Lithuania, Latvia and the Russian district of Pskov.

Before 8,000 BC the waters of the Baltic ice lake broke through to the ocean in central Sweden to the north of the Billingen mountains. As a result of this, the level of the Baltic Sea dropped 20-30 metres. Estonian territory increased by a remarkable extent.

In the eighth millennium BC the climate in Estonia became considerably warmer. Birch and pine forests appeared, elks, bears, beavers and other animals of the forest belt settled here. The first known human settlement in Estonia also dates from this period.

Ancient Times. The period from the arrival of the first inhabitants to the loss of ancient freedom at the beginning of the thirteenth century AD is called the **Ancient Times**. This majority of the period can be studied primarily due to the remains of human activities. Among them are former settlements, fortified settlements, burial mounds, sacrificial grounds, fields, and places where metal was worked, as well as tools and utensils, arms and ornaments made in the Ancient Times. All these – either immovable or loose – are called **antiquities**. This contrasts with later periods, where written source become the primary tool of research.

Researching the Ancient Times. The Ancient Times are studied by archaeologists who carry out archaeological excavations. Science and natural history also provide important information for archaeologists. The amount of radioactive carbon (carbon 14) in charred timber can be measured and, on the basis of this, the age of the wood can be calculated. This method, called radiocarbon dating, does not give the exact date, but a rough interval of +/- 25 years or more. At the same time the age of some end-pieces of logs can be calculated to the precision of one year. Also there is the **dendrochronological scale**, which calculates the changes in the thickness of the annual rings of tree growth. For example, in Estonia this scale goes back to the eleventh century AD. By comparing the rings of growth of the trees from the excavations with this scale, it is possible to find out the exact time of its growth and cutting.

Zoologists identify to which species the excavated bones belong, and botanists examine from which plants and trees the seeds or pollen found came.

Anthropologists study the skeletons obtained from burial places and identify the race, gender, age and sometimes even the illnesses suffered, nutritional condition, and others. **Numismatists** examine the coins discovered among treasures and from excavations. They identify the place and time the coins were minted, as well as trade relations by the composition of the treasures found. Sometimes silver coins can reflect quite interesting details. For example, it was common practice in the Ancient Times to examine by biting to see if the silver was genuine. Thus, by carefully studying the tooth marks on the coins, it is possible to identify in how many transactions the silver coin had been used.

In all, representatives from many branches of science can contribute to the dating, identification and study of materials obtained from archaeological excavations. In writing a survey of Estonian prehistory, all of the above are used. In addition, the analyses of **ethnology,** or the study of folk life are also considered, as many of the buildings, artefacts, customs, method of work and others with roots in the Ancient Times have been preserved. **Folklore** that often depicts old traditions is also worth using. Even **language** can provide essential information on the Ancient Times. The data from comparative linguistics on the development of related languages, the etymology of loanwords in the Estonian language and others gives an estimation of earlier migration routes by tribes and peoples, as well as their contacts with peoples from other linguistic families.

Written sources of both close and distant neighbours give some evidence of Estonia in the Ancient Times. Some historians have argued that Estonians are among the peoples living outside the borders of the Roman Empire who were mentioned by Roman historians and geographers. Scandinavian and Icelandic sagas provide more reliable data on the ancestors of Estonians. Although they were written down only in the thirteenth century AD, they depict the events of several earlier centuries, the descriptions passed on by oral tradition over generations. East Slavonic chronicles mention some events that took place in the last centuries of the Ancient Times. Among western and northern European chronicles where entries on Estonia are rare, the Chronicle of Henry of Livonia is the richest in information. Although the Chronicle mainly describes the adoption of Christianity by the people of Estonia and Latvia and its struggles, it also provides valuable data on the social order, internal relations, fortified settlements, everyday life and religion of the Estonians.

Periodisation of the Ancient Times. The Ancient Times cover a period of more than eight and a half thousand years in Estonian history, from the middle of the eighth millennium BC until the end of **the Ancient Fight for Freedom** in the first quarter of the thirteenth century AD. The **Historical Times** have lasted for only a little longer than seven and a half centuries, from the year 1227 until today. Thus, the Ancient Times make up the predominant part of the entire history of Estonia.

During these centuries, significant changes took place in people's ways of life, of which can be divided into distinct periods. Archaeologists distinguish between the **Stone Age**, **Bronze Age** and **Iron Age**, which in turn are divided into sub-periods. The periodisation is based on the primary materials used for making tools and artefacts.

The **Palaeolithic Era** or Early Stone Age started with the beginning of mankind and ended with the end of the Ice Age in northern Europe. There is no evidence of human settlement in Estonia from that period.

During the **Mesolithic Era** or Middle Stone Age, which lasted from the first half of the ninth millennium BC until the end of the sixth millennium BC in Estonia, tools and artefacts were made of stone, horn and bone.

These tools of stone, horn and bone were still used in the **Neolithic Era** or Late Stone Age (from the first half of the fifth millennium BC until the middle of the second millennium BC). However, at this time such tools were crafted better and new improved tools came into use as well. Pottery appeared as a necessary innovation at the beginning of the Neolithic Period.

In the **Bronze Age** (from the middle of the second millennium until the fifth century BC) bronze objects spread to Estonia. As copper and tin, components of bronze, are not found in Estonia, stone and bone objects remained dominant aside from individually imported bronze tools.

The **Iron Age** is divided into four sub-periods according to object types, burial customs and changes in lifestyle: **Pre-Roman Iron Age** (from the fifth century BC to the first century AD), **Roman Iron Age** (from the first to the middle of the fifth century AD), **Middle Iron Age** (second half of the fifth century to the end of the sixth century) and **Late Iron Age** (from the ninth to the early thirteenth century AD).

Attempts have also been made to periodise the Ancient Times by other principles, using social and economic relations, family structures and so forth.

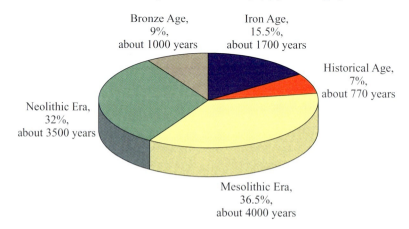

Periodisation of Estonian History (by percentages).

Bronze Age, 9%, about 1000 years

Iron Age, 15.5%, about 1700 years

Historical Age, 7%, about 770 years

Neolithic Era, 32%, about 3500 years

Mesolithic Era, 36.5%, about 4000 years

2. Stone Age

Settlements of the Mesolithic Era. In 1967 in the village of Pulli near the Pärnu River, geologists discovered under a three-metre stratum of sand and clay a thin dark vein containing pieces of coal and animal bones. The **Pulli settlement**, with remains of an ancient settlement from the **first half of the ninth millennium BC,** is the oldest known human settlement in Estonia.

Before Pulli was discovered, the **Lammasmägi settlement in Kunda** was thought to be the oldest. The first inhabitants settled there in the second half of the eighth millennium BC. At the time, Lammasmägi was a small island in the shallow Lake Kunda. Many objects have been found in archaeological excavations of the settlement, especially from the bottom of the former lake.

Today several other settlements as old as Kunda or slightly more recent are known. The finds are very similar to those from the Lammasmägi settlement. All the Mesolithic settlements in Estonia belong to the so-called **Kunda culture**. Kunda culture was spread in all countries on the eastern coast of the Baltic Sea, from southern Finland to the mouth of the Vistula in Poland.

The people of Kunda culture set up their settlements near bodies of water, where they could catch fish and hunt animals thirsty for water. Lakes and rivers offered better opportunities for travelling than thick and barely permeable forests.

Although fireplaces have been found at the settlements' excavations, no remains of dwellings have been discovered yet. The people probably lived in conical tents consisting of some covering over a frame of poles. The covering was made of branches, skins, bark, and in wintertime, turf. In the middle of the tent there was a fireplace surrounded by stones that provided light and warmth during the dark season, as well as fire for cooking.

Tools and ways of life. The tools used by Stone Age men were made of stone, bone and horn, as

Flint objects found in Pulli (arrowheads, as well as scraping, cutting and shearing tools)

well as wood, although wooden objects have not been preserved to this day.

Among minerals, **flint** was used most of all. After splitting the mineral, the sharp edges of flint can be used for cutting. As flint was quite rare in Estonia, pieces of **quartz** were commonly used as well.

In the Mesolithic Era relatively small tools – only a few centimetres long – were used to abrade fat from animal skins, to smooth the surface of bone and wooden objects, and so forth. Horn and bone were worked and cut with carving tools that had strong protruding knobs. Small sharp chips of stone were fastened to a groove hollowed into the edge of the bone tool with a special lute. Arrowheads were also chipped out of flint.

Crystallite minerals, which were worked by polishing, were used for making bigger tools. They were not yet common in the Mesolithic Age. The **stone axes** of those times were of irregular shape and uneven surface, as only the blade was polished. The axes did not have an eye, as the blades were fixed to the wooden handles simply with straps. Smaller axes or **wedges** were sometimes made with an axe-head made of horn. A hole was hollowed to one end of a thick horn for the end of the wedge, and an eye was bored to the other end for the handle.

The people of Kunda culture mostly used **bone** and **horn** for making various tools. They made special carefully polished fishing spears that had protruding barbs on one side. Strong ice picks made of long bones were used for making holes in the ice, giving evidence that ice fishing was practised. In the second half of the Mesolithic Era, fish was also caught with fishhooks made of bone, as well as with primitive nets. Harpoons that had bigger and stronger barbs were used for hunting aquatic animals, most importantly seals and beavers.

Hunting wild animals was important as well. The bones found from the settlements indicate that elks were caught most often (two-thirds of all bones found in Kunda), though the amount of beavers was also quite big. Aurochs, bears, wild boars and goat were game of less significance. Dog bones found from both Kunda and Pulli indicate that dogs were hunters' friends.

Origin of the earliest inhabitants. There is no satisfactory answer as of yet to where the **original home** of the people of the Kunda culture was. Current theories suggest they came from the south. Some of the objects found in the Pulli settlement are made of high-quality black flint, a material not found in Estonia. Deposits of that type of flint are found in southern Lithuanian and Belarus. The Pulli people may not have originated from there, but it was likely that they brought that type of flint with them while they passed through the area. Anthropological analysis of skeletons from a Kunda culture burial mound in Latvia indicates a **Caucasian origin**

Tools made of bone and horn used by Kunda culture.

A wedge in a horn axe head.

of most of the inhabitants, which also supports the theory of their southern origin. However, these ancient people cannot be linked to any contemporary European nation.

Linguists show that some common words in Estonian are not characteristic of either Finno-Ugric or Indo-European languages. It is thought that words like "meri" (sea), "mägi" (hill), "haug" (pike), "rääbis" (whitefish), "eile" (yesterday), "häbi" (shame), "must" (black), "sugu" (gender, kin) and others come from the language of so-called Proto-Europeans who inhabited Europe before the Indo-Europeans – to which the people of the Kunda culture could have belonged. According to certain data, the first representatives of Finno-Ugric tribes arrived here also during the Mesolithic Age. Some suggest that the entire Kunda culture belonged to Finno-Ugric tribes, but there is no firm evidence supporting that hypothesis. However, the first inhabitants of Estonia were certainly one component in the long development of the local population.

The beginning of the Neolithic Era. The use of pottery marked the beginning of the Early Stone Age (or Neolithic Era, spanning the first half of the fifth millennium to the middle of the second millennium BC). The first earthenware was made of thick clay mixed with pebbles, shells or even plants. The shape of the vessels resembled big kettles with pointed bottoms, which were kept upright by digging a hole into the earth or by surround the base with stones. It is not clear, however, from where pottery skills came to Estonia.

Comb-pottery culture. Around the beginning of the fourth millennium BC (or around 2500 BC), a type of more elaborate earthenware arrived in Estonia. Their outer surfaces were decorated with dimples and rows of small indentations. From such decorations the culture is called **comb-pottery culture**. Most archaeologists associate the emergence of comb-pottery culture with the arrival of new tribes to Estonian territory.

The new arrivals were hunters and fishermen, like the people of Kunda culture. However, their skills in making tools and utensils were much more advanced. Flint objects were sharpened not only at the edges, but their surface was also evenly worked. Several types of carefully polished axes and wedges made of crystalline minerals were widespread.

The **burial customs** of the comb-pottery people are also better understood. The dead were now buried within the settlement, sometimes even under the floor of the dwelling. The dead were buried with some knives, scrapers and ornaments – amulets made of animal fangs and tusks, figures made of bone, and also amber, probably for use in their "next life." In the settlement of Tamula, a burial site was discovered with a boy holding the bones of a crane's wings in his hands alongside other objects in the grave.

The finds indicate not only a developed religion but also high **artistic achievement**. Small figures of animals, birds, snakes and men, used as ornaments, were carved from bone and amber. At the same time, it is likely that the people believed the figures possessed magical qualities and protected their owners, maybe even granting the strengths and abilities of such animals and birds.

The spread and origins of comb-pottery culture. Antiquities from comb-pottery culture are found throughout the eastern coast of the Baltic Sea, from northern Finland to eastern Prussia, as well as areas east of Estonia. Contacts were frequent among different regions. For example, amber from the south-eastern coast of the Baltic Sea is found everywhere, even in the

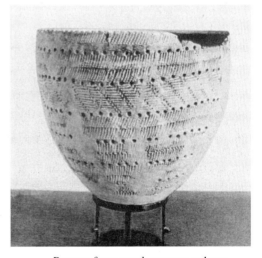

Pottery from comb-pottery culture.

comb-pottery settlements in northern Finland. Tools made of slate from the Russian region of Ladoga and Finland, as well as tools made of flint from the upper course of the Volga River, have been found in ancient settlements in the southern Baltic areas.

Archaeological cultures relatively close to the comb-pottery culture have also been discovered further east up to the Ural Mountains. They are associated with early Finno-Ugric tribes. According to some linguists, the original home of the Finno-Ugrians was located somewhere between the Kama River, its tributaries, and the Ural Mountains.

The people of the comb-pottery culture are considered to be direct ancestors of the later **Baltic Finns**: Estonians, Finns, Livonians, Karelians, Vepsians, Ingrians (or Izhorians), and Votics. Material found at comb-pottery burials confirms this hypothesis. A reconstruction of a skull found in the settlement of Valma shows a man with a broad face, high cheekbones and amygadaloid eyes, resembling those of Finno-Ugrians living in Siberia.

The spread of comb-pottery culture in approximately the same territories where Finno-Ugrians have lived or where place names are characteristic of them supports the theory as well. Besides, there are no other later archaeological cultures with a similar territorial reach associated with Baltic Finns. However, the people of the comb-pottery culture cannot be considered as Estonians yet.

Boat-axe culture. **In the beginning of the third millennium BC (or about 2200 BC)**, new tribes from the south arrived in Estonia. The culture is known as **boat-axe culture** after well-polished battleaxes with bored eyes that resemble a boat. Pottery decorated by cord imprints and specific burial customs were characteristic of the new tribes as well. The dead were laid on their sides, huddled together, with their knees pressed against their breast and one hand under the head, buried in graves dug into the earth. Burial places were located usually away from the settlements either on a nearby hill or by some body of water.

Objects placed into the graves were made of bones from domesticated animals. This indicates that the tribes of boat-axe culture practised **animal husbandry**, the raising and breeding of goats, sheep, cattle and pigs. Some studies argue that they already began cultivating the land. Thus the beginning of agriculture in Estonia can be associated with boat-axe culture.

The original territory of boat-axe culture was located somewhere between the Dnieper and Rhine rivers. They moved to the north in search of new and better grasslands. These people were **Indo-Europeans**. A reconstruction of a skull found in a burial place in Ardu shows a man with an oblong head, high face and thin nose, supporting this theory.

For many centuries the tribes lived side by side with the comb-pottery people. Their relations appeared to be peaceful, as available archaeological data do not show armed conflicts. Unfortunately, there is also no evidence of the merging of the two cultures. According to some opinions, this process finished no earlier than by the middle of the sec-

A man from comb-pottery culture (reconstructed from a skull found in Valma).

ond millennium BC. In the last forty years the dominant theory indicated that descendants of the boat-axe culture became predominant south of the Daugava River, becoming ancestors of the **Baltic tribes**: Lithuanians, Latvians and Old Prussians. Descendants of the comb-pottery culture remained predominant north of the Daugava, laying the foundations to the languages and peoples of the Baltic Finns.

Using the same theory, Baltic loan words like "härg" (ox), "oinas" (ram), "hein" (hay), "hernes" (pea), "seeme" (seed), "vagu" (furrow) and "kirves" (axe) connects the Estonian language with boat-axe culture.

Boat-shaped axes.

However, serious doubts to whether boat-axe culture actually played a crucial role in the development of the Baltic peoples have arisen. At the same time, the influence of this culture in ethnographical processes cannot be denied either. For example, characteristics of boat-axe people exerted an influence on local inhabitants. Blue eyes and light-coloured hair, regarded as typical of Estonians, were not typical of the comb-pottery people. The boat-axe people placed a certain role in the development of such characteristics by Estonians; however, such characteristics developed more so from contacts with Germanic tribes during the Ancient Times and from close connections with Germans, Latvians, Swedes, Danes and Poles through the last few centuries.

A man from boat-axe culture (reconstructed from a skull found in the Ardu burial site).

3. Early Metal Age and Roman Iron Age

Beginning of the Bronze Age (middle of the second millennium until the fifth century BC). The first metal tools arrived in Estonia three and a half thousand years ago. While in many other places the introduction of bronze marked the beginning of rapid developments in economic and social relations, this was not the case in Estonia during the first half of the period. Copper and tin, necessary for making bronze, are simply not found in Estonia. At first it was too expensive to import bronze objects in great numbers. Only the most necessary tools – first of all, axes – were obtained. Most of the other objects were still made of stone, horn and bone, though the skills in working those materials developed even further. For example, at least from its outward appearance, bronze objects were imitated by horn or bone.

Fortified settlements. During the middle of the Bronze Age, local people began to fortify their settlements by building fences from limestone and defensive walls from logs. Four or five such settlements from the ninth to sixth centuries BC are known around coastal regions in Estonia. The culture of the time is known as **Asva culture**, named after the best-known fortified settlement of the time on the island of Saaremaa.

The fact that settlements were fortified shows that valuables acquired by the people attracted foreign attention and needed to be stored. Archaeological finds indicate that such valuables included herds of cattle and bronze.

In the second half of the Bronze Age, **cattle breeding** became the main source of subsistence. About eighty per cent of all bones found in fortified settlements came from bred animals. Sheep, goats, cattle were bred at the time, as well as pigs and horses to a lesser extent. Traces of grain on fragments of pottery indicate that **tillage** was an additional source of subsistence. However, horn hoes indicate that the activity could not be of a large scale.

Hunting and **fishing** provided additional food. On the island of Saaremaa, seals were the primary game. Nine-tenths of the bones found belong to them. Seals were usually hunted early in spring when the food supplies gathered in autumn dwindled. A successful hunt brings plenty of meat, waterproof pelt, as well as fat usable for lighting.

The inhabitants of fortified settlements already knew how to recast bronze. Broken or worn objects were used for this purpose. Complicated axes and spearheads were made. Fragments of casting moulds for making jewel pins, necklaces and bracelets indicate that there must have been sufficient supplies of bronze.

Increasing amounts of imported metal indicate the development of **trade**. In the second half of the Bronze Age, Estonia's close ties with central Sweden, the island of Gotland and south-eastern Finland became obvious. The appearance of pottery characteristic of Asva culture in overseas settlements gives evidence of the active lifestyle and migration of the local people.

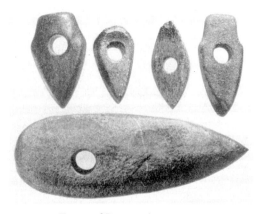

Types of Bronze Age stone axes.

An archaeological excavation at Jõelähtme, displaying the stone cist graves.

The **oldest iron tools**. Compared to bronze, iron was an even better material. Iron tools and weapons were stronger, sharper and more durable. In the fifth century BC, the first iron objects arrived in Estonia. The oldest iron objects found in Estonia, including a sword, large knife and awl, are from a stone burial site in Jäbara in Ida-Viru county. However, during the **Pre-Roman Iron Age (fifth century BC until the middle of the first century AD)** only occasional iron objects spread to Estonia from neighbouring areas. Rarely available and expensive, iron object could not displace bronze and stone yet. Thus the Pre-Roman Iron Age, compared with the Bronze Age, did not change the lives of people much. At that time, people lived in fortified settlements and mostly lived on cattle breeding and maintaining close ties with foreign lands. Therefore both the Bronze Age and Pre-Roman Iron Age are commonly called the **Early Metal Age**.

Burial mounds and sacrificial stones. Contacts with peoples from the west influenced the customs and beliefs of Estonia's inhabitants to a remarkable extent. While earlier the dead were buried in graves dug into the earth, during this time the dead were laid to rest on the surface in **stone cist graves**. The burial mound consisted of a circle of boulders with diameters of three to eight metres and a cist in the centre, bearing a north-south orientation, in which the dead was buried. The space between the cist and circle was filled with smaller stones and the cist itself was covered by a conical pile of stones. Sometimes there were several cists in one circle, or the grave could be surrounded by two or three stone circles. As a rule, the man was buried in the central cist, probably the head of the family as the significance of that role increased. If there are several graves in the mound, then the others are situated between the central cist and the stone circle. One of Estonia's oldest group of stone cist graves (36 graves) was discovered in Jõelähtme adjacent to the Tallinn-Narva highway. Stone cist graves were the predominant type of graves in Estonia until the first century AD.

Some **ship-shaped graves** were also built in Estonia, modelled after similar types from Gotland. The surrounding stones in this model were laid out in the shape of a ship. The dead were buried in smaller stone cists in the ship-shaped graves after cremation. The two best-known ship-shaped graves are located on the peninsula of Sõrve on Saaremaa.

Alongside the stone cyst graves some of the most mysterious antiquities – **small-dimpled sacrificial stones** – spread in Estonia. Over 1,750 of the erratic boulders are found, adorned on which are numerous dimples of five to ten

Early Metal Age and Roman Iron Age

A small-dimpled sacrificial stone in Tumala (on Saaremaa).

centimetres in diameter. The original meaning of the dimples is not known. It probably has to do with the cult of stones originating in Scandinavia that may have been connected to the cult of ancestors.

Iron smelting. Economic development accelerated by a remarkable extend after the local people learned how to smelt iron themselves. **Bog iron ore** is found in many places. The ore, which resembles brownish clods of rust, was crushed and put with charcoal into a conical reduction furnace made of clay and stone that stood about a metre high. Air was pumped into the furnace with bellows to keep the coals smouldering to provide the necessary heat. Coal also played an important role in reducing iron from ore. One furnace-full of ore would usually yield a few kilograms of iron, which had to be worked several times before the smith could forge it into a knife or axe. According to the most recent data, iron smelting began in Estonia about **2,000 years ago**.

Progress in tillage. Progress was made in all areas of life with the use of metal tools. They were most important in the development of agriculture. While earlier people practised hoe tillage in small fields, now, thanks to metal axes, slash-and-burn clearance spread. The trees were felled and wood was left to dry for some time. Ashes from the burnt wood were good fertilisers. For some years the burnt-over fields yielded well, but as the fertility of the soil decreased with use, the fields were abandoned for a new forest to grow. Slash-and-burn clearance was more widespread in southern Estonia, where it remained very important for many centuries.

In areas where the topsoil was thin, woods grew slowly. Already in the Pre-Roman Iron Age, **rotating agriculture** began to develop. Cultivated land was simply allowed to lay fallow over some years and used as a pasture.

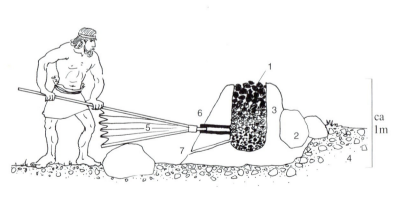

Reconstruction of an iron reduction furnace.
1) coal and bog iron ores;
2) rocks;
3) clay furnace;
4) ground;
5) bellow;
6) air passage;
7) opening for discharging slag.

Dung fertilised the soil and later it could be ploughed again.

The lands in western and northern Estonia, as well as on Saaremaa, were most suitable for primitive tillage, as the limestone subsoil was thin but fertile. The oldest remains of such fields in Estonia, as well as on the entire eastern coast of the Baltic Sea, were discovered in Saha-Loo, one kilometre west of Lake Maardu. The plots of land, which were only a few square kilometres, were surrounded by oblong beds of stone piled up during stone-clearing or by round heaps of field stones. The age of the Saha-Loo fields is estimated at two and a half thousand years.

The establishment of fields allowed people to build **settlements**. Dwellings were often built adjacent to lands suitable for cultivation.

Several contemporary villages in northern and western Estonia may have had their origins in these early settlements. Therefore, the age of a number of Estonian villages exceeds two thousand years. Intensive agriculture and long-term settlement in one location shaped an intense loyalty and fondness of Estonian for their native place.

Centuries of ascent. The period from the middle of the first century until the middle of the fifth century AD is called the **Roman Iron Age**, as at that time the huge Roman Empire exerted influence all over northern Europe, including Estonia.

It can be argued on the basis of the magnificent finds from burials that this period was a period of ascent in the history of Estonian tribes. **Tillage** and **animal husbandry** became the basic fields of subsistence for the local inhabitants. This resulted in an increase in wealth and population. Central Estonian lands, where the soil was less favourable for cultivation, were also taken into use. As a result, the population density increased as well.

Crafts, especially metalwork, flourished alongside agriculture. Bronze was at this point imported to Estonia in huge quantities and several intricate types of brooches, pendants, bracelets, necklaces and rings were made. Some of the ornaments were even decorated with multicoloured enamel.

Now the trading interests of Estonians were directed southwards – to the Roman Empire. Merchants from the Empire and its provinces also arrived at the south-eastern coast of the Baltic Sea.

They were primarily interested in amber and fur from forest creatures. A Roman historian once mentioned that in Rome, one would pay "more than for a living man" for even the smallest amber object. Nordic pelts were highly appreciated for their long and thick fur.

It was possible that grain grown in Estonia was bartered with northern and eastern neighbours for fur, which in turn was resold. Trade towards the south operated through the Baltic tribes. The people of Virumaa (north-east Estonia) had direct contacts with people from the mouth of the Vistula River via the Baltic Sea. Some goods from the Roman provinces were also imported; for example, several brooches, bronze coins, glass beads and even a bronze lamp was found in Kavastu, near Tartu. Local craftsmen developed ornament types that had spread north, along with bronze, from the Baltic tribes.

Burial customs also changed remarkably. Stone cist graves were still built constantly, but now their "inner structure" consisted of rectangular walls built from larger stones. These burials are called **enclosure graves**. A cist was usually a few metres wide and three to ten metres in length, laid out one at a time and formed one grave.

The burials in the enclosure graves were cremations. The remains of bones, together with numerous offerings of ornaments, were strewn among the stones. As the bones and objects were usually scattered, it is difficult to estimate the exact number of cists. An average of ten to twenty remains were buried in each enclosure grave from approximations made on the basis of found ornaments.

Estonians first mentioned. Roman geographers and historians also described the peoples living on the coast of the Baltic Sea. The "Aestii" people were first recorded by Tacitus in 98 AD. It is generally believed that "Aestii" refers to the Baltic tribes. However, it is also possible that the ancestors of Estonians were among them as well, because the area settled by Baltic Finns reached significantly further to the south at the time. Another theory suggests that

The "walls" of the Jaagup enclosure graves after excavation.

Estonians could have been considered as the „Fenns" that was used to describe the Finns in Roman sources.

According to some characteristic burial customs and the distribution of different ornament types, Estonia can be divided into **three** major cultural areas: West Estonia, North and Central Estonia, and South Estonia. Their borders mostly overlap with respective groups of dialects, folk costume and folklore known in later periods. Thus ancient tribal areas can be distinguished already in the Roman Iron Age. At that time a large part of northern Latvia also belonged to South Estonia as the same population lived there. The fact that the Roman Iron Age was a peaceful period without wars probably favoured the remarkable economic progress. In fact, no fortified settlements are known and no weapons either individually or as burial offerings have been found. Therefore there were probably no major armed conflicts between the different parts of the country, nor an external threat.

4. Troubled Centuries

The building of fortresses. In the Middle Iron Age (from the second half of the fifth century until the late eighth century) peace became more elusive. The settlers began to build fortresses. They were built in particular abundance in about the seventh and eighth centuries. The fortresses remained in constant use until the end of the Ancient Times.

For the building of fortresses, hills with sharp inclines and of suitable size were chosen. Artificial earthworks fortified the naturally less-protected slopes of the hill. In South Estonia the earthworks were mostly made of sand and were held together by walls made of logs. In North and West Estonia the exterior and interior of the earthworks were laid as a drywall of limestone slabs without any binding material. Log walls were erected on the edge of the slope, but also on the other sides of the fortress. In addition, a ditch was dug outside the earthwork.

About **120 ancient fortresses** used in the second half of the first millennium or the early centuries of the second millennium are known in Estonia. According to their outward appearance they are divided into four major groups.

Hill fortresses were erected on single hills naturally protected from all sides.

Cape fortresses were built on the end of a hill ridge, which resembles a cape. They offered good natural defences from three sides. An artificial bank was laid on the remaining side. From above they usually resembled triangles.

A reconstruction of a cape fortress.

The "Kalevipoeg's bed" of Alatskivi.

Hill and cape fortresses were the most common fortress types and can be found throughout the Estonian mainland (excluding West Estonia).

The so-called **"Kalevipoeg's bed" fortresses** were built on drumlins, usually on their higher central parts. As they were naturally well protected from the sides, banks and ditches had to be built on the two ends only. Seen from afar they resemble a huge bed with high ends, hence the traditional name after Estonia's mythical hero. The "Kalevipoeg's bed" fortresses were mainly spread in the northern part of the Tartu region.

Ring fortresses are characterised by a high artificial mound built all around the yard of the stronghold. The strongest ringed fortresses were built on Saaremaa and In West Estonia.

The first three groups of fortresses were typical of the eighth to the eleventh centuries. The ring fortresses were built mostly in the twelfth and thirteenth centuries, although similar strongholds with lower mounds may have been used even earlier.

Until the middle of the eleventh century, the fortresses were constantly settled. The settlements were also located in their immediate neighbourhood, as the danger of military attacks and raids was great and foreign troops often arrived out of the blue. The arms and burnt layers of earth found during excavations recall the battles fought. For example, the fortress of Rõuge had been burnt down as many as six times between the eighth and eleventh centuries.

Burials and hidden possessions. In the Middle Iron Age, burials in old-style graves continued. New stone cist graves built in this period were simply piles of stones without any internal structure. Adding weapons in the grave was an important change. They were considered to be necessary in the afterlife, just as if still alive.

From the fifth and sixth centuries, ornaments, weapons and tools were more frequently hidden. Besides bronze ornaments, more valuable gilded or golden objects were found buried in **silver hoards**. The biggest such finds were from Kardla in Tartu district, where silver brooches, a necklace, a bracelet and a thin golden necklace were hidden in a stone cist grave from an earlier period.

Aside from treasures the finds also consisted of iron objects, mainly spearheads, fragments from swords and long blades (so-called battle knives) and sometimes tools. Such finds usually emerge from swampy areas.

Ornaments and weapons were hidden mostly in case of danger. However, the collection found in swamps may also be sacrifices thrown into the water or bog pool.

The building of fortresses, as well as the inclusion of weapons in burials or in major ar-

Troubled Centuries 25

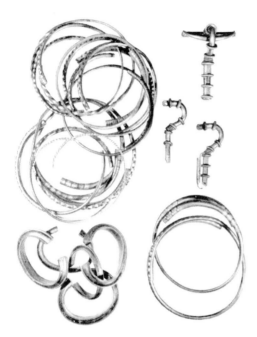

Silver and gold jewellery from the treasure found in Kardla.

chaeological finds, indicates an upsurge of warfare. This was not caused only by minor hostilities between Estonian regions, but also by the migration of tribes and peoples in neighbouring regions during the second half of the first millennium — which affected Estonia to some extent.

Events in the south. At that time **East Slavonic peoples** began to exert influence on the northern part of east Europe. In about the sixth and seventh centuries, a part of them gradually moved northwards from their original home between the Vistula, Dniestr and Dnieper rivers. Near the mouth of the Dnieper and Daugava rivers they encountered the Baltic tribes. A part of the latter was assimilated into the Slavonic group, while others withdrew northward.

Until then the Baltic Finns had lived in northern Latvia. Now a large number of **Baltic** tribes arrived in the region and in the following centuries the natives merged with the newcomers. Only the western part of Latvia remained the possession of the Livonians. Some pockets of ethnic Estonians were preserved in northern Latvia until the nineteenth century.

The Baltic tribes may have even tried to push further north to the territory of contemporary Estonia. The building of numerous fortresses in the south-east of Estonia in the seventh and eighth centuries indicate this as well. The fortresses evidently proved effective, as the border between the Baltic tribes and Estonians was fixed provisionally just south of the current Latvian-Estonian border.

Danger from the sea. In the Middle Iron Age, contact with overseas lands livened up again. Several objects of Scandinavian origin have been found in Estonia, especially the marvellous gilded items from the fifth and sixth centuries discovered in a stone cist grave in Proosa near Tallinn. Peaceful trade contacts contradict the descriptions of military campaigns to Estonia by Scandinavian sagas.

Around the **year 600**, the King of the Swedes, **Ingvar**, landed in Estonia with his army. A huge battle ensued when a large Estonian force confronted the invaders, and the Swedish King was killed in battle. According to a saga, Ingvar was buried on the Estonian coast. Ingvar's son, however, apparently led a victorious retaliation campaign the following summer.

In the Viking Age (800-1050 AD), contacts with Scandinavia became closer. Estonia laid on the Viking trading routes to Byzantium and the Orient, evidenced by the discoveries of silver

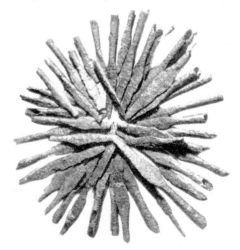

Arms found at the junctions of the borders of Järva, Alempois and Nurmekund regions, close to Rikassaar.
Were they offerings or for denoting some agreement?

Arab coins and spearheads and swords made by Western forgers.

At the same time the sagas depict Viking **military campaigns** in Estonia, boasting of conquests along the eastern coast of the Baltic Sea. However, archaeological finds fail to confirm this. The Vikings did not achieve any lasting success, and the sagas even testify to their serious defeats. For example, Halfdan the White, son of the Norwegian King, was supposed to have been killed in Estonia, while Estonian pirates captured Norwegian Queen Astrid and her son Olaf and enslaved them. In the first half of the eleventh century, several **runic stones** dedicated to the memories of Vikings killed in Estonia were erected. This shows that Estonians managed to stand up to a strong enemy and even conduct counterattacks.

Fateful centuries for related eastern tribes. For many millennia the ancestors of the Votics, Vepsians, Karelians, Merya, Muroms and other Finno-Ugric peoples lived to the east and north-east of Estonia. In roughly the eighth and ninth centuries AD, East Slavs began arriving in those areas. The newcomers mainly settled in places like Old Ladoga, Novgorod and others, which were located at important waterways and were inhabited already by Baltic Finns, Balts, and Vikings. More and more East Slavs arrived and by about the thirteenth to fourteenth centuries, they had managed to merge with the native population. This had great effects on the development of the northern part of the East Slav population. For example, several Finno-Ugric characteristics can be detected in the dialect, folk customs and even anthropology of their descendants in northern Russia. Place names from the Finno-Ugric period have also been preserved in those areas. For instance, many linguists believe that the names of rivers ending in Russian with *-va*, such as the *Moskva* (Moscow), are Finno-Ugric in origin.

It is often suggested that some East Slavs also tried to settle in Estonia. **Sand barrows** with cremated remains found in the eastern part of Southeast Estonia can be associated with East Slav migrants from the Middle Iron Age. However, the sand barrows were built already in the fifth-sixth centuries and have traits in common with a Finno-Ugric tribe closely related to Estonians, sometimes even with the predecessors of the Setus (a Finno-Ugric people closely related to Estonians that live on both sides of the Russian-Estonian border around Pechory). Recently some Russian archaeologists have also suggested that analogous mounds found in the Russian regions of Pskov and Novgorod also belong to the earlier Baltic Finns and Balts.

Relations with Kievan Rus. According to the famous East Slav chronicle "**Tales of Old Times**", some East Slavonic tribes invited three

Excavations of sand barrows in Suur-Rõsna.

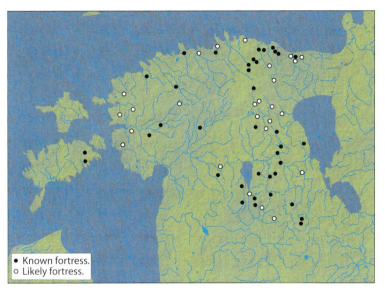

Estonian fortresses between the years 700-1050.

• Known fortress.
○ Likely fortress.

brothers – Riurik, Sineus and Truvor – from Scandinavia to rule the emerging state in the year 862. However, the history of Kievan Rus really begins when Oleh, a friend of Riurik, captures Kiev and unites many East Slavonic tribes.

In the ninth and tenth centuries, relations between Estonia and Kievan Rus were peaceful. East Slavonic chronicles called Estonians and other Baltic Finns living east of Lake Peipsi the **Chudes**. The Chudes played an important role in Kievan Rus. They helped Oleh to conquer Kiev, took part in campaigns to Byzantium and served in fortresses established on the southern border against nomadic peoples. Mikula Chudin, a famous Kiev aristocrat, compiled "The Code of Yaroslav's Sons" together with his princes. Several names of signatories of treaties between Byzantium and Kievan Rus in 911 and 944 are typical of Baltic Finns.

In the late tenth century, relations deteriorated between Estonians and Kievan Rus. Vigorous Rus princes attempted to extend their possessions at the expense of Estonia and tried to subjugate the local people. According to East Slavonic chronicles, Yaroslav the Wise conducted a victorious campaign against the Estonians **in 1030**, built a fortress in Tartu and named it **Yuriev** after his Christian name Yuri (George). However, this was not the date of the town's founding. Archaeological excavations indicate that an earlier Estonian fortress and extensive settlement had existed many centuries earlier.

The East Slavs were defeated in another campaign against the Estonians in the year 1054. Ostromir, a citizen of Novgorod who led the campaign, was killed. Subsequently the fortress of Keava in Harju region was taken in a campaign led by Prince Izyaslav. In the year 1060, Izyaslav imposed duties on the Estonian tribes called the **Sossols** in the chronicles. However, the latter soon drover the tax collectors out, recaptured Tartu the next spring and pushed as far as Pskov in battle. There a major battle was fought where, according to the East Slavonic chronicle, a thousand East Slavs and countless Sossols were killed

The years 1030 to 1070 were noteworthy in the entire history of Estonia, since it showed that Estonians had become a force strong and organised enough to defend their freedom and to fight successfully against the aggressions of a great power. The fact that there is no evidence of campaigns by East Slavs in the following half century testifies to the influence of that victory.

5. Estonians in the Late Ancient Times

The **early part of the second millennium was a period of remarkable development in the life of Estonians.** The population increased greatly and the country soon became densely populated. The majority of North Estonian villages known in later times already existed by the early thirteenth century. Only the more swampy south-western part of the country, coastal areas and some islands, remained uninhabited. At the end of the Ancient Times, at least 150,000 people lived in Estonia.

Areas of subsistence. Cultivation of the land was the main area of activity, which by this time had achieved a high level. Estonians had become one of the northernmost peoples mainly subsisting by tillage. Iron ploughs, which was introduced around the seventh and eighth centuries, contributed to the development of plough farming. Different types of ploughs were used according to the thickness of the soil. With thin soils in North and West Estonia the single-blade **hooked plough** was used, while with thicker layers of earth in Central and South Estonia the two-blade **forked plough** was used. While barley was grown in earlier times, winter rye became widespread from the eleventh century. The proportion of wheat, oats, peas, beans and other crops was smaller.

Ploughland was the unit of land measure. A ploughland corresponded to a field that could be worked with one plough. Usually one farming family used one ploughland. In farming the two-field system was used. Every year one part of the field was sown and the other part lay fallow. Alongside the introduction of winter rye, a more efficient **three-field system** began to spread. In one part of the field was the winter crop, in the second part the summer crop would grow, and the third part lay fallow. The three-field system became predominant and prevailed until the nineteenth century.

Besides tillage, **animal husbandry** was also practised. Cattle, horses, sheep, goats, pigs and hen were bred. In West Estonia where meadowlands were larger, more cattle were bred. In South Estonia a rather larger number of pigs were raised.

Hunting and **fishing** were also of some importance. However, among the bones found during the excavations of fortresses and settlements, those of wild animals make up only some ten per cent. Elks, wild boars, goat, rabbits, beavers, ermines, pine martens and squirrels were the primary game. Fishing was done in fresh water sources inland. On the seacoast there was no permanent settlement that could have fished the sea.

Wild apiculture was also of appreciable importance. Honey was the only sweetening agent and there was great demand for wax in western European markets.

Development of crafts. Each family made most of the necessary tools and utensils, dwellings, clothes, and means of transport for their own use. In some fields, special craftsmen were employed.

Iron smelting and **iron working** had become an important special craft. Local smiths, who used iron smelted from bog iron ore, made most of the everyday tools, such as knives, axes, sickles and scythes. In the late Ancient Times, major **iron smelting centres** developed in Virumaa regim and on northern Saaremaa, where hundreds of tons of iron were smelted for local use and supply of other regions.

The work of **armourers** was especially remarkable. They made quality spearheads decorated with silver, jewelled hilts of swords, and probably even some blades.

Some masters specialised in **bronze ornaments**, which were made in large numbers. Women used to wear numerous ornaments – long-linked chains, jewel pins, elegant horseshoe-shaped brooches, necklaces, rings and bracelets around both arms. Clothes were interlaced with small bronze rings and spirals, which formed original patterns. In the late Ancient Times when **silver ornaments** came into fashion, silversmiths came to the forefront.

In connection with the introduction of the potter's wheel, **pottery** also became a specialised craft.

Exchange of goods. Trading between Estonians and their closest neighbours – Livonians, Finns, Karelians, Votics and the Baltic peoples – became more and more extensive. As trading routes that linked the western and southern coasts of the Baltic Sea with Russian towns passed through Estonia, long-distance trade missions flourished. Trading missions reached as far as Pskov and Novgorod, and traders from Saaremaa were often found on Gotland – the most important commercial centre in the Baltic Sea area. In the second half of the twelfth century, German merchants were commonly encountered on Estonian roads.

Bartering predominated. The main goods imported to Estonia were silver, bronze, iron, salt, better weapons, fine cloth and other luxuries coming mostly from the west. In return, fur and wax, which were in high demand in western Europe, were exported. Written sources indicate that Estonians also resold properties and prisoners seized on raids.

Because of their favourable position **commission trade** played an important role (for example, goods were purchased not only for personal use but also for resale). Novgorod and its vast non-farming hinterlands were provided with grain. The fur, wax and other raw materials received in return were sold in west and north European markets. Probably a part of the goods obtained there were resold at a profit to Russia.

Exchange of goods was a profitable activity as evidenced by numerous treasures, consisting of silver coins and ornaments, hidden in the earth in the final centuries of the Ancient Times. While thousands of oriental coins arrived here in the ninth to eleventh centuries, western European silver coins dominated later times. **Silver** was already a generally recognised exchangeable commodity. Finds of scales, pieces of ornaments among treasures and halves of coins indicate that the value of goods was assessed on the basis of silver.

Trading posts developed on the intersections of major roads where central fortresses and settlements were situated. More craftsmen who of-

Silver treasures from the fortress of Muhu.

fered their products lived there as well. In Tartu an early **urban settlement** started to develop. Tallinn became the most important trading centre on the coast. However, in the late Ancient Times, there were no real towns with special town charters in Estonia yet.

Dwellings and villages. Estonians lived predominantly on the land. Log cabins were divided into a living room heated by a stove and a front room. As grain usually do not ripen in the field at this latitude, it was dried in the heated room or barn. Gradually a universal **granary** came into use, which in the following centuries became a dwelling and workplace characteristic to Estonians.

Farms were usually located close to each other and formed villages. The chronicler Henry of Livonia, whose attitude towards Estonians was hostile, could not help but praise the beauty of local villages. He mentions the village of Kareda in the Järva region as remarkably nice, large and populous. According to the particular landscape, different types of villages sprung up in Estonia. In West, Central and North Estonia, as well as on Saaremaa, farms were located close to each other in the middle of fields, forming **huddled villages**. On the drumlins of East Estonia, farms were established in a line, forming a **linear vil-**

lage. In South Estonia there were **dispersed villages**, where farms were scattered far away from each other.

Parishes and regions. Villages in a localised region formed a parish, which was the most important administrative unit in Estonia. In the early thirteenth century, there were about **45 parishes** in Estonia. Parishes were united into larger units called **regions**, basically due to external threats. There were **eight regions** in Estonia: Virumaa, Rävala, Järva, Harju, Läänemaa, Saaremaa, Ugandi and Sakala. In Central Estonia, where external danger was less of an issue, some parishes (sometimes called mini-regions) like Alempois, Nurmekund, Mõhu and Vaiga, which did not join any region, were preserved.

By the end of the Ancient Times, some notable tendencies of **co-operation** between regions indicate the development of elements of statehood. According to the Chronicle of Henry of Livonia, even annual joint consultations of county elders were supposedly held in Raikküla.

The development of the Estonian nation had started. The people themselves and their neighbours usually used the names of the regions. At the same time, written sources already used the common names "Estonia" and "Estonians."

Assemblies and noblemen. In the eleventh and twelfth centuries, the Estonian population was still relatively united. Free individuals formed the majority of the population. The most important issues were discussed together at assemblies. Fortresses were built together, while pastures and highlands were public property. However, it is thought that field were used individually by families.

The increase in private property was accompanied by **material inequality**. Those already wealthier increased their wealth even more by trading or by loot from military campaigns. They used prisoners taken during campaigns were enserfed, though usually as servants instead of slaves without rights.

In most cases wiser and more influential men with higher social positions in the villages and parishes became **elders**. The nobility, called "elders," "the rich" or "the better" by Henry of Livonia, also began to develop. They were more numerous in South Estonia. The authority of individual nobles was so great that entire villages were named after them. For example, Henry of Livonia on several occasions referred to the village of Lembitu, one of the most influential elders of Sakala.

Military standard. Relations with neighbours remained peaceful for the most part. Once in awhile mutual raids and campaigns occurred. The situation became more serious as state-like unions developed in neighbouring areas. These

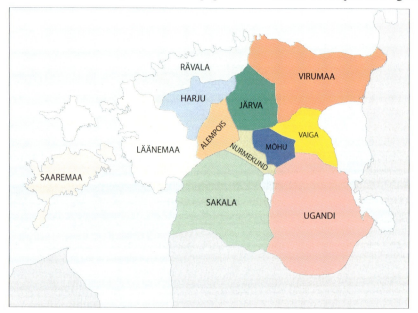

Ancient regions of Estonia.

new groupings could raise larger military units for their campaigns, which posed a threat to Estonia's freedom. A serious attempt had been made already by Kievan Rus in the middle of the eleventh century. Thus the need for arrangements to meet the changed circumstances arose.

In the middle of the eleventh century several smaller fortresses were abandoned for larger and stronger ring fortresses. Especially strong fortresses were erected in **West Estonia** and on **Saaremaa**. For example, in order to erect the 580 metre-long and 8-10 metre-high wall of the fortress in Varbola (which stands partially today), more than 32,000 horse-loads of limestone were needed — which had to be chipped, carried to the fortress site, and placed with precision. The gates of the fortresses were fortified with special care. For some fortresses long gateways with multiple gates were built to defend the entrance. In these sections higher defensive towers were also built.

The excavated gateway of the fortress of Varbola.

The gate of the fortress of Varbola (reconstruction).

Spears were an important component of the Estonians' weaponry. Smaller and lighter javelins, as well as bigger and stronger spears, were used. Quite a few men, mainly horsemen, also used swords, battle-axes and clubs. Bows and arrows were used somewhat less. Armature mainly consisted of shields, though some wealthier men could also afford chain mail made of iron links. There is, however, no evidence of helmets used by Estonians.

A **district army** consisted of both cavalry and infantry. Primitive siege craft was also known. At sea, the men of Saaremaa were skilful on their speedy ships, which resembled Viking ships. Until the Ancient Fight for Freedom, the military level of Estonians was sufficient for repelling the attacks of close neighbours.

Relations with neighbours. To the south of Estonians lived the ancestors of Latvians: Lettgallians, Selonians, Semigallians and Couronians. An extensive area by the Gulf of

Estonians in the Late Ancient Times

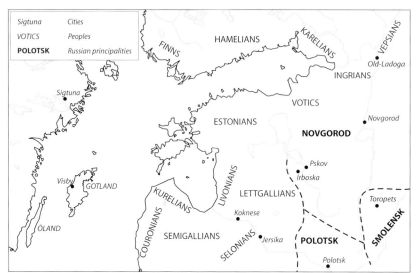

Estonians and their neighbours.

Riga and in northern Couronia belonged to the Livonians and Kurelians, **kindred Finno-Ugric peoples** to the Estonians. According to Henry of Livonia, disputes and armed conflicts erupted quite often between Estonians and Lettgallians, with the Lettgallians apparently suffering more. In the south, Lithuanians were a much stronger enemy, evidenced by several desolating looting raids to Estonia. In the twelfth century, Swedish and Danish state and church authorities continued their attempts to subjugate Estonia and christen the people. However, there was no decisive outcome. At the same time, Estonians themselves became more active in organising military and looting raids to other areas on the coast of the Baltic Sea.

In the year 1170, the navy of the Danish King fought a battle against the Estonians and Kurelians, who were raiding the coast of the island of Øland for two days. In the **year 1187**, the "pagans from the Eastern Sea" captured and burnt down **Sigtuna**, Sweden's most important town at the time. Estonians, Kurelians, Karelians or a joint army of peoples living on the eastern coast of the Baltic Sea are thought to be responsible for the sacking of Sigtuna, which remained in ruins. However, Estonians, especially those living on the coast and on Saaremaa, had good relations with Kurelians, Finns, Karelians and the people of Gotland.

The danger from the east diminished in the twelfth century as Kievan Rus had disintegrated into smaller parts. At that point, only minor conflicts with the nearby **feudal republic of Novgorod** occurred. At times the rulers of Novgorod organised raids that mostly affected East Estonia. During the years 1111-1116, Estonia had to fight the army of Prince Mstislav of Novgorod three separate times. Hi successor, Prince Vsevolod, also organised three campaigns during the years 1130-1134. The three campaigns did not bring any lasting conquests. This is confirmed by East Slavonic chronicles, which also depicted counter-raids by Estonians. In the second half of the twelfth century, Estonians apparently became the initiator of conflicts.

Thus in the year 1777 "Estonians of the entire country" organised a large campaign against Pskov, though that was followed by a counterattack. In 1190 the ships of "seaside Chudes" also came under attack on Lake Peipsi, perhaps in anticipation of a major campaign planned by the Estonians. Subsequently the troops of Novgorod and Pskov conquered Tartu in the winter of 1191-1192 and the fortress of Otepää the following summer. However, the invading army quickly departed thus the victory did not bring south-eastern Estonia under Slav rule.

In the late Ancient Times, a relative balance of power reigned over the eastern coast of the Baltic Sea. Although the Estonians did not have a state yet, they were organised well enough to repulse conquest attempts by neighbours.

6. Ancient Estonian Religion

Religion was the most important aspect of the spiritual life of ancient Estonians. However, there was no single ancient Estonian religion nor fixed customs characteristic of the entire Ancient Times. In the course of the long period, religious views underwent several changes. New customs came about due to changes in areas of activity. The religion of Stone Age hunters and fishermen certainly differed from that of Iron Age people practising tillage and animal husbandry. Close contact with neighbouring tribes and peoples also resulted in changes in religious views. Although the Estonian territory is small, quite a few regional peculiarities developed in religious practice. This also supports the theory that there was no single religion with defined rules. Unfortunately, there is only a vague idea of this aspect of the lives of ancient Estonians, as very few sources reflecting ancient beliefs and thought have been preserved. There are mere allusions in some older written sources, but most of the information were obtained from folk traditions and folklore collected at the end of the nineteenth and beginning of the twentieth centuries. Sorting out information that comes from the Ancient Times is an extremely complex task. Unfortunately, the examination of ancient cult sites by archaeologists failed to yield considerable results as of yet.

The Palivere sacrificial tree.

Force. Force was one of the central notions and elements of ancient beliefs. It was believed that people, like all other living creatures, possess a special force or power besides their physical body. There was also force in certain objects, places, and in the sky. The latter became clearly evident during thunderstorms.

Words also could contain force. Using words, spells could be cast, curses could be placed, and illnesses could be cured. The individuals able to do so had to possess a special force themselves. Such individuals were called **wizards** or sorcerers. These people usually un-

Sacrificial stone.

derstood nature better and could "direct" its forces. The wizards passed their knowledge from generation to generation, which included knowledge of herbal qualities and sensitivity to natural phenomena, which allowed them to predict the future with some accuracy. Estonian wizards, as well as those of their eastern neighbours, were very famous. According to East Slavonic chronicles, "Chude" wizards were usually preferred above their own.

Force was not distributed evenly. The existence of force must have been a reason why some stones, springs and trees were considered sacred while others, some more spectacular in appearance, were not.

Animals and human beings held most of their force in their heads, hearts, blood, nails, hair, fur, and teeth. The teeth and tusks of beasts were worn around the neck or attached to clothing from the Stone Age to the end of the Ancient Times, probably for the bearer to take possession of the force of the animals or even just for protection.

A slain enemy was often beheaded or had his heart removed, in order to destroy his force. Hair of slaves was chopped off to take away their force and break down their resistance. Young women also had their hair cut off when they married, to ensure their total submission to men.

It was also possible to take hold of an animal's force by eating its organs and drinking its blood. The Chronicle of Henry of Livonia depicts a startling example. In the year 1223, warriors from Sakala captured the Danish bailiff of Järva region, Hebbe. The Chronicle described how the warriors "plucked out the heart of Hebbe, who was still alive, and roasted it over a fire, dividing it amongst themselves and eating it to be strong against the Christians."

Soul. The soul bore the uniqueness of an individual and was very important in keeping the physical body alive. While sleeping, a person's soul could escape the body temporarily, move around, and sometimes even settling in another person's body. In the case of death, the soul left permanently. Opinions differed on where the departed souls end up after death. In some areas it was believed that the soul of dead people could be transferred to insects, thus it was forbidden to kill "animals of the soul" like beetles, spiders, ants, and others. However, the predominant belief at the time was that the soul simply continued in a new "home," such as a sacred grove or cemetery.

Belief in the afterlife was important as well, which affected burial customs. Ornaments, tools, utensils, weapons, and even food, were put into graves for the dead. Food and drinks were also taken to the burial sites later, sometimes for commemoration meals.

The Setu people, a kindred Finno-Ugric people living in south-east Estonia, have preserved this custom even today. Once a year, relatives gather in the cemetery, sit down by the nearest grave and have a meal after commemorating the dead. Some pieces of meat are placed at the edge of the grave and a drop of alcohol is poured on the cross.

The souls of the dead continue to influence the lives and destinies of their families. In late autumn, between St Michael's Day and St Martin's Day, it was the **time of souls**. At that time the souls of the dead roamed, possibly visiting their homes. To treat them, a table was set offering the best food, as during the autumn harvest and butchering time fresh foods, such as meats, bread, dumplings and porridge, were available. In many places, food was taken behind the farmhouse to the loft, onto the poles for drying grain in the barn or to the sauna. The sauna was heated for them and water, soap and birch whisks were readied for taking a traditional sauna. The time of souls was also a quiet time, as noise displeased them.

Attitude towards nature. Nature was connected closely with the lives of ancient Estonians. People believed that they were a part of nature, and also believed that animals, birds, insects, plants, trees, as well as bodies of water, the Sun, and the moon, had souls. Such attitude towards nature is called **animism**. In fact, animism is characteristic to all peoples at a certain stage of development.

Ancient Estonians in their relations with natural objects followed the maxim, "treat others as you expect them to treat you." If someone harmed or destroyed anything, the respective soul could exact revenge; for example, the forest could misguide the traveller, water could drown the swimmer, the earth could infect the healthy with disease. Therefore a friendly attitude towards nature prevailed. All aspects of nature were regarded as equal and respected as such. Ancient Estonians were far from acting as if they were the masters of nature.

Spirits, fairies, gods. To the ancient Estonians, there were also spirits and fairies that guarded and protected nature, such as forest "fathers" and "mothers," meadow "fathers" and "mothers," as well as field and water spirits. In North Estonia they were usually called fairies, probably a loan word from ancient Germans.

Some fairies also lived in the farm or nearby areas. As late as the nineteenth century, **Tõnn**, a home fairy, was still kept in many places around Pärnu and Viljandi, while the Setu people kept **Peko** in their granaries. The latter was taken out on festive occasions connected with fieldwork and cattle breeding only. Home fairies were usually more important and have been considered demigods.

Compared with the ancient religions of neighbouring peoples, Estonians had few dominating so-called greater deities. This is the most characteristic feature of ancient Estonian religion. However, the notion of a god itself was known a long time before.

Henry of Livonia named only **Tarapitha** as a deity. The name has been interpreted at times as a war cry or prayer, "Taara, help!" (in Estonian, "Taara avita!"). According to the Chronicle, Taara was born in Virumaa and later flew to Saaremaa, where he became a deity. Some experts in ancient religions think that Taara is a borrowing from the Scandinavian Thor, the god of thunder. At the same time, eastern Finno-Ugric peoples – the Khants and the Mansi – have gods with similar sounding names. Therefore some researchers argued that the Cult of Taara may have come from a more distant past and may not have been a Germanic borrowing. It is also possible that the later cult of Uku, another known deity, could have spanned the Ancient Times.

According to a description by Henry of Livonia, Estonians even had "statues and faces of gods" on a hill (probably Ebavere) in a beautiful forest near the border with Virumaa that were cut down by Christian priests. However, religious experts believe that these were probably not statues depicting deities, but rather in memorial of dead companions in order to preserve their force. The Estonians who witnessed the destruction of the figures were quite surprised to see that no blood flowed from them. This reflects the belief of the times that a statue could entirely replace the person it depicts.

Places of sacrifice. Spirits, fairies and gods were neither well nor ill disposed towards people by nature. However, it was necessary to be on good terms with them. Sacrifices or offerings were brought to please them. There were special cult or sacrificial sites for this purpose, such as sacred groves or a single tree, springs, stones, or rarely hills, lakes and rivers. Oaks and linden were regarded as **sacred trees**. The ground under the trees was sacred, thus cattle were not allowed to go there and branches, leaves or berries were not picked. Branches were often decorated with ribbons, yarn and strips of cloth.

On the surface of some **sacrificial stones** there were dimples with diameter 0.2 to 1 metre of either natural origin or man-made. In some places some so-called small-dimpled sacrificial stones found widely in the Early Iron Age were still used in the late Ancient Times.

Sacrificial springs have various names: sacred, health, life, weather, eye, and more. The name often signified the characteristics of the spring or the water from it.

Sacrificing usually took place on festive days, as well as before and after major endeavours. **Thursdays**, which was a "sacred day" for Estonians, was considered the most suitable day. Milk, meat, blood, wool, grain, and on important occasions, animals, were the offerings. There is also evidence that people – usually captured enemies – were sacrificed sometimes.

Prophecy, **sorcery and magic**. Prophecy, sorcery and magic were important components of sacrifices. They allowed for the prediction of the outcome of a coming raid or some other endeavour, as well as influencing the outcome by sacrifice or sorcery. According to Henry of Livonia, the will of the gods was revealed during animal sacrifice. If the animal fell on its right side, it indicated acceptance by the gods or fairies, predicting success for the endeavour. However, falling on its left side was a bad omen, which indicated divine opposition.

Sometimes the choosing of sacrificial victims fell upon the gods. For example in Tartu, during the Ancient Fight for Freedom, the gods were called to choose whether the victim would be a fat German priest or the stout ox on which he rode by which leg the ox crossed a spear laid on the ground. In the Tartu case, as well as another similar situation documented from the Livonians, the gods "chose" the animal.

Magic was based on the belief of a mutual relationship between objects and phenomena that could be influenced. For example, it was necessary to clean the "weather spring" to bring rain during a drought. In case of heavy and long-lasting rain, the same spring was plugged.

Healing magic was also very important. Several healing springs were known in Estonia. The water of the eye spring was supposed to cure eyesight, while corresponding springs cured skin troubles, ear problems, and others.

The Saula sacrificial spring.

Some Stone Age pendants made of bone and horn.

Offerings were given to the spring for its water. Primarily silver coins or ornaments were offered, but poorer people just gave small silver scraps. Common offerings could also be thrown into some springs.

Influences of Christianity. Although the ancient beliefs were predominant during the late Ancient Times, Christianity was not completely unknown either. Estonians had close contacts with neighbouring Christian peoples like Swedes, Danes and Slavs. The influence of Christianity can be seen in the changes of some customs. Starting in the eleventh century, burials of bodies became more common than cremations. In the new type of burial, the dead lay with their heads pointing west, similar to Christian burial customs. Among the ornaments worn in the twelfth century, there were even some cross-shaped bronze pendants.

Since merchants from Scandinavia, Gotland, and the Russian principalities visited Estonian regularly, the existence of churches or chapels was possible.

From the second half of the eleventh century, the Catholic Church already showed great interest in spreading Christianity in Estonia. According to the Chronicle of Adam of Bremen, Archbishop Adalbert of Bremen appointed the monk **Hiltinus** to be bishop (Bishop Johannes) of the peoples of the Baltic Sea around the year 1070. However, the missionary work spanning two years failed to yield any results and he returned his crosier. Around 1167, the French monk **Fulco** was ordained the Bishop of Estonia. Later the Pope allowed **Nicolaus**, an Estonian-born monk living at the Stavanger Monastery in Norway, to be his assistant. Fulco is supposed to have visited Estonian in the early 1170s.

The Chronicle of Henry of Livonia even mentions a few baptised Estonians, such as Tabelinus, the elder of Pudiviru, who was baptised on Gotland.

Some elements of Christianity also spread to East Estonia from the Russian principalities. This is confirmed by the appearance of Slavic religious terminology in Estonian, such as "rist" (cross), "raamat" (book) and "papp" (priest).

Apparently the attitude towards the baptised and the new religion in general was not hostile. The fierce and uncompromising fight against Christianity in the early thirteenth century was caused by the fact it was forced upon the native population.

7. First Period of the Ancient Fight for Freedom (1208-1212)

Antecedents. In the 12th century the German invasion to the east ("Drang nach Osten") started, which at a later time began to influence the future fate of Estonians to a considerable extent. At first the Germans crossed the Elbe River and reached the southern coast of the Baltic Sea. In 1143, the town of **Lübeck** was founded in the territory of the subjugated Western Slavs, which also served as a starting point to events that followed.

At that stage German traders began to move on the Baltic Sea and soon achieved a significant position on **Gotland**. From there they travelled to Russian towns by familiar trading routes via the Daugava River or the Gulf of Finland. On the way they met and traded with Estonians, Livonians and other Baltic peoples.

On the advice of merchants, **Meinhard**, a chorister of the Augustinians, came to the Livonians living at the mouth of the Daugava and began preaching Christianity there around 1184. In 1186, he was ordained as **Bishop of Livonia**. Theoderich, a monk and Meinhard's assistant, became known as well. At first they tried to make the impression that spreading the faith was their only aim. A church and a stone fortress were built in Uexküll (Ikšķile in Latvia today). The latter was offered to the Livonians on the condition that they adopt Christianity. Some Livonians were baptised. Among the baptised was **Kaupo**, elder of Turaida, who became an enthusiastic supporter of the Germans.

In the summer of 1191 Meinhard sent Theoderich to Estonia, likely as a missionary. According to the Chronicle, the "pagans" threatened the monk because of a solar eclipse, as the Estonians believed that he would eat up the sun. Astronomical data indicates that on Midsummer night, 23 June 1191, a solar eclipse really did take place.

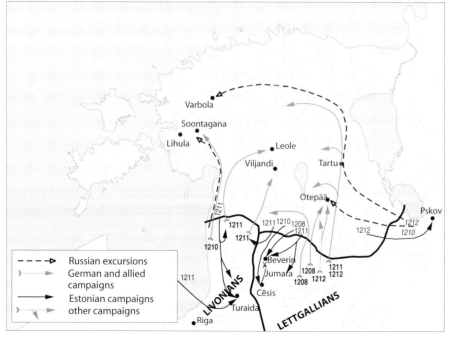

Military campaigns in the years 1208-1212.

Soon the real plans of the Germans became evident to the Livonians. The baptised men washed themselves in the Daugava River and declared that thereby they return their christening to Germany. After Meinhard's death, **Berthold** was named the new Bishop of Livonia. At once sharp conflicts arose between him and the Livonians, thus the Bishop returned to Germany.

Beginning of the invasion. Backed by the Pope, Berthold gathered a strong army of crusaders and came back to Livonia in the summer of 1198. However, he was killed in the first battle held against the Livonians, despite the German victory.

Albert, the Canon of Bremen, an energetic and power-hungry man, was ordained as the next Bishop of Livonia. He became the main organiser and leader of the war of conquest. Albert gathered a powerful army of crusaders, sailed to the mouth of the Daugava, and in **1201** founded the town of **Riga** on a Livonian settlement. Riga became the bishop's residence and the main base for the ensuing conquest. The entire territory planned for subjugation was dedicated to the Virgin Mary, thus Estonian and Latvian territories were then called **Mary's Land** (Maarjamaa).

In 1202 a special religious order of knighthood – the Brotherhood of the Knights of Christ – was founded. Professional soldiers became members of the Order. They wore long white coats bearing a design of a red sword and a cross. Therefore the order was called the **Order of the Sword Brethren**. The Master of the Order was at the head of the organisation. The members of the order were divided into different categories. Knight-brothers, whose duty was fighting, were the most important. Priest-brothers dealt with church issues. Among servant-brothers there were squires, armourers, cooks and other craftsmen.

By such a strong military force the Germans managed to subjugate the Livonians living at the Daugava and Gauja rivers and convert them to Christianity. It was even easier to subjugate the Lettgallians as several of their chiefs handed their lands over to German rule without any remarkable resistance.

Invasion into Estonia. The struggle for Estonia began **in 1208**. In fact, the Germans, as well as the Danes, had conducted raids on the Estonian coast already earlier. Encounters with men from Saaremaa had also taken place, but these were just occasional skirmishes. **Ugandi** became the first victim of an ongoing onslaught. According to the Chronicle, this was motivated by an incident from long ago. Even before the town of Riga was founded, the inhabitants of Ugandi were accused of attacking German merchants travelling to Russian lands and of stealing their goods. Now demands were made for the repayment of stolen goods. The Germans were supported and encouraged by the Lettgallians, to whom Estonians were supposed to have caused great harm from military campaigns. The Estonians rejected the demands. According to the Chronicle, several rounds of negotiations failed to yield any results and finally the envoys left, "threatening each other with very sharp spears".

In the autumn of 1208, the Germans punished Ugandi with their allies. The plundering of the land, burning of the villages and killing the people started at once. One of the most important centres of Ugandi – the fortress of Otepää – was set on fire. Then the inhabitants of Ugandi, together with those from Sakala, retali-

Seal of the Order of the Sword Brethren.

Knights and bowmen of the Order of the Sword Brethren.

ated with a counter-raid on the lands of the Lettgallians. Thus, the ancient fight for freedom had started for Estonians, the victims and results of which no one could yet imagine.

Siege of Cēsis. In 1210, another counter-raid by Estonians into Latvia took place. A great joint army laid siege to the fortress of Cēsis (Wenden in German), which had become one of the most important **strongholds** of the Order. Estonians were quite eager and successful. They tried to set fire to the fort with big stacks of wood and erected a tall siege tower. The defenders of the fort had a difficult time trying to repel attacks from above and below. The chronicler boasts that many Estonians died from bowmen's arrows, but at the same time concedes that spears from Estonians killed some of the Cēsis defenders. The battle for the fortress lasted three days and the defenders could not have held their positions for much longer, but on the fourth day the besiegers suddenly left. The Estonians had received word that a major army from Riga was approaching to help the defenders of the fortress. Without waiting for the arrival of the reinforcements, the men of Cēsis together with their allies – Livonians and Lettgallians – began following the Estonians.

Battle of Jumara. The Estonians crossed the Gauja River and, on the next day, prepared a trap by its tributary – the Jumara (Ümera in Estonian). The pursuing force thought that the "pagans" had rashly fled. Scouts had confirmed this as well. The German group led the expedition, followed by the Livonians and the Lettgallians.

In the forest on the banks of the Jumara, the hidden Estonians delivered an unexpected blow on the enemy. The ambush was successful. Several men of the Order were killed, and the Lettgallians and Livonians also suffered losses. At first the Germans tried to regroup around the battle flag, but when the allied troops fled, they had to withdraw as well. The Estonians followed their enemies, killing some and capturing others. Of the hundred prisoners taken, some

Estonian warriors and their weaponry.

were killed at once and others taken back to the Jumara. According to the Chronicle some of the fourteen men were burned alive, while crosses were cut on the backs of others with swords before they were killed.

The victory in the battle of Jumara gave optimism for the future. Although the number of Germans who took part in the battle was small, the victory added to the self-confidence of Estonians. The announcement of the Germans' defeat was sent to all districts, with the promise to be like "a single heart and spirit against the Christians."

Siege of Viljandi. Gradually the struggle intensified. In the early spring of 1211, the biggest military operation pursued by the Germans was the **siege of the fortress of Viljandi**. At first nearby lands were plundered, food was taken and people who had remained in the villages were killed or captured. Some prisoners were taken to the fort where they were killed to threaten the defenders, and the bodies were tossed into the moat.

In the first encounter near the gate of the fortress, the defenders managed to repulse the Germans, causing them great losses and allowing them to loot the enemy's equipment. The besiegers built a siege tower, filled the moat with trees and pushed the tower against the fortress. From there they threw spears and shot at the defenders with bows. The Estonians in turn tried to set the siege tower on fire. Here the Germans also used catapults for the first time in their campaign. It was used for firing stones at the fort day and night, causing quite serious damage. Finally the Germans succeeded in destroying one wall, but there was another wall behind it. The Estonians also managed to put out the fire in the parts of the fort that were ablaze. They even restored the fortifications by the next morning.

Unable to conquer the fort in five days, the Germans started to negotiate on the sixth day. As the fort suffered from the lack of water, and there were also many wounded or killed inside, the elders made peace with the besiegers. Only priests were allowed into the fort, who than began sprinkling holy water on the fortress, houses, men and women. A general christening still did not take place; it was postponed "due to the tremendous bloodshed." Having taken the sons of the elders and noblemen hostage, the foreign troops hurried back.

The offensive by Estonians. Estonians soon responded to the siege on Viljandi with a series of counter-raids. Besides inhabitants from Sakala and Ugandi, the men of Läänemaa and Saaremaa also took part in these raids. The territories of the Lettgallians and the Livonians – allies of the Germans – were plundered "so that one army after another, one left and the other came." By the summer of 1211, a plan for a serious offensive was composed. The aim of the offensive was to conquer the fortress of Turaida belonging to Kaupo, the ally of Germans, and, after that, attack Riga. According to the co-ordinated plan, the army of mainland Estonians of the Ridala and Rävala regions and the navy of Saaremaa gathered at Turaida on a set day. The fort was besieged and the offensive began. The besiegers promised to stay there until the fortress was taken or when the Livonians agreed to join them in an attack on Riga.

Soon German reinforcements arrived from Riga and a fierce battle broke out between them and the besiegers. Livonians and German bowmen also rushed out of the fort. The Estonians remained between the two attackers. They were forced to withdraw, but still managed to gather on a hill between the fortress and the Gauja. The battle lasted from dawn to dusk and finally the Estonians had to sue for peace, as their losses were great, and agreed to be christened. But at night they boarded their ships instead and tried to flee to the Baltic Sea by the Gauja. Unfortunately, the Germans had built a bridge with defensive towers on the banks of the river, and the Estonians were met with arrows and spears. The following night the Estonians abandoned their ships and fled by foot.

The Estonians suffered great losses, but the Chronicle has exaggerated them; 2,000 men killed, about 2,000 horses remained for the Germans and over 300 ships seem to be very serious exaggerations.

The opposite camp now felt more confident. Germans, as well as Lettgallians and Livonians, organised new campaigns into Estonia. Some reached over the Emajõgi River and even once to Järva region. In addition to the horrors of war, the **Plague** had broken out. It spread contagiously in the territories of the Lettgallians and the Livonians, as well as in Sakala and Ugandi. Both camps clearly needed a breather, thus favourable conditions for peace talks developed. At first peace was made between Estonians and the Livonians and Lettgallians. In the spring of 1212, the Estonians and Germans also reached a mutual agreement. The **Turaida armistice** was to last for three years.

Relations with Russians. Tense relations with the Russian principalities apparently also forced the Estonians to sue for peace. In 1210, the troops of Prince Mstislav the Brave of Novgorod and Prince Vladimir of Pskov laid siege on the fort of Otepää for eight days. Because of a lack of water and food supplies, the Estonians had to seek peace. Paying 400 marks in silver (about 80 kilograms), they bought themselves off the siege.

In 1212, Mstislav the Brave once again came to Estonia with a big army, this time heading for the Järva region. Henry of Livonia wrote that since they found no Germans there, they moved on to the Harju region and laid siege on the fortress of Varbola, which belonged to Estonians. After a couple of days the defenders offered silver and for 700 marks the Russian army turned back and headed home. However, an unpleasant surprise was waiting in Pskov. With the army gone, Lembitu staged a raid on Pskov with his unit and began killing local people. But when the Russians began making noise, the Estonians fled quickly with loot and captives. Thus, in the first period of the fight for freedom, the relations between Estonians and Russians were rather tense. To a certain extent Pskov was even the Germans' ally, since the daughter of Prince Vladimir married the brother of Bishop Albert. According to the Chronicle, a "big group" of Russians took part in a German raid into Soontagana at the turn of 1210 and 1211. This information is confirmed by arrowheads used by Russians that were found at archaeological excavations in the stronghold of Soontagana.

8. The Struggle in the Years 1215-1221

Looting raids into Ridala and Sakala. In early 1215, the Germans together with allied forces undertook a major campaign into Ridala in northern Läänemaa. This came as a complete surprise to the Estonians, as the peace of Turaida was valid up to spring. The Germans argued that only the Ugandi and Sakala regions and the southern parishes of Läänemaa had participated in the peace deal. This, of course, was a violation of the truce. Having arrived at Ridala, the foreign army was divided into groups and began to raid nearby villages. Merciless killing and looting lasted for three days. On the fourth day they turned back to Livonia "with great joy," together with horses, cattle and prisoners.

In the spring of the same year, an army of Germans and their allies arrived at Sakala. At first they made raids in the northern parts of the district. After that they converged at the fortress of Lõhavere (Leole), of which the elder was **Lembitu**. The Estonians in the fortress bravely resisted the first attackers and "put the fear in them." The besiegers, however, managed to set the fort on fire on the fourth day. The Estonians could not extinguish the fire and thus were forced to come out and surrender. But during the christening the foreign army forced their way into the fort and robbed it clean. Lembitu and other elders were taken prisoners, but were released after giving their sons as hostages.

The manoeuvre of three units. After the raid of Ridala and the capitulation of the fortress of Leole, the Estonians initiated decisive action. A large-scale plan for a counter-attack was drafted with the final aim of **fully destroying the local German colony**. According to the plan, men from Saaremaa were to close the mouth of the Daugava River and surround Riga. The task of

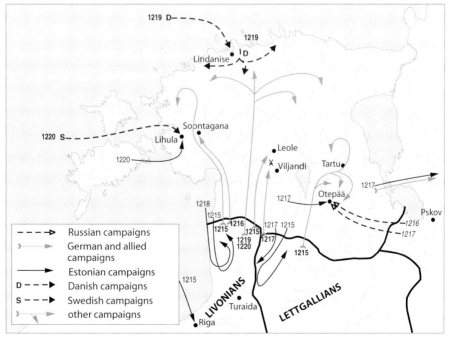

Military campaigns in the years 1215-1221

Lõhavere fortress mound (fortress of Leole).

men from Läänemaa was to attack the Livonians of Turaida, while those from Sakala and Ugandi had to hold down the Lettgallians to prevent the latter, as allies of the Germans, to go and help Riga.

In late April or early May 1215, men from Saaremaa closed the mouth of the Daugava. They brought old ships with them and build logjams at the same place filled with stones, through which German ships could not pass. Some of the men rowed to Riga and camped on a plain near the town. When the enemy's strong army charged out of Riga, they withdrew to the mouth of the Daugava to wait for reinforcements. Suddenly two crusaders' ships came into sight from the sea. As the pursuing army from Riga had also arrived, the two forces trapped the Saaremaa men. Considering their lesser numbers, they were forced to break for the sea away from the Germans.

At the same time the units of other regions were active in the territories of the Livonians and the Lettgallians. They did not achieve any remarkable success because the people had already taken shelter in forts. The planned joint operation did not yield the results that had been expected. The participating forces were simply not sufficient.

Naval battle in the New Port. After the Estonians' joint operation failed, some crusaders returned to Germany. In June 1215, nine ships began their journey. However, upon encountering a storm the next night, they had to seek shelter in the New Port (Uus-Sadam) on Saaremaa.

When the Estonians found out that the ships came from Riga, they immediately responded. They called for help to all of Saaremaa and sent messages to all Estonian districts. They closed the narrow harbour mouth quickly by sinking "wooden constructions" filled with stones to the bottom of the sea. The Germans landed secretly in Saaremaa, cutting foliage with their swords, but the people of Saaremaa managed to take eight of them prisoners.

The Estonians surrounded the German ships with 200 of their own boats and ships. With the help of the southern wind, the besiegers directed large boats, on which dry wood was burning, towards the enemy's ships. When the fire, which rose higher than the enemies' ships, reached them, the wind suddenly turned east and carried the burning boats away to the sea. The Estonians rowed around the enemies' ships and wounded many of them with spears and arrows, but could not take any of the ships. Only after two weeks did the Germans managed to break out of the blockade and escape to the open sea.

The Surrender of Ugandi and Sakala. In the summer of 1215, Germans and especially Lettgallians undertook several devastating raids into Ugandi. According to the Chronicle, they were so frequent that foreign troops were looting almost without break. The enemy promised to fight until the Estonians adopted Christianity or they would be exterminated. The situation of Ugandi was now hopeless. There was no help available and the danger from the Russian principalities had to be considered as well. Therefore envoys were sent to Riga suing for peace. There the old claim – to return the properties taken from German merchants – was once again put forward. The Estonians answered that since the Lettgallians had killed the thieves of these properties, they could not possibly return anything. Finally the Estonians agreed to be christened. Those in Sakala, frightened by the fate of Ugandi, also made peace and asked priests to come and complete the christening. The christening of Ugandi and Sakala that followed remained incomplete, as the priests did not dare stay for a longer time and hurried back.

The christening at Ugandi arouse great indignation in Pskov. Prince Vladimir not only threatened, but in fact made a looting raid into Ugandi in the autumn of 1216. After that, the people of Ugandi, with their new allies – the Germans – started to fortify Otepää. On the Epiphany (6 January) 1217 a joint raid into Russian lands was made. The time was suitable as, according to the Chronicle, the Russians were rejoicing with feasts and celebrations at that time. Forces from Ugandi came home from the counter-raid with prisoners, cattle, horses and other loot.

Victory at Otepää. Only now did Pskov and Novgorod begin to realise the danger from the German side. They decided to move against them together with the Estonians. First of all, they formed an alliance with Saaremaa. The lat-

Otepää fortress mound.

ter had planned already joint action against Riga in 1216 with another Russian principality, Polotsk. However, the sudden death of Prince Vladimir cancelled that joint endeavour.

In February 1217, a big Russian army arrived at **Otepää**. Men from Saaremaa, Harju and even those previously baptised from Sakala joined them. The besiegers of the fortress of Otepää were estimated at 20,000 men. The naturally well-protected fort was strongly fortified and thus the siege lasted for seventeen days.

Some 3,000 men, headed by the Master of the Order, travelled from Riga to help the besieged Germans. Near the fortress a battle broke out between them and the besiegers. The Germans managed to force their way into the fortress, though losing many men in the process. Inside the situation had become critical. The extended siege reduced food and fodder supplies to a minimum. Horses even ate each other's tails due to hunger. On the third day after the arrival of the German reinforcements, negotiations began. According to the peace treaty, Germans were required to depart from Otepää, but also from all of Estonia. This was their greatest defeat in the crusade so far.

The **battle of St Matthew's Day**. Estonians tried to advance the victory at Otepää further. It was considered important to maintain the alliance with the Russians and envoys were sent to Novgorod with many gifts. Novgorod indeed promised to help. Estonians themselves also started raising troops. Lembitu became the main organiser. In the few years, the Germans had made campaigns and looting raids to the regions of Harju, Läänemaa, Järva, and even Saaremaa. Therefore Estonians from all over the country joined the army. The chronicler Henry of Livonia mentioned that warriors from Sakala, Ridala, Harju, Viru, Rävala and Järva – altogether about 6,000 men – gathered at the Paala (now Navesti) River in Sakala. There they waited for the troops from Novgorod.

Having heard of the Estonians' plans, the enemy hurried to stall the arrival of troops from Novgorod. Some 3,000 selected warriors soon arrived at Sakala. From there the army moved forward, ready for battle, with the Germans in the middle, the Livonians on one side and the Lettgallians on the other wing. On **St Matthew's Day** (21 September) 1217, the two armies met 10-11 kilometres from Viljandi, probably near the site of the Risti chapel. The Estonian unit were waiting in the woods and from there it sprang on the enemy in three groups.

Fierce fighting ensued for many hours. The Estonians were most successful on the Livonian wing, forcing them to retreat. However, the Germans decided to break through the centre of the Estonian unit, which eventually decided the outcome of the battle. Step by step they succeeded in doing this and the Estonians had to retreat. A part of the Germans then went to help the Lettgallians on the side "fighting bravely and holding out for a long time" against the men from Sakala, according to the Chronicle. Now, surrounded by enemies on both sides, they tried to withdraw and regroup. The force from Sakala suffered heavy losses and Lembitu and several other elders were killed. The Estonians that started to attack on another front met the resistance of the Livonians and a new group of Germans who had just arrived, forcing the Estonians to retreat as well. According to the Chronicle, the Germans chased the fleeing Estonians into the woods and swamps, and killed up to a thousand of them. The enemy's losses were not recorded, but the Livonian elder Kaupo was mortally wounded in the battle.

After the battle, foreign troops camped in Lembitu's village and looted nearby territories for three days. The elders of Sakala that were still alive made peace again and offered hostages. The battle of St Matthew's Day was a serious defeat for the Estonians, but this did not break the resistance. The Germans did not feel secure either. Bishop Albert even realised that they could no longer cope with the situation on their own. In the summer of 1218, he met King Valdemar II of Denmark and asked for his help.

Danes **conquer northern Estonia**. Denmark had made attempts earlier to conquer some Estonian territories, but up to that point Estonians had managed to repulse these attempts. In the summer of **1219**, after careful planning, a large

Seal of Danish King Valdemar II.

Danish navy arrived at the **port of Tallinn**. King Valdemar II himself led of the campaign. Several other high state and church officials also took part in the campaign. The Danes took the Estonians' fortress without meeting any resistance. Local elders and envoys even appeared friendly towards them.

Actually the Estonians secretly organised a force and, after three days (on the evening of 15 June), attacked the Danish camp from five fronts. At first the Estonians were successful. They even managed to reach the tent of Theoderich, who had been named the bishop of Estonia. Theoderich was killed and the enemy was forced to retreat. Suddenly, approaching from a distance, a unit of western Slavs, headed by Prince Vitslav, attacked the Estonians. The Danes regrouped their forces and secured a victory. According to some legends, a red banner with a white cross, which fell from the sky during the battle, had actually brought the victory. Later it became Denmark's national flag: the *Dannebrog*.

After the victorious battle, the Danes built a strong stone fortress in Tallinn. The christening of the people of Rävala region followed this, which was a year-long struggle. The Danes tried to subject other northern Estonian regions as well, which aroused protests from the German camp. In late 1219 and early 1220, they launched looting raids into Järva, Virumaa and Harju regions and baptised part of the local population.

Since baptism was the outer sign of subjugation, a peculiar **victor's christening** took place in 1220. The chronicler Henry of Livonia complained that Danish priests sent their assistants further into areas in Virumaa and Järva and let them erect wooden crosses in villages as if the christening had already taken place. The Danes were also rumoured to have forbidden the people of Virumaa to adopt Christianity from German priests. The chronicler writes that because of this, the Danes hung Tabelinus, the most famous elder of Virumaa. Such disputes clearly showed that spreading Christianity was only a pretext for conquering the country.

The **Swedish royal army is smashed.** In the **summer of 1220**, **the Swedish army** headed by the young King Johan and his bishops invaded Läänemaa. They settled in the fortress of Lihula and turned it into their stronghold. The Swedes moved around in Läänemaa, baptised the people and started to build churches. Having left his escort in Lihula, King Johan returned to Sweden. In the early morning of 8 August when it dawned, a big army from Saaremaa arrived at Lihula. The fort was encircled and set ablaze in the course of the fierce battle. The Swedish invasion ended in complete defeat and the fort fell into the hands of the Estonians. According to the Chronicle, almost all of the 500 Swedes were killed and only a few escaped and reached Tallinn. For Estonians, this was a very important victory raising new hope and belief in their own strength. The Swedish elite army was smashed and thus the entire attempt at conquest fell through.

9. Final Stage of the Fight for Freedom (1222-1227)

Saaremaa on the offensive. The Swedish defeat at Lihula incited men from Saaremaa to continue their fight. In 1221, they made an attempt to conquer Tallinn together with warriors from Rävala, Harju and Virumaa. They laid siege on the fortress for fourteen days and repulsed all allies of the Danes. Unexpectedly, four ships came into sight at sea, to which the attacking force believed was the Danish King's army. They ended the siege and left.

In 1222 the Danish army, lead by King Valdemar II, landed on Saaremaa, where they began to build a stone fortress. The island's inhabitants immediately attempted to hinder the building of the fort, but their attempts were repulsed this time. When the building of a preliminary wall to the fortress was finished, Valdemar II left Saaremaa, leaving his men there.

Saaremaa's inhabitants immediately organised a counterattack. They raised a force composed of men from all villages and parishes, and requested assistance from Läänemaa. Representatives of Saaremaa went to Varbola where a catapult, presented by the Danes, was located. They studied its construction carefully, which allowed them to build seventeen such weapons. They were set up in front of the Danish fortress and a serious siege began. For five days they fired stones into the fortress with the catapults. The defenders suffered great losses. Arrows shot by bowmen also killed some of the men from Saaremaa, but this did not stop the siege.

Finally the Danes had to accept the proposals of the besiegers. The fortress surrendered to Saaremaa. Most of the Danes were allowed to leave, but seven of them and the brother of the Bishop of Riga were taken hostage. The victorious side also destroyed the fort to such an extent that not a single stone was left in its walls.

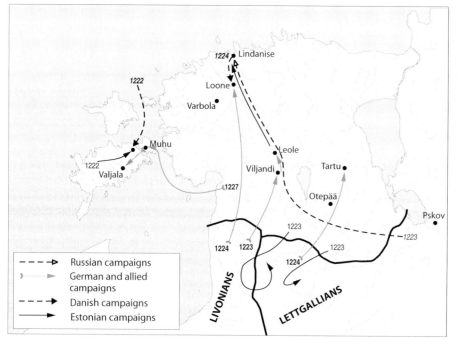

Military campaigns in the years 1222-1227.

The general offensive by the Estonians. Encouraged by the victory, the men of Saaremaa now planned to push their enemies out of the entire country. The message of their victory was sent all over the country, inviting all Estonians to follow in their example. Envoys hurried to the mainland where they instructed others on the construction and use of catapults and other arms. At first the fort of Varbola was liberated, where some Danes and their priests were killed. The men of Viru and Järva were more reserved. They gathered their priests and sent them to Tallinn.

Those in Sakala were considerably more militant. On Sunday, 29 January 1223, they forced their way in the fortress of Viljandi during a church service. Brothers of the Order, servants, tradesmen and even a bailiff were killed. The other Germans were put in chains. Some men went further to the fortress of Leole, where they told the local men to act in the same way. Subsequently the same Sakala force arrested Hebbe, the bailiff of Järva, and took him to Viljandi. Hebbe's heart was torn from his chest while he was still alive, roasted it on a fire and eaten together ritually "to become strong against the Christians".

The elders of Viljandi sent a message of victory to Otepää and Tartu, inviting all Estonians to follow in their example. To the men of Tartu they sent swords covered with the blood of Germans, as well as horses and clothing gained from the victory. Soon Otepää and Tartu were also free. The bodies of their dead enemies were left, as in Sakala, scattered over fields upon which birds and dogs preyed.

Throughout Estonia there were action against the enemy. By quick and decisive action the entire country was liberated. Only the attempts to liberate Tallinn failed. Everything that symbolised Christianity was destroyed and ancestral customs were revived. The dead, buried according to Christian tradition, were exhumed and cremated according to ancient customs. Individuals, as well as houses and fortresses, were washed to remove the christening. Those prisoners taken by Estonians were exchanged for hostages held by the Germans. The envoys of Sakala were sent to Riga with a message declaring that peace would be appreciated, but "the Christian faith would never be accepted as long as there is a single one-year old or one-ell tall boy in the country."

The strongholds were reinforced, catapults were built everywhere and the handling of bows taken from the Germans were taught to one another. Soon foreign troops undertook new raids into southern Estonia, to which the Estonians responded with counter-raids. In the spring of 1223, Estonian forces launched a major looting raid in the district of Jumara. A strong German force hurried there upon learning about it. They made an unexpected attack on the Estonians while they were crossing the Jumara River. Although the Estonian forces "bravely resisted," according to the Chronicle, the Germans won the second battle of Jumara.

In the summer of 1223, an 8,000-strong army of Germans and their auxiliary forces arrived at the fortress of Viljandi. A violent siege lasted for two weeks. Both sides used catapults, bows and other effective weapons. The enemy could not completely conquer the fortress. The Estonians, however, were forced to surrender because of numerous fallen men and a lack of water, and were obliged once again to adopt Christianity.

Co-operation with Russians. Already in 1222, Estonians realised that their own forces were not sufficient. So they quickly established contacts with Pskov and Novgorod. The negotiations were successful. This time their renewed allies did not confine themselves only to future promises, but also sent an auxiliary force. The allied warriors were stationed at Tartu, Viljandi and some other fortresses, where arms, money and other belongings taken from the Germans were distributed to them.

The elders of Sakala even sent their envoys to Suzdal with money and numerous gifts. The Grand Duke of Vladimir-Suzdal sent his brother, Yaroslav, to Estonia in late 1223. The men from Saaremaa who had come to meet him invited the 20,000-strong allied army to take part in the siege of Tallinn. While passing through Sakala, Yaroslav heard that recently the Germans, after conquering the fort of Viljandi, hung the Russian defenders of the fortress. This filled the Duke with rage that he exacted "great punishment" on Sakala. Together with the Estonians, the army of Yaroslav laid siege on Tallinn for four weeks, but could not conquer the town. According to the Chronicle, Yaroslav's forces

Final Stage of the Fight for Freedom (1222-1227)

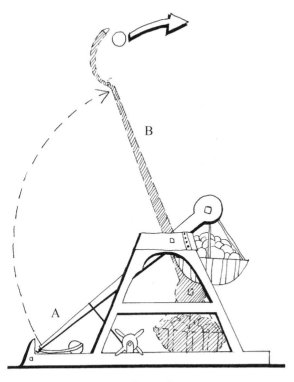

Catapult.
A - loading position, B - firing position.

left angrily and returned to their homeland, though looting villages in Rävala on their way back.

In late 1223, Prince Vyachko arrived in Tartu with two hundred men. Vyachko had been granted from Novgorod the right to govern in Tartu and all other districts in which he could subject to his power. This was, in fact, an attempt to establish a Russian principality in Estonia. The people of Ugandi were forced to endure everything since assistance to the fight against the Germans were needed urgently. The districts that refused to pay tribute to Vyachko fell under looting raids.

Defence of Tartu. The Germans gradually succeeded in extending their power in Estonia and by the summer of 1224, **Tartu** had remained the only point of resistance on the Estonian mainland. The town had withstood two sieges. The Germans made thorough preparations and arrived at Tartu with a great force for the third time on 15 August. They once again tried to persuade Prince Vyachko to break off from the Estonians, but the Prince rejected the proposal, hoping for the arrival of reinforcements promised to him.

A serious siege began. Bigger and smaller catapults were built that were used for throwing stones and hot iron – or so-called fire-pots – into the fortress. In eight days a tall siege tower was built and was gradually pushed closer to the fortress. By digging from below, the besiegers also hollowed the earth surrounding the fortress. They placed stacks of wood together and set them ablaze, allowing the flames to reach the fortress. The defenders fired stones with their catapults, and attacked the besiegers with arrows. Even at night the two sides did not let each other rest, as war games were held and men shouted at one another, struck swords against shields, banged drums and blew whistles and trumpets.

Finally the Germans decided in favour of storming the fortress. The soldier who breaks into the fortress first was promised great honours and prizes of horses and the most important prisoner – with the exception of Vyachko. They already decided to hang Vyachko.

The Germans indeed succeeded in storming the fortress. About a thousand Estonians, both men and women, were killed. At the same time many Russians, including Vyachko, were also slain. According to the Chronicle, only one man, a vassal of the Grand Duke of Suzdal, was left alive. He was sent back east to give an account of what had happened in Tartu.

With the fall of Tartu, the entire Estonian mainland fell under foreign rulers. Only Saaremaa remained free for the time being.

The finale on Saaremaa. In January 1227, when the sea was covered with thick ice, the Germans raised a strong force. According to the Chronicle 20,000 men set off for Saaremaa. From the mouth of the Pärnu River they moved on the frozen sea. As the ice was supposed to have been very slippery, they reached the **fortress of Muhu** only on the ninth day. Seeing such a big army, the men of Muhu offered peace and promised to adopt Christianity. Most of the

Germans did not agree with this, therefore they laid siege to the fortress. The first attempt at storming the fortress was repulsed by stones and arrows. The besiegers fired stones into the fort by catapults, erected a siege tower and hollowed the earth around the fortress.

The men of Muhu fought bravely and only on the sixth day did the superior forces succeed in pushing their way into the fort, where a massacre then ensued. The fortress's properties, horses and cattle were robbed and the fortress was burnt down.

From there the foreign army proceeded to **Valjala**, which was the biggest and strongest fortress on Saaremaa. Looting raids were undertaken to nearby villages and the ill-gotten goods were collected near the fortress. Catapults were readied and preparations were made to erect a siege tower. Estimating the situation that had developed, especially the fact that the fortress was full of people and that the fortress did not offer shelter from stones and arrows, the leaders of Saaremaa opted for peace. The Germans, figuring that a siege would result in more casualties than the taking of Muhu, agreed to negotiate.

At first, the Germans demanded that the sons of elders be given as hostages. They were baptised at once. Having consecrated the well in the courtyard of the fortress, a number of priests began baptising men, women and children. Soon envoys from other forts and parishes on Saaremaa began to arrive, asking to be christened. Thus the priests baptised the people on the entire island.

The Estonians' Ancient Fight for Freedom had come to an end and together with this the ancient times or the ancient independence period had also ended.

Reasons **for the defeat**. For about twenty years, Estonians had defended their country and their people as well as they could. Their enemies conquered the land with systematic looting raids. Estonians had to survive fifty such desolating campaigns and try to respond to these campaigns with counter-raids.

The odds were in their enemies' favour. The knights of the Order were professional warriors with good training and experience. They could use the best and most advanced weapons of the time. They also could recruit more men continuously. In addition to the Germans, Estonians also had to fight against strong military powers like Denmark and Sweden. The most important and most influential force in Europe, the Roman Catholic Church, also stood behind the conquerors. The indulgence promised by the Pope and the hope for quickly becoming rich constantly attracted new crusaders.

The conquerors were good diplomats. They subjugated the Livonians, Lettgallians and Estonians one by one and made use of and intensified the disagreements among them.

The united actions by Estonians, the organisation of the army and armament was adequate for single campaigns. Up to then it had been sufficient, but this was no longer the case against a systematic conquest. However, in the course of the struggle Estonians improved themselves quickly; they took new arms into use, learned how to lay siege to strong fortresses, and fought field battles successfully. For a long time they were able to meet their enemies equally. One of the enemies, Sweden, was even defeated. But the long war exhausted the people, despite having sacrificed everything. Finally, the Estonians suffered primarily from the lack of manpower.

The Estonians had not developed their own state yet and the contacts between individual districts were loose. This prevented a united resistance. The lack of co-operation with nearby neighbours – the Lettgallians, Livonians and Lithuanians – was also a weak point. In the ini-

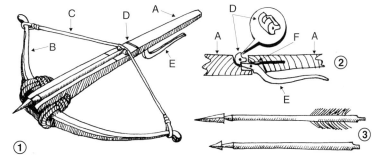

1) crossbow
2) safety mechanism of the crossbow
3) arrows/bolts

A) the stock
B) the bow
C) the cord
D) the safety disc
E) the safety lever
F) the steel spring.

A view of the courtyard from the ruins of the fortress of Valjala.

tial stage of the fight for freedom, forces from Russian lands were a serious problem as well. Although later some joint operations were arranged with Pskov and Novgorod, the Estonians had to offer concessions – enticing them into fighting with money and gifts, enduring their looting raids, and in a sense acknowledging their pretensions for supremacy in some districts. In addition, the Russians did not always adhere their agreements and this seriously hindered the Estonians' plans for action.

Although the Estonians were finally forced to surrender, the ancient fight for freedom occupies an important place in its history. Indeed, everything was done to preserve freedom. The brave resistance of their ancestors inspired the Estonian people to continue the fight for freedom and independence for centuries to come.

II Middle Ages

10. The Lands and Peoples of Old Livonia

The victors divide the land and their reign over the lands begin. Subjugating the Balts required much energy and time from the Germans. The Lithuanian tribes went unconquered but after long struggles the Couronians and Semigallians, too, were subjugated in 1267 and 1290, respectively.

The territories that were conquered in Estonia and Latvia were known as **Livonia**. The region of Northern Estonia, put under the rule of the Kingdom of Denmark, was known as **Estonia**. This region's development, both in terms of economy and standard of living, was shaped following the models of feudal Europe.

The burden from the Ancient Fight for Freedom forced Estonians to accept foreign rulers on their native land for the time being; the final fate of the land was pushed further into the future. Whenever possible, the Estonians put up resistance to the foreign rulers to protect their natural way of life, but the latter proved to be stronger.

The victors divided the land amongst themselves, already considering themselves the legal lords of the land. However, their camp was also divided into groups rivalling for power. Thus, Livonia never managed to become a united territory. The land was divided into individual regions headed by so-called **reigning princes**. Their territories were similar to small feudal states.

The King of Denmark also held the title Duke of Estonia. A lord lieutenant represented him in the Tallinn fortress. From this time onward Rävala was considered a part of Harju region, and the territory ruled by Denmark was generally called **Harju-Viru**. Estonia was ruled by relatively independent reigning princes – the **Bishop of Tartu**, the **Saaremaa-Läänemaa Bishop** and the **Livonian Order**. The period of feudalisation in Estonia is called the period of **Old Livonia**, but is also known as Estonia's middle age or age of the Teutonic Order.

Secular power in Estonia was held by the largest military force in Old Livonia – the **Livonian branch of the Teutonic Order** (or the **Livonian Order**), located in Marienburg. The Livonian branch of the Teutonic Order was formed from the ranks of the Order of the Sword Brethren, which was delivered a devastating defeat by the Lithuanians in the battle of Saule in **1236** and thus ceased to exist. The spiritual order of knights, originally formed to promote religion, was soon out of the control of the bishops. Power and material interests shifted to the forefront. The ranks of the knights had also thinned. In the name of strengthening their numbers, they also opened their rank and file to "less suitable" men, including even escaped criminals.

The most important person in the Livonian Order was the **master of the order**. Although he was officially subordinate to the Grand Master of the Teutonic Order in Marienburg, the Order was relatively independent throughout the middle ages. Territories belonging to the Order were primarily Latvian regions and the Estonian areas of Sakala, Järva and small counties in central Estonia (see map). In addition, the Order held land in Läänemaa region and on the Estonian islands Hiiumaa and Saaremaa. While Riga was the first capital city of the feudal state, the capital was later moved to Cēsis (known then in German as Wenden), the largest fortress held on Latvian territory. The Order's land was divided into **smaller administrative units – commanderies** and **bailiwicks**, governed by the corresponding authorities – commanders and bailiffs. They ruled over the Order's manors, which were headed by governors. In the internal structure of the Livonian Order, the **brotherhood of knights** were the most important. They wore uniforms of white coats decorated by a black cross. In the fourteenth century, there were 200-300 knights in the Livonian Order. Members of the organisation were called

half-brothers – they were smiths, bakers, shoemakers, etc. **Priest-brothers** who held church offices were also of high-esteem in the order. Every-day life of the order was kept running smoothly by the fortress managers, treasurers, millwrights and kitchen masters and others.

The **Archbishop of Riga** was the highest religious authority of Old Livonia. He presided over the churches of the Bishop of Tartu and the Saaremaa-Läänemaa Bishop, as well as over the Bishop of Couronia in Latvia.

The Bishop of Tartu presided over the ancient Ugandi county and the southern part of Vaiga; the capital city of the Diocese was Tartu. The **Saaremaa-Läänemaa Diocese** consisted of two main areas, Läänemaa region and the island of Saaremaa, in addition to a slue of smaller islands. Constant disputes arose because parts of this land territory were under the rule of the Livonian Order. At first, Vana-Pärnu served as the capital city of Diocese. However, this area met the path of the enemy's military expeditions all-too-often and, as a result, the bishop soon moved to Haapsalu. The **Bishop of Tallinn** held spiritual authority in northern Estonia, which was under Danish rule. He reported to the Archbishop of Lund in Sweden.

Nonetheless, the state structure established by foreign rulers was not entirely new; the previous circumstances and conditions in Estonia had also played a role in its formation. For the most part, territories were mapped in accordance with the boundaries of the ancient counties.

F**oreign rulers and the natives of the land.** At first, the domination by the victors was not so absolute that it would have enabled them to do things only as they saw fit. As the land was conquered, verbal or written **treaties** were made with the Estonians region by region; these agreements primarily set out the losers' obligations but they also afforded **some rights**.

For the most part, the customs and traditions of ancient Estonia were left in place. Indeed, administering justice over the peasants was put in the hands of the feudal lords, but the court also included some representatives of the native people, who as seekers of justice or "hirsnik" proclaimed the verdicts. The judgements were

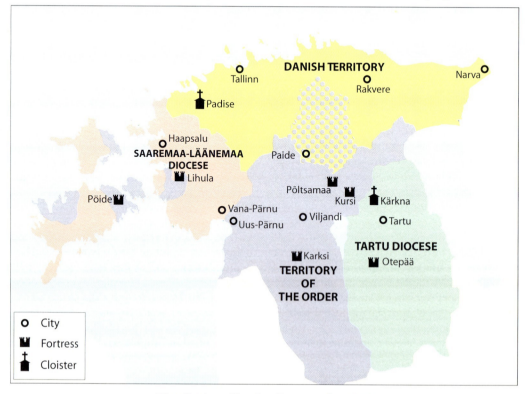

Distribution of land in Estonia after 1237.

Treaty of 1241 between the people of Saaremaa and the Livonian Order

made based on customary practices. The representatives of the villages came from among the peasants themselves.

Even during this period the Estonians were considered to have a military force of considerable strength. While the new lords usually had to force them to go along with the military expeditions, there were also instances of allied relations between the descendants of the elite from the olden times, such as those between Saaremaa and Virumaa.

The **greatest dependency** was experienced by South Estonia – Sakala and Ugandi, along with their small neighbouring regions – which had suffered severely during the war. Läänemaa and especially Saaremaa gave in to the conquerors under much more advantageous conditions. In essence, Saaremaa managed to maintain independence. Legally speaking, the situation of the people of Harju region and Virumaa fell somewhere in the middle.

Today, the relationship of **Saaremaa** with the Germans is best known. After the Battle of Saule in 1236, the people of Saaremaa freed their land, and it was not until the year 1241 that the master of the Order managed to force them into submission and to sign an agreement. Once again, the people of Saaremaa agreed to accept Christianity and to pay a moderate tax. Governing was left to the local elders. The bailiwick, as representative of the foreigners, visited the island only once a year to preside over the court.

Under the agreement signed with the Order in 1255, the people of Saaremaa also managed to maintain their political rights by agreeing to support the Order in the case it came under attack. Eight representatives of Saaremaa are even recorded by name as having participated in the negotiations.

The defeat of the Livonian Order in the Battle of Durbe of 1260 encouraged many Baltic peoples, even some from Saaremaa, to join the fight. This uprising brought retaliation by the Order and its allies, leading to the savage pillaging of Saaremaa in 1261. Nonetheless, a treaty was signed yet again.

In essence, **two entirely separate worlds** existed on the Estonian territory: that of the conquerors and that of the conquered. The Germans and Danes did not feel very secure in their position and, for that reason, efforts were made to keep the surrounding people as spread apart as possible. In general, Estonians were not allowed to live within the fortresses – and so the churches, cloisters and fortresses built as strongholds remained as foreign bodies in the country.

Records from the thirteenth century and the early decades of the fourteenth century document many attempts, especially in Harju region and Saaremaa, to regain Estonia's independence. However, one can certainly claim that there was even more resistance to the foreign powers than that which has been recounted on paper.

The legal situation of the native people worsens. Those people who had accepted Christianity were deemed free individuals and, at first, their property ownership was left untouched. However, the economic conditions faced by the peasantry became more difficult. **Trade** and **seafaring**, as profitable occupations, were left to the city folk. This loss was especially painful for the people of North and West Estonia and the people of Saaremaa, for whom maritime trade had always played an important role, especially considering the poor soil of those areas. The **tools** and **methods of tillage** remained the same. Although the foreign lords did nothing to further agricultural development, the Estonians – as the succumbed people – had to provide for them, as well.

Along with baptism immediately came the "obligations of Christians." The main tax was payment of the **tithe**, meaning one-tenth of the farm's harvest. At first this was paid in grain, but later this was extended to a cattle tithe and other additional taxes, such as timber and hay. There was also a lighter, pre-determined natural tax – called a **hinnus**. In addition, the peasants had to provide for the local priest, as well as pay a church tax in the amount of one-tenth the tithe. The people also had to contend with possible fines, not to mention preparing gifts that might be demanded by the nobility during court proceedings. It was far from every year that the harvest or economic year even made it possible to pay all of these various taxes. If at the end of the year the peasant was indebted to the lord of the manor, this debt was reason enough to cut back on the peasant's personal freedom and to give him additional obligations. Such were the exhaustive consequences of the crop failure and resulting starvation in 1315, which was particularly devastating to the peasantry in Harjumaa.

The hard work of building fortresses and churches, as well as roads also rested on the shoulders of the people. After some time, once the new lords had moved into their manors, the people were also subjected to **corvée**. Although this responsibility only consumed a few days per year at first, it began to demand increasingly more time.

The peasants kept their personal freedom. They had their own land and were entitled to use community property (common goods). The Estonians were also permitted to conduct trade. Compared with the period of independence, however, the situation seemed unjust.

Many Danish sources from the fourteenth century noted a great danger, which haunted the local authorities and especially the city of Tallinn, due to the "frequent attacks of the devils." Tallinn, as a convenient port, had already played an essential role in the economic situation of surrounding villages prior to the ancient fight for freedom. It was in specifically this region that the Harju-Viru vassals took arbitrary action against peasants. A large part of the Estonia's manor estates of the time had been built up around Tallinn, bringing their ruling vassals significant income. Previously, the people of this region had been rather wealthy and they moved about quite freely; the new situation made them quite angry. Economic pressure further antagonised the already mounting political tensions, and the people were even more determined to restore freedom.

11. Relations between Foreign Rulers. Cities, Churches and Fortresses

Foreign powers between themselves. The entirety of Estonia's Middle Ages is characterised by the struggle for power between the reigning princes and the cities as well as between the authorities of church and state.

Because it seemed the land had been conquered for the purpose of spreading Christianity, the Archbishop of Riga considered himself to be the highest authority. On several occasions, tensions between the Archbishop and the Livonian Order escalated to military conflicts. The first **civil war** in Old Livonia broke out in 1297. The city of Riga and the Archbishop, as well as the bishops of Tartu and Saaremaa-Läänemaa, formed a united front against the Order. The Livonian Order put its military prowess to use, and managed to destroy the united front of the spiritual reigning princes. As a result, in 1304 the Order led the other local political powers in Paide to form a **confederation** against the city of Riga and the Archbishop.

The unstable situation and constant complaints by both sides forced the Pope to send his own special emissary, who composed a protocol on a roll of parchment 30 metres long. This historical document informs us of many specific wrongdoings by the order and describes many events that occurred in Old Livonia during the eighth century.

In order to become the sovereign, the Order sought to include the Archbishop in its ranks. Nevertheless, this plan did not succeed and the conflict continued.

Immediately following the defeat, the Order opposed the King of Denmark. This conflict could not even be resolved by the so-called **intermediary state** – made up of Virumaa, Järva and Läänemaa – which was established by the Pope's emissary **Modena Wilhelm** and subordinated directly to the Roman Pope. But it was not long before Danish forces from one side and the Order's military from the other destroyed the intermediary state. Almost immediately these two forces collided with each other. The Order proved to be the stronger side, and after suppressing the Estonian supporters of the intermediary state, the Order moved on to deliver a blow against the Danes. The Tallinn fortress was forced to surrender in the summer of 1227.

Another Papal nuncio attempted to solve the conflict in Old Livonia by creating a separate "Papal state." The Sword Brethren refused to leave Toompea fortress in Tallinn peacefully. In 1233, the Sword Brethren and vassals supportive of the Pope engaged in bloody battle on the grounds of the fortress and in front of the cathedral. The vassals, who included some Estonians, were severely defeated. Nearly one hundred opponents of the Order were killed. The murdering even continued at the church altar, where some of the vassals had gone in search of refuge. Thus, the possibilities of creating a Papal state directly subordinate to Rome had been exhausted. The Sword Brethren conquered its fortresses and demanded a high price from the

The majority of settlers coming to Livonia came from territories of North Rhine-Westphalia.

vassals and peasants there. The King of Denmark also lost his territories here as a result of these events.

The dispute was not resolved until 1238, with the signing of the **Stensby** agreement between the Danes and the **Livonian Order**, the successor of the Order of the Sword Brethren. The King of Denmark regained Tallinn as well as Harju region and Virumaa. Järva was left to the Order. The agreement also outlined a military alliance for the plans of conquest to the east. The King was to receive two-thirds of future conquests, the Order one-third.

The Stensby agreement secured the Danish hold in Estonia, kept the region from belonging entirely to the Livonian Order, and was to be the foundation for the Roman Catholic advance to the east. The foreign powers continued to quarrel and reconcile. The peasants, however, had nowhere to go from their homes and so they continued to be caught in the middle of looting raids and military expeditions in the times of civil war.

The **making of the local nobility.** Following the conquest and distribution of territories, the victors settled in the local areas. However, members of the Sword Brethren and later the Livonians Order, clergymen, and the merchants right on the heels of the conquerors were still sparse. In order to build up colonies, the authorities called upon noblemen, especially Germans, to resettle in the areas. Already during the fight for freedom, Estonian villages were being feudalised in preparation for the necessary institutionalisation needed for governance of the land. The number of applicants seeking land increased during peacetime. Bishops and the Danish King were particularly zealous in granting new fees, because vassals were obligated to serve in military battles at the beckon of their reigning princes. Only the Order did not require additional military forces, and for this reason the Order also feudalised little land. In general, similar **vassalage** to that of Western Europe began to be accepted in Estonia. Over time the land given to vassals began to be considered as private property, passed on from father to son.

Local **gentry** began to emerge, with the families of more important vassals grabbing more and more land for themselves. Vassals did not settle on their properties immediately. At first they used the property simply as a place to collect taxes and a mill was usually built there for reprocessing these duties.

Manor estates emerged most quickly in Harju-Viru. The local vassalage had achieved a relatively high level of independence soon after the conquest and caused a lot of problems for

Danish audit book   *A page from the Danish audit book*

the Danish authorities. In the **Danish audit book** (*Liber Census Daniae*) that dates back to 1241, only three estates are named in the list for Estonia. However, it is likely that more manors were in existence by this time. The list shows the Danish King as having 115 vassals, most of whom were German; less than ten Danes were found on the list of vassals. About ten per cent of the King's vassals were Estonians.

The Estonian vassals were clearly nobles, or descendants of nobles, from the freedom fighting days. Many of the nobles from the olden days had fallen in battle. Many had melded into the peasantry. Yet the conquerors treated those who remained with respect.

Nonetheless, capture of the land was a deathblow to the old Estonian nobility. Most of those who kept "their position" Germanised very quickly. For example, the Maydells, a Baltic-German family of nobility even in the twentieth century, was most likely of Estonian background as their coat of arms is decorated with three fish (the Estonian word *maidel* means gudgeon, a small type of fish).

The new landowners migrated from many German regions, especially from the Rhine and Westphalia. For them, Livonia was foreign and they regarded the natives with blatant distrust and contempt.

The earlier manors were small – an average of five plough-lands. The most common ways to enlarge one's estate were to take farms by force or to buy up land left empty as a result of war or epidemic.

Initially, the landlords lived in large farmhouse type buildings, which never had a chimney and only had one heated room. The manor itself, however, was usually larger than the farmhouse and included outbuildings and stables. The entire estate was enclosed in a strong wooden fence. It was not until the mid-fourteenth century that vassal citadels were built instead of such manors. Until then, the nobility had to find refuge in the palaces of the bishops or the order in the case of a revolt by the peasants.

In 1343, Harju-Viru had a total of 23 manors, of which 21 were in Harju. There are also accounts of manors in other areas of Estonia, but these are scarcer. There were also two so-called collective landlords, meaning cloisters outside of the villages and cities, one in the Tartu Diocese in

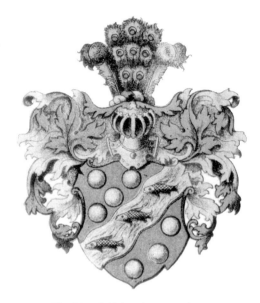

The Maydell family coat of arms

Kärkna and in Harju region in **Padise**. The cloisters' wealth enabled them to build mighty strongholds.

Relations between Old Livonia and its neighbours. The foreign policies of the feudal states of Old Livonia were based on the desire of the Teutonic Order and the Pope to increase their own power. Their main adversaries were the principalities **Novgorod** and **Pskov**, and **Lithuania**.

The area settled by Lithuanian tribes had been an obstacle for the Germans in their journey to the eastern coast of the Baltic Sea. The Lithuanian tribes grew much stronger throughout the thirteenth century, when Grand Duke Mindaugas united a large part of the land. In the battle of Durbe in the summer of 1260, the Lithuanians completely destroyed the Order's military. The Lithuanians' success in retaining independence also had an inciting effect on the other Baltic peoples. Because of this, the Livonian Order was persistent in its attempts to subdue Lithuania. The Lithuanians themselves were just as persistent in their own military expeditions.

In 1263 the Lithuanians penetrated deep into the Order's domain, reaching as far as Läänemaa and burning down Old Pärnu on the way. In 1270 they made their way through Läänemaa to Saaremaa. On their return journey to the mainland with their loot, however, the Lithuanians were met on the sea ice near **Karuse** by a strong army of the Order. The Germans took a terrible beating in this battle; the Order Master, killed in battle, was buried in the Karuse church.

Relations with eastern neighbours were marked by attempts to expand the influence of the Roman Catholic Church to Russia. The main activity occurred in the beginning of the 1240s.

The Swedish crusaders, deployed from Finland, were struck hard by Prince Alexander at the Neva River. In the following autumn and winter, it was the Russians' turn to suffer; they lost Pskov and other fortresses to the Germans. The Germans found that this was the time to begin colonisation of the conquered lands. However, the so-called **Ice Battle** on the frozen Lake Peipsi occurred in **1242**, in which the Order's army, surrounded while having their Estonian reinforcements flee, was crushed permanently by forces led by Russian Prince Alexander Nevski

Regardless, the Russians had to accept the fact that Estonia and Livonia would remain under the rulers from the West. The Germans were forced to accept that their conquests stopped at the Narva River and Lake Peipsi. Later looting raids by both sides had no effect on this balance.

The struggles gained momentum again in the 1320s. With Pskov now under Lithuanian rule, the Lithuanians and Russians joined forces. Their force charged across the Narva River and made its way all the way to Tallinn. The Livonians retaliated by surrounding Pskov, but this effort was also unsuccessful.

In 1340 a new conflict broke out between the Order and the people of Pskov. By April 1343, the Order's military was again in Russia.

Developing cities.

Once lands had been conquered, the emerging cities began to play an ever-increasing role in Old Livonia. This quick growth was largely possible thanks to the fact that some of the city folk had already settled in before the German invasion. The cities primarily emerged from the centres along trade routes, as the trade posts enjoyed benefited from protection by the fortresses.

The conquerors were quite active in strengthening their strongholds. The necessary master builders and craftsmen were called in for this purpose. Craftsmen were needed to serve the authorities and military forces who moved in to these fortresses. Additional goods soon had to be transported in to the fortresses and villages, and this brought the settlement of more merchants. In 1230, the Sword Brethren invited 200 German merchants from **Gotland** to Tallinn and other centres in Northern Estonia, promising them several kinds of benefits. These merchants are believed to have settled around St Nicholas's Church (Niguliste kirik) area in Tallinn, thus also creating the foundation of the future citizenry. Two city parishes in the lower part of Tallinn – of St Nicholas's Church and one in the vicinity of St Olaf's Church (Oleviste kirik) – had already been established in the thirteenth century. Construction of homes and businesses was underway. Tallinn was granted its freedom as a city with its bylaws in 1248.

Tartu had already developed into a large city-like settlement in the days of freedom. Right after the land was conquered, merchants, builders, craftsmen also startled to settle in Tartu once the lands were conquered. Tartu was declared a city in 1262.

Toompea fortress

The city of **Vana (Old) Pärnu** developed as the Saaremaa-Läänemaa Diocese on the right bank of the estuary of the Pärnu River. After the Lithuanians burned down the city, the Bishop took up residence in the **Haapsalu** fortress, and a city soon emerged there, as well. But another new city – **Uus (New) Pärnu** (henceforth refereed to as simply Pärnu) – was founded near the Order's fortress on the left bank of the Pärnu River. **Paide** and **Viljandi** were the other settlements near the Order's fortresses to become cities in the thirteenth century. To the east, the centres under Danish control, **Narva** and **Rakvere**, were declared cities in the first half of the fourteenth century. By the middle of this century a total of nine cities had emerged. Their citizenry flourished: the thick fortress walls provided good protection to the merchants, craftsmen and simple immigrant settlers. This time also marked the beginning of the Estonian townspeople.

The other settlements with good chances of expanding to city stature thanks to their location on much travelled trade routes were Otepää, Lihula, Koluvere, Valga, Kirumpää and Vastseliina.

Building strongholds. The households of merchants and craftsmen to emerge around the marketplaces and churches needed solid protection. Although the primary buildings of the cities had long been built of wood, the people did their best. A fortress wall of limestone was built to surround Tallinn in the thirteenth century. The Danes did their best to fortify and add to the wall already in the beginning of the fourteenth century. At the same time, walls were being built around Tartu; the same occurred in Viljandi, Pärnu, Narva and Haapsalu in the fourteenth century.

The reigning princes were primarily concerned with their own safety and that of their vassals. In a short period, Estonia was relatively covered with **stone fortresses**. At first the conquerors used the ancient Estonian strongholds, adding to and rebuilding them. Work on the first stone fortress in Estonia was started in 1224 in Otepää. This fortress is also the oldest known brick construction. Upon their victory, the Danes immediately began building their grand fortress on Toompea in Tallinn. This was built following

Sculpture of two Estonian women gossiping in the Karja church.

the proper four-cornered wall design of a so-called **castle fortress**. One of the most grand of the Orders' fortresses was built in Viljandi in the thirteenth century. The fortress in Viljandi included Estonia's most powerful **convent** (home of the members of the Order). Another type of fortress being built in this time period was the **tower fortress** – the fortress of the Order in Paide, for example.

All of this immense building activity was commissioned by the new ruling powers: building masters were called in from abroad but the hard labour was completed by the subjugated Estonians.

Architecture and the art of sculpting. Very noteworthy monumental buildings and accompanying masterful sculptures have been preserved from the early middle ages in Estonia. The large majority of these preserved works of art are church or **sacred architecture.**

Whereas thirteenth century churches reflect the **Roman** style of building with some Gothic influences, the additions and new buildings of the first few decades of the fourteenth century were primarily High Gothic. From the turn of the century, city churches were made taller, while rural areas saw new churches being built ad wooden churches being replaced with churches made of stone.

Dome churches (cathedrals) and city churches emerged as mature architectural works. In Tallinn, The limestone Dome Church (Toomkirik), St Nicholas's Church, and St Olaf's Church towered above Tallinn. The architecture of the dome church in Haapsalu and the church in the city of Viljandi also deserve mention.

Differently from the other cities, Tartu was the capital city of **brick architecture**. The largest sacramental building in Estonia stood atop dome hill – Tartu's Dome Church (Toomkirik) with two spires. Also worthy of great attention is St John's Church (Jaani kirik) built in the lower part of the city; obvious French characteristics are reflected in the extraordinary richness of its terracotta sculptures.

The rural churches form a separate group of **Järva churches** from the thirteenth century, which might carry influences of Gotland. The Nõo Church in the Tartu Diocese has preserved its appearance from that time.

An altogether different group of churches is that of the **Saaremaa churches**, the most remarkable of which are the churches in Valjala and Karja. The Valjala church was the first in which **dolomite** from Saaremaa was used. In addition to the plenitude of this fine material, the openness of the people of Saaremaa in their communications with other peoples – even after the ancient fight for freedom – fostered the productive creativity seen on the island.

The majority of building masters and sculptures arrived in Estonia from foreign lands. The most influences came from the Rhine and Westphalia areas of Germany and from Gotland. It was through contacts such as these that Estonian art became included in European art history.

12. The St George's Day Uprising: 1343-1345

Political history. By the beginning of the 1340s the political situation in Harju-Virumaa had become quite complicated. The land still belonged to the Danish King, who was not capable of controlling the headstrong local vassals. Under such circumstances, it was wiser for the King to simply sell Estonia for a good price. By doing so, he would be relieved of the difficulties involved in governing a faraway land across the sea and would gain needed money for his country. The King's steps in this direction were followed closely by all forces that hoped to control Northern Estonia's fate: **the vassals of Harju-Virumaa, the Livonian Order, and the native people of the land**.

The vassals feared new barons would take away their relatively extensive freedoms. On many occasions they managed to receive the King's promise that Estonia would not be sold. The Livonian Order, previously forced to accept that North Estonia was given to the Danes, now considered itself the certain future governor of the land. In principle, the sales agreement had already been made between the Teutonic Order and Denmark, as well. At the time the land was changing hands between landlords and the foreign powers dealing amongst themselves, the people of Harju decided to use the situation to their own advantage. With the goal of getting an overview of the political situation, their delegation even approached the Danish King to get an idea of his plans.

An extensive attempt was made to gain back the freedom that had been lost for five generations. For this reason, the event should be considered a continuation of the age-old struggle for freedom.

The revolt was thoroughly planned and was kept so successfully secret from the Germans that the first blow took the enemy by complete surprise.

The uprising begins. St George's Day (23 April), had become one of the most notable days in the folk calendar, and the selection of this day as the beginning of the uprising may have had a very

Saha Chapel near Tallinn – a possible starting point for the uprising.

strong psychological influence. After all, the day marking the beginning of spring fieldwork and letting out of the cattle was the most important beginning of the calendar year. They wanted to start the new agriculture year as a free people. On St George's Day it was customary to light a bonfire, blow horns and cause as much noise and commotion as possible to protect the cattle and horses from predators and to ward off any other possible dangers. But the lighting of the signal fire on this particular night may have been a clever planned move by the revolters. This tactic gave the people involved in the revolt a camouflaged signal that the Germans did not immediately understand. It was certainly very effective to begin the revolt at night, thus catching the enemy off-guard, sleepy and unable to put up a fight. The unexpected start of the revolt was so frightening to the Germans that they recalled it with horror for a long time to come.

Ruins of Padise Cloister

Despite the anger toward the oppressors, the uprising did not turn into an indiscriminate rampage. The general plan was adhered to and such discipline guaranteed initial success. Estates and churches throughout Harju region were burned. The captured Germans were killed. Chronicle records state that the few Germans who escaped fled barefoot and half-naked to Tallinn and Paide, in search of refuge behind fortress walls. The conquest of the heavily fortified **Padise Cloister** was a significant military victory for the revolters. The cloister was set on fire, and 28 monks were killed. In just a short time, nearly **all of Harju** (except Tallinn) was freed of foreign rule.

The revolters assembled after the implemented strike. They elected four supreme leaders, who are referred to in the chronicles as **kings**. It is quite possible this was a name used by the Estonians themselves. In Estonian, the word "*kuningas*" (king) is an old Germanic term that initially referred not to a monarch but rather, simply a leader or military commander.

A joint force of what sources estimate at 10,000 men took position below Tallinn and set up camp in the immediate vicinity. In the days of freedom, Tallinn had primarily been a port and trade area, but to the foreign rulers it was the essential and most securely fortified centre. Therefore, conquering the city was a mission of both principle and strategic importance. After taking a realistic account of their capabilities, the revolters decided ask for assistance from the **bailiff of Turku**, who was the Swedish King's deputy governor of Finland. This was a wise move diplomatically because, at the time, Sweden was at loggerheads with Denmark, and thus could realistically attack Tallinn.

The bailiff received the Estonian delegation warmly and promised to be in Tallinn soon with a large force. Acceptance by the Swedish au-

Ruins of the Order's fortress in Paide in the mid-19th century.

thorities as a political partner increased the faith of the revolters in their own capabilities. Although the treaty meant that in case of a victory Estonia would be subjugated to the Swedish King, this move was seen not as a new conqueror but rather as a diplomatic agreement; as such, it was considered to hold promise of much more advantageous conditions.

Meanwhile, a revolt also broke out in **Läänemaa**. This reaction shows the reasons behind the revolt were not hidden in the unique situation experienced in Harju region but that the cause of the uprising was more general in nature. The events in Läänemaa followed a similar course to those in Harju; all captured Germans were killed, with the revolters later assembling – this time in the centre of the Saaremaa-Läänemaa Diocese, at Haapsalu. The peoples of Harju and Läänemaa had previous ties and experience in co-operation from their ancient freedom-fighting days.

Involvement of the Order and the Paide Negotiations. Despite the strong disagreements among the foreign powers, the entire German population turned to the only possible saviour – the **Livonian Order**. The Order's northernmost stronghold at the time was the Paide fortress, governed by the bailiff of Järva. Refugees and pleas for help arrived from both Harju and Läänemaa, and in turn, the bailiff informed the Order Master **Burchard von Dreileben**, who was engaged with his troops in battle against the Russians at the Pskov border. The Order Master immediately turned back from his military expedition to solve the most impeding problem of the moment. Although the revolt was not directed against the Order, the general threat it posed was realised by all. Also, standing as the defender of all Germans opened an opportunity for the Order to again become involved in matters of North Estonia.

It can be believed that the people of Harju had used the Order's business in the region of Pskov region knowingly, seizing the advantage of the moment. By now it had become imperative to keep the Order from getting militarily involved. For this reason, the Estonians agreed to meet with the Order Master in **Paide** to begin negotiations. The kings hoped that by seemingly participating in negotiations they could stall long enough for reinforcements to arrive.

The Estonians arrived for negotiations in Paide on 4 May 1343. Their delegation was comprised of the four kings and three soldiers. The other side was also represented at the highest level – in addition to the Order Master, a gathering of important officials was present. The Bishop of Tallinn looked after Danish interests at the negotiations. It is also likely that chronicler **Bartholomäus Hoeneke** himself was present at the negotiations, chronicling what he saw with a certain bias, justifying the Order's behaviour.

It was recorded that the Order Master accused the Estonians of killing many Germans and that he ordered the emissaries be imprisoned. An armed conflict followed, leading to death of the entire Estonian delegation.

For the Estonians, the death of their military leaders was most tragic. The military was left without its trusted leaders, and this in itself was a significant blow to their fighting ability.

The Order attacks. At the time of the negotiations, a part of the revolters' forces had approached the southern border of Harju. After assembling its forces in Paide, the order began its march toward Tallinn. Armed conflicts followed. The Germans were attacked twice at their stopovers in the village of Kämbla, but both attacks were unsuccessful. These attempts were followed by a larger battle in a bog near the village of **Kanavere** in Kose parish. Although the armour-weighted men of the Order found it difficult to fight in the bog, they achieved a victory despite great losses. Fallen Estonians outnumbered the Order's losses.

The road to Tallinn had now been cleared and the Order's army had made it to within seven kilometres of Tallinn, near the village of Mõigu, by 14 May; it was here that they conducted their final plan. Considering the Estonian's elevated position at **Sõjamäe** Ridge, between Lake Ülemiste and the Sõjamäe and Rae bogs, they would have had to retreat to swampy land that would have posed difficulties for the knights. Although the Estonians had agreed at earlier negotiations to surrender, the soldiers of the Order demanded the murderers of their relatives and friends be punished. It is claimed that the Estonians had retreated to the swamplands right at the start of the battle but to no avail – 3000 Estonians were said to have fallen. According to the chronicle, only one young German lord had been killed. The chronicler also described what he called the best witness of the Estonians' fighting spirit – when the residents of the city later went to look at the battleground, one injured soldier among the dead jumped up and tried to kill one of the people nearby.

But the Estonian army was in no way completely destroyed. Yet it could no longer be assembled to determine the political fate of Harju-Virumaa. The Order's forces set up camp right below the Tallinn fortress walls. Frightened by these events, the Danes entrusted the defence of the city to the Order. Burchard von Dreileben himself moved with the larger forces to Läänemaa, where they forced the revolters who had surrounded the Haapsalu fortress to surrender.

At precisely the agreed-upon time – 18 and 19 May – the **Swedish forces**, led by the bailiffs of Turku and Vyborg, arrived in Tallinn by ship. Unfortunately the events had evolved more

Memorial of the Battle of Kanavere

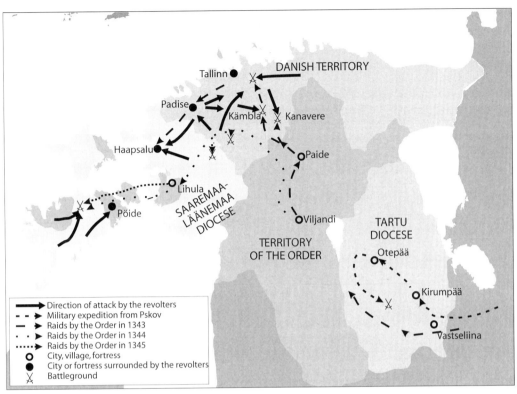

Events of St George Day's Uprising.

quickly than planned and the reinforcements simply turned around and sailed home.

Delegates from amongst the revolters also turned to the Russians in their search for help. According to the writings of a chronicler, a 5000-strong army from Pskov charged from the Tartu Diocese to Otepää. The Germans were forced to assemble their troops in South Estonia. Although the troops from Pskov turned around towards home, the Estonians were given a temporary reprieve.

The uprising of the people of Saaremaa and the final victory by the Order. On 24 July, the day before St James's Day, revolt broke out on Saaremaa. The people of Saaremaa had for some time enjoyed more freedom than the mainland Estonians and their known fighting spirit persisted. Their uprising was apparently influenced by the events on the mainland. The people of Saaremaa set out to surround the foreign power's main stronghold – the **Pöide fortress**. After being held siege for eight days, the captured supporters of the Order surrendered under the condition they be allowed to vacate the fortress freely. However, once they stepped out of the protective fortress, they were all stoned to death.

Despite the Order's success at Tallinn, the situation became quite complicated. In addition to actual combat at the Russian border and on Saaremaa, there was also information of an ongoing uprising in Harju and tensions elsewhere in Estonia. The forces were wearing thin and for this reason the Order Master turned to the Germans' Grand Master with an urgent plea for help by "making him aware of this horrible situation." In late October, large reinforcements had arrived; in November the main forces and reinforcements moved together toward Harju, threatening to kill the entire population. The people of Harju took cover in two fortresses, probably in **Varbola** and **Loone** (Lohu). Paying the price with losses from within their ranks, the Order managed to conquer both. Harju was so savagely destroyed that records chronicled three years later still described it as "an empty and forsaken land."

The winter that followed was relatively mild, and it was not until February 1344 that the Order's troops could charge across the ice to Saaremaa. For an entire day, they attacked the strongly fortified fortress in **Karja**, in the place known as the hills of Koolja. The Order's own chroniclers were usually conservative when reporting on the Order's losses, but in this case a chronicler from Prussia recorded the Germans as losing 500 men. Nevertheless, the fortress was finally conquered and the king of the Saaremaa people, **Vesse**, was hung by his tightly tied elbows. The victory by the Order was not final. Warming weather forced them to rush in their departure and Saaremaa was free once again.

It was not until the winter of early 1345 that the Livonian Order managed to pull together their forces and deliver the final blow. For the expedition to Saaremaa, the they pulled in the forces of the various dioceses. Livonians, Latvians, mainland Estonians, Kurelians, Semigallians – they were all forced to go on the expedition to conquer Saaremaa. The troops made an eight-day stopover in Karja and pillaged the surrounding area, after which the people of Saaremaa agreed to surrender. The terms were harsh ones. Saaremaa had to give hostages, destroy their own fortress and bring their arms to Lihula. For the coming years they were obliged to build as punishment the **Maasilinn** fortress and they were forced stop building the fortress of their diocese in Kuressaare. Even so, it was not possible to subjugate the people of Saaremaa with any means other than a definite treaty.

Summary. The fight for freedom that began on the eve of St George's Day in 1343 lasted for nearly two years and directly involved three large regions, which together accounted for nearly one-third of Estonia's territory. Tensions also rose in other counties, and the Livonians also revolted. The events became extremely dangerous for the foreign rulers because the revolters had also received international recognition. Despite some differences in the living conditions and their methods of warfare, the objective of the uprising was common to them all – restoration of their lost freedom. Therefore, the St George's Day Uprising, was a continuation, the final act, of the ancient fight for freedom. Indeed, the Estonians truly defended their freedom through the very last opportunity.

13. Peasantry in the Fourteenth to Sixteenth Centuries

The peasants' situation, social and national composition. Widespread punishment of peasants followed the St George's Day Uprising, as did general lawlessness. The feudal lords now gave significantly less consideration to peasants' rights than they had even before the uprising.

In order to ensure their power, the nobles proceeded in even greater numbers to settle in rural estates. Brute military force was increasingly used to discipline disobedient peasants.

In the fifteenth century, and especially its second half, international trade saw a new phenomenon, which also had an impact on Old Livonia. The manufacturing industry began to develop in Western Europe, giving rise to cities and a need to import **grain**. The local merchants – particularly those from the Netherlands – often visited Estonian ports and paid a good price for grain, especially for rye.

As the wealth of the nobility grew, new manor estates were built and older estates were expanded. By the mid-sixteenth century, the number of manor estates in Estonia had already grown to number over 500.

More and more nobles and wealthy city folk acquired luxury items and other expensive products, and in doing so they gave a boost to maritime trade, which was already developing quickly, when they first arrived.

As the opportunities for marketing grain increased, so did the feudal lords' interest in increasing the volume of crop. The burden carried by the peasants also increased. **Corvée** became the primary means for renting farmland, especially at private manors. In manors held by the Order or by a diocese, rent paid in money was still of most importance.

Coins from the Middle Ages.

The tithe was no longer limited to one-tenth of the crop, and in fact often reached as high as one-fourth of the grain crop. In the middle of the fifteenth century, manor lords began to demand more and more money for rent instead of collecting many of the smaller taxes of lesser importance. By the beginning of the next century, many private manors had started to demand solely **monetary rent.**

The peasants fought against these increased demands in many ways: they made complaints against the manor lords, failed to pay their dues, stood up to the manor slave-drivers, and even resettled elsewhere. In the border regions, it was mostly single young men who journeyed to Russia, Sweden and Finland. Some of the peasants managed to get settled in cities, where extra hands were in high demand. The departure of peasants was detrimental to the estates for two reasons: it was a loss of labour as well as of taxpayers.

Records of fugitive peasants being punished date back as far as the late fourteenth century. At first, fines were arbitrarily collected from the deserting peasants.

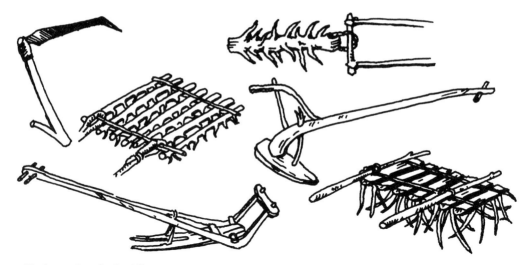

Tools used in the Middle Ages: 1) half-scythe, 2) harrow made of the crown of a spruce tree, 3) wooden harrow, 4) wooden plough, 5) forked wooden plough, 6) brush harrow.

In the early fifteenth century, fugitive peasants were sought out and returned to the estates. The generally accepted principle was "either man or debt." This phrase meant that a manor lord who hired one of these escaped peasants was to either return the peasant or pay off the unpaid dues.

As it was more important to find peasants able to work, the feudal lords in Old Livonia started to sign agreements with various countries for the extradition of fugitive peasants. The only way for the feudal lords to block the desertion of the corvée was to be united in their stance. The first such agreement known to have been made was by the Tartu diocese and renewed in 1458. All fugitive peasants were to be extradited; **rural police courts** were established to ascertain the fugitives' identities and return the peasants to the estates. The same process was soon adopted in the territories of the Order. Similar agreements were signed between the Order and the various dioceses in the early sixteenth century.

Now united, the nobles also took it upon themselves to claim the peasants as personal property, to sell them, give them away, exchange them or bequeath them. By the beginning of the sixteenth century, most Estonian peasants had lost their basic personal freedom. The age of serfdom had arrived.

However, the economic and legal situations of all peasants was not equal.

Ploughmen were in the majority. This name was given to them after the calculation of plough-lands, although the sizes of the various lands actually differed greatly, ranging between one-half and five plough-lands in size. In the fifteenth century, one plough-land was considered between eight and twelve hectares. The larger farms needed to hire **farmhands** and **housemaids**. It was at these manor estates that peasants performed their corvée.

In conjunction with new lands being taken into use in the first half of the fourteenth century, a class of peasants called the **one-legged** emerged. This group was mostly made up of the younger sons of the ploughmen – there was no longer room for them at their fathers' homes and so they settled a small farm of their own somewhere on the outskirts of the land. Such farms had a sure place on the island of Hiiumaa, for example, as it became increasingly populated. The so-called one-legged usually worked for the manor one day a week, or with "one leg at the manor," so to speak. After time, these farms also grew and thus so did their dues.

It was much more advantageous to be a **yeoman**. They paid the tax in money and were freed of the statute labour. The highest class among the yeomen and peasants in general was the **freelanders.** There were but a few of these Estonians with special rights – they were the descendants of the ancient Estonia nobility and ownership of their farms was documented on the basis of enfeoffment. The freelanders were not subject to the duties faced by regular peasants but they were required to serve in the feudal cavalry in times of war.

After the St George's Day Uprising, the Estonians were no longer obliged to serve in the military as allies of their oppressors, but they were still taken along on larger military expeditions. Instead, the authorities intensified the building of strongholds in the cities, as well as in the countryside, and this brought about an increase in the exhausting construction and compulsory conveyance work.

In the sixteenth century, the general wealth experienced in Old Livonia also improved the situation of peasants compared to that experienced in the previous century. Although still without rights, the peasant proprietor could manage to achieve some wealth in the case he had good relations with the manor. The average plough-land had anywhere between three and five males capable of working and several horses, oxen, cows and numerous other animals.

The **three-field system**, which had already started to take root at the change of the thirteenth and fourteenth centuries, had become the norm in farming. The communal farming lands were divided into narrow individual strips of land, making farming the land all the more difficult.

As Old Livonia faced less internal and external struggles in the fifteenth and sixteenth centuries, the population continued to grow. Whereas the population at the end of the Ancient Fight for Freedom numbered about 100,000 people, the population of Estonia in the mid-sixteenth century had grown to 250,000 to 280,000 people.

Some of the population increase was accounted for by the **German** and **coastal Swedish settlements**. The Germans lived primarily in the cities. The attempt by the Germans to expand settlement of the land with their own peasantry had failed. The Swedes' arrival to the Estonian islands and the western and northern coasts had already started in the second half of the thirteenth century. To counterbalance the local peasantry, the reigning princes allowed Swedes to purchase their lands to become landowners in the mid-fourteenth century.

Steady **Russian settlements** began in the middle of the fifteenth century near Alutaguse on the northern coast of Lake Peipsi.

The first record of Jews in Tallinn date back to 1333; the earliest mention of the Romany in the region were recorded in the first half of the sixteenth century.

Nonetheless, the land's development and population growth was primarily due to the perseverance and vitality of the native people.

Intellectual life of the Estonians. After the conquest, the German influence poured into all areas of culture. For example, the Middle Ages saw a significant amount of German vocabulary adopted into the Estonian language.

The imagination of the Estonians was largely influenced by the fact that Christianity had beaten their gods in the Ancient Fight for Freedom. The religious beliefs of the time were put in doubt even by the simple observation that no

Estonian folk costume of an unmarried woman, sixteenth century

blood flowed from the statues of gods when they were destroyed by the German priests, or that the people responsible for axing down sacred trees and forests were not immediately struck down as had previously been believed. All of these factors prepared the way for acceptance of the Christian God and saints, especially because they had already become familiar in the age prior to the oppression.

Forced to follow the superficial customs of the Catholic Church, the people associated these customs with their earlier understandings and beliefs. It was more so, taking into account that these new rituals were relatively similar to the old views of worshipping saints and relics.

The people began to expect the same type of assistance from the saints as they were used to asking of guardian spirits. Secretly continuing their worship of sacred forests, trees, rocks, springs and rivers, people kept bringing them offerings and started to also bring offerings – wax figurines, money, etc. – to churches and chapels. Popular offering spots were the Saha Chapel in Tallinn and the Risti Chapel near Viljandi, for example. The mixing of elements of Christian and ancient beliefs also played a part in the clever move by the Catholic clergy to build new houses of the Lord on the sites of the natives' former sacred places. It is likely the offering stone of Tartu's Dome Hill (Toomemägi) was also moved slightly from its original location to accommodate the new Dome Church put in its place. In this way, the new religious leaders ensured that (at least outwardly) it would seem people were attending church more frequently, while they also managed to curb pagan worship.

Priests in many dioceses complained that people continued pagan worship both in the churches and chapels and in the nearby areas.

To some extent, Estonians continued to worship Taara and to a lesser extent, the spirit of Uku. For the most part though, the people accepted the Catholic saints, the cult of which included a great amount of pagan elements. The names of the saints were left the same but their name days were changed to match with everyday chores and earlier customs. In addition to St George's Day, there was also St John's Day (24 June), which marked the beginning of the harvest, and St Michael's Day (29 September), which marked the end of field work and the slaughter of sheep and goats.

Special foods were prepared on these days, nature was observed carefully and weather predictions were made.

The saints to gain the most popularity through their adaptations to local customs were George (Jüri in Estonian) the guardian shepherd, Peter (Peeter) the "god of fish," Catherine (Kadi) the guardian of lamb, Anthony (Tõnn) the guardian of domesticated animals and particularly pigs. Perhaps Antonius was the most popular. Not of one man, Anthony was the guardian at each farm; each farmstead had its own special chest for tributes made to Tõnn.

In the fourteenth century Estonians still bore ancient names. It was not until the end of the fifteenth century that they started to use Christian names adapted into Estonian, such as Andres, Hans, Jaan, Laur, Mart, Mihkel, and so on.

Whereas cremations were still the primary burial method at the end of ancient times, this custom had been generally lost in the thirteenth century. Although religious leaders demanded the dead be buried in the vicinity of the church, very many were buried in the village. Respect toward the **souls of forefathers** remained characteristic of Estonians.

The arrival of Christianity in Estonia brought along belief in Heaven and Hell, as well as in the demon of fortune, the werewolf, and other extraordinary evil powers. Witches and messengers of the Devil wee also unknown in Estonia until the arrival of the strangers. **Witch-hunts** began. A new tendency toward bleaker and saturnine elements seemed to take over the people's belief.

Estonians had to adjust to several principles unfathomable to them. For instance, until this time Estonians had never known two opposing forces struggling with one another: good and evil, right and wrong, demonic and godlike. It took them hundreds of years to become completely accustomed to the two extremes.

The Catholic religious services were conducted in **Latin**, and it was not until near the end of the Order's rule that priests were required to speak Estonian. Despite all of the efforts made, the people's understanding of Christianity remained scarce. In the sixteenth century – three hundred years after the land was official Christianised – Estonians were still often referred to as "new Christians."

14. Domestic and Foreign Relations. From the St George's Day Uprising to the Reformation

Influence of the Livonian Order grows. A large change on the political map of Old Livonia was a direct result of the St George's Day Uprising. Denmark was no longer capable of holding on to its faraway province – Estonia. Indeed, in 1346, the King finally sold Estonia to the Teutonic Order for 19,000 silver marks (Cologne marks). In the following year, **1347**, the grand master gave governance of Harju-Viru to the **Livonian Order Master**. The Order ruled with a much steadier hand than the faraway Danish king, and this forced the vassals to join in tighter co-operation to protect their privileges.

The division of Estonia's other administrative regions was left as it had been under Danish rule, but it became increasingly clear that the Order was the most powerful ruler in Old Livonia. It was also undoubtedly the largest landowner in Estonia.

The prestige in which the Livonian Order was held among local Germans had increased during the suppression of the Estonians' uprising, and the Order's leading role seemed generally unshakeable at the time. The bishops, nonetheless, put up an intense resistance.

During restructuring of church life and activities, the canons of the Archdiocese in Riga and the Tartu Diocese began dressing in black robes instead of the white robes that were similar to the white coats worn by members of the order. The Order even saw this change of dress as an attempt to undermine its authority; protest was filed while the manors of the Archbishop and his canons were occupied. This chain of events is referred to as the so-called **wardrobe dispute.**

In the second half of the fourteenth century, the dioceses of Old Livonia became, to a greater or lesser extent, dependent on the Livonian Order. Only the Tartu Diocese managed to maintain its independence. In the last decades of the century, opposition to the Order was led by the bishop of the Tartu Diocese, **Dietrich Damerow**. Damerow had previously served as secretary to Emperor Karl IV of the Holy Roman Empire. Dietrich Damerow was originally from Prussia and he had studied at university in Paris. His extensive connections throughout Europe and his outstanding diplomatic skills enabled him to find a significant amount of foreign aid. He even offered the Tartu Diocese to be subjugated to the Queen of England, but the long distance separating the two entities left this plan unfilled. However, Damerow was joined by the Duke of Mecklenburg in north Germany and by many other German nobleman, as well as by Grand Duke Vytautas of Lithuania and the Archbishop of Riga. Five-hundred Victual brothers, known pirates of the Baltic Sea, also arrived in Tartu to assist. But everything, in fact, was determined by

Grand Duke Ivan III of Moscow

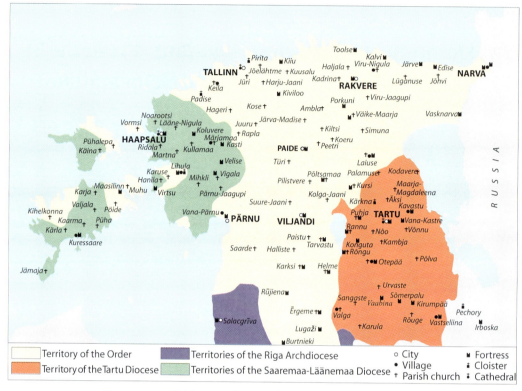

Governance divisions in Estonia through the mid-16th century.

the Order's military expedition in **1396**. The land of the Tartu Diocese was plundered; all fortresses, except the Diocese's main stronghold on Dome Hill, were conquered.

The Danzig Congress. As these events carried international importance, the conflict was resolved at a large meeting held in Danzig (now Gdańsk, Poland) in 1397. The Danzig Congress was quite impressive in terms of representation. In addition to representatives of all political powers in Old Livonia, Grand Master Konrad von Junginen of the Order, and many secular and religious authorities were also present. It was decided that, henceforth, the Archbishop of Riga had to be a member of the Livonian Order. At the same time, however, it was ruled that the Order could no longer demand the participation of the dioceses and its vassals in military activities. This decision significantly cut back the Order's influence. Another disadvantage to arise for the Order was the Harju-Viru vassals' demand for a new privilege, which is today known as Grand Master Konrad von **Junginen's letter of pardon**. This privilege extended the vassals' right to inherit property to include the feuds, thus strengthening their situation yet further. The vassals now wielded significant political influence.

Internal struggle continues. The internal struggles in Old Livonia continued throughout the fifteenth century. The Teutonic Order had been defeated by the combined forced of Poland and Lithuania in the **Battle of Grünwald** in 1410. The weakening of the Grand Master's authority caused the situation of the Livonian Order to worsen. Another threat to the Order was posed by the conflicts within the Order itself. The Archbishop of Riga was released from the grip of the Order, and the Order Master's relationship with the Bishop of Saaremaa-Läänemaa also became strained.

The role of the vassals continued to gain importance, especially in Harju-Viru. Internal issues were to be resolved at gatherings called

men's days. Generally speaking, the vassals tended to lean toward supporting the Order over the bishops. Cities, too, started to co-ordinate their interests at meetings of their representatives – called **cities' days**.

Starting in 1421, more general **diets** (*Landtage*) were held in Old Livonia; these meetings were convened more or less once a year. Many important issues were covered at these meetings: the most important foreign policy matters were discussed and decided upon, internal disputes were settled, taxes were set, and steps were taken to address the issue of escaped peasants. In 1435, the diets were organised to include **four representative groups**: 1) the Archbishop of Riga and other church authorities; 2) the Order Master and officials of the Order; 3) representatives of the vassalage, led by those of Harju-Viru; and 4) representatives of the cities (Riga, Tallinn and Tartu). The inclusion of the new powers – vassals and the cities – held significant importance.

The diets were held in the "geographic centre" of Old Livonia, either in **Valga** or **Valmiera**, and over time they became the centre of local politics in the fifteenth century. Despite their importance, these meetings did not serve as a uniting factor for the various political powers. It was not made mandatory for anyone to adhere to the decisions made at the diets. If even one representative group at the diet was against a particular decision, that decision did not take force. Because of this, the diet was incapable of resolving its own internal disputes. Unanimity was most often achieved in matters related to keeping the peasants under control.

In 1507, a decision was passed to forego the auxiliary military unit force up of peasants. Estonians were forbidden to bear arms. Although the untrained peasants army was of little importance in the era of cannons and professional soldiers, the decision also showed a certain fear of possible revolt by the native people of the land. Political fragmentation and internal conflicts continued up until the last days of Old Livonia.

F**oreign policy.** In the late fourteenth century, the political situation of already fragmented Old Livonia worsened. During the Teutonic Order's downfall following its defeat in the Battle of Grünwald, the Livonian Order also found it difficult to serve as a force uniting Old Livonia in case of foreign aggression. At the same time, neighbouring countries signed treaties of alliance and became all the stronger.

Poland and Lithuania had formed a personal union in 1385; this agreement stipulated that the King of Poland and the Grand Duke of Lithuania would be one and the same individual. The Scandinavian countries of Denmark, Norway and Sweden also signed a treaty by which they followed a common foreign policy. When the Danish kings again decided they wanted to own North Estonia, they again took the title of Duke of Estonia. Meanwhile, Russia was becoming a unified state, headed by the Principality of Moscow. In the fifteen century and the first half of the sixteenth century, Russia was considered the main possible threat.

During the days of rule by Grand Duke Ivan III, Novgorod was annexed by Moscow. In the

Order Master Wolter von Plettenberg's tombstone in a church in Cēsis

The Herman fortress in Narva and the Ivangorod fortress

year 1480 when Russian troops were engaged in a war against the Tatars, the leaders of the Order found it to be the appropriate time attack Pskov. Despite meticulous preparations, they did not manage to take the city. In retaliation, Moscow, Novgorod and Pskov united their armies to launch a mighty expedition to Livonia in the winter of 1481. The Order Master was not capable of taking action against the invaders and allowed the enemy to plunder the land for an entire month without any retaliation or punishment. The most important stronghold to be conquered by the enemy was the city of Viljandi, which they proceeded to burn to the ground. Nonetheless, they did not succeed in conquering the fortress.

One of the primary goals of this expedition was to frighten the Livonians with extraordinarily merciless and cruel treatment.

Moscow did not yet have the necessary force to completely conquer Livonia, and a ten-year armistice agreement was signed in the autumn of 1481. However, the strength of Old Livonia had been diminished and Ivan III maintained a foreign policy with the clear goal of expanding Russian territory at Livonia's expense. In 1492, he ordered a fortress, Ivangorod, to be built on the eastern bank of the Narva River, directly across from the fortress of Narva. In 1494, the local Hanseatic trade office in Novgorod was shut down; the German merchants were imprisoned.

The military forces of Old Livonia were temporarily united by **Wolter von Plettenberg**; although born in Germany, he had grown up in Narva and thus had a good understanding of the Russians' ambitions. He served as the Livonian Order Master from 1494-1535. In order to strengthen the land's defence capabilities, he made efforts to smooth some of the internal tensions. To some extent, he succeeded.

The Order Master found that it would be necessary to deliver a decisive blow against the Russians, causing them to abandon completely any aspirations for the Orders' territory. Because ongoing fears have already become a burden for the land and maintaining a professional army on hand for a long period of time was too expensive, the attack had to completely unexpected and one of great force. The diet decided to collect a special war tax from all of the representative groups. Despite their relative wealth, some of the nobles and towns avoided paying the tax and, thus, only half of the sought amount was actually collected.

All preparations having been completed, Plettenberg and a sizeable army invaded Russia in late summer of 1501. Sources recorded the number of troops at 80,000 men – an apparent exaggeration. Nonetheless, this force was undoubtedly the largest army in the history of Old Livonia. At the same time, the Russians – also with a significant army – were on their way to Livonia. The chance meeting occurred just as the Livonians had crossed the border into Russia. After a small battle, the Russians fled.

Plettenberg did not attempt to take Pskov, as contagious diseases were spreading quickly through the ranks. Therefore, they quickly turned back to Livonia. In the same year, the Russians managed to conduct large-scale **looting raids** through Viljandi, Tartu, Järva and Virumaa, causing devastating damage to the land. Tatars were included among the Russian cavalry for the first time, and they immediately gained a reputation for their characteristically savage treatment of the peasantry.

Plettenberg attacked Pskov again in 1502. And this time, his forces met with success. The largest battle occurred at Lake Smolino, at which the Russians were forces to retreat. The passion for counter-attacks previously shown by the eastern neighbours had dwindled significantly by this time, and an armistice agreement was signed in 1503. It was extended later on several occasions.

Although the victory of the united Old Livonian army had been smaller than hoped, Plettenberg had secured peace within the territory's borders for many decades to come. This, in turn, was advantageous for the cultural and economic development of Old Livonia.

15. Cities and Trade

Legal organisation of the cities. For cities, the most important means of recognition was legal stature, based on the rights of the city.

The legal organisation of Estonian cities were usually modelled after, or even directly copied from, the practices of neighbouring countries. Tallinn, Narva and Rakvere – the cities that had developed under Danish rule – were given the rights of the **Lübeck Law on Cities**. Tartu, Viljandi, Paide and New Pärnu were given the **Rights of Riga** (modeled after Hamburg). Although Old Pärnu was also influenced by neighbours, its development was more locally oriented; Old Pärnu was subject to **Bishop's Law**, imposed by the Bishop of Saaremaa-Läänemaa. The legal status of its capital, Haapsalu, was also determined by the bishop.

According to the rights of the city, the **magistrate** (*rat* in German, meaning council) ruled the city. The number of members of the magistrate varied by city, and grew in proportion with the city's population. The Tallinn magistrate was the largest and most powerful city authority; in the fifteenth century it usually consisted of 24 members, of whom half performed their duties in odd-numbered years, followed by the second half who served during even-numbered years. In the mid-fifteenth century, the rotation of magistrates was replaced with a system in which the aldermen of the 14-member magistrate served their life-long duties continuously. The magistrate was supplemented with four **bürgermeisters**, who served as the magistrate's board of directors. The **syndic**, selected from among educated lawyers, held a position of importance nearly equal to that of the *bürgmeisters*. In smaller cities the magistrate had fewer members. Tartu was an exception as it was the only city besides Tallinn to also have four *bürgermeisters*. Magistrates were appointed for life. New members were selected from among society's elite (the wealthiest) and appointed by the magistrate itself.

The reigning princes were represented at the magistrate level by **the town bailiff**, who held

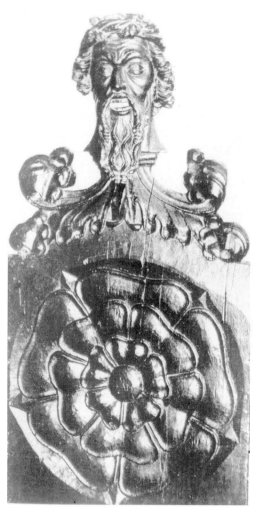

The rose as a symbol of kept secrets – from a carving decorating a bench in the Tallinn Town Hall.

Viru street (in Old Town Tallinn) at the start of the nineteenth century.

relatively little influence, especially in the larger towns and cities. The residences of the reigning princes, meaning the castles of the dioceses or the Order, did not usually belong to the city. The areas surrounding Toompea Castle in Tallinn and Dome Hill in Tartu were practically towns in themselves. Relations between these areas and the actual cities were usually very strained if not to say downright hostile.

Responsibilities of the magistrate included taking care of the city's entrances, welfare and security. It was also the responsibility of the magistrate to implement measures for promoting trade and handicrafts, for representing the city's interests in dealings with other cities and reigning princes, for maintaining the churches and schools, providing for the poor and the ill, and so on. The magistrate was also the city's highest **judicial authority**.

The magistrate looked after the security of the city's residents. Ordinances were passed to address fire hazards, curfews (quiet hours in Tallinn started at 9pm), and so on. Steps were taken to ensure that feasts and celebrations would not undermine the cities' wealth and prestige; for example, limitations were placed on the amount of food that could be ordered and the number of musicians and entertainers that could be hired for the celebrations. The magistrates also competed with one another in terms of luxury and fashion. Tallinn women were strictly forbidden to wear styles of clothing popular in Tartu. Everyone was to dress in fashion appropriate for their particular status.

The citizenry was also quite active in the goings-on of the city. Such activities were organised and co-ordinated through various representative and professional unions and associations. Guilds were the most prominent of these organisations.

S**mall towns and villages**. In the second half of the sixteenth century, the number of cities in Estonia remained about the same. One of the many factors contributing to lack of growth in large settlements was that cities strongly warded off any potentially competitive trade centres (villages, for example). At the end of the Order era, Estonia had fourteen villages and small towns. In addition to the earlier settlements, the following new names had emerged: Helme, Keila, Kuressaare, Laiuse, Pirita, Põltsamaa, Vastseliina, and Viru-Nigula. One reason why these towns didn't grow into cities is that they only had a slight German population. Nonetheless, small towns and villages of the time had many traits similar to those of cities. In Keila, for example, the municipal government established a guild, which was headed by the *bürgermeister.*

T**rade**. The wealthier businesses belonged to the Great Guild; the association of individual merchants and businessman was a guild-like organisation called the **Brotherhood of Blackheads**. The name of the latter originated from the group's coat-of-arms, which bears the group's guardian angel, Saint Mauritius. Estonians were not permitted to become members of these guilds and they only participated in the city's business as small merchants.

The importance of Estonian cities as **foreign trading posts** stemmed largely from their geographic location on trade routes between Western Europe and Russia. **Tallinn, Tartu, Viljandi and (New) Pärnu** were also members of the new association of trade cities, known as the Hanseatic League. In particular, the blossoming of Tartu and **Narva** into growing cities is attributed to their position as trade posts located on the way to Russia. The latter, Narva, was in a constant dispute with Tallinn, and thus was not included in the Hanseatic League. Tartu played a large role in the activities of the Hansa office in Novgorod.

Of Estonia's own products, **grain** held the greatest importance. The majority of goods were transported for sale in Flanders and Holland. Grain was also temporarily transported to Russia. Fish, furs, stone for buildings, and tombstones, and to a smaller extent, linen and seal blubber, were exported to markets abroad.

Woollen cloth, canvas, salt, herring, wines, beer, spices, metals products and luxury items were the primary transit products transported to Russia through Estonia. Some of these products were also put on Estonia's domestic market. For example, archaeologists in Tartu found extraordinary painted glass beakers, dating back to early fourteenth century Venice. **Salt** imported from Portugal and France was stored in Estonian facilities for future shipment to Finland and Russia. Local merchants received large compensation for trading salt. It has been even been said that Tallinn was built on salt.

Russian goods transported to the West through Estonia included furs, tanned leather, wax, fat, linens and hemp. Russians came with onions, cabbage, radishes, and so on for sale on the Tartu market.

Communicating openly with the world resulted in the receipt of various exotic packages. For example, In 1534, the Bishop of Tartu was presented with a camel from a duke in Moscow. As a note of thanks, he sent back a turkey that had been brought back from Germany. It is also recorded how the people of Tallinn once admired a lion that passed through Tallinn on its way to Moscow.

Aside from the primary land routes and sea routes, the riverboat passage extending from Lake Peipsi to the Pärnu Cove was an essential **artery** providing access to Tartu, Viljandi and both New and Old Pärnu; this river route was still in active use even in the mid-sixteenth century.

This unique Viennese glass beaker from the early part of the fourteenth century was found in an archaeological dig in the city of Tartu.

Domestic trade also increased. Representatives of the Order and the gentry, and even members of the clergy, engaged in active trade between the cities and villages. Estonian participation in trade was primarily seen at market sand on church holidays in small towns and villages. Of course, the peasantry was also able to sell the fruits of its crop at marketplaces in the cities.

Craftsmen. In medieval cities, it was common that most of life's necessities were produced locally. It is recorded that Tallinn had 73 various professions. Nonetheless, only the strongest of these professional groups united to form guilds. The nearly 20 guilds that had been founded in Tallinn by the mid-sixteenth century followed regulations and activities as set out in their guild **charters**, approved by the magistrate. Some guilds actually united several professions in one. In Tallinn, for example, cabinetmakers, wood carvers, glass smiths and painters were all joined in one. A particularly interesting thing to note is that Tallinn even allowed unions to be formed for several occupations that were not officially certified – boatmen, coachmen, beer servers, and so on. The majority of these were Estonians. In fact, Estonians also belonged to many of the prominent guilds. Some guild charters, however, only allowed Germans as union members. Tallinn had two small guilds for craftsmen – the **Canute** and **Oleviste** guilds. The Canute Guild primarily consisted of Germans, while the Oleviste Guild was comprised of primarily Estonian members. In addition, the craftsmen of Toompea were united in the craftsmen's guild called the **Dome Guild**. All of the guilds were headed by elected guild elders. Each guild had its own traditions. For example, a guild might conduct large celebrations, or so-called festivals, twice a year.

Each **guild** also had its own customs. These were mainly related to the process of acquiring the status of master craftsman. The number of years required for a journeyman's service was not always pre-determined; length of the service often simply depended on when a master's position would become available. Once a position became available, the candidate had to meet several requirements: honest background, completion of the required years as journeyman, apprenticeship in other cities, completion of a masterpiece. Upon meeting the aforementioned qualifications, the journeyman was also expected to host festivities for his fellow guild members, to become a citizen of the city and be married. Life was easier for those who married a master's child or widow. It was not common for a master to be allowed more than two journeymen at a time. Apprentice status was rare among guilds in Estonian cities until sometime in the sixteenth century.

It was essential to the livelihood of craftsmen that merchants and tradesmen did not flood the market with imported handicrafts. The likelihood of such oversupply actually happening was quite high because of Estonia's location on transit routes. In the early sixteenth century, the Tallinn Tailors Guild managed to influence the magistrate to pass a statute limiting the sale of imported articles of clothing to pants made of local materials. Guilds competed fiercely with individual workers in the same field who lacked the required master's certification. Tallinn shoemakers even had the authority to have such hacks jailed.

The increase in political activity was greatly due to the wish to regulate the circulation of money. Both Tallinn and Tartu minted their own currency.

The appearance of cities. The wealth and prestige of medieval cities was quite literally reflected in their appearance. The larger cities managed to build up their centres in areas surrounded by protective stone walls. Old Pärnu, Rakvere and Paide, as well as the more important villages, were forced to stop with simpler ramparts of mud and timber. Moats surrounded these city fortresses and walls.

The **Tallinn** city wall was the most impressive of them all. The wall stood at an average height of eleven metres; it circled the city in a wall approximately 2.35 kilometers long. The wall was fortified with 46 wall and gate towers. Some places along this circle were even protected by a double wall. The **Tartu** city wall was a bit smaller, with only 18 towers. Narva and Viljandi were also heavily fortified and stood out with the impressive fortresses that belonged to the Order. In Haapsalu, a relatively small city, the city wall was 1.2 kilometres long.

In terms of the land they encompassed, Tallinn (35.3 hectares) and Tartu (27.6 hectares) territories were even larger than Old Livonia's most important city, Riga (27.4 hectares).

The cities could not fit their growing populations and thus the poorer citizens moved to the **outskirts**.

At first the buildings in the cities were most of wood, which meant they were a constant fire hazard. The blazes were particularly devastating in the larger cities. It was not until the early fifteenth century that buildings in Tallinn and Tartu were mostly of stone; Narva and Viljandi did not reach this stage of development until the sixteenth century. These conditions resulted in continual building activity.

Due to shortage of space, the city streets were narrow, as were the plots of land on which the houses were built. Even for the wealthiest businessmen, these limitations only allowed for houses to be built with narrow facades and high, pointed gables. The outbuildings, such as sheds, stables, coach houses and so on, faced the courtyards. The homes of craftsmen were usually more modest in appearance.

Relative to other European cities, Tallinn began building its streets as early as the mid-fourteenth century. The Market Square (Town Hall Square) was covered with 10,100 flat cobblestones of limestone in 1370.

The Market Square, lined by small shops, was the hub of city activity. The Town Hall – the building of highest social importance – was also established on one side of the square. The town hall currently standing in the Tallinn Town Hall Square was completed in 1404 as one of the most charming Gothic-style buildings in the Nordic countries. Tallinn's town pharmacy was opened in 1422. The city also had many other establishments connected to the health of its citizens, such as barber shops, saunas, and so on. Nonetheless, the generally low level of sanitation caused diseases to spread easily, and the most devastating of these was the **plague**. People suffering from leprosy were isolated in hospitals dedicated specifically for those with the disease. These special

Towers along Tallinn's city walls.

establishments, built a bit outside of the city, were called **almshouses**. Today, Tallinn's Old Town and its many architectural monuments continue to reflect the character and feel of a mediaeval city. Tallinn truly was one of the most beautiful cities in Northern Europe. In terms of both size and beauty, Tartu vied for the same title. For example, in 1414, the renowned traveller and observer Ghillebert de Lannoy named Tartu as one of the most beautiful cities he had ever seen in his 51 years of travel through Europe and the Far East. In the first half of the fifteenth century, a member of one of the Russian churches wrote: "But the city of Tartu was large and of stone, the buildings were pleasant and, never before having seen such beauty, were in awe. The churches were a-many and the cloisters were large...They also had hills and fields, the gardens were pretty."

Population. The population of Tallinn in the fifteenth century reached between 7000 and

8000 people. In Tartu, the population was between 5000 and 6000. During the days of the Order, the population in Viljandi could have been slightly over 1000. Narva was slighter lower, and the rest of Estonia's cities and towns were yet smaller. City residents accounted for up to eight percent of Estonia's entire population.

In the cities, **Germans** played the greatest role. However, when including all labourers and outlying districts, **Estonians** (called non-Germans at the time) still held the majority of the population in all of Estonia's cities. The service sector in Tallinn also included a noteworthy amount of Finns and Swedes. A significant number of Russians resided in Narva and Tartu.

These cities would not have been able to develop and remain standing without the local population, however. This observation was also noted by the city magistrates. At times, plague and other deadly diseases added to the already low life expectancy rate, wiping out up to half of the cities' residents. The necessary inflow of residents to the city came from the peasants who fled from working at manor estates. The vassals of Harju-Viru apprehended the peasants especially viciously. The city magistrate, however, ruled that according to the rights of the city, if a person has been in the city for one year and one day (actually, it was one year and six weeks) then the city would defend the person. In 1535, the magistrate even ruled to have the famous estate-owner **Johan von Uexküll of Riisipere** executed for torturing a peasant who had fled from his service. The nobleman was brought before the court at the request of the dead peasant's brother, a street cleaner in Tallinn.

16. The Catholic Church and Reformation

Organisation of the church on Estonian territory. At the beginning of the Crusades directed at the peoples living on the east coast of the Baltic Sea, the institution of the Catholic Church was nearly one thousand years old. For those at the top of this hierarchic power, secular interests – including territorial demands – had become a tradition. These interests were often pursued through means of aggression. In addition to what were in essence secular aspirations (power, land, property), the crusaders' religious order of knights had also been given an assignment by the Pope – to free the peoples, to proclaim forgiveness and the only true faith. The actions of the religious order of knights soon brought to light their actual nature, however, causing the majority of the clergy to develop a cool attitude toward the proclaimed values of their predecessors.

The organisation of church states in Old Livonia was built up on already-existing rules. Locally, the highest religious authority in Old Livonia was the **Archbishop of Riga**, whose holy province in Estonia included Tartu and Saaremaa-Läänemaa. The Bishop of Tallinn was subordinate to the Archbishop of Lund.

The bishop was the director of church life and the highest judge in matters of religious crimes in his jurisdiction. Synods, or parochial visits, were conducted to oversee religious matters in the diocese. The parochial visits made it possible to review the work of priests as they proclaimed the word of God and taught the people, and to detect any shortcomings in religious life. Bishops' responsibilities included swearing in spiritual leaders of lower positions, blessing churches, chapels, alters, church bells and tools of the church, as well as conducting the more formal church services in cathedrals.

The main church of the diocese also included a **cathedral chapter**. This was the name of the highest council, usually consisting of twelve canons. The chapter was headed by the priest, who was followed in importance by the dean. In

(Reconstructed) Front and side views of Dome Church in Tartu.

addition to heading the economic life of the diocese, the priest led the chapter, while the dean handled the order of religious services and discipline in general.

The most influential right held by the cathedral chapter was election of the bishop. However, final approval of the nominated candidate was given by the Pope, who often named bishops according to his own preference or selected them from among those close to him. Of local chapters, the Tartu chapter was most consistent in utilising its rights, but even so, one-third of the bishops in Tartu at one time or another had been personally appointed by the Pope. The cathedral chapter served as an advisory body to the bishops in regard to managing religious life and ruling territories and, in essence, its members were state officials. When the role of bishop was not filled for some reason, the cathedral chapter acted as ruler. It was the duty of the canons to carry out the formal **mass** services. Mass was characterised by the musical nature of the **liturgy**. The clothes and attributes that accompanied mass services were very luxurious, as were the church interiors and furnishings. Everyday caring for the soul was usually passed on to regular clergymen.

The habit common to canons in the fifteenth and sixteenth centuries – to interfere in secular life – caused them to become increasingly removed from the original principles of common monastic life. The canons used their position foremost as a source of income. They primarily lived on their manor estates as regular manor lords; only on occasion did they stay at the cathedral. It was not until the early fourteenth century that the canons began acquiring personal homes on *Toomemägi* (Cathedral Hill) in Tartu or on *Toompea* (Cathedral Hill) in Tallinn.

This superficial attitude toward their occupation often resulted in breaches of religious ethics, such as living with women, carousing and other entertainment. Another frequent occurrence was that the same individual would belong to the Tartu, Tallinn and Saaremaa-Läänemaa chapters. There were even instances where foreigners who had never set foot in Livonia managed to receive Papal appointment to local canon positions while

Dome Church in Tallinn.

also receiving income from many other dioceses, in Germany or Italy, for example. Nonetheless, the majority of clergy members active in Estonia had origins in Old Livonia dating from the fifteenth century. The percentage of locals was even higher among priests.

In the medieval churches of the larger cities, there was a plenitude of alters located in the larger cities' churches (28 alters in St Nicholas's Church in Tallinn, 24 alters in St Olaf's Church). Each alter had it own dedicated clergyman. Wealthy families, guilds and other brotherhoods were quick to have their own alters built, so that a clergyman would pray daily for the their salvation

Religious life in rural areas. Although the diocese kept numerous clergymen and assistants, the majority of religious healing in rural areas was done by the priest of the local parish. The number of parishes continued to increase throughout the Middle Ages; by the sixteenth century, there were 97 parishes in Estonia.

The centre of the parish was the **parish church**. **Chapels** were often established in the outlying areas of parishes, where the religious duties usually assigned to priests were carried out by vicars. Priests were provided for by the income they received from the small plot of land allotted to each, as well as by the **church tithe** (one-tenth of the estate's total tithe) and donations made by church parishioners. Because the Livonian Order and the rural noblemen supported the church with material goods, they were free to choose their own clergymen, often members of the more prominent local families. In later years it was not even necessary for the candidates to have the education and skills necessary for fulfilling the duties of a priest.

Practical duties given to priests included sharing the seven sacraments (rites believed to have been ordained by Christ and held to be means of a divine grace or symbol of a spiritual reality conducted by the church – baptisms, confirmations, holy communions, confessions, last rites, ordaining priests, weddings – with the parish and teaching the word of Christ. It was also the duty of priests to teach the peasants the Lord's Prayer and "Ave Maria," the Ten Commandments and other lessons necessary for salvation. Unsanctioned marriages and washing off the baptism were sins punishable by death. However, these and other measures adopted to improve religious life were of little help. In general, even the simplest religious principles remained unknown to the common man. In the early sixteenth century, **Bishop Johannes IV Kievel** conducted many extensive visitations in his jurisdiction of Saaremaa-Läänemaa, which brought to light the disorder of the churches, the greed of the religious men, and much more. For example, Bishop Johannes IV dismissed one priest in Kaarma for allegedly taking a cow or ox, sometimes by force, for each funeral he conducted. The same man was known as a goods trafficker. While he was on a two-month visit to Riga, seven unburied corpses awaited his return.

One of the more famous religious leaders of Old Livonia, **Johannes Blankenfeld**, also demanded that order be established in the churches. Blankenfeld was the bishop of Tallinn and Tartu, and later went on to become the Archbishop of Riga.

Cloisters. In addition to the official church organisations that existed in mediaeval Estonia, there were also many cloisters of various religious orders. At first, life in the cloister meant quiet service of the Lord, away from all external and disruptive influences. But before long only the **Cistercian** Order, the oldest religious order in Estonia, remained in such isolation. The aim of its members was to do their work in isolation – gardening, raising cattle and tilling the fields. They established a cloister in Kärkna (near Tartu) in the thirteenth century and another in Padise in the fourteenth century. Later, a female branch of Cistercians was formed, with established cloisters in Tallinn, Tartu and Lihula.

Many orders of **Dominican and Franciscan** mendicant friars, who were much more active in social life, also settled in Estonia. Based on their activities, the Dominicans were called the "preaching brothers." Their cloisters were located in Tallinn and Tartu, and in the sixteenth century, they also established a cloister in Narva. Due to their attire, the Franciscans were called the "grey brothers;" they established cloisters in Tartu, Viljandi and Rakvere.

Both of these two orders emphasised preaching the word of God, and united this with their excursions. Such travels called for knowledge of the local languages. For the Dominicans,

Coat of Arms of Johannes IV Kievel

knowledge of the local language was in fact one of the requirements in their daily routine. In this way, the Dominicans could be compared with folk teachers. They conducted sermons in both German and Estonian at their cloister in Tallinn.

The monks had strong support from the locals. However, such popularity was frowned upon by members of local religious authorities. In the fifteenth century, the Dominicans of Tallinn found themselves in a dispute with the cathedral chapter, which claimed to have the sole right to provide schooling. Masked priests forced their way into the cloister during one of the holy sermons; singing a taunting song, they suggesting the landlord turn the church into a pigsty and horse stable instead. The monks retaliated with a similar tactic, charging into Candlemas Day mass at St Nicholas's church.

Construction of the only cloister of the **Augustinian Order** in Estonia began in 1407. This was the mixed cloister (nuns and monks) in Pirita, dedicated to St Birgitta and the Virgin Mary, modelled after the Vadstena cloister in Sweden.

As the Catholic church followed the fall of its top leaders, simple mortals were becoming more religious. This increased interest seen in the early sixteenth century gave way to a time of increased population at cloisters in Estonia. There was also increased respect toward the remains of saints. Several cloisters and churches claimed to have belongings or body parts of deceased saints. The most popular destinations for pilgrimages were the Vastseliina Fortress chapel, the St Nicholas's Church in Pärnu, Mary's Chapel in Viru-Nigula, and St Birgitta's cloister. It is said that Tartu's Toomkirik (Cathedral) preserved the thumb of a saint, which later turned into a priceless sapphire. Local places of worship were also visited by pilgrims from abroad. Estonians, too, made pilgrimages to holy destinations in Europe.

The cloisters, with their vast land territories, were so-called **collective manor lords**. They claimed taxes and services from Estonians but also made positive contributions of their own. Several types of fruit trees were brought to Estonia through the cloisters. The monks taught locals several types of handicrafts, not to mention better tilling methods. Also, the first water mills in Estonia were built by the cloisters. The female branches of the orders helped tend to the sick during epidemics, as well as in everyday life.

T**he Reformation.** Opposition to the Pope-led church arose in the beginning of the

Ruins of the St Birgitta Cloister

sixteenth century. The opposition occurred on two levels – **political and spiritual**. Opposition on the political level took the form of greed by religious leaders, noblemen and wealthy city folk; hungry for the church's treasures and lands, they tried to gain control of the church to access its riches. The other opposition came from those clergymen of the new thinking fighting for deeper cultural changes and against the feudal organisation of the Catholic Church. They preached the Gospel, believing salvation was possible only through the love of Christ in return for faith; for them, the Holy Bible was the only theoretical basis for Christianity.

The Reformation was begun by **Martin Luther** in Wittenberg, Germany in the year **1517**.

The reformers came to Tallinn from Germany, by way of Riga in 1523. Within the following year, three evangelic preachers were already active in Tallinn. Their work was all the more productive due to the fact that the population already harboured some resentment toward bishops, Dominicans and the better known Catholic priests.

Hermann Marsow, a disciple of Martin Luther, was the first Protestant preacher to serve in Tartu; he arrived in late 1523. The new ideas also gained popularity in Tartu, thus irritating the Bishop, who soon forced the preacher to leave. Marsow moved on to Tallinn. Alongside Johann Lange, a priest at the church of St Nicholas, Marsow became one of the primary figures of the new faith.

By 1525, the Reformation had spread to Narva, Viljandi and (New) Pärnu; however it took longer to reach the smaller cities.

While Protestantism was quickly accepted in cities, and even emerged as a strong force against monks and catholic priests, the rural areas still stepped out in defence of the latter in 1525. This was due the noblemen's old-fashioned nature in general, as well as the unfriendly relations between the vassalage and cities.

The most adamant Catholic supporters were Order Master Wolter von Plettenberg and the Archbishop of Riga Johannes Blankenfeld. Although Blankenfeld had previously participated in the humanistic movement in Europe and favoured internal reform of the Catholic Church, he became a staunch opponent to the Protestants. In addition to being the Archbishop of Riga, he was also the Bishop of Tallinn and Tartu. Having previously held many honourable positions in the religious hierarchy of Europe, he now dedicated his life to Old Livonia, attempting to preserve the prestige of the Catholic Church and its independence from the Livonian Order. As we can see, the two primary defenders of the Catholic Church could not manage to agree among themselves, while the Reformation continued to gain momentum.

Plettenberg did his best to keep the peace in the rural areas even when Riga refused its subordination to the Archbishop. The Order Master wrote a stern letter of reprimand to the town council in Tallinn. Upon its reading, large protests erupted in the city; these later became known as **iconoclasm**. On **14 September**

Dominican Cloister in Tallinn

1524, a mass of 400-500 rioting Germans and Estonians charged into the church of the Dominican cloister, the Church of the Holy Spirit and St Olaf's Church, destroying icons, alters, treasures, etc. Only of St Nicholas's Church was left untouched, as the padlocks on the church doors had wisely been tinned shut.

In January 1525, a mass of hundreds of Tartu residents, led by the popular German preacher and furrier **Melchior Hoffmann**, actually waged an attack against the bishop's guards on Cathedral Hill in Tartu. Two Estonian and two German residents of the city were killed in the battle. While the bishop's fortress remained untouched at first, the cathedral church and the houses of the canons, as well as all of the downtown churches, were thoroughly pillaged. The Tartu council found this behaviour by the residents to be dangerous and Hoffmann was forced to leave the city.

Iconoclasm followed in Viljandi, Pärnu and (New) Pärnu. As a consequence of the pillaging and constant pressure, some cloisters, including the Dominican cloister in Tallinn, decided to end their activities. The largest church in the city, formerly belonging to the Dominican cloister, was given to the Estonian congregation.

Although the teachings of Martin Luther had been generally accepted, the Livonians did not associate these principles with their author and, thus, we cannot consider these events or reformation as a knowingly Lutheran one. The reformation became known as Lutheran much later.

The peasants took the message of the reformation to be that all men are equal before God. This caused disturbances in North Estonia and in the Tartu diocese. Fearing an uprising by the peasants, the gentry initially supported the Order and the bishops in their fight against the reforms.

While the church as ruler in Northern and Central Europe lost its territories and most organisations of the Catholic Church were being shut down, the anti-reform forces in Old Livonia managed to maintain some of their position. A large contribution toward this was made by Order Master Plettenberg. As opposed to the Teutonic order, which ceased to exist as a religious order of knights, the Livonian Order continued its activities independently in **1525**.

Even though the majority of vassals had converted to Protestantism by the 1530s, the political aspects of the reformation went unfinished.

Melchior Hoffmann

Catholic bishops, cathedral chapters, the Livonian Order and most cloisters remained active throughout the age of the Teutonic Order, and took on a relatively large importance domestically.

17. Education and Culture

Catholic education. In the mediaeval age, school was inseparable from the church. The primary objective of school was to groom clergymen.

Even back when the land was being conquered, it was considered important for the priests to know the local language. For this reason, young boys (taken hostage) were schooled abroad to become members of the clergy. This type of schooling subsided once the land had fallen to its conquerors.

Cathedral and **monastic schools** were active in the bosom of the Catholic Church.

While there is no known specific data about cathedral schools in Estonia, it is likely that such schools operated parallel to all three of the cathedral chapters – in Tartu, Haapsalu (previously Old Pärnu), and Tallinn, as early as the mid-thirteenth century. Cathedral schools groomed future canons but, starting in the fifteen century, individuals aspiring to higher positions in the church were required to have completed university-level education.

Most such studies were completed at **German universities** in Rostock, Erfurt and Leipzig, but also at universities in Bologna, Paris, Prague and elsewhere. Records even document the names of some Estonian university students of the time. If their financial status permitted such studies, then the Catholic system did not forbid such opportunities. As far as it is known, the most exemplary Estonian student was **Johann Pulck**, a student at the university in Rostock; in the sixteenth century Pulck was even a member of the cathedral chapter of the Saaremaa-Läänemaa Diocese.

Despite the fact that both the chapter and the council often supported young people wanting to study abroad, the trip overseas was out of the grasp of many would-be students. Another problem was that the more talented students usually did not return to their homeland upon completing their studies, and if they did, it was typically after

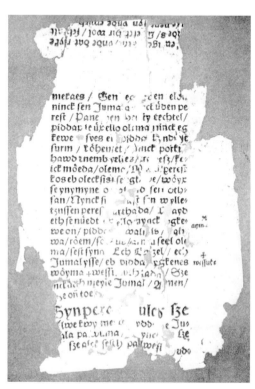

A preserved page fragment of the catechism by Wanradt and Koell.

a long period of time. This problem brought about the establishment of the **higher school for Latin**, where children from rural areas could prepare and study for the priesthood. The proposal to establish such a school was discussed at numerous diets in the sixteenth century. Bishop Kievel was also a driving force in this undertaking. Old Pärnu was selected as the location for the school; a scholar from the university in Rostock was invited to accept the position as director of the school, and even managed a trip to review the conditions there. Still, the school never came to be due to the Reformation.

Records show that an Estonian-language catechism was published at the initiative of Bishop Kievel, with the aim of grooming the children of rural areas.

While the only remaining documentation of specifically monastic schools is in regard to the **Dominicans of Tallinn** and the Cistercians of Kärkna, it seems likely that many of the cloisters had their own schools. Such schools had access to the libraries of the cloisters; the library of the Dominican cloister remains today. As this cloister primarily gained members from among the local population, many of the schools' students were Estonians. In the mid-fifteenth century, the superior of the cloister was **Henricus Carvel**.

Town schools. In order to gain the basic skills and knowledge necessary for successful careers in the times of the trade boom, children from towns also needed schooling in secular matters. While the town schools (also called Latin schools) did indeed function alongside the town churches, they were directly subordinate to the town council. In addition to religious subjects, the children were taught to read, write and do arithmetic. A great emphasis was put on the Latin language and literature.

The first city school in said to be a school founded in 1432 in Tallinn, near St Olaf's Church. Schools were next established in Narva, (New) Pärnu, Paide, Tartu and Rakvere.

Lutheran education and the printed Estonian word. While the Reformation caused development of the Catholic schooling system to come to a standstill, the new church opened up even greater opportunities for public education, including Estonian language studies. After all, the Bible had been proclaimed the basis for the true religion.

In Lübeck in 1525, a **book of common prayers** was also published with explanatory texts in Estonian, Livonian and Latvian. Nearly all copies of the book were destroyed by the Lübeck council, which called the publication Lutheran foolishness. Although no copies are known to be in existence today, the books is nonetheless referred to as the **first** known printed matter in the Estonian language.

Still, the new religious movement, which demanded religion to be taught in the native language of the land, could not manage without such a book. Soon a **Lutheran catechism** was compiled in Tallinn. The book was put together by Pastor **Simon Wanradt** of the Church of St Nicholas and translated into Estonian by **Johann Koell**, an Estonian preacher from the Church of the Holy Spirit. The catechism by Wanradt and Koell was printed in Germany **in 1535**; the text in Low German was printed on the left-hand side, while the text in Estonian on the right-hand side. It was but a few years before the council also deemed this a forbidden book "due to the many mistakes" in it. It is likely that the so-called mistakes were errors in reference to the already-accepted Lutheran principles of the time. In a lucky coincidence, 11 pages of the book were used in the binding of another book and were thus recovered. It is believed that an Estonian catechism was also in wide use in the 1550s but, unfortunately, no copies of this catechism have been found.

Even back in those days, translators were faced with the problem of which Estonian dialect to use for translations. The issue of dialect

Doorknocker (1430) on the Suurgildi *(Great Guild) building.*

became more acute as publication of books in the Estonian language started to intensify.

As early as the sixteenth century, many attempts were made to translate the Bible and hymns into Estonian. High-quality translations called for well-educated Estonians. One translation of the Bible had been started by a student of the Tallinn town school, **Hans Susi**, who died of the plague in 1549. He had been a talented young boy, whose grandmother contributed a rather large sum of money toward his education. Stricken with the plague, the boy asked the money intended for his schooling be passed on to educate another boy. This so-called **Susi capital** had already previously been added to a fund, collected from sums bequeathed for the education of poor children and other donations. Tallinn shoemakers decided to provide shoes for such students at no cost. It is not known how much progress was made on Bible translations at that time because complicated issues kept these translations from going to print and no manuscripts have been found.

Despite the pro-education position of the Lutheran church, nothing of essence changed in the conditions of schools in Old Livonia after the Reformation. The number of cloister schools dropped dramatically; the majority of schooling was carried about by **town schools**. Resident and noble families looked for instructors to provide their children with **home schooling**.

Records indicate an increase in the number of young men who left Livonia to study at universities throughout Europe.

Architecture, textiles and the fine arts in the second half of the Middle Ages. In Estonian architecture, the period of feudal splintering is known for its variety of styles. Various types of room characteristics, architectural forms, and decorative solutions were brought to Estonian towns and parish centres by influential residents and their contracted architects and designers; architectural characteristics from Western and Northern Europe became especially popular. Accepted and adapted for local conditions, these styles gave rise to unique groups of buildings that differ greatly from buildings found elsewhere in the world. Examples of such distinguishable architectural works are the three-nave churches in central Estonia and the single-nave churches in Läänemaa and Saaremaa. Small, brick churches were typical of the Tartu Diocese. In general, rural church architecture blossomed in parallel to the rise of the manor estate economy in the second half of the fifteenth century.

The most vivid examples of Estonia's architectural accomplishments are found in north Estonia – Tallinn, in particular. Public buildings and homes were designed in the Late Gothic style and remain intact today. Some fine examples from the golden period of Estonian architecture include Tallinn's Town Hall. Large homes of the wealthier city residents, the *Suurgildi* (Great Guild) building and the

The Suurgildi *(Great Guild) building in Tallinn.*

Oleviste (St Olaf's) guild building, all of which date back to the mid-sixteenth century. Two- and three-nave churches were re-built as glorious, late Gothic **basilicas**, in line with the stylistic preferences of the wealthier population. It is significant to note that the Tartu cathedral was also rebuilt for this reason.

The strongest influence on paintings, wood sculptures and textile arts were primarily influenced from **German** styles, and later by those of the **Low Countries.** These woks were usually crafted by the guild masters contracted by town halls, guilds, and wealthy individuals. The artists' circle also included artists of Estonian nationality.

Wall murals were one of the more important forms of painting during this period, but only few of these works remain today; most of the wall murals still in existence in Estonia are found in the churches that once belonged to the Saaremaa-Läänemaa Diocese. A number of well-know European mural painters worked in Tallinn. Famous German master craftsmen were also commissioned to paint in local churches. One of the best known artists in Lübeck in the second half the fifteenth century was **Hermen Rode**, who painted the side alter of the Church of St Nicholas; the other master craftsmen of Lübeck, **Bernt Notke**, painted the main altar of the Church of the Holy Spirit. Notke's greatest work was the mural entitled "Danse Macabre;" only 7.5 metres of this extraordinary mural remains today. It is believed that this mural was commissioned by one of the churches or cloisters in Tallinn.

In the fifteenth and early sixteenth century, the Tallinn foundry boasted many talented casters, primarily the casters of church bells and cannons, whose works were also commissioned from elsewhere in the Nordic countries. Cast in Tallinn, the church bell still hanging in the Church of the Holy Spirit today is the oldest church bell in all of Estonia.

Churches were rather rich in terms of gold and silver. During the iconoclasm of the Reformation, such articles were indiscriminately destroyed and stolen. In difficult times – especially times of war – articles of silver were confiscated from churches and guilds and then melted down and cast as coins. For this reason, very few of such artistic treasures remain today.

Urban culture saw a breakthrough in **Renaissance art** in the 1520s and '30s. At the time, Estonia's most renowned painter of the mediaeval era, **Michel Sittow**, worked in Tallinn. The young Tallinn native later went on to become an acclaimed Renaissance painter throughout Europe. He was commissioned for works in such faraway places as Spain, and later served in royal court of the King of Denmark. Sittow's works can be found in many museums around the world.

R**ussow's Chronicles.** In the second half of the sixteenth century, **Balthasar Russow**, a minister practising in Tallinn's Church of the Holy

Fragment of "Danse Macabre" by Bernt Notke.

Fragments of the main altar in the Church of St Nicholas (work of Hermen Rode, 1482).

Spirit, wrote **"The Chronicles of the Livonian Province"** in Low German. This work is one of the most important sources on the Estonian Middle Ages in existence today. The first publication of the chronicles, printed in Rostock in **1578**, was read by a wide public. Thanks to its popularity, a second and third publication of the work soon followed. As a resident of Tallinn, Russow was strong in his criticism of the nobility and pointed out the intensifying suppression of the peasantry. It is believed that Russow was an Estonian, the son of a Tallinn coachman. The primary content of the chronicles was in regard to the Livonian War. However, the chronicles also give a vivid and interesting depiction of life and conditions in pre-war Livonia. Customs and habits of the ruling strata are discussed at length, as are the numerous festivities. Accusing the noblemen and Catholic Church of all vices, Russow discusses the carefree and extravagant lifestyle enjoyed by the upper classes in Old Livonia in the critical pre-war period. Russow's chronicles are the primary source for getting to know the history of this period in history.

III The Period of Warfare

18. The Livonian War

International background. Already by the final quarter of the fifteenth century political changes had begun in countries surrounding the Baltic Sea. Emergence of such large centralised states as Russia, Poland-Lithuania, Denmark and Sweden by the middle of the sixteenth century sharpened particularly the question of hegemony over the Baltic Sea.

Denmark ruled over the Baltic straits. **Sweden**, then master of Finland, attempted to widen its influence further east. **Poland**, borders of which had again reached the Baltic by the fifteenth century, was gaining power. Lithuania, united with Poland, stood out in military strength.

The **Grand Duchy of Moscow**, having expanded to other Russian regions, bordered Livonia and the fight for the eastern Baltic coast emerged among its main foreign policy goals. Strengthening of Russia's economy led to wider trade interests and broader ties. But when Old Livonia's powers in 1539 barred Russians from direct trading with foreign merchants visiting its towns, Russia's interests were greatly compromised. Relations were also hampered by the fact that Livonia, wary of Russia's excessive strengthening, set direct limitations to transit of specialists (doctors, craftsmen, etc.) and certain goods (copper, tin, lead, etc.) to Russia from Western Europe. Old Livonia with its political disunion remained the only weak link in the chain of countries around the Baltic. Under such circumstances, it became a subject to territorial claims by all the latter, most notably Russia.

Diplomatic prologue. Danger from the East had caused great distress in Livonia by the early 1550s. Tartu's town council ordered the city walls checked and prepared for possible attacks. For the moment, however, peace remained. In 1554, nobles of the Order Master and Bishop of Tartu were instructed to extend it by a further 30 years. The delegation also had an obligation not to make concessions in standing trade policy. Moscow, however, was still resting on glory from victory over the Kazan Khanate and openly claimed unlimited trade freedom for its merchants. It was also demanded that the Tartu Diocese pay a tax to Russian tsar of one mark a year per capita. The Russians argued that Livonia was a territory under Russian rule and princes from past centuries had allowed German nobles to settle there only under provision that taxes would be paid correctly. Such invention greatly surprised the Livonians, who nevertheless decided to accept the harsh condition to avoid war. Truce was concluded for 15 years. The "Tartu tax" was to be paid in three years.

In the same year of 1554, an envoy from the Tsar arrived in Livonia and had the Archbishop of Riga, Order Master, and Bishop of Tartu endorse the conditions of the **treaty** in his presence. That was done, though sneakily and with hopes of cunning tax evasion, thus fixing legality of the questionable tax on paper forever. This was a great victory for Russian diplomacy.

In 1556-57, the Order once again battled with the Archbishop of Riga and his ally, Poland. The war showed the weakness of Old Livonia's powers once again. Such experience naturally just increased the appetite of its neighbours. Clashes were ended by **Pasvalys Peace Treaty**, by which the Livonian Order formed an anti-Russian alliance with Poland-Lithuania. The treaty was, however, to enter into force in five years, after the expiry of the Russian-Polish truce.

Also in 1557, the truce with Russia expired. Envoys from Old Livonia arrived in Moscow in the autumn to find Tsar **Ivan IV (the Terrible)** in absolute confidence. The Astrakhan Khanate had surrendered to him a year earlier, while favourable peace treaties were concluded with the Crimean Khan and the Swedish King. Russia was now free to deploy its forces at Livonian borders. The meeting started without a customary handshake from the Tsar. When it was apparent that the delegation had not brought the tax proceeds, the choice was made – Russia prepared for war.

The "Tartu tax" was not, of course, the cause for war, but by breaking the payment promise, the powers over Livonia provided a reason for attack. Two questions were vital now: who would help and to whom to surrender.

The countrymen once again sought ways to reinforce their status. **Envoys from Saaremaa** visited the future Swedish monarch Johan in Turku, proposing to put their island under the Swedish crown.

The war breaks out. On 22 January 1558, Russian forces, led by Tatar Khan Shah Ali, invaded the Tartu Diocese. At least a quarter of the army comprised of Tatars. Additional units simultaneously entered Latvian territories and Alutaguse. The short expedition was more of a reconnaissance, looting and scaring mission. Some important nobles were attending a lavish wedding in Tallinn at the time, and landlords could only worry about their holdings. That was why Order Master **Fürstenberg** was unable to gather a force for counterattack. Only peasants resisted, engaging in a bloody battle with the invaders at Jõhvi church. Shah Ali, having returned to Russia, wrote the Order Master, offering Livonia peace in return for quick payment of the tax due.

Still, the tax proved impossible to collect and peace remained elusive. In the spring of 1558, Russian forces attacked again, seeking to completely conquer Livonia. Siege and bombardment of **Narva** began in early April. The bombs inflicted much damage, causing occasional fires. The town was held, but as no help arrived from the rest of Old Livonia and the town had primarily relied on Russian trade, those favouring surrender prevailed. In the morning of 11 May, an all-out blaze spread through town. Defenders retreated to the castle, accompanied by many citizens seeking protection from the fire and enemy. Soon it was decided to lay down arms, as conditions offered were also quite favourable. Every individual wishing so were allowed to leave freely. The town retained its trade rights. The invaders acted politely, trying to impress positively towns not yet conquered.

Meanwhile, about 60.000 Russian troops, led by prince Shuisky arrived in south Estonia. Still

Ivan IV (the Terrible)

unable to put up resistance, the Order Master retreated to Latvia. The take-over of Kastre fortress by the Emajõgi River allowed Russians to transport by water to **Tartu** with no resistance their heavy siege cannons. The town was taken on 18 July, exactly a week from the start of the attack. Seemingly forgetting their actual situation, the Bishop and town council proposed to the attackers stringent surrender conditions. Shuisky surprisingly accepted them all and Tartu retained all its rights for the time being. The fall of the town marked the end of one local state – the Tartu Diocese. The Bishop himself was allowed to settle at Kärkna monastery, but was soon sent to Russia. A majority of Tartu's German citizens were deported to Russia a few years later.

A relatively effortless conquest of Narva and Tartu, two towns of major importance, was of great strategic and moral importance of the Russian army. The victor claimed to have seized 552 cannons and large quantities of gunpowder in Tartu. A list of smaller fortresses – Rõngu, Rakvere, Laiuse, Põltsamaa, Toolse, and others – were taken in August. Russian troops arrived at Tallinn, but did not undertake a siege of the city at the time. In the autumn of 1558, leaders of the Livonian Order attempted broader counterattack, but achieved no breakthroughs and direct war activities on Estonian territory faded.

Under mediation of Danish nobles, a six-month truce was concluded in April 1559.

Local powers used the brief suspension to seek **foreign assistance**. The party friendly to Poland took lead in the Livonian Order. Its head, **Gotthard Kettler**, assistant to Order Master, superseded Order Master Fürstenberg and secured his election to the seat.

In the autumn of 1559, the forces of the Order and Bishopric made an attempt to take back the Tartu Diocese. Rõngu fortress was conquered and victory was declared at battle at Tõravere, but Tartu and Laiuse did not fall.

In September 1559, the Bishop of **Saaremaa-Läänemaa** completed a transaction with Frederik II, the new King of Denmark. The King purchased the diocese for 30,000 thalers and handed it over to **Duke Magnus**, his brother. Magnus, 19 years of age, and his party landed in Kuressaare in April 1560. The ambitious youngster, sworn in as Bishop, also bought himself bishop's titles in Couronia and Tallinn and planned to acquire lands yet unconquered by the Russians. Having hired deserted mercenaries and adventurers of all varieties, he set out to loot several mainland areas. Doing so, Magnus was drawn into conflict with the Order, but a truce was concluded, suspending hostilities until the next spring. The King of Denmark summoned his brother to report.

Military **defeat of the Livonian Order.** Russian troops started a fresh attack in 1560. On 2 August, the last field battle of the Order took place at **Hoomuli** mansion near Ērģeme. Trying to prevent Russians from advancing towards Viljandi from Latvian areas, the Order's land marshal attacked 12,000-strong force with his 500 horsemen. The Order's force was surrounded and completely eliminated.

Local resistance had now scaled down to defence of fortresses. The latter were mainly manned with mercenaries, whose morale had often fallen due to unpaid wages and despair. Even the mighty **Viljandi** fortress was simply handed over to the enemy after just a few days of siege. Former Order Master Fürstenberg was captured and sent to Russia, where he died. Forces of the Order were in control of just Tallinn, Pärnu, Paide and the surrounding areas.

Uprising by Estonian peasants. For the local peasantry, the war resulted in nothing but suffering and duties. Villages were unprotected from looting and military raids by both sides. The people were burdened with taxes to cover for payments to mercenaries. Peasants were conscripted as well.

In some occasions, the peasants exploited the loss of power of their oppressors with acts of revenge. Some Germans were executed and mansions burned. Considering the Russians enemies of their enemies, the peasants had sometimes assisted them as spies and guides in the early days of the war. It soon turned out, however, that the Russians were trying to win over local landowners by various facilities. Peasants had no chance but to stand for themselves.

In September 1560, an uprising ensued, gripping most of **Läänemaa** and **Harjumaa**. As the chronicler Russow wrote, the peasants had decided "not to submit to the nobles or perform any corvée, but to seek complete liberation from it or to utterly destroy and uproot the nobles." As the uprising spread, peasant leaders emerged. It was written in Renner's chronicles that the peasants "chose a non-German blacksmith their king and set him on a carriage; 12 guards ran by side and one rode in front with a bagpipe – he was his music-man. The king's head was crowned with two hats encircled by thorns, this was his crown." The peasants attempted to talk with the Tallinn town council, apparently hoping to take advantage of its hostilities with Harjumaa-Virumaa vassals. The

Duke Magnus

town council, however, advised the peasants to end their rebellion.

The rebel parties started to gather at **Koluvere** fortress, where many nobles had sought refuge. Unexpectedly, the peasants were attacked by a strong troop of horsemen comprising of nobles from Läänemaa, who at first destroyed a 300-strong peasant party and then the smaller rebel squads. A total of 200 peasants were believed to have been killed at Koluvere. Their "king" was taken to Kuressaare and drawn and quartered. Other leaders of the uprising were tortured and executed as well. The uprising occasionally flared until 1561, but its spine had been broken.

This was one of the largest peasant uprisings in Estonian history.

Change of sovereigns. The advance of Russian troops and the peasant uprising prompted the powers of Old Livonia to seek new, stronger superiors.

Due to Order Master Kettler's ties with **Poland**, most fortresses unconquered by Russians were manned by Polish troops in late 1560.

But many in Tallinn found Denmark and, in particular, Sweden more appealing. There were also hopes to achieve better trade conditions under rule of the latter.

In 1561, the Swedes drove the Poles from Toompea in Tallinn. Subsequently, the knights of Harju, Viru and Järva, and the city of Tallinn surrendered to Swedish King Erik XVI, on 4 and 6 July, respectively. **Swedish rule** was thereby imposed over **North Estonia**.

On other Livonian territories, the Livonian Order Master and Archbishop of Riga swore allegiance to Sigismund II August, the King of Poland. **The Livonian Order then ceased to exist**.

In 1561, Magnus returned to Kuressaare, bringing a large amount of money and ten battleships. The Danish King sent with him the vice-regent, who was to guide the army and foreign policy. The **Saaremaa-Läänemaa** Diocese thus ceased to exist and was directly united **with Denmark**.

The mediaeval political division were now of the past. **The year 1561** thereby marked the end of the Old Livonian era. In 1563, the conflict between Sweden and Denmark grew into the seven-year Nordic War, with Livonia once again becoming a battleground. During the war, the Swedes invaded the island of Hiiumaa, which provided a valuable base for attacks on Saaremaa. Main battles were fought on the islands, though some activity was also seen in Läänemaa, where Sweden fought the Poland-Denmark alliance.

King Erik XIV of Sweden

King Frederik II of Denmark

A distinctive role was held by special German mercenary horsemen squads, which comprised of former servants and mercenaries of the Order, such as **nobles** deprived of their estates, various adventurers, as well as occasional Estonians. Some of those rose up against the Swedes and conquered the town of Pärnu, subsequently handing the important base over to Polish forces.

After indecisive events, a **peace treaty** was concluded between Denmark and Sweden in 1570. Danish rule was now limited to the island of Saaremaa.

Several changes in the division of power between the Baltic countries fighting over Livonia had occurred by late 1560s. In 1569, the Kingdom of Poland and the Grand Duchy of Lithuania entered the Union of Lublin, creating a commonwealth – *Rzeczpospolita* – which naturally considered Livonia to be its territory. A coup in Sweden in autumn of 1568 brought Johan III, brother-in-law of the King of Poland to power. That resulted in improvement of ties between Sweden and Poland. Commands of both armies in Livonia signed a truce, later even teaming up against Russia.

Birth of the so-called Livonian Kingdom. Magnus, in loggerheads with the King of Denmark and having lost sole power over Saaremaa, aspired to expand his domain and sought assistance from the King of Poland. But as negotiations were fruitless, he sent envoys to the Tsar of Russia in 1569. Ivan the Terrible now sensed an opportunity of establishing a **vassal kingdom** under Moscow's influence. He cherished Magnus by calling him "the King," promised help against the Swedes, and prompted him to marry his niece's daughter. The capital of the new kingdom was originally planned at **Põltsamaa**. The young Duke was in his turn satisfied and delighted by his lavish reception in Moscow.

In late August of 1570, the new Livonian "King" arrived near **Tallinn** with a large Russian force and a few mercenaries. The city was besieged. The sea route remained open, but did not supply enough ammunition and food for the city. The plague devastated the besieged city through the winter. In March, however, it spread to the besiegers. After almost seven months of siege, Magnus's forces set fire to their camp in mid-March 1571. The Russian army left Estonia, and Magnus in turn departed for his "capital"

King Sigismund II August of Poland

Põltsamaa with his Germans, fearing Ivan the Terrible's rage over the failed siege.

Among towns, Tallinn and Paide were now under Swedish rule, while Pärnu were under Polish control. Kuressaare, granted town rights by Magnus in 1563, were under Danish rule together with Saaremaa. The remaining towns, as well as most of Estonian territory, were under Russian rule.

Russian troops score important victories. Up to that time, most of the opportunist adventurers-mercenaries, in search for a more favourable regent, had remained with Magnus. But in late 1571, several of their cavalry units attacked Tartu – then under Russian rule. The attempt was unsuccessful and leaders of the traitors turned to serve the King of Poland instead. Magnus seriously feared that such conduct by his men would finally enrage Ivan the Terrible. The fear materialised and the Tsar arrived in Livonia heading a large army. In 1572-73, the Russians took Karksi and Paide from the Swedes, but were defeated in a battle

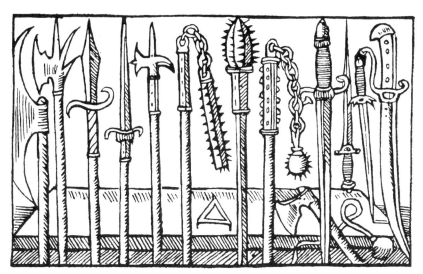

Sixteenth century weaponry (contemporary sketch)

near Koluvere. The Tsar was, however, still merciful towards Magnus. In addition to new land grants, he replaced his ally's bride, who had passed away, with her 13-year old sister. After a lavish wedding in Novgorod, the couple settled at Põltsamaa.

The war raged on. Swedes, using Tallinn as their base, shipped mercenaries from Germany, Scotland and England. In 1574, Swedish forces attacked Põltsamaa. They were unable to take the fortress, but managed to burn the surrounding village to ashes. Magnus, in critical condition, once again received assistance from Russia. Using Russian and Tatar forces, he managed to conquer almost all of Estonia, including Pärnu and Saaremaa, during **1575-76**. Polish forces were driven from the country, while Sweden retained only Tallinn and Harju region.

Peasantry in combats. The situation was depressing for the local people. In addition to the movement of armies and mercenaries subject to three separate masters, the peasants who defiantly farmed on had to put up with terror by gangs of former peasants, who had abandoned work for looting. The final blow was delivered by **the plague** that had repeatedly raged through the 1570s. Despite all that, the land was more or less able to supply the towns, looting armies, robbers and, to some extent, themselves. Long-lasting sieges often resulted in **famine** for the surrounding areas.

Units of peasants that had fled to Tallinn and common townspeople were formed in the Swedish army in 1576 and prepared for guerrilla warfare against the Russians. The goal was looting in enemy territory, but surprise attacks on Russian troops and even attacks on fortresses were carried out. The approximately 400-strong force was headed by a journeyman minter named **Ivo Schenkenberg**. His outstanding courage won Schenkenberg the title of the "Livonian Hannibal" and his peasants the "people of Hannibal" among enemies. Due to the same excess courage, however, the unit was later in 1579 surrounded by Russians near Rakvere. Victory over the grossly outnumbered rebels was held as a considerable achievement. The wounded leader was taken to Pskov and cruelly executed together with his men.

In addition to the peasant force from the city, several other self-styled peasant squads attacked the enemy. Among the largest was the unit of **Ohtra Jürgen**.

End of the Livonian Kingdom. The Tsar no longer had confidence in Magnus's commanding abilities and sent his own army under Russian commanders against Tallinn. In late January of **1557**, the army reached the city walls of Tallinn – a symbolic moment when Estonia's future was to be decided. The city was bombarded with large cannonballs and firebombs, but did not fall. The defence was well-organised, Schenkenberg's troops acted defiantly as well. After a seven-week siege the Russians once again burnt down their camp and pulled out.

During the hard times, Magnus begun to seek a new master. Ivan the Terrible was displeased and had the traitor imprisoned. Duke Magnus was later allowed to leave for Kuramaa, where he chose to serve Poland-Lithuania instead. Russian forces subsequently took Põltsamaa and eliminated the Livonian vassal kingdom.

End of the war. Poland had so far only modestly interfered in the fighting on Estonian territory. But with the crowning of **Stefan Bathory** in 1579, extensive military campaigns against Russia were launched. Polish cavalry successfully invaded Tartu region later in the year, and even some of Russia's own territories were taken the year after.

Poland and Sweden acted independently in different Estonian regions. Both, however, pursued the goal of taking back lands fallen under Russian rule.

While Russia concentrated on fighting Poland, Sweden gained ground in Läänemaa and Virumaa. In 1581, Swedish troops, assembled in Finland, crossed the frozen Gulf of Finland under the leadership of **Pontus De la Gardie**. After a siege, Rakvere was taken, followed by several smaller fortresses. Haapsalu resisted for the longest, but surrendered as well. Narva was taken by storm and the Swedish commander allowed his troops to arbitrarily kill and loot for some 24 hours. After Paide was taken, **the entire northern part of Estonia was under Swedish rule** and the battles carried over to Russia.

The cruelty of Russian troops during looting raids (from a contemporary leaflet)

Russia was now attacked from both sides of Lake Peipsi. Large chunks of Russia fell to Polish forces, but their siege of Pskov was unsuccessful. With the truce of **Jam Zapolsk** concluded in mid-January **1582**, Ivan the Terrible regained Russian towns and lands from the Poles, but had to surrender all Livonian fortresses under his control. **South Estonia** was thereby transferred **to the rule of *Rzeczpospolita***.

In 1581 and 1582, Swedish forces scored victories throughout Ingria up to Lake Ladoga. In **1583**, at the estuary of the **Plyusa River**, a truce was concluded between Sweden and Russia as well, leaving the Swedes with all of west and north Estonia, as well as areas conquered in the Ingria.

The Livonian War was over. A short break occurred in the fighting era. The **balance achieved was, however, temporary**. The land remained divided between the kings of Poland, Sweden and Denmark. Little commonality could be found in the administrative practices in the regions. Estonia therefore experienced even deeper divisions than during the days of the Old Livonian Order and dioceses.

Pontus de la Gardie

19. Estonia under the Three Kings

The Polish era in south Estonia. Upon the surrender of the Livonian Order and the Archbishop of Riga to the King of Poland, the Livonian nobility had demanded that their privileges remain unaltered. The **Sigismund August privilege**, named after the King, in fact did restore the nobles' former estates and fixed serfdom for peasants. The Lutheran faith was to be maintained and all offices filled by Germans. Through the entire war era the local nobility had proven untrustworthy, so Poland was satisfied that the province should be closer associated with the state and should be Polonised. To pursue that, Stefan Bathory began appointing Polish and Lithuanian nobles to leading posts.

The Polish era in Livonia began with an administrative shake-up. The Livonian **constitutions** were enforced in 1582. The highest official was, as until then, the **vice-regent**. Land was divided into three: the Tartu, Pärnu and Cēsis **prefectures**. A prefect for life was appointed for each by the King. The prefect's powers were, however, limited mainly to leading the nobles' cavalry.

In 1589, the prefectures were renamed duchies and the prefects, respectively, to dukes – just as in Poland. Prefects (later dukes) were further divided into sub-prefectures, headed by royal appointees who were not subordinate to the prefect. There were nine sub-prefectures in Estonia.

Representative organ of the local nobility was the **Diet**, which also comprised of representatives of larger towns. Work of the Diet was closely associated with Polish-Lithuanian state authorities. The Diet elected its representatives – two Poles, two Lithuanians and two Germans – to the Polish *Sejm*. Higher offices were similarly divided among the three nationalities. Courts of the prefectures did not consider matters concerning peasants. The latter were judged by landowners and, on state lands, the sub-prefects. The peasants were still considered attached to the land.

The share of Polish and Lithuanian nobility increased among landowners, reaching 30 per cent by the end of the sixteenth century. The new landowners oppressed the people, as had the Germans. The situation facing the peasantry was somewhat improved only by the fact that most lands were nationalised and oppression was lighter there than in nobles' estates.

During the last decades of the century, Polish authorities attempted to restore the country's economy. Duties were harmonised and placed in effect. This favoured the peasants' initiative in farming. Farms emptied by the wars were populated primarily on attitude towards Poland, therefore most new settlers originated from the

King Stefan Bathory of Poland

state's core areas. The period of growth was, nevertheless, terminated in the last decades of the seventeenth century by continual war and the economic decay of the state. Attitudes towards the peasantry were also changed; everything was now taken from them.

The Livonian War's legacy to the new authorities included thoroughly impoverished towns. Steps taken for their revitalisation were fruitful to some extent. Tartu, Viljandi and Pärnu rose again as trade centres. The lead among them was Pärnu, now united, with its valuable port. As a result of war, Old Pärnu had economically perished. Stefan Bathory in 1584 granted town rights to **Valga**. The development of towns in Old Livonia was, however, largely influenced by continuing uncertainty. The magistrates quarrelled with the sub-prefects. New decay in towns was triggered by the war of early seventeenth century. As Poland failed to secure sufficient development prospects for the towns, townspeople often welcomed the arrival of troops from the economically more liberal Sweden.

Re-institution of Catholicism was considered the main priority for the Polonising of the new domain. Another important consideration was Sweden, enemy number one, being Lutheran. **Counterreformation** was launched, naturally favoured by the Pope, who eyed spreading the faith even to Russia.

Counterreformation began from the youth perspective. The main part in shaping practical education was played by the Jesuits, formally called the Society of Jesus, acting against the reformation throughout Europe.

The main Jesuit centre in Estonia was established in Tartu, the importance of which was repeatedly stressed by Polish authorities. Members of the order arrived there in 1583 and immediately started to form a **college** – an organisation of priests and secular brothers living together. Important directions to better regulate activity by the Jesuits were provided by a leading counterreformation missionary, Papal envoy **Antonio Possevino**, who visited Tartu in 1585. A **grammar school** was founded in the college and soon provided education for about 70 students. In addition, the Jesuits founded an **interpreters' seminary** in Tartu. Besides languages and basic clerical training, bookbinding, tailor-

A Jesuit (contemporary sketch)

ing and other skills, as well as printing, was taught there, for the graduates were to be future publishers of translated books. In both the grammar school and seminary, lessons were taught in Latin. In spring and autumn, the students performed dramas in Latin. There were several Estonians studying in both institutions.

Property of the Jesuit college included two churches and several dwellings. In addition, economically supportive holdings were obtained, for example, in Rõngu.

The Jesuits' success was based on their ability to exploit local conditions. Their appeal remained low in towns. But peasants, who met Jesuit priests during their long travels and attended their simple, emotional sermons, expressed considerable sympathy.

To instruct the clergy on divine services in Estonian, relevant books had to be issued. The translation and publishing activities of college members were rather quick. Of books issued in Estonian, only,one, the 1622 small Latin book of common prayers, "Agenda Parva," has survived. It includes prayers, as well as texts in Polish, Latvian and good South Estonian dialect. Only a few books of the era survived, as most of them were destroyed by the Lutherans during the forthcoming Swedish era.

Seal of the order of Jesuits

Aspirations of the Jesuits on fields of culture, education and book publishing deserve high appreciation.

The Polish era in south Estonia was cut short. Even less was done for a peaceful arrangement of local life. The changes planned were not able to take root under circumstances at the time and brought about no long-term influence. The Catholic counterreformation stopped short. Legal status of the peasantry was still framed with relations to serfdom.

The Swedish era in North Estonia. North Estonia, now under Swedish rule, was titled the Estonian Duchy. Local nobility retained wide influence. Swedish kings fixed all previous rights and privileges of the nobility. The Swedish state originally received large estates, as former lands of the Order, Bishop and churches were acquired, plus lands of the nobles having fled Estonia or fought against Sweden. More lands were therefore in state ownership rather than of the nobility.

State lands were administered by a Tallinn-based **governor**, the highest local royal representative. Due to continuous wars the governor also served as army commander, supervising the maintenance and defence of fortresses, equipping and transporting of troops, as well as proper fulfilment of the cavalry service obligation. Another main task of the governor was checking proper submission of state taxes by the peasants. Assistants appointed by the King assisted him in all fields.

The province was divided into seven **fortress fiefdoms**: Tallinn, Paide, Rakvere, Narva, Haapsalu, Koluvere and Lihula.

State estates were locally administered by bailiffs, who gathered taxes and acted as judges. As supervision over bailiffs' actions was weak, they often overtaxed peasants, but withhold the resources from the state. King Karl IX once commented that most individuals who had served as bailiff for half a dozen years could be justifiably hung. To simplify investigations into misconduct, Karl IX in 1600 ordered the **levelling of taxes** in all of North Estonia. The tithe was replaced with a fixed corn tax and number of duties were slashed. Tax levels remained roughly even with those of late Order era. Varying local conditions, however, hampered a complete levelling. As for corvée obligation, it is known that, for example, in Haapsalu in 1597, a man with a pair of oxen and a labourer (male or female) per each plough-land had to be submitted for 200 and 260 days, respectively.

The peasant population decreased considerably during the wars, but the amount of corvée labour had not, thus the number of days of labour increased in the early Swedish era.

Despite extensive obligations, submission to the bailiff was less burdening for peasants than life in a private estate. In **private estates**, the nobility's powers were nearly unlimited. When North Estonian vassals submitted to Sweden in 1561, all their standing privileges were fixed by the King. The landowner had full reign on all life over his property. The state had to apply for landowner's permission for any activities in the noble's premises. The landowners' only notable obligation was cavalry service: one fully equipped horseman per 15 plough-lands had to be submitted to state service on demand.

The kings had given emptied Estonian estates to members of prominent Swedish noble families already during the Livonian War. Germans were nevertheless still dominant among the local nobility. Nobles formed the **Estonian knighthood**, which had its own authorities and officials. Such noble self-rule was parallel and in competition with state authority.

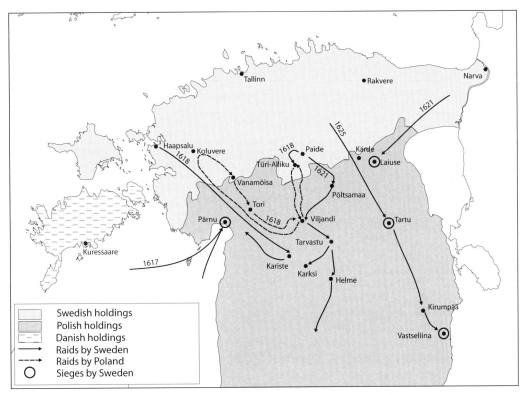

Main events of the wars between Poland and Sweden

The Diet, attended by all landowners, was the highest authority of the knighthood. The Diet was chaired by head of the knighthood. Estonia was divided into **four counties**, or districts: Harjumaa, Virumaa, Järvamaa and Läänemaa. Each had a police chief from the ranks of the nobility. The Swedish kings had stood against "non-Christian beating and corporal punishment" of peasants, but the landowners actually cared little. The need for improving peasants' conditions was notably stressed by Karl IX. He demanded that peasants should have the right to send their sons to schools. As the Swedish *Riksdag* included representatives of the peasantry among those of other classes, the King demanded equal legal protection to Estonian peasants as well. He condemned the serfdom that remained, claiming civilised people had abolished it long ago. In general, the extensive reform plans by Carl IX pushed for both legal and administrative "Swedification" of the province. Yet the King's statements about life here remained hollow and actual steps were not peasant-friendly.

All the reform plans offered by the kings were met by fierce resistance from local landowners. On the other hand, the King could not manage without support from the nobility. Money shortage and other problems forced the state to grant more estates to the nobility and make other concessions. By 1620, as much as four-fifths of Estonian lands under Kingdom of Sweden were in private ownership.

Saaremaa under Danish rule. The fate of Saaremaa differed greatly from that of other Estonian regions due to smaller losses during the war.

Danish authorities enforced the nobility's standing privileges. The nobles formed the **Saaremaa knighthood**. This largely limited the actions of state authorities, but the Danes firmly enforced authority of their state. Influence of the knighthood was weaker on Saaremaa than in the rest of Estonia, but the cavalry service required was more stringent; of lands, two thirds were held by state and the remaining were in private ownership. The state conducted **reduction**, or the confiscation of land from the landowners. The nobles were deeply annoyed by the move and even attempted to break away from Denmark to establish their own state.

State lands were administered by a royal **vice-regent**, assisted by a number of lower-ranking officials. The land was divided into **departments**, headed by administrators, who were assisted by elders elected among peasants, called taskmasters and overseers.

Departments were divided into smaller administrative districts. The peasants were judged by local courts, which comprised of the vice-regent and secretary, as well as so-called assistant justices from among the peasantry.

The rights of peasants were more extensive on Saaremaa than on the mainland. Relatively satisfactory living conditions are reflected by rich and spacious dwellings. Estate duties, in particular the corvée, were, however, a heavy burden to the countrymen of Saaremaa as well.

A number of influential persons, merchants and craftsmen were among those to flee from the mainland to the island during the Livonian War. The village expanded and by rights granted by Duke Magnus in **1563**, **Kuressaare** became a town. Kuressaare also acted as Estonia's westernmost grain exporting port.

The kingdoms continue land division. Neither Sweden nor Poland was fully satisfied with their holdings. In **1600**, the war for Livonia broke out again. At first, while the main Polish forces were engaged in battles on the state's southern border, the Swedes claimed victories. They took all of Estonia and north Latvia, reaching Riga.

A while later, however, the mighty Polish cavalry took over the momentum. The front occasionally moved north from even Tartu and Paide.

Serious **famine** accompanied the hardships of war in 1601-02, the main blow being naturally born by the peasantry. Desperate people sought sustenance even by cannibalism. Many, however, did not escape death by starvation.

Battles lasted until both Poland and Sweden turned, for a while, to invade Russia.

When **Gustav II Adolf**, son of Karl IX, was crowned King of Sweden in 1611, he immediately concluded a truce with Poland and extended it further following that.

After reaching a favourable peace with Russia, Sweden resumed fighting in Estonia and Latvia. Success was now with the troops of Gustav II Adolf, who took Riga in 1621 and Tartu in **1625**.

In 1629, a truce was signed in **Altmark** (now in Poland), by which Poland surrendered all territories north of the Daugava River to Sweden. The truce was later extended.

The 70-year war era had ended with the annexation of mainland Estonia to the Kingdom of Sweden.

Saaremaa remained under Danish control. But after the **1643-45** Denmark-Sweden war, Denmark had to surrender Saaremaa to Sweden under the **Brömsebro** peace.

All of Estonian territory had thereby fallen under the rule of the **Swedish state**. The Swedish era in Estonia had begun.

IV Swedish Rule

20. The Establishment of Swedish Rule over All of Estonian Territory

Administration. With the establishment of Swedish rule over the entire Estonian mainland, a new administration developed – which remained unchanged for a long time even after the end of Swedish rule in Estonia. As it was earlier, Estonian territory did not form one administrative whole but remained divided between two provinces. The four North Estonian regions (Läänemaa, Harju, Järva and Virumaa), which were awarded to Sweden from the Livonian War, formed the **Estonian province**. The **Livonian province** with Riga as its capital consisted of territories conquered from Poland in southern Estonia and northern Latvia. The Pärnu and Tartu regions, covering all of South Estonia, belonged to the Livonian province. **Saaremaa**, which was united with Swedish possessions only as a result of the Brömsebro Treaty with Denmark in 1645, formally belonged to the Livonian province but continued to preserve a special status. Unlike other districts, Saaremaa had its own lord lieutenant, nobility, and church administration (consistory), and its taxation system differed from Estonia and Livonia. The island of **Ruhnu**, which belonged to the diocese of Couronia, was the last piece of Estonian territory to fall under Swedish rule following the Oliwa Peace Treaty in 1660. Swedish rule, however, did not reach Setumaa, the south-eastern corner of Estonia that remained, as in the Middle Ages, under Russia.

The King appointed the **governor-general** of the Estonian and Livonian provinces. The governor-general of Estonia lived in Toompea Castle in Tallinn, while the governor-general of Livonia in Riga Castle on the shore of the Daugava River. They commanded the armed forces on their administrative territory, appointed and inspected the work of civil servants, checked the province's incomes and expenses. The governors-general also took care of postal services, road and bridge maintenance, as well as public order.

Nobility. Besides governors-general and other Swedish state officials, local nobility and town councils also exercised power. In the 1630s, a **Livonian** nobility developed alongside their **Estonian** counterparts, which had grown out of Harju-Viru vassalage. On **Saaremaa**, while under Danish rule, an independent nobility was formed and it survived the unification with Swedish-held lands. The nobility united local landowners defended their rights before Swedish state authorities and, at the same time, solved all local problems that did not directly belong to the spheres of interest of the King and the governor-general. Members of the nobility gathered at **diets**, which on average convened every three years. In the meantime, twelve (six on Saaremaa) **councillors**, elected for life among the most respectable noblemen at the diets, managed the affairs of the nobility. While the magistrates usually discussed the most important matters, the head of the nobility (in Livonia known as the regional marshal) had to solve everyday problems. New magistrates were usually elected from among former marshals.

Judicial authority. The judicial system established under Swedish rule was preserved until the end of the nineteenth century. To maintain public order, **judges** were elected from amongst local landlords. Their task was to arrest and return fugitives peasant, to investigate minor crimes committed by peasants, and to punish those convicted.

On a district level, **district courts** investigated the cases of peasants and other commoners. Serious offences and all cases brought by noblemen were solved on the provincial level at the **Estonian Supreme Provincial Court** in Tallinn and at **Livonian High Court,** which operated in Tartu for a long time. The Swedish King remained a final appeal possibility for those dissatisfied with the court verdicts. The King's ruling remained the ultimate decision in judicial matters.

Swedish state power and Baltic nobility. As the Estonian nobility and Tallinn had come under Swedish rule of their free will, the privileges of local nobility and towns that were in ways more extensive than those of their counterparts in Sweden were preserved. Sweden's attitude towards Livonia, which was considered a conquered province, was different. King Gustav II Adolf assigned Governor-general **Johan Skytte,** who was appointed to the office in 1629 in Riga, to integrate Livonia into Sweden quickly by introducing the Swedish administrative and judicial system. Due to the death of Gustav II Adolf in 1632 Skytte's quick-paced work remained unfinished. The aristocracy that came to power in Sweden quickly reached an agreement with the Livonian nobility and in 1632 Skytte was recalled from Riga. The Swedish high aristocracy, who in the following decades acquired significant amount of land in Estonia and Livonia, was as interested as the Germans in the preservation and expansion of noble privileges in the Baltic provinces. Therefore, by the middle of the seventeenth century, the Livonian nobility and towns gained similar rights to those in Estonia. Such a situation lasted until King Karl XI came to power in 1672.

Population. When a long-term armistice was finally signed between Poland and Sweden, there were probably few people who remembered the pre-war days. The land, exhausted from continuous wars, offered a depressing view. A great deal of farmland had not been tilled for decades and had therefore grown over with bushes. Some of the towns, settlements, strongholds, manors and villages lay in ruins. The population had fallen catastrophically. In the 1620s the number of local peasants was estimated to be **less than 100,000.** In fact, the number may have been a bit bigger, but still over half the population had perished during the wars. The areas that were more densely populated and relatively more prosperous suffered most in the wars. In Järva region, 90 per cent of the farms were neglected. The outskirts of Tallinn, western part of Virumaa, Viljandi region and western Tartu region were ravaged to a similar extent. Saaremaa and Hiiumaa, the vicinity of Karksi and Helme (Viljandi region) and areas near the Russian border suffered minor losses only. Some peasants who fled to Russia during the war had built Estonian villages on the eastern coast of Lake Peipsi.

A monument to Swedish King Gustav II Adolf in Tartu.

In the 1630s the lands were put to use again. In order to enlarge the labour force quickly, landlords invited new people to villages, exempting the new settlers from all kinds of taxes usually for three years. With such incentives, peasants from less fertile lands moved to the ravaged but more fertile lands. About one-third of Estonian peasants resettled at that time, either moving in search of a new home or remaining in a new area after being displaced by war. The peasants searched for better farmlands, as well as more lenient landlords. The conditions were quite favourable for moving, as in some places there were no landlords at all, in others they had only recently moved into a new manor and were not familiar with local circumstances.

In late 1630s, the population of Saaremaa made up about a quarter of all Estonians. However, a significant number of them moved to free lands on the mainland. They usually settled in the regions of Läänemaa or on the western coast, but sometimes even in eastern Estonia. During the wars, landlords in Läänemaa had already attempted to forcibly settle people from Saaremaa.

In the second quarter of the seventeenth century, numerous representatives of other peoples also arrived in Estonia. In some places they even formed the majority of the population, settling in many empty villages close to one another. There are more precise data available on South Estonia concerning the location of settlements. As much as 17 per cent of the peasants there were immigrants. The figure was probably about the same in North Estonia.

Russian peasants were most numerous among the foreigners who settled in Estonia. Craftsmen, merchants and fishermen also came from Russia. In general the Russians lived in eastern Estonia, for example in Alutaguse, but also further from the border. Later, at the end of the seventeenth century, the so-called Old Believers – Russians who were persecuted for opposing reforms in the Russian Orthodox Church – settled on the northern and western coasts of Lake Peipsi.

Finns also made up a large number of newcomers to Estonia. The gathered in villages in Viru and Harju regions, where they made up 20 and 12 per cent of the population respectively. A part of the Finnish newcomers were settled by state authorities, while others left Finland to escape compulsory military service. At first the Swedish kings disallowed the enserfment of Finnish and Swedish peasants. However, in the course of time, such royal interference diminished and the Finns were forced to fulfil heavy manorial burdens as well.

Latvians, who mainly settled in the vicinity of Valga, formed the third big group of newcomers.

In all members of at least ten foreign nations lived among Estonian peasants; besides the aforementioned groups there were Poles, Germans, Lithuanians, Swedes, Hungarians, and even Dutch and Scots.

The foreigners arrived in the course of several decades. As most of them lived scattered among Estonians, they soon adopted the local language, customs and ways of work. They were assimilated as early as the seventeenth century. Only some Russian villages, including those on the coast of Peipsi, remained unchanged.

Despite a significant flow of foreign immigrants, the native population itself had the final say in their preservation. After the end of the wars the number of Estonians grew quite rap-

A Russian village on the shores of Lake Peipsi during the seventeenth century.

The cabin in Kärde, according to folk tradition, in which the Swedish-Russian peace agreement was signed.

idly. The people who survived were mostly young and that proved to be extremely vital. Nothing hindered the establishment of new families, as there was plenty of free land. Former cottagers got their own farms, though at times the landlords forced some of them into farming. Favourable circumstances supported the high birth rate. Events of the Russian-Swedish War in 1656-1658, the plague of 1657 and others caused setbacks. Because of these reasons the population growth was halted temporarily, but by 1695, the Estonian population is estimated to have been over 350,000 people. The land was once again filled with children.

Russian-Swedish War 1656-1661. Although, according to the peace treaty, Estonia, Livonia and Ingria belonged to Sweden, such a solution satisfied neither Russia, Poland, nor Denmark. In 1655, Swedish King Karl X Gustav waged a campaign in the course of which he occupied Couronia, Lithuania, Eastern Prussia and a great part of Poland. The Baltic Sea was becoming Sweden's internal sea. The Russian Tsar Alexei I Mikhailovich was especially disturbed because Lithuania, which he had regarded as his future possession, had fallen into the hands of the Swedes.

In the late autumn of 1655, Russians started to prepare extensively for a secret attack on Estonia, Livonia and Ingria. In the early summer of 1656, the Tsar initiated war, hoping at last to conquer the lands remained elusive to him. Attempting to secure a victory, he directed the siege of Riga in person. However, Riga withstood the siege. The taking of **Tartu** in the autumn of 1656 remained his biggest victory. The strongholds of Vastseliina and Vasknarva also fell into the hands of the Russians.

At the end of 1658, an armistice was signed in the village of Vallisaare near Narva. However, Russia was forced to conclude a final peace in **Kärde** (Laiuse parish) in **1661** as Sweden ridded itself of its opponents in the south and threatened an attack. Thus, Russia had to abandon its conquests in Estonia and Livonia. Sweden had reached the pinnacle of its power.

21. The Strengthening of Royal Power. Everyday Life under Swedish Rule

Reduction. In 1660, four year old Karl XI came to the Swedish throne. He began his reign independently in 1672, bringing with him a remarkable change in the relations between the crown and the nobility in the Baltic provinces. Having inherited an empty treasury, Karl XI started to take back state lands given to private individuals by his predecessors – the so-called **reduction**. In Sweden such steps had been taken earlier as well in order to increase the state's income, but this had not touched the Baltic provinces. A decision of the Swedish parliament in 1680 extended the reduction to Estonia and Livonia.

Such a step by the Swedish parliament triggered strong **opposition** among the Baltic nobility, who regarded the reform as not only detrimental to their economic interests, but also as a violation of their rights. The nobility believed that only local diets – and not the Swedish parliament, whose decisions were said to be invalid for Estonia and Livonia – were entitled to legislate. After the parliament gave the King full powers to carry out the reduction in 1682, it became much more difficult for the Baltic nobility to oppose it.

As a rule, only the manors given to nobility during Swedish rule were subject to reduction. There were more of them in Livonia and therefore the local nobility was more eager to criticise the activities of Swedish authorities. However, this gave an opposite result to what had been expected; the King became indignant and thus demanded that portioned manors – the lands given to private ownership already before the establishment of Swedish rule – were to be taken back as well. Therefore, four-fifths of the lands were subject to reduction in Livonia. In Estonia the respective figure was 54 per cent and on Saaremaa 30 per cent.

Unlike in Sweden, the manors were not divided in the Baltic countries. The manors which were taken back were usually rented to their former owners who had to give a part of their income as rent to the Swedish state. After the manors were given back, state income increased significantly. Together with this the state of education and church improved.

The reduction did not change the status of manors taken back by the state only. The manors, which remained in private property, were once again made subject to feudal law. For example, they were not freely transacted (buying, selling, exchanging, pawning), and such transactions required royal approval. Thus **state control** was established over all landed property of Baltic manors.

Rearrangements in Livonia. The reduction caused growing discontent among landlords with Swedish state authorities. Several Livonian noblemen called for a boycott of the King's orders. **Johann Reinhold Patkul,** an educated district magistrate but known for his spiteful character, numerous legal proceedings against his brothers, and maltreatment of servants, became leader of the Livonian nobility's opposition. In 1695 Patkul and his collaborators were put on trial at a special court in Stockholm. They were accused of insulting the King, criminal writings, and rebellious activities. Patkul was sentenced to death and his property confiscated. However, he succeeded in escaping abroad where, on the eve of the Great Northern War, he became one of the fiercest plotters against Sweden.

To break the opposition of local nobility, Karl XI named the capable and loyal **Jacob Johan Hastfer** governor-general. Representatives of the state were unyielding in their demands and thus managed to carry out the reduction.

As a punishment, the King dissolved the Livonian nobility's council of district magistrates and subordinated the diets of nobility to the governor-general. There were also no more assessors named from among district magistrates in the High Court and consistory. Thus the self-government of the Livonian nobility was practically abolished. Swedish royal power succeeded in breaking the backbone of the Livonian nobility's power and in establishing its will by the end of the seventeenth century.

In 1694 a new administrative division came into force in Livonia, the purpose of which was to fit district borders to the Estonian-Latvian ethnic border. The border of two **districts** ran somewhat further north from the present national border, leaving the town of Valga and its outskirts to the Latvian side.

Swedish King Karl XI.

The state of peasants. The reduction brought about significant changes in the state of peasants. Although earlier Swedish royal power had attempted already to bring the status of local peasants closer to that of Swedish peasants, all of these attempts remained unrealised. Unlike Swedish peasants who were free and even represented in the parliament, serfdom was preserved in the Baltic provinces. In 1645, the new organisation of land exploitation issued by the Estonian governor general Gustav Oxenstierna confirmed **serfdom** – the attachment of peasants to the soil – in North Estonia. In 1668, Governor-general Clas Tott of Livonia published an order of land police, which also stressed the peasants' status as serfs. The amount of statute labour was actually fixed by the will of the landlord and it increased together with the growth of manor fields. So, until that time, living under Swedish rule had worsened rather than improved the situation of the peasants.

With the reduction, a large part of private manors went back to the state and the power of landlords over peasants diminished. As the manors were taken over, the peasants were called together and they were told that from then on they were subjects of the King only. It may be argued that reduction liberated the peasants of the reduced manors of serfdom. As state authorities were interested in increasing the income from crown lands, they could not allow overexploitation of the peasants. Therefore a thorough evaluation and mapping of the lands accompanied the reduction, and after that the amount of statute labour was in conformity with the actual economic capacity of the farms.

In the reduced manors, **registers of socage holdings** were introduced in which all the peasants' duties towards the manor were fixed. Precise fixation of duties restricted the power of manor stewards. **District bailiffs**, officials appointed by the state, started to fulfil police duties, replacing the judges of district courts from the nobility.

Peasants were given the right and opportunity to bring an action against tenants or stewards of an estate for a violation of existing laws – even to the King himself. Suspicious – probably not without reason – of local Baltic Germans, Estonians often undertook long journeys to Stockholm in order to present their petitions and written complaints to state offices. Improvements in the lives of peasants have often been recalled as the "good old Swedish times".

Landlords. During Swedish rule, Baltic landlords were still predominantly Germans. Swedish grand noblemen who acquired manors in Estonia and Livonia usually chose to live in their homeland, renting their manors to local Germans. Although some landlords of Russian, French and even Scottish origin are known from the early Swedish period, they were soon germanised.

Local nobility was characterised by arrogance and class pride. Conflicts with town citizens, when the latter wore fancy clothes or travelled in more luxurious coaches, were rather frequent. In the seventeenth century, the type of clothes a certain class of people was to wear, the number of guests to invite to their parties and the sorts of food and drinks to serve were prescribe strictly. Therefore among the Livonian noblemen who were degraded to the status of tenant farmers and to a great extent deprived of the right to have their say in the country's government felt offended.

During the Great Northern War, Russian Tsar Peter I (the Great) skilfully manipulated the nobility's change of heart caused by the reduction in his own interests, promising to restore their former privileges. Thus Peter the Great gained surprisingly quick support from the Baltic German nobility.

Agriculture. By the late seventeenth century, the number of manors in Estonia reached over 1000. The number remained at the same level, not counting later auxiliary or dairy farms, until the beginning of the twentieth century. Landlords emphasised grain as the main source of income, making Estonia the northernmost country to export grain. Rye was, however, the most common crop. The traditional three-field system dominated tillage both in manors and peasant farms. Fields between farms were divided into long narrow strips. Oxen were used predominantly as beasts of burden. Quite a few cows were kept as well. Due to the poor transport infrastructure, it was possible to produce milk for sale in suburban manors only.

The large amount of stones in the fields hindered the increase of grain production. Stone

Johann Reinhold Patkul.

clearing began in farmlands, but also in manors starting on Muhu and Saaremaa. At first the stones were simply gathered into piles; later they were used to make stone fences. The crop usually depended on fertilisation. As usually less cows were kept in manors, the crop yields were even better from the fields of peasants. In turn, the manors compensated by increasing the cultivation area, which dependent on peasant labour. While the number of fields cultivated by peasants was four times bigger than those of manors before the Livonian War, it was reduced drastically by the end of the seventeenth century. This of course brought about an increase of statue labour performed by peasants.

Statute labour became the most important duty of peasants. It was divided into so-called **harness duty** and **foot duty**. Harness duty was the most difficult for farm households. It was generally required to send a man with a horse or a pair of oxen and a harness to the manor for three to six days a week for the average farm. If there were urgent seasonal work (such as construction, carting dung, burning fields, etc.) in the manor, peasants were forced to carry out **additional labour**. In winter, the most difficult task was **manor carting**. For example, it could mean peasants in south-east Estonia were forced to transport grain to Tallinn, Pärnu, or Riga – treks over 150-250 kilometres long.

In addition to statute labour in the manor, peasants had to give the landlord a portion of the farm's agricultural and goods production as payment in kind.

According to the law, noblemen also had more rights to the woods than peasants. In the second half of the seventeenth century, peasants were forbidden to hunt elks, wild boars and roe under the threat of corporal punishment. However, peasants were forced to participate in bear and wolf hunts as drovers.

Estonian waters were still rich in fish. Significantly big catches came from Lake Peipsi. For the Russians living on its coasts, fishing was the main source of livelihood and they dominated local fishing. However, the poaching of fish in other inland bodies of water upset Swedish authorities.

Compared with the Middle Ages, the role of apiaries diminished by a considerable extent.

Towns and trading. The late sixteenth and seventeenth centuries brought about great changes to Estonian towns. Up to that time small inland towns were able to participate in trading, but new circumstances offered possibilities for lively economic activities at **seaports** only. Transit trade between Russia and western Europe, which had played a significant role in the development of Estonian towns, now proceeded through two water routes – via the port of Arkangel and the White Sea, and to a lesser extent via Narva and the Gulf of Finland – and one land trade route – from Pskov to Riga via Vatseliina or Aluksne.

Thus the seventeenth century meant economic prosperity for **Narva**. **Tallinn** maintained it position as well, but could no longer stave off the rise of border towns. The situation in Tartu, a former important trading centre, deteriorated, and the town lost much of its glory. Pärnu, as well as Haapsalu and Kuressaare, were only of minor importance as centres of export.

During the Middle Ages, towns acted rather independently in their economic activities. However, state control gradually took over more aspects of such activities and subordinated them to state interests. Only Tallinn preserved its traditional independence fixed in town bylaws, and for some time even continued to mint its own coins. As the Swedish central authorities were especially interested in Narva, the town was more dependent on the state. It was even discussed whether to name Narva as the second capital of the Swedish state. The town councils of Tartu and Pärnu also preserved their rights in principle, but due to economic problems and resulting conflicts, they were subordinated to the direct supervision of the governor-general. At this point currency was minted in Riga only.

Other towns were enfeoffed to some powerful noble family, thus becoming totally dependent on them. The appearance and legal status of Viljandi, a former member of the Hanseatic League, suffered from an especially significant decline. Although the population fell in other towns aside from Tallinn and Narva, by the end of Swedish rule some six per cent of the total population was urban – a high figure at the time. This could also be the reason why the number of towns in Estonia did not increase during Swedish rule.

Besides Swedish ships, those of England and Holland increased their activity in the Baltic Sea. Although most of the trade between Eng-

A house in Narva from the Swedish era.

land, Holland and Russia went through the White Sea, a number of Englishmen and Dutchmen also settled in Narva. The English even had their own clergy in Narva. The role of Russian merchants in Narva remained significant.

The economic boom in early modern western Europe also brought about growing demand for various foodstuffs, as well as other goods like shipbuilding material. Estonian ports met the demands, as local and imported goods from Russia were exported. The biggest demand was for **grain**, which were dried in local barns. Grain made up two-thirds of trade, some times as high as 85 per cent, of Tallinn's export. In the 1690s, the high level of export before the Livonian War was exceeded twofold. This is why the Baltic countries were called the **granary of the Swedish state**.

Flax was another important article exported to the west. However, as fax was grown only at a small scale in Estonia, much of it came from Russia. Hemp was also exported from Russia. Narva was the main port handling exports for flax and hemp. Local products such as tar, birch tar, spars, boards and planks, alongside other goods necessary for shipbuilding, were also exported. Among Russian goods, the importance of fur diminished in Europe, but export of leather increased due to the demand for footwear.

Salt was the most important imported article, and Tallinn remained the main storage site from where salt was shipped to Russia and Finland. Salt was acquired abroad in exchange for grain usually. The import of various metal goods, luxuries, spices and alcohol continued. Tobacco, writing paper and various fruits were new imported goods.

In the economic life of towns, shopkeepers who specialise in a specific merchandise (such as wine, woollen cloth, foodstuffs, etc.) served an important purpose. **Peasant shopkeepers**, which sold essential commodities to other peasants or exchanged them for agricultural products, had the widest range of customers.

In all towns except the multinational Narva, German merchants dominated. The rise of an Estonia to the position of an influential merchant was a great exception. Knowing this, the career of **Pulli Hans**, an Estonian merchant in Tartu who became a citizen and member of the Great Guild, is especially remarkable.

Crafts. Besides trading, crafts remained an important field of activity for townspeople. In the seventeenth century, traditions that had developed earlier began to flourish. The relations among masters, journeymen and apprentices were precisely regulated. The organisation of guilds became stricter than before. According to the craft order enforced in Tallinn, only the craftsmen belonging to a guild were allowed to work in the trade. The number of guilds grew, sometimes by the specialisation from a larger branch. At least three masters of such a speciality were required to form a new guild. In the case of need, masters in small towns were included as members of the appropriate guild in Tallinn (in Estonia) or Riga (in Livonia).

In 1675, St Olaf's Guild, which at the time included many craftsmen of Estonian origin, was closed. German masters refused to take

Coins from the Swedish era.

them into Canute's Guild, rendering a large part of the former guild members to commoners without the rights of a citizen. Such a stiff attitude of Germans was a reaction to the increase presence of Estonians and their roles in towns. The Germans fought to preserve their leading position, though remaining a minority in population in Tallinn and other towns.

Larger enterprises, or manufactures, based on production from manual labour, represented another form of the crafts industry. Brickyards and limekilns were the oldest among them. In the sixteenth century, sawmills were also built. The De la Gardie family owned the Hüti glass factory (derived from the German word *Glashütte*, glass chamber), which was a new type of business. In the middle of the seventeenth century, glass for windows, bottles, bowls and others were made there.

Narva was the primary centre of manufacturing. The enterprises processing the hemp and flax exported from Russia for re-export were successful. The Narva copper works made sheets and plates from copper exported from Sweden. Timber from Ingria was processed into planks and boards in the local sawmill. There were copper works in Tallinn as well, though in 1664 one was rebuilt into a paper mill, using wood scraps as raw material.

Distribution of bread to starving children (illustration by Ott Kangilaski).

The **famine of 1695-1697.** The so-called **Great Famine** of 1695-1697 was the most devastating to occur in Estonia and it remained in the memories of the people for a long time.

In 1694, the climate was unfavourable for crops. The following summer was cold and rainy thus hay could not be made and the rye would neither bloom nor ripen. An early frost in autumn destroyed the summer crop. In some places there was not even enough seed grain.

March and April of 1696 were very cold months, and it rained throughout the summer months. The crop failure was even bigger than in the previous year. In the spring, peasants began dying of hunger and it continued unabated throughout the year.

The spring of 1697 revealed the many corpses from under the melting snow. Orphans and the elderly had almost no hope of survival. Desperate peasants rushed into towns, but starvation lurked there as well. According to a chronicler, "day and night such complaints of distress and hunger were heard in towns and villages, and on roads and streets that would have made even a stone scream."

Despite local authorities and towns having significant supplies of grain in 1696, they did not support the starving people very much. At the time when people died *en masse* of hunger in the "granary of the state" (Estonia and Livonia), they exported grain to Sweden and Finland where there was also crop failure. Some landlords and merchants reaped enormous profits from the grain trade.

The miseries of the Great Famine ended only in 1698. The rich and populous parishes of central Estonia suffered especially hard. The number of people that died from hunger in Estonia is estimated at **70-75,000 people**, or roughly 20 per cent of the population. Most of the victims were buried where they fell, often into mass graves outside cemeteries. According to a Danish envoy that travelled throughout the Baltic countries, it would take thirty years for the affected areas to recover. But in less than three years, the **Great Northern War** broke out.

22. Spiritual Life in the Period of Swedish Rule

The **organisational foundations of the Lutheran Church could be laid only after Swedish rule became firmly rooted in Estonia.** As a result of the Livonian War, the condition of the church was miserable. The buildings were destroyed or devastated, and most of the congregations had lost their clergymen. Besides material losses, customs from the ancient religion started to spread again among the peasants. The dead were buried in old burial mounds, baptism and church weddings were abandoned, and there were even less of those who went to Communion. Pastors were lacking in education and morals. For example, it became evident that in Kirbla, beer was served instead of wine at Communion.

Military activities, which continued at the beginning of the seventeenth century, brought about another setback so that everything had to be started from square one. **Joachim Jhering** proved to be the most energetic bishop in Estonia during Swedish rule. It was he who managed to establish a firm basis to the Lutheran church in Estonia while holding his position (1638-1657).

In Livonia, the supremacy of Catholic Poland hindered the activities of the Lutheran Church. Before Livonia was subordinated to Sweden, there were only five Lutheran pastors in Livonia's rural congregations. Following the Estonian example, a Lutheran church administration – **consistory** – was established in Livonia.

A superintendent-general, with powers nearly equal to those of a bishop, stood at the head of the clergy. After the University of Tartu was founded, the Livonian church administration was transferred to Tartu and mostly university professors served as superintendents-general.

The most prominent superintendent-general in Livonia was **Johann Fischer** (1675-1699), who was called the new Livonian apostle. The promotion of education, the publishing of popular literature and the organisational consolidation of the church in Livonia were Fischer's main accomplishments. The establishment of Swedish rule in all of Estonian territory coincided with the Thirty Years War in Europe – a confrontation of Europe's Catholic and Protestant states. As Sweden became the main support of Protestantism in this war, supporting the Lutheran Church was an essential part of Sweden's state policy in the following decades. Swedish authorities also regarded the church as an institution contributing to making Estonia and Livonia more Swedish faster. This brought a great deal of attention from authorities to the local church. This included a negative attitude towards any religious movements or sects that deviated from orthodox Lutheran doctrine.

The local Lutheran church tried to oppose the spread of new religious movements, especially Pietism, which spread to the Baltic countries

A portrait of Swedish cleric Abraham Winkler, a teacher at Tallinn's Dome Church (Toomkirik).

from Germany with support from state authorities. Students known as supporters of the Reformation movement were hindered from going to universities. Some pastors supporting Pietism were dismissed and deported from the country. In many respects the fear of the spread of Pietism was unreasonable and the fight against it weakened the religious movement.

During Swedish rule, Lutheranism became the predominant religion in Estonia. As destroyed churches were restored and new ones built, the material state of the church improved. The level of education for pastors also improved by considerable extent. By the end of Swedish rule, the majority of them had university education and was able to deliver sermons in Estonian. The peasants' attitude towards the church also became more favourable. In order to deal with the economic matters of congregations, **church wardens** were elected from among the peasants, which in turn brought the peasants closer to the church.

Fight against heresy. In the seventeenth century, Lutheranism remained alien to most Estonians. In the Middle Ages, the ancient Estonian religion had mixed with Catholic traditions, thus the eradication of such was not an easy task for Lutheran pastors. Regarding the beliefs of the people as superstitions and as such extremely harmful, the pastors destroyed places of sacrifice that had been taken into use again during periods of warfare. A great peasant disturbance in Osula in the parish of Urvaste in 1642, known as the **Revolt of Pühajõe**, is also connected with heresy. A local landlord built a water mill on the Võhandu River, though the peasants believed it to be sacred. The peasants considered the failure of crops that devastated the country to be revenge for polluting the river, and therefore destroyed the mill and the dike. Although the army sent there successfully put down the revolt, the local pastor had to acknowledge that the peasants "don't know anything about God or his word, nor belief nor the Commandments. Their blindness, heresy, idols and sorcery goes beyond all bounds."

Relying on the support of Swedish authorities, the Protestant church showed special eagerness in the persecution of witches. At that time **trials for witchcraft** occurred throughout the country. Often more active and talented people like folk doctors fell victims to such trials.

Anonymous denunciations also gave grounds to suspect a person for witchcraft. In 1623, Superintendent-general Samson published detailed instructions on how to recognise a witch and how to handle them. Such a "guide for the identification of witches" gave an impetus to new trials. At first the accused faced an "ordeal by water." The hands and legs of the accused were tied and was let down to the water with a rope. It was believed that an innocent person would sink to the bottom, and a witch would remain on the surface. If the "ordeal by water" showed the accused of being a witch, the person would be forced to confess of the most absurd accusations while under cruel torture. Burning on a stake was common punishment for witchery, but towards the end of Swedish rule putting to the sword was more common. However, death penalties became quite rare at later witch trials, and the convicts were punished by being put in the pillory near the church and were beaten. The last death penalty executed from a witch trial in Estonia was carried out in 1699.

Promotion of public education. To reinforce the influence of Lutheranism, the authorities considered it necessary to spread literacy. Initially **parish clerks** (assistant to a pastor) were supposed to teach reading to peasant children. However, literacy spread with much difficulty as there were few parish clerks and their education was lacking.

The training of teachers became the main task. **Bengt Gottfried Forselius**, who grew up in a family friendly to the peasants, assumed this extremely difficult task. He was born around 1660 in the district of Harju, parish of Harju-Madise, to a family of a Swedish pastor who came from Finland. Forselius also spoke good Estonian and German. After studying in a higher education institute in Tallinn and for some time at a university in Germany, the young teacher started to teach peasant boys for free.

In 1684 a **teachers college** was founded at **Piiskopimõisa** near Tartu, in order to train Estonian schoolteachers and parish clerks. Forselius was the only teacher of the school. The tuition was two years and most of the pupils came from the vicinity of Tartu. The main emphasis was placed on fluent reading and religious instruction, while some hymns, bookbinding, German and calculating was taught. Forselius introduced a new method to acquire the ability to read more quickly by asking one boy read aloud and the others to follow the text silently. From 1686, a new printed alphabet book written by Forselius himself came into use.

The landlords who did not like the peasants' aspirations towards education started to spread rumours about the harmfulness of the schools. For example they argued that the pupils were recruited to the Swedish army after finishing the school or that the teacher asked for an enormous tuition fee.

In order to break the opposition, the energetic Forselius went on a long journey to Stockholm with two of his best pupils – **Ignatsi Jaak** and **Pakri Hansu Jüri** from the parish of Kambja. The pupils also demonstrated the excellent abilities of Estonian boys to King Karl XI.

In 1688, Forselius made another trip to Stockholm where he was appointed the inspector of Estonian and Livonian peasant schools and given "the permission and power" to establish schools wherever necessary. On his way back, however, young Forselius was killed in an autumn storm on the Baltic Sea. The work of the teachers college stopped. However, there was optimism about the future of public education. Within four years about 160 young Estonian men had received tuition at the seminary.

There is evidence of 41 peasant schools, most of them in South Estonia, while Forselius was active. In **1687**, the Livonian Diet decided that landlords must build a school in every parish and pay the wage of the local teacher. However, the progress in building schools was slow and teaching usually took place in a barn dwelling. Although there was still some opposition among the nobility, soon there were schools in most parishes of Estonian territory.

Besides schools, **home teaching** played an important role in teaching children to read. Children who could not learn to read at home were required to attend schools. By the end of Swedish rule, the percentage of Estonians who could read was remarkably high. According to Chilian Rauschert, a progressive pastor from Sangaste, even herdsmen read books while looking after their cattle. He also expressed the opinion that "the Estonian people are like fallow land, which yields good crop if the brushwood growing on it is cut down."

B.G. Forselius en route *to Stockholm.*

The **Estonian written word.** Besides promoting popular education, the translation of the Bible into the vernacular was also considered to be important by the Lutheran Church. The figurative style of the Bible demanded not only very good command of the Estonian language but also the derivation and invention of several new words by the translators. This in its turn required standardisation of the literary language. The division at the time of the Estonian language into North Estonian and South Estonian literary languages made this task even more complicated.

The spelling of the earliest Estonian printed matter was completely free. Only in 1637 did **Heinrich Stahl** write the first **Estonian grammar**. However, this work only aimed at adapting the Estonian language to the rules of German. Stahl made much use of foreign letters such as: ch, ck, f, ph, tz, and x. Although Stahl's Grammar remained far from the colloquial language, it was considered to be an authoritative and indisputable survey of the Estonian language for decades. Forselius made a proposal to use the phonetic system of spelling taking Finnish as an example, but it was rejected due to the opposition of conservative pastors. The argument that the phonetic system of spelling would be more familiar to the flock did not find any support as, according to pastors supporting Stahl's system, the peasants pronounced their language in a wrong way and carelessly. The system of spelling was an issue at the so-called **bible conferences** at the manor of Liepa near Cēsis in 1686 and at Pilistvere in 1687, but no agreement was reached. In fact, these were the first conferences on the Estonian language. Deriving from this dispute, **Johan Hornung** published an Estonian grammar in Latin in **1693**, drawing up the rules of North Estonian orthography, borrowing ideas from both schools of thought. These rules, known as the so-called **old system of spelling**, remained in force until the middle of the nineteenth century.

The inability to reach an agreement over the spelling system was the main reason why the bible as a whole was not published during Swedish rule. Still, in 1686, the New Testament was published in the South Estonian literary language, translated and edited by **Andreas Virginius**, pastor of Kambja, and his son **Adrian**. This was also the first book exclusively in Estonian. A manuscript translation of the Old Testament and a North Estonian version of the New Testament were also completed, but due to the Great Northern War they remained unpublished.

Mostly religious texts were published during the Swedish Rule. In 1632-1638, Heinrich Stahl published an extensive four-volume "Hand- and Home Book for the Estonian Principality in Livonia," of which text was printed in parallel in German and Estonian. The book consisted of passages from the Bible, hymns and a small Lutheran catechism, and was mostly meant for pastors with a poor command of the Estonian language. In the middle of the century the first attempts to print Estonian hymns considering rhyme and metre were made. Martin Gilläus, a Tartu University graduate, is known as a translator of hymns. Some of his translations are in use even today.

Preface to the New Testament intended for peasants.

Estonian secular poetry started to develop alongside religious hymns. Besides French, Estonian was introduced in *salons*. It became customary to present poems (for example wedding songs) written in Estonian for major family events. Poems written in the language of the native population could be found even at the headings of dissertations. Reiner Brockmann, pastor of Kadrina and later professor at a Tallinn higher educational institute, remains in the history of literature as the best-known author of so-called Estonian occasional poetry.

The authorities allowed the printing of books in the South Estonian literary language in Riga and those in North Estonian in Tallinn. In 1631-1710, at least 45 books were published in Estonian, in addition to some other small printed matter. Taking into account that literacy was widespread, several official announcements of the governor-general were also published in the local language.

The beginning of Estonian journalism also comes near the end of Swedish rule. In 1675, a German weekly "Ordinari Freytags Post-Zeitung" began to circulate in Tallinn.

Gymnasia **and Tartu University.** The ideas of humanism, which emphasised the importance of science and education, were very popular in seventeenth-century Europe. In the Swedish Kingdom, *gymnasia* –institutes of secondary education – were founded and the founding of the University of Uppsala – the only institution of higher education – was also supported in every way. A similar organisation of education was, of course, also introduced in the new province. The active student life in Tartu under Polish rule also caused the Swedish authorities to show serious initiative in this area.

The first governor general of the province, **Johan Skytte**, played an important role in organising the educational system in Livonia. Skytte was an educated young man and taught King Gustav II Adolf and also served as chancellor of the University of Uppsala.

The first seal of Tartu University.

On his initiative, the so-called **Academic *gymnasium*** was founded in **Tartu** in **1630,** where the system of teaching was quite similar to that of universities. So it became a preliminary step to becoming a full university. In 1631, *gymnasia* were also opened in **Tallinn** (later named the Gustav Adolf *Gymnasium*) and in Riga.

As early as 1631 Skytte submitted a petition to the King to reorganise the Tartu *gymnasium* into a university. In June 1632, Gustav II Adolf signed the founding charter of **Tartu University.**

The opening ceremony took place on **15 October 1632** and it was named Academia Gustaviana after the King. In his speech at the opening ceremony, Johan Skytte announced that not only noblemen and citizens, but also peasants, could study at the university. However, in reality the latter had no opportunities to enter a university.

According to European tradition there were four faculties at Tartu University. Studies began at the Faculty of Philosophy, which gave necessary preliminary knowledge. The essential university education was acquired in the higher faculties of Theology, Law and Medicine. The duration of studies was normally nine years. In order to acquire a broader education one often studied in several different universities in suc-

Johan Skytte.

cession. This was possible as Latin was in use as the language of tuition all over Europe. One did not have to finish a certain school in order to become a student and sometimes even ten-year-old boys matriculated (registered in the matriculation roll). Fourteen to seventeen year-old students were quite common. On the acceptance of new students, a special ceremony was carried out, in which traditionally the new student candidates, in odd masks, were laughed at during a party.

The main forms of study were **lectures** and **disputes**, the latter useful in developing performance and debating skills. Students became eligible for scholarships after passing term examinations.

Numerous Swedes, Finns and Germans studied at Tartu University. There is also evidence of one Latvian student. However, there is no clear indication of any students of Estonian origin. Still, Johannes Freyer from Tallinn, who started his studies in 1642, is believed to have been an Estonian. Several university teachers and students were interested in the native people, studying Estonian history and folk culture.

The university worked in Tartu until the Russians seized the town in 1656 during the Swedish-Russian War. Some of the professors and students who fled from the war tried to continue their activities in the rooms of Tallinn *Gymnasium*, but after a while such activities lulled.

In 1690, the university was reopened in Tartu. As the conditions in the town were quite poor, the university moved to **Pärnu** in **1699**. In contrast to Tallinn, the university was highly appreciated in Pärnu and despite the war the continuation of its activities was supported in every way. As Pärnu surrendered to the Russian army in August 1710, the university also stopped functioning. The property of the institution was taken to Sweden, while professors and students had fled or died of the Plague.

Decorative **art and architecture.** While the first decades of the seventeenth century almost entirely belonged to the Renaissance, by the middle of the century, Baroque had become the leading style in all fields of art. Woodcarvers produced works with expressive forms. The most famous and productive masters in this field in Tallinn was **Christian Ackermann,** whose works of art have been preserved in the town's churches as well as other public buildings. Stonemasons decorated buildings and made magnificent tombstones adjacent to them. Several **circled crosses** erected at cemeteries in the countryside were probably also cut by town masters. The circled cross as a symbol of sunlight was widely taken into use in the seventeenth century by wealthier West and North Estonian peasants and manor officials of Estonian origin. The texts on these crosses were usually carved in capital Latin letters.

Baroque wall and ceiling paintings spread, made to the order of the town council, brotherhoods and wealthy citizens. The artists also started to paint more portraits.

During Swedish rule, Estonian towns preserved their mediaeval looks to a great extent. Large-scale building activities were undertaken in towns where the wars had caused great damage and fires: Narva, Tartu and Pärnu. Minor

The spire of Tallinn's Niguliste (St Nicholas) Church.

towns where wooden buildings dominated had suffered from irreparable damage. Their economic state did not allow them to achieve any appearance better than that of a small town.

Swedish authorities organised building activities in towns according to their aims. The new building policy was most efficiently carried out in prosperous **Narva,** where living standards were rising. The Dome Church, Town Hall and commodities exchanges became the most remarkable public buildings. The new style – **Baroque** – which had become predominant in Europe, prevailed in these buildings and in the architecture during Swedish Rule.

The new style also changed the towns' skylines. Taller buildings were built with gorgeous Baroque spires, as can be seen today on top of Tallinn's Town Hall, Dome Church, Holy Ghost Church and St Nicholas (Niguliste) Church.

The Livonian War had proved that in the era of cannons the town wall and towers were not able to provide firm defence for citizens. Therefore the Swedish authorities started to build a new type of fortifications – **bastions.**

The pulpit of Tallinn's Dome Church (work of Christian Ackermann from 1686).

Bastions were earthen pentagonal terraced fortifications. Walls held the embankment together. Inside there were rooms for ammunition and defenders. The cannons were placed on a higher terrace in the middle of the bastion and it was possible to fire in many directions. Simulta-

The Narva bastions.

neously with the building of bastions, earthen intermediate banks and other supportive structures were built.

Most large-scale building work was designed to create a new fortifications system in Tallinn. However, only three of the eleven bastions were completed. Attempts were made to develop analogous fortifications systems in other towns, most successfully in Narva. The building of major fortifications brought along new taxes, which put a strain on the economy and brought about the need for a large labour force. The building deadlines dragged on and instead of the more powerful bastions, smaller quadrangular redoubts were built.

Still, the state authorities had been quite right at estimating the need for new fortifications and soon their quality was put to the test.

Peasant culture. Peasant culture preserved its traditional character and changed slowly. Periods of relative economic wellbeing diversified it, but basic values were passed on from generation to generation.

Rye bread remained the main dish for Estonians, and fish, especially salted herring, some of which was even imported from Finland, was usually eaten alongside the bread. Everyday bread was made of grain, and mixed with chaff, ground by a hand mill or at the mill. Of new edible plants, lentils came into use. Flour or barley porridges, as well as peas and beans were constantly favoured even at festive meals. However, the peasants' table was the fullest at **weddings,** which have even been described as wasteful. At Christmas the peasants' food was more abundant as well.

Besides everyday light ale and mead, plenty of home-made beer and spirits was consumed at weddings. At the end of the seventeenth century, spirits were distilled not only in towns but to a large extent also in manors and farms, using rye, and, more seldom, wheat. In order to sell beer and spirits, the landlords started a campaign to build **taverns.** Frequenting taverns became quite popular among the peasants. Here village news spread, while taverns at bigger crossroads brought travellers, who in turn also brought news from faraway places. People also traded and played music in taverns.

Tobacco had only just started to spread. In light of that, few peasants smoked at the end of

A bridal attire from Halliste in the late Swedish times.

Swedish rule. Generally soldiers of the Swedish garrisons were the most eager buyers of tobacco.

Barn dwelling was the predominant type of farmhouse. The whole family lived in one room where grain was dried. It was usually surrounded by adjacent rooms and therefore completely dark. Only the oven mouth and pine splinters gave some light. As the oven stood at the wall of the threshing room, the cattle that were kept there in winter also received some warmth.

The import of new fashion, mainly from Sweden, had great impact on the development of **folk costume**. Skirts with stripes lengthways, women's pot-like caps, men's cloth caps in North Estonia, pleated skirts, men's knee breeches and others are all examples of this new influence. **Bagpipes** were also a substantial element of peasant culture.

23. The Great Northern War (1700-1721)

The Baltic countries on the eve of the war. In the second half of the seventeenth century, the Swedish Kingdom was at the height of its power. The Baltic Sea had almost become its inland sea, so that even Denmark, which charged duty on all other foreign ships, could not charge Swedish ships. Poland, Denmark and **Russia** opposed Sweden's hegemony in the Baltic Sea. They all had claims to parts of Sweden's possessions. By the end of the century a favourable opportunity presented itself. Russian-Polish relations had improved, and thanks to a peace treaty both states were for some time relieved of Turkish danger on their southern borders. Sweden's allies England, France, and the Holy Roman Empire were occupied with their mutual problems.

Sweden's internal conditions were problematic. The famine of 1695-1697 crippled vital parts of the state. In 1697, King Karl XI died. The new King Karl XII, who came to the throne at the age of fifteen, was rather inexperienced. A part of the Estonian and Livonian nobility were politically opposed to Sweden and ready to acknowledge the King of Poland as their master.

In 1699, **August II (August the Strong)**, Prince-elector of Saxony who was elected king of Poland, **Peter I**, the Russian Tsar and **Frederik IV**, King of Denmark, formed an alliance against Sweden. According to the agreement, Estonia and Livonia were to be subordinated to Poland in case of victory.

Despite its difficulties, Sweden maintained its military power. Its mines and manufactories produced over 30 per cent of the world's cast iron and steel, which enabled the production of good weapons. A great number of free peasants allowed the maintenance of a cheap, effective and patriotic army that gave Sweden an advantage compared with European mercenary troops.

Beginning of the war. The Great Northern War broke out during the eve of **12 February 1700**, as the **Saxon** troops of August II, concentrated in Couronia, attacked **Riga**. The Livonian governor-general had been aware of the danger and took precautions. The Saxons laid a long and unsuccessful siege on Riga. In the summer of 1700, Danish troops conquered some Swedish possessions in Germany. However, as the Swedish army rapidly moved to siege Copenhagen, Denmark was forced to make peace immediately. In the autumn, Russian troops were concentrated near **Narva.** In the latter half of October, the main force started fierce bombardment of the town under the command of Peter the Great. At the same time **Boris Sheremetyev**

Russian Tsar Peter I (the Great).

The Great Northern War (1700-1721)

Swedish soldiers in the Great Northern War.

invaded Virumaa, going as far as Rakvere with 5000 cavalrymen and mercilessly devastating the land.

In such a situation Karl XII, the young Swedish King, acted skilfully and decisively. In early October he landed in Pärnu with his main force, having decided to attack the Russians first.

The Battle of Narva. From Pärnu the Swedish army moved through Tallinn to Rakvere, where provisions necessary for the men and horses had been gathered in haste. On its way further, the Swedish advance guard met Sheremetyev's cavalry at Pühajõe. Despite the Russians' favourable position on the high right bank of the river, they were routed with little trouble. Swedish war bulletins wrote about an Estonian peasant named **Stephan Raabe** (Ronga Tehvan in Estonian), who was said to have led the troops to the rear of the Russians, guaranteeing the quick success.

Having arrived in Narva, Karl XII with his 10,500 men faced the Russian army of 30,000 men. On the day before the battle, Peter left his soldiers for unknown reasons, leaving the handling of troops to Duke de Croy of Austria.

Under cover of fog the Swedish troops moved right in front of the Russian defence. On **19 November** at 2pm, Karl XII gave the command to charge. A snowstorm had just developed with the wind blowing from behind the Swedes and directly against the Russians. Russian troops fled from the battleground but as the bridges were destroyed, many drowned in the cold current of the river. The parts of the Russian army command that consisted of foreigners went over to the Swedish side. Some isolated Russian units withstood bravely, but they also surrendered before nightfall. A great part of the Russian battle equipment, including all cannons, fell spoils of the winner.

After their brilliant victory at Narva, the Swedes also organised looting raids beyond the Narva River. Due to a lack of men and arriving winter, continuing the campaign was out of the question. The Swedish army with their young King stayed at **Lauise** for the winter.

In 1701, Swedish royal troops left Estonia. Military activities continued in Lithuania and Poland. Small garrison and field troops under the command of Anton **von Schlippenbach** were left to defend Livonia.

The Great Northern War (1700-1721)

in Pärnu. Henceforth the troops of von Schlippenbach could no longer prevent the looting raids by Russian forces to Livonia and Estonia.

In 1703, the Russians mercilessly devastated the entire eastern part of Estonia up to the Viljandi and Järva regions. Sheremetyev wrote to his Tsar with overt content: "There is nothing left to be devastated in the enemy's land. Men, women and children have been taken prisoners by the thousands, as well as horses and cattle. Anyone who couldn't be taken along were stabbed or cut to pieces. All of Livonia and a part of Estonia are so empty that the settlements exist only on map. To my mind all those who are hiding themselves in bogs and woods side firmly with you." However, all Estonian towns were still in the hands of the Swedes, and their navy had full control over Lake Peipsi.

In the early part of May 1704, an arranged Swedish fleet sailed towards Lake Peipsi from Tartu. Due to the lack of caution, the Swedes fell into a trap set by the Russians near **Kastre**. There was no manoeuvring space in the narrow river and the big ships were not able to offer any resistance. In order not to surrender the flagship to the Russians, the crew blasted it and went down with the ship. The other ships fell to the Russians. Having placed Lake Peipsi under

Stephan Raabe.

Russia's success. Having come to terms with the defeat at Narva, the Russians concentrated new troops in Pskov under the command of Boris Sheremetyev. In September 1701, 20,000 Russians invaded south-east Estonia in three places, but were forced to retreat by 2,000 Swedish defenders. After receiving reinforcements, the Russians came over the border again at the end of December. An attack in winter came unexpectedly. At the manor of **Erastvere** near Kanepi, Russian troops, outnumbering the Swedes by three to one, gained their first important victory in the Great Northern War.

The battle of Erastvere was the first in a number of defeats Swedish field troops suffered in Livonia. In July 1702, the Swedes were defeated in a battle near Valga at the manor of **Hummuli**. Retreating Swedish soldiers were even seen

Swedish King Karl XII.

their control, the Russians could now use the waterways for transporting heavy siege cannons to both Tartu and Narva.

In June 1704, Peter I again attempted to besiege **Narva** and, after that, **Tartu**. The lack of success bombing Tartu made the Tsar nervous and he came to lead it himself. At the command of Peter I, the troops started to demolish the old defence from the side facing the river. On 12 July, the raid began and in the next morning Tartu surrendered. The troops that concentrated at Narva also took the town in a raid on 9 August.

E**stonian peasantry in the war years.** For Estonian peasants, the war brought about terrible suffering. In the areas living under a reign of terror, tillage did not occur. In the first years of the Great Northern War, many families tried to resettle in the western parts of Estonia. People also sought shelter in the woods and bog islands.

The war also brought about an increase in the duties of peasants, as Swedish policy was based on the principle that the country in which the war is held covers the war expenses. The troops marching through would take everything they needed arbitrarily. Peasants were constantly taken as assistants for the building of fortifications. The duties of

Russian soldiers in the Great Northern War.

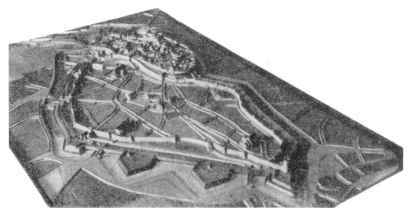

Tallinn's fortifications for the Great Northern War.

Events in Estonia of the Great Northern War.

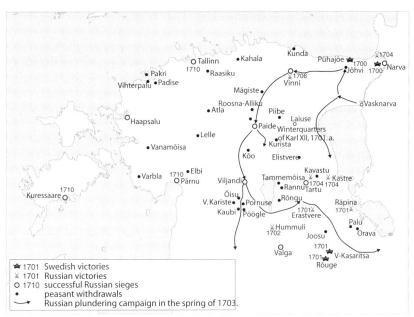

- ✠ 1701 Swedish victories
- ✗ 1701 Russian victories
- O 1710 successful Russian sieges
- • peasant withdrawals
- → Russian plundering campaign in the spring of 1703.

lodging and compulsory conveyance were also exhaustive. In 1700, there were already some peasant disturbances. Usually the peasants refused to fulfil their duties and sometimes plundered the manor. Most of these revolts took place in south-eastern Estonia, where a number of peasants had already fled to Russia.

Attempts were also made to recruit Estonian peasants to the Swedish army. Groups of soldiers headed by an officer would move around in the country forcing the peasants to join the Swedish army often by swindling or violence. At the same time, many Estonians joined the army voluntarily, even to be relieved of their duties at manors. Units of **militia** were formed of local men, whose arms were limited to old guns and swords taken away from Russians. Still, the peasants showed remarkable fighting spirit. For example, the commandant of Tartu distinguished the bravery of two militia battalions at the town's defence. Approximately 15,000 Estonians were recruited into the Swedish army during the Great Northern War, of whom a number were promoted to became officers.

The war continues. After Tartu and Narva were conquered, military activities in Estonia ceased for a while and were limited to mutual looting raids into enemy territory. In **1708**, active warfare began again in Estonian territory. The most important battle was held at the fields of Vinni manor, which ended with the defeat of the Swedes. This was also the last significant field battle in Estonia.

However, the final results of the Great Northern War remained unsettled. The Russians were afraid that Karl XII would return to Estonia and Livonia and were not sure that they could keep the conquered territories. In the winter of 1708, all the citizens of Tartu and Narva were **deported** to Russia with their families, and in the summer of the same year Tartu was blown up almost entirely. **Käsu Hans**, the pastor of Puhja who is considered to be the first poet of Estonian origin, has described this event in a "lamentation."

In the **battle of Poltava** held in late June 1709, Peter the Great completely smashed the Swedes' main force. Now it was no longer in the Swedes' power to hold Estonia and Livonia in their possession. In early 1710, Riga surrendered to prevailing Russian troops, followed by Kuressaare and Pärnu in August and Tallinn in September. The Plague, which in some garrisons had killed more than a half of the soldiers, also weakened the resistance of the siege. On **29 September 1710** an **act of surrender** was signed in the manor of Harku near Tallinn, according to which the Swedish army surrendered and the Estonian nobility and Tallinn recognised Russia's supremacy.

End of the Great Northern War and Estonia's annexation to Russia.

Although as Tallinn surrendered and open military activities ceased, the suffering of the Estonians had not yet come to an end. In the years 1710-11, the Plague epidemic that had started to spread in the Swedish army killed more than a half of the peasant population that had survived the war in 1710-1711. Three-quarters of Tallinn's population died of the Plague.

The population decreased to **120-140,000** people. The country was in a state of chaos and bands of robbers (peasants and former soldiers) – so-called looters – stomped about. Some of them had also arrived from Russia.

After Tallinn surrendered, the Great Northern War continued for another dozen years. Although the Swedish army was smashed, its navy remained quite strong. The lack of funds caused difficulties for the state. Until then the war was at the expense of the provinces, but now the war started to drain Sweden itself. Karl XII was ready to give up his Baltic possessions to Russia but instead wanted to unite Norway that had been a Danish possession. In a campaign against Norway in 1718, the King was killed. The Swedish military command still tried to continue the fight with Russia, but a defeat in a decisive naval battle in 1720 left the country's coast open to the forces of the enemy. Therefore the **Uusikaupunki Peace Treaty** was signed in **1721,** according to which Russia got Estonia, Livonia, Ingria and a part of south-east Finland including Vyborg. It gave the Finnish territories occupied during the war back to Sweden and paid a two-million thaler reparation. Sweden got the right to import duty-free grain from Estonia and Livonia for a remarkable sum at the time: 50,000 roubles.

V Under Russian Rule

24. Estonia after the Great Northern War

Devastated land. The Great Northern War devastated Estonia more than any other war in the country's history. A high price was paid by Estonians for Russia's "window to Europe," which cost the lives of more than half of Estonia's population. By the end of all military activities, 120-140,000 people survived – less than the total population of the early thirteenth century.

The barren land offered a miserable view. Folklore speak of churches surrounded by overgrown woods and people searching for each other by footprints. Fields untilled for many years lay fallow, while cattle herds perished.

The manors were also in poor shape at the beginning of the eighteenth century. The manor houses of those days did not differ much from the barn dwellings of peasants: straw roods, narrow windows, and walls built of wooden logs.

A scarcity of food and shoddy clothing demonstrate the poverty of the time rather than wealth. However, the land recovered from the devastation of war surprisingly fast. The ensuing longer period of peace allowed for quick growth in the population. Empty farms were re-inhabited by new settlers. By the middle of the eighteenth century the population already reached the pre-war level, and by the end of the century it exceeded **half a million**.

Baltic exclusive order. Although Russia's victory profoundly changed the balance of force in northern Europe, Russia did not feel certain of a lasting supremacy over the conquered territories. Sweden's defeat was not so drastic as to preclude a desire to retake the lost territories. Russia's advance also made west European states watchful, resulting in countermeasures being taken. In such a situation it was important for Russia to secure the support of the local Baltic German nobility.

In order to gain the support of Baltic nobles, Russia began a **restitution** of those properties taken over during Swedish rule. This began even before the end of the war. Even those noblemen that fled to Sweden could get their manors back if they returned by a certain date. Such a step definitely helped solicit the support of the Baltic nobility for Russia. Together with their manors, the former rights of the nobility over peasants were also restored.

The main aspects of the administrative order in the Baltics were fixed in the 1721 Uusikaupunki Peace Treaty between Russia and Sweden. The Baltic nobility and towns retained extensive self-rule in the Russian Empire. Standing laws and tax arrangements were enforced. Estonia and Livonia were further isolated from the inner Russian provinces by prevailing Lutheran faith, German-language administration and customs border.

The highest representatives of the Russian central power were the governors-general appointed to Tallinn and Riga. Those offices were, as a rule, filled not with Russians but foreigners having made career in the Russian army. The Swede Otto Gustav Douglas, Dane Woldemar Löwendahl and Holstein Prince Peter August von Holstein-Beck held the governor general's office in Tallinn, while Peter Lacy and George Browne, both Irish, the post in Riga. The main concern of the state authority was to maintain government forces in the province and to supervise tax collection. As high officers, the governors-general often visited St Petersburg and showed little interest in Baltic affairs. Actual power was left to the two administration aides appointed from among local nobles.

The noble self-rule in Estonia, Livonia and Saaremaa was executed by the knighthood, whereby the organisational structure of the Swedish era was retained. Noble gatherings – the Diets – no longer comprised of representatives of towns, as had been customary before. The knighthood attempted to impose their control over the church as well, claiming seats in ruling church authorities.

Governor-general Otto Gustav Douglas.

In 1730s to 1740s the special members' lists of the knighthood, or peerage books, were drawn up. Only registered nobles had political and economic privileges in Estonia and Livonia. The peerage books were to protect the privileges of local hereditary nobility from German and Russian newcomers.

The Baltic nobility's self-rule was substantially supported by Germans invited to the St Petersburg court during the era of Peter the Great. It was even planned to unite Estonia and Livonia into a separate vassal state, which would have been tied to Russia only through the Tsar himself. For the administration of court and financial procedures, special authorities were established in St Petersburg for the Baltic provinces: the board of justice for Estonian and Livonian matters and the chamber office for Estonian and Livonian matters.

Self-rule was retained in local towns as well. Smaller ones devastated by the Northern War had been taken by nearby landlords and townspeople, like peasants, were forced into corvée. Paide and Rakvere demanded reinstatement of their rights by Russia, but their claims remained unanswered in St Petersburg. Political rights were no longer held by all townspeople, but citizens only. Citizenship was granted by the town council. For Estonians, the way to citizenship was largely blocked throughout the eighteenth century.

The towns did not form an anti-knighthood front. Achievement of that goal was hampered by internal quarrels over trading rights and frequent disagreements between town councils and its citizens. Such clashes were most notable in Tartu, of which satisfaction with the authorities was seldom heard.

The Baltic nobility's unlimited control over local matters was executed only on the expense of the rights of the local people – the Estonians. The highest officials of the self-government, the district magistrates and town councillors, were not elected, but appointed for life by the magistrate board or the town council, respectively.

On the other hand, the Baltic special order acted as a fence between Russia and the Baltics, helping to maintain local cultural individuality and prevent colonisation – which would have been possibly fatal to the native people. It also enabled ties to Western Europe, thereby providing faster development compared to Russia's inner provinces.

Agriculture. Grain trade, the main source of income for estates and farms throughout the eighteenth century, played the main role in the agricultural revival. The privilege of duty-free trade favoured continuing grain export to Sweden. A new grain consumer arose in the form of about 50,000 Russian troops stationed in the Baltics. To provide for them at lower expense, the government occasionally prohibited grain exports, drawing fierce criticism from the Baltic nobles.

Grain spirits soon became the main export to Russia, the income being characterised contemporarily as "a silver rain over Estonia." It was in the eighteenth century that virgin forests were cut to heat the distilleries. Long trains of barrels headed for St Petersburg through the winter.

The distillery refuse was used to fatten oxen, which were also delivered to the St Petersburg market. This was a foundation to more extensive cattle breeding in the estates. That, on turn, improved fertilisation of the land and the yield as well.

State of peasants under Russian rule. Peasants who earlier tried to assert their rights in the Swedish capital now tried to find similar support in St Petersburg. In 1737, a miller from the manor of Vohnja in Virumaa, **Jaan**, submitted a written complaint to the Empress against his persecuting landlord. The state authorities then asked the nobles to explain the rights of the peasantry in the Baltic countries. The explanatory letter in **1739** from Baron Otto Fabian Rosen, a district magistrate of Livonia, became widely known as the **Rosen Declaration**.

According to Rosen, local peasants were serfs, of whom the landlord could bequeath, exchange and sell like any other manorial property. The peasants belonged to the manor like all other property. In order to use the land, the peasants were required to perform statue labour, the amount of which was unlimited according to Rosen. The magistrate believed that judicial authority over the peasants belonged to the nobility only, not the state.

The Rosen declaration corresponded to the attitude of landlords at the time. The state also began to support such a policy. Thus, under Russian rule, the peasants lost all the rights they gained during Swedish rule. They were now relegated to simply **serfs without rights**.

However, economic interests of the landlords protected the peasants more than state authority and law. Unlimited exploitation would have resulted in the ruining of the farm, as well as the manor itself due to flight of peasants. Until the middle of the century there were still empty farms in Estonia where runaway serfs could settle. In later times, runaway serfs fled overseas to Finland and Sweden, as well as the Russian province of Pskov. Entire villages of peasants fleeing from Livonia appeared at the foot of the Pechory monastery.

Illustration of a watermark from a paper produced at the Räpina paper mill.

Trade, industry and crafts. From the middle of the eighteenth century, trade began to enliven again after being at a standstill from the country's absorption into Russia. As **maritime trade** accounted for the main part of income for state coffers from the Baltic region, the Russian government eagerly intervened in the organisation of local trade. Bans on the import and export of certain goods, which protected the rights

The Räpina paper mill.

The porcelain produced in Põltsamaa rarely survived in tact to this day. On the left are fragments discovered in a dig by archaeologists, on the right is a reconstruction of a vase.

of local craftsmen and merchants, were lifted as they decreased the income of the state.

Attempts by the government to increase activities in the newly-built port of St Petersburg hindered the development of trade. Various advantages and privileges were given to the Russian capital's port that in turn reduced the share of trade in Tallinn, Narva and Pärnu.

Among **exports**, grain, timber, flax and hemp still played a major role. Among **imports**, peasant goods predominated: salt, iron, tobacco and herring. The nobility and well-off citizens also demanded luxury goods and textiles.

In manors, distilleries, sawmills, brickyards and limekilns continued to operate. Their production usually covered the needs of surrounding manors. The manufactories that were founded during Swedish rule were either destroyed in the war or had ceased operations. In 1734, a **paper mill** was founded in the manor of **Räpina**, which is believed to be the oldest industrial enterprise in Estonia that is still active today.

In the second half of the eighteenth century, the establishment of manufactories increased. Woldemar von Lauw, an enterprising landlord, was active in **Põltsamaa**. Having started his business with the production of bottles, he continued with glass for windows and mirrors, and even started to produce expensive porcelain at Põltsamaa. Manufactories also sprung up in towns, producing some of the most sought-after goods at the time: candles, soap, tobacco and starch.

In the eighteenth century guilds, with its mediaeval restrictions and regulations, still influenced crafts in towns. As the economy enlarged, it became more difficult to preserve the monopoly of the guilds. The support of provincial authorities was needed to protect local merchants and craftsmen from competitors in the east and west, usually by strict orders and bans. In order to guarantee livelihood to local merchants, they were given the monopoly of purchasing such goods. All others could purchase the same goods only for personal needs.

25. Estonia in the Second Half of the Eighteenth Century

The Baltic policy of Catherine II. In the summer of 1762, **Catherine II** came to the Russian throne. Her reign (1762-1796) brought about significant changes in the relations between the Baltic nobility and Russian state authorities. The new Tsarina sought to abolish the existing privileges on the empire's outskirts and to subordinate them to absolute imperial rule. The significant improvement of Russia's international standing also enabled the enactment of the new policy. There was no considerable opponent that could tear the Baltic provinces from Russia. On a grand tour to Estonia and Livonia in the summer of 1764, Catherine II emphasised the inseparability of the Baltic provinces with the Russian Empire and pressured the local nobility to co-operate more eagerly with the central authority.

George Browne (1698-1792), governor-general of Riga, became the central figure at the implementation of the new Baltic policy. Following the political doctrines of the time, Browne tried to regulate all aspects of life in a military style, from agriculture to the postal service. However, one cannot ignore Browne's attempts to improve the condition of Estonia's peasantry and promote education.

In the summer of 1767, Catherine II invited elected representatives from all over the empire to Moscow in order to discuss Russia's new code of laws compiled by the Tsarina herself. The new code of laws threatened to abolish the former special status of Estonia and Livonia. This compelled the Baltic representatives to energetic counter-activities to avoid the extension of the new code to the Baltic region.

Although the Russian nobility believed that the laws of Russia had to be valid in the conquered provinces as well, the new code of law was not passed. However, Catherine II did not give up her plans of closer integration between the Baltic provinces and Russia.

Creation of a regency. In the late 1770s, Russian authorities began making preparations for extending the new administration, passed in Russia in 1775, law to the Baltic provinces. As expected, the Baltic German nobility resisted, but Catherine II promised to make manors hereditary property in compromise. This ended unstable property relations and constant threats of seizure by the state.

In **1783** a new administrative system, known as **regency** (1783-1796) was established in the Baltic provinces.

Riga Governor-general George Browne (from J.C. Brotze).

District magistrate of Livonia, Baron Carl Friedrich Schoultz von Ascheraden, supported improving the lives of peasants.

The former **administrative division** changed as new districts were formed.

In addition to the four districts of the province of Estonia (Läänemaa, Harju, Järva and Virumaa) a fifth district, centred at Paldiski, was created. However, it existed during the regency only.

In Livonia, the Viljandi region was separated from the district of Pärnu and together with the southern part of Tartu district formed the region of Võru after the new town was founded in 1784. Thus, together with Saaremaa, there were five regions in the Estonian part of the province of Livonia.

The town of Narva and surrounding areas remained in the province of St Petersburg, while the Setu (Pechory) district stayed in the province of Pskov. Some Estonian areas at the present southern border belonged to the districts of Valmiera and Valga, with most of the latter being Latvian territory.

In 1783, all **regional centres** received town bylaws. From then on until the end of Russian rule there were 12 towns in Estonian territory: Tallinn, Tartu, Narva, Pärnu, Kuressaare, Haapsalu, Paide, Rakvere, Viljandi, Valga and the new towns **Paldiski** (1783) and **Võru** (1784).

However, **political reforms** were much more significant. The political organisation of the Baltic provinces was unified with that of Russia. A common vice-regent was appointed as the head of both provinces. The permanent executive bodies of the Baltic diets were abolished. The new government of the nobility and towns was based on completely new principles. All estate owners in Estonia and Livonia acquired equal rights, regardless whether they belonged to the nobility or not. In towns, all property owners received voting rights irrespective of their nationality or occupation. For governing the towns, town councils were created that also represented less wealthy groups.

The taxation system was also thoroughly reformed. At this point a **head tax**, which has been in effect throughout Russia since the Peter the Great days, was established in Estonia and Livonia. In order to register the taxable population, **censuses** began. As the records of censuses have almost entirely been preserved in the archives, they are considered an important source material for studying Estonian history.

The establishment of regency included a number of democratic elements, as it imposed restrictions on the former mediaeval system of local government. At the same time, the new administrative system was aimed at the assimilation of all borderlands of the empire with Russia, completely ignoring any historical, religious or ethnic differences. In order to avoid an increase of tension between the state authority and the Baltic nobility, the former method of government was in principle restored after the death of Catherine II.

Positive regulations. As the ideas of the Enlightenment spread, the question of improving the state of the peasantry in Livonia gradually became more substantial. Johann Georg **Eisen von Schwarzenberg** (1717-1779), the pastor of Torma, criticised the feudal manor economy as unproductive, lacking in perspective, and in need of essential innovations. In his essay "A

Patriot's Description of Serfdom of Livonian Peasants," Eisen considered it necessary to abolish serfdom and replace the unproductive system with monetary rent that would favour economic enterprise.

Only a few landlords expressed the desire to modernise their manors. Most of them did not feel any interest or need to change. Therefore the diet of the Livonian nobility that gathered in the winter of 1765 was surprised when Governor-general Browne made demands to improve the condition of the peasantry alongside other proposals. The nobility, used to the passivity of the central authority in regard to the state of peasants in Livonia, considered the governor-general's speech an interference into the nobility's internal affairs and expressed firm opposition to the attempts at reforms. As Browne stood firm to his demands and referred to the support of the Tsarina herself, the nobility relented and accepted the proposals.

In April 1765, Browne enacted the so-called **positive regulations** or protective regulations, which relieved the plight of the peasantry. Peasants were given the right to ungrounded property. The peasant that has fulfilled the obligations towards the manor could take the remainder of the agricultural production to the market. Firm limits were set to manor duties and the landlords could no longer raise them at whim. Corporal punishment was limited to 30 lashes. Peasants were also given the right to file complaints against landlords not following the regulations.

Compared with the Rosen declaration, the positive regulations were beyond a doubt a step forward. However, the status of the peasantry remained far behind the level reached at the end of Swedish rule. The peasants still remained under the authority of landlords as serfs and the Russian state showed little interest in whether the protective regulations were strictly followed or not.

In **1784** a large-scale peasant revolt (the so-called **head tax disturbances**) erupted. The peasants believed that the establishment of regency and the implementation of the head tax meant liberation from their manorial obligations. In several manors in Livonia, the peasants refused to perform labour.

To quell the disturbances, military units were sent to manors. This resulted in confrontations between peasants and soldiers. The height of the disturbances (the so-called **Orchard War**) took place in Räpina, where five Estonian peasants were killed. In the manor or Karula in Võru region, women joined the fight by throwing stones at soldiers arresting the peasants.

The people of Põltsamaa (from A.W. Hupel).

The Russian-Swedish War of 1788-1790. Throughout the eighteenth century, Sweden did not abandon the idea of re-conquering Estonia and Livonia – lands lost during the Great Northern War. The first attempt in **1741-1743** ended for Sweden with a further loss of territories in Finland. In **1788**, Swedish King Gustav III began a new war against Russia, taking advantage of yet another Russian-Turkish conflict. Most of the military forces that defended Estonia and Livonia were sent to the front against Turkey. Sweden's strategy foresaw an army offensive in Finland and a landing in Ingria, with the goal of conquering St Petersburg. By this, Sweden hoped to force Russia into territorial concessions. The military activities got stuck. The Swedish navy did not gain predominance in the Baltic Sea, and the army failed to defeat Russian troops in Finland.

In March 1790, a small Swedish military unit unexpectedly landed in **Paldiski**, forcing the local 500-strong garrison to surrender. However, capturing Paldiski was of little military significance. The Swedes hoped for more success with **Tallinn**, with the goal of crushing the Russian navy. Despite their predominance and forceful attacks, the naval battle on 13 May 1790 ended with a Swedish defeat. As Sweden found no success in Finland as well, the Peace of Värälä was concluded in the same year, restoring the pre-war situation.

Prior to the war, Gustav III hoped that the **Baltic nobility**, not satisfied with the implementation of regency and the restriction of their privileges, would support Sweden's conquest plans. However, the early months of the war showed the nobility's **loyalty to the Tsar** and not many welcomed the Swedes. The peasants and townspeople were clearly pro-Swedish during the war. Rumours spread amongst the people that Swedish forces would land on the Estonian coast soon. In the summer of 1788, a large number of peasants – some armed – gathered in the woods near the coast waiting for the landing. The **flight** of peasants to Sweden and Finland also increased remarkably during the war years.

The Russian government in turn was forced to organise basic defence in Estonia and Livonia during the war. As there were not enough regular troops, the government issued permission for the formation of voluntary **rifle corps** in Estonia. In the autumn of 1790, there were already 10,000 members of the navy and army in Tallinn alone. To the Estonia people, the war brought about **extra obligations** in the form of fortifications, transport responsibilities, housing troops, and others. The latter was often accompanied by conflicts between peasants and Russian soldiers.

26. Spiritual Culture in the Eighteenth Century

Cultural influences in the eighteenth century. The incorporation of Estonia into Russia did not change the local cultural orientation. Russia, which only recently started to aspire towards Europe, was culturally backward and could not exert any remarkable influence on the Baltic countries. However, cultural contacts with Germany intensified. Young Baltic German noblemen studied at German universities. Many intellectuals from Germany found work in the Baltic countries, where there was a lack of pastors, lawyers, doctors and private teachers.

Although the Baltic provinces were among the most developed regions of the Russian Empire, the level of cultural development in the Baltic countries in the eighteenth century should not be overemphasised. The devastating and destructive influence of the Great Northern war affected spiritual life even more than the economy, hampering the natural development of the local peoples for decades.

The Lutheran Church after the Great Northern War. After the Great Northern war, the Lutheran Church continued to play the central role in spiritual life, although in difficult conditions. Many congregations were left without pastors; some of them fled, while others were deported. As the activities of Tartu University were discontinued, theological training also ceased, in turn making it more difficult to nominate new pastors. Churches were ravaged or destroyed in the war.

Although state authorities acknowledged the leading role of the Lutheran Church in the religious life of the Baltic provinces, the influence of the Church had diminished compared with earlier times. No bishops were appointed in Estonia or Livonia. In Livonia the ecclesiastic superintendent-general continued as the head of the church organisation, while in Estonia one of the councillors performed these duties. The interference of the nobility in church matters was very common in the first half of the eighteenth century and usually the will of the nobility was forced on the Church.

Pietism. Even during the time of the Great Northern War, a new religious movement – piet-

A view of Tallinn (E.H. Schlichting).

A view of Viljandi (W.S. Stavenhagen).

ism – began spreading to the Baltic region from Germany. Those following pietism were dissatisfied with the deepening conservatism of the Lutheran Church. They sought a deeper understanding of the faith in making life more ethical.

In the 1720-1730s, pietism acquired a dominant position among local pastors. With their energy and diligence, priests adhering to pietism helped the Church overcome the crisis after the Great Northern War.

Followers of pietism also managed to bring Lutheranism closer to the people. One of their aims was to replace the earlier cramming of religious dogma with explanations, in order to make them more understandable. The publication of religious literature also reappeared. In **1739** a full translation of the **Bible** appeared in Estonian for the first time. The laborious task was accomplished by Anton Thor Helle, the pastor of Jüri.

The **Moravian movement.** As pietism remained basically within the theological circles, it was the **Herrnhut** (named from the German town of Herrnhut, where it originated) movement that brought the ideas of pietism closer to the people. Through travelling German craftsmen, it arrived in Estonia in the early 1730s and was quickly adopted by the peasantry.

The Herrnhut movement preached piety, humility and morality, as well as social equality and fraternity. Although the Herrnhut movement did not break from the official Lutheran Church, they formed their own congregations and chose their own preachers. Often the even gathered outdoors. The biggest congregations built their own meeting houses.

At first, they fought against everything associated with the old beliefs. Old places of sacrifice, ornaments and objects of "boasting" – bagpipes and violins – were destroyed. As a result of the Herrnhut influence, taverns were frowned upon and many were closed as a result. Great emphasis was placed on morality. On Saaremaa, where the movement was especially strong, not a single crime was registered in 1740-1745.

Within a decade, the number of congregation members increased by 10,000, not counting the numerous listeners and sympathisers. Most pastors favoured the Moravian movement, as this brought the people closer to the religion.

The movement of the Moravians played an extremely important role by increasing the self-consciousness of peasants. The rules of the congregations allowed all members to sound off, thereby offering an opportunity of self-realisation. The requirement of equality, which forbade discrimination on the basis of wealth or social standing, also had to be met.

In many places, the movement exceeded the bounds of religion and members began pushing social claims.

Tallima Paap, a peasant from Rõuge, preached that the power of landlords is evil and does not have to be obeyed. People must live as one friendly community with common property and common work. When they become strong enough, they would take over the manor's property as well. Those following the Herrnhut move-

The manor of Keila-Joa (W.S. Stavenhagen).

ment often went to extremes in their demand for morality. For example, the aforementioned Tallima Paap demanded that even married couples should not have sexual relations, as everyone was supposed to live like brothers and sisters.

As the Church and nobility were no longer able to keep the Moravian movement under control, Tsarina Elizabeth prohibited the movement in 1743. However, the prohibition could not abolish the movement. In the early nineteenth century a new wave of Moravian thought spread in Estonia.

Rationalism. As the ideas of the Enlightenment spread, a new religious movement – rationalism – gained popularity. The rationalists looked at the sanctimonious nature of pietism with taunting superiority. They set education and enlightenment of people as their aim. The sermons of rationalist pastors often offered practical knowledge and clear advice.

The rationalists' concept of society was original as well. While pietism explained social problems by the poor sense of morality among the peasantry and saw redemption by total religious piety, the rationalists criticised the social organisation of society – especially serfdom – in the Baltic provinces.

Johann Georg **Eisen von Schwarzenberg**, pastor of Torma, who represented the older generation of rationalist pastors, drafted several agricultural projects (see chapter 25) and worked out a plan to colonise free German peasants in the Baltic countries. Besides working on growing fruits and drying vegetables, Eisen was also the initiator of vaccinations against smallpox in Estonia – which was the most dangerous infectious disease of the time.

August Wilhelm **Hupel** (1737-1804) was a prolific man of letters who handed down valuable descriptions of his time to the people of today in his German collections of articles, "Topographic Notes from Estonia and Livonia" and "Nordic Writings." Hupel was also active spreading literature and organising reading societies. With Peter Wilde, a local doctor, he published the first Estonian-language newspaper, "Lühhike õppetus..." ("Short Instruction...").

Public education. The Great Northern War had a devastating effect on the state of education. There was a lack of schools, leaving parish clerks teaching prayers and spelling as their only teacher. The school itself was usually housed in a farm building and was open in winter months only when there was less work on the farm

In the second half of the eighteenth century, the first attempt at establishing compulsory education was made. The diet of **1765** approved a plan creating a school system. The plan, compiled by Superintendent-general Zimmermann, provided the foundation for schools not only in each parish, but also in bigger manors. Due to the indifferent attitude or even opposition of the landlords, this plan was not fully put into practice. Many noblemen were convinced that the peasants' place was in the fields, thus needed no education to do such work. In 1787 Governor-general George Browne again had to reassert compulsory education.

The Stone Bridge of Tartu.

In the province of Estonia, the process of establishing schools was even slower.

Printed matter. Despite a loose network of schools, literacy made remarkable strides among the peasants. Children were mostly taught to read at home. Under these circumstances, the need for the Estonian printed word arose.

The majority of publications for the peasantry consisted of the Bible, prayer books and hymnbooks. In the second half of the eighteenth century, the availability of Estonian secular writings increased. The first known **almanac for rural-folk** was published in 1731. The almanac of those days comprised of numerous instructions in many areas of life, such as farming, healthcare and others. They also published weather forecasts for the coming year, which the peasantry followed with great interest. Astrological advice was equally important. The stories published in "almanac tales" were of special importance. For the most part these were adapted from German translations. A typical representative of such literature is "A Nice Book of Tales and Instructions" (1782) by Friedrich Gustav **Arvelius**, which promoted obedience to the landlord and naively praised the humility of peasants.

However, the life and instructions of Ramma Joosep, one of the main characters of the story who displayed unending loyalty to his master, became an object of admonishment among the peasantry. Friedrich Wilhelm **Willmann**, the pastor of Karja, was more popular among peasants with his popular stories and his storybooks were often read until they fell apart.

Architecture. The poor economic circumstances after the Great Northern War hindered the development of architecture for decades. The only outstanding example of architecture in the first half of the century is the Palace of Kadriorg. The construction was commissioned by the central government and began in 1718. As for its architectural appearance, the Palace of Kadriorg resembled the palaces build during the same period in St Petersburg and its outskirts, where regular French-style parks surrounded a palace built in the prevailing Italian Baroque style.

In the second half of the century, increasing prosperity enabled Baltic German landlords to build fabulous mansions as well. The manor of Palmse is one of the best examples of the period's architecture.

In the 1770s, a new **Classicist** style gradually took the forefront in Estonian architecture. Buildings from that period bear traits of both Baroque and Classicist styles. In 1773, the rebuilding of Toompea Castle in Tallinn was completed. In 1784, the Tartu Town Hall was finished as well. Classicist architecture, with its strict proportions, antique arches and columns, and an abandonment of the numerous details of Baroque, became predominant in the mostly-rebuilt Tartu, which was heavily devastated by the Great Northern War and many fires. After the great fire of 1775, almost all of the city required rebuilding. The Stone Bridge over the Emajõgi River was built as a present by Catherine the Great. Also built at the time are the **university buildings** on Toomemägi, which contributed greatly to the image of Tartu. The architect was Johann Wilhelm **Krause**, later professor of Tartu University.

27. The Abolition of Serfdom in Estonia

Early symptoms of crisis in the manor economy. Until the late eighteenth century, Baltic landlords were not very interested in economic innovations. Prices of grain were still high and Russia's internal provinces remained a strong market. The first symptoms of crisis appeared as late as the end of the eighteenth century, when consumption by landlords began exceeding the economic capacity of the manors.

Relations with Germany brought about attempts to raise living standards. However, that required significantly higher expenditures due to the poor circumstances in the Baltic region. In the late eighteenth century, magnificent manor houses with parks and ponds were built instead of wooden buildings. More expensive and exotic foods appeared on the tables. Trotters were brought from above. Foreign wines replaced beer. However, the obsolete manor economy could no longer cover such expenses. This forced many landlords to borrow more and more money. To cover the debts, production was increased.

The landlords tried to do this the old fashion way – by increased tillage and peasants' duties. It became more and more evident that this was not the solution to the crisis.

Attempts to carry out reforms. In the late eighteenth century, groups of landlords in both Estonia and Livonia started to look for a way out of the developing crisis. However, a discussion on the issue of the peasantry at the 1795 diet of the Estonian nobility failed. The majority of landlords still opposed any reforms.

The unjust situation of the peasantry in the Baltic provinces also diminished the prestige of the Russian Empire in Europe. Due to the greater openness of the Baltic region, local agricultural relations were more visible to Europe than the lives of Russian peasants – which were not any better than their counterparts in Estonia and Livonia. Democratically disposed intellectuals also contributed much to the introduction of agricultural conditions in the Baltic region.

Garlieb **Merkel** described the economic and legal situation of the Livonian peasants in his book, "Latvians, Especially in Livonia, at the End of the Philosophical Century," published in Germany in 1796. His straightforward and open style deeply impressed European readers. Johann Christoph **Petri** was also sharply critical towards serfdom in his book, "Estonian and the Estonians" (1802).

Tsar **Alexander I**, who reigned from 1801 to 1825, was ready to change the social and economic situation in the Baltic countries. Reforms in this region would no way affect the interest of landlords in Russia proper. In order to apply pressure on landlords, the central authorities used its position in granting out loans to the nobility who were being crushed by debts. Alexander I hinted to Jakob von Berg, a ranking official

Garlieb Merkel.

*Põltsamaa castle
(W.S. Stavenhagen).*

of the Estonian nobility, that acquiring a loan would involve the state of the peasantry.

The agrarian reform laws of 1802 and 1804. At the 1802 diet of the Estonian nobility, under the economic and political pressure from the central authorities, the regulation of the peasantry proposed by von Berg was adopted without any significant disputes.

In historical literature the regulation is called "Everybody..." ("Iggaüks" in Estonian), after the first word in the Estonian text. The most important aspect of the law was the establishment of a **hereditary right to farms**. This meant that when a peasant had fulfilled his duties to the landlord, the latter could not be evicted from his family home and the farm was passed down to the sons in case of the farmer's death.

In Livonia a similar law was passed in **1804**. Besides the hereditary right to farms, the Livonian law also provided a **standardisation of statute labour**, for example, by harmonising it with the farm's economic capacity. For this purpose, farmlands needed to be properly measured and its yield to be accurately estimated, establishing the amount of labour required that could not be changed at a landlord's whim. It was also prohibited to sell or expropriate peasants. The landlords' right to punish peasants was restricted to a two-day incarceration or fifteen lashes, while farm-owners were deprived of that.

In 1804, the demand of fixing duties to the manor was also enforced in Estonia. However, the agrarian reform law in Estonia did not foresee a measurement and estimation process.

Although peasants in Livonia and Estonia were still serfs, the relations between the manor and peasantry became more regulated. The hereditary right to farms and the right to own ungrounded property aroused a lasting interest by peasants to increase their wealth.

Parish courts, where peasants themselves were judges, were established in Estonia and Livonia. Although the parish courts of those times remained under the control of the landlord, the establishment of such courts contributed greatly to the rise of self-esteem and sense of justice among peasants. This was the first step towards the establishment of self-governance by peasants.

Unrest in North Estonia. The regulations of 1804 did not satisfy either side. Landlords felt that the laws were too binding on them, while the peasantry expected more – especially in the reduction of manor duties. It was rumoured that the landlords had concealed the real law and had published a fake. In the autumn of **1805**, unrest spread from Livonia to Estonia. As the agrarian

An Estonian farm at the end of the eighteenth century in Pärnu region (by J.C. Brotze).

reform law in Estonia was much more conservative to that of Livonia, the peasants felt that the landlords did them an injustice. Due to the growing unrest in manors, the landlords requested help from the military. Units were sent to calm the peasants. A major incident broke out in **Kose-Uuemõisa** in Harju region. The local landlord, von Rosen, was frightened as rumours spread that the peasants wanted to murder him in order to be admitted to the imperial court and to reclaim their rights there. The peasants gathered in the manor and killed a captain of a Russian unit that was sent there for assistance. There were also casualties on the peasants' side. Only after reinforcements arrived with guns did the peasants return to work for the manor again.

The **Napoleonic Wars and Estonia.** Although the Napoleonic Wars did not touch Estonia directly, the events on the Baltic Sea created a stir in the coastal areas. In May of 1801, famous British Admiral Horatio **Nelson** made a raid with his squadron upon Tallinn. During the next few years, British warships moved in Estonian coastal waters, seizing fishing boats and merchant ships, often in demand of water, food, cattle and more from the coastal dwellers. On Hiiumaa, there was even an attempt to form a local defence force among the peasantry, but the central government did not allow it. In August-September 1809, British warships alongside Swedish allies blockaded the Russian navy for several weeks at the port of **Paldiski**. In **1812**, Napoleonic troops (the corps under Marshal MacDonald) invaded Couronia, though the drive ceased near Riga. Estonia remained outside of the immediate area of conflict.

For Estonians, the war brought about additional duties. Constant military activity demanded more and more men – **conscripts**. In Estonia, regular conscription started in 1797. In 1812, men were called up three times. In 1807, a **home defence** or **land militia** was formed to support the regular army. The unit of K. von Nieroth was formed in Tartu in 1812, which pushed as far as the outskirts of Paris in its campaign. In the Russian-French conflict of 1812, many leading posts were filled by Balts, such as the Russian minister of war at the time and later General Field-marshal Michael Andreas **Barclay de Tolly**.

During the war, the **economic depression** deepened due to the extraordinary obligations (accommodating troops and their provisioning, duty of compulsory conveyance, etc.), Russia's association with the continental blockade (which caused a slump in grain prices), and the crop failure and famine that afflicted Estonian in 1806-1808.

The **emancipation from serfdom.** The continuous pressure of the central government to the nobility was partly due to ideological consideration. Napoleon had abolished serfdom, liquidated class privileges and began implementing reforms in the conquered territories.

This forced the tsarist government to more concessions, at least in the Baltic provinces. After discussions with the nobility, legal concessions followed, though economic power remained in the hands of landlords. The agrarian reform law of 1807 in Prussia became a model. **Tsar Alexander I** on 23 May **1816** confirmed the new regulations for Estonian peasants, and three years later on 26 March **1819** did the same for Livonian peasants.

The nobility renounced all its former rights over the peasantry. Estonian peasants were joyously declared **free from serfdom**. At the same time, however, the landlords retained ownership of all land. To continue living in their farms, the peasants still had to rent the land from the landlord. Thus peasants were still required in a way to perform labour dues. A "free" **lease** replaced the earlier fixed obligations. This meant the annulment of the limitations established by the 1804 law, giving landlords an opportunity to dictate requirements to the peasants. The peasants had to accept the conditions or else the landlord could lease the land to another peasant.

Thus the abolition of serfdom did not bring about any remarkable change to the life of peasants at first. They were formally granted personal freedom, but the possibilities to enjoy it were limited.

In order to guarantee a workforce for landlords, restrictions on the freedom of movement of peasants remained for a long time. Although peasants could go from one landlord to another, they were not allowed to settle in a town or to leave the province.

The emancipation from serfdom also included the introduction of **surnames**. Until then, peasants were known only by their Christian name, and the name of their farm and father (such as Mart of Kahvre Hans). Now surnames, or **free names**, were added. As the names were usually given by the landlords themselves, German or characteristically German surnames spread among Estonians. The situation changed with the Estonianisation of names in the latter half of the 1930s.

Agriculture after the abolition of serfdom. There were over 1000 manors and about 60,000 farms in Estonia in the first half of the nineteenth century.

Grain remained the primary income for the manor. However, the manor economy based on statute labour could no longer compete on the European market. The decline of grain prices in the 1820-1830s reduced the landlords' incomes by a remarkable extent. To increase incomes, fields were enlarged and farms – sometimes entire villages – were "manorised". The new fields required an additional workforce, thus the landlords had to raise the rent again. Such a way of management exhausted the farm economy beyond all limits, creating insecurity and indifference among the peasantry.

More enterprising landlords studied the possibilities for new sources of income, such as raising sheep for wool, breeding dairy cattle, and cultivating potatoes for distilling spirits. However, only a small group of landlords showed any interest in agricultural innovations. Most continued to push along in the same old way, squeezing the last resources out of the system by statue labour.

28. The First Decades after the Emancipation from Serfdom

Self-governance of peasants. Up until the nineteenth century, the **manor** – an administrative unit that included the lands of both manor and village – played a central role in organising the everyday lives of peasants. At the beginning of the nineteenth century, the **rural community** – the self-governance of peasants as a social class – started to develop in parallel with the manor. Peasant regulations of the early nineteenth century enabled the establishment of **parish courts**. The courts consisted of three members: one nominated by the landlord, another elected from amongst the farmers, and the final from amongst farmhands. These courts dealt with mutual disputes and property claims among peasants, as well as manor duties and minor violations. In the 1820s, parish courts were renamed community courts.

Common responsibility for the **common granary** also united the community of peasants. This was a supply of grain from which the peasants could borrow in an emergency. To keep a supply of grain, peasants had to build a granary and contribute a certain amount of grain a year. Both the communal granary and the grain were the common property of the peasants, and landlords only had the right to supervise.

Relief for the poor was also the task of the community. The community supported its members who were unable to work or were destitute. The latter were usually sent to so-called rotations, going from one farm to another where they were given shelter and food for a couple of weeks. Later special community poorhouses were built.

The abolition of serfdom also required a more clear-cut definition of such self-governance, as it still depended heavily on the landlord after the 1816 and 1819 peasant regulations. For examples, landlords convened the community's general meetings and sanctioned all decisions. Heads of communities – a **parish elder**, with assistants in Estonia and two **churchwardens** in Livonia – were elected from amongst the peasantry. These officials had to be approved by the landlord, who also had the right to dismiss them. Besides, the landlord maintained police authority over the community. The self-governance of peasants was freed from nobility control as late as 1866 with community reform.

A parish judge.

Estonian peasants (E. von Gebhardt).

Composition of the peasantry. In the nineteenth century, the peasantry was divided into **manor and village folk**. Among the latter **farmers**, who actually managed the farm but had to fulfil manor duties, were central. The heads of the farm worked on the fields while their children often worked with **tenants** on the fields of the manor, performing the labour dues. There were also **cottagers** who owned a small piece of land and a cottage on the outskirts of bigger farms. Their labour force was used at farms for urgent seasonal work.

Manor folk formed a socially and economically prominent group amongst the peasantry. These people received their subsistence from manors, with some acting as "enforcers" (such as overseeing socagers, bailiffs, etc.) and others as artisans.

By the middle of the nineteenth century, farmers made up about 40 per cent of the total population of peasants, followed by tenants at 30 per cent, cottagers at 20 per cent, and manor folk by 10 per cent.

Peasants' obligations. The community was also responsible for the fulfilment of the obligations of peasants. This was based on a system of **mutual observance**.

Labour dues, which were divided into regular weekly dues and extraordinary labour services required for seasonal work, continued to be the primary **manor obligation**. The fulfilment of labour dues was calculated in so-called harness days, when peasants went to manor fields with draught animals and inventory, or in foot days. Various natural duties and taxes in favour of the manor became additions to labour dues. From the middle of the nineteenth century, the gradual transition from labour duties to monetary rents began.

Among **state obligations** on the peasantry, the head tax and conscription were the most important.

The **head tax** was introduced in Estonia in 1783, with the original tax rate at 70 kopecks for each male individual. However, the head tax gradually increased by more than fivefold, and poorer peasants had great difficulty paying it. Usually the landlord paid the head tax for peasants, but of course in demand for additional labour or other duties in return. State peasants, most of which lived on Saaremaa, paid their head tax themselves.

The obligation of state **military duties** – conscription, or so-called "blood tithe" – was established in Estonian in 1796. At first, conscription was carried out without rules. In those days, it was literally a manhunt, called in folklore as conscript abduction. Later (1816 in Estonia and 1829 in Livonia), a system of drawing lots was introduced. Farmers, schoolteachers, and community officials were exempt from conscription.

In Livonia, peasants could exempt themselves for life by paying a special fee starting in 1819 (at first it was 300 silver roubles, increased to 1500 later). Peasants of North Estonia gained this right as late as 1861. The community was also obliged to supply conscripts with money, provisions for the journey, and clothes. The landlords could punish insubordinate peasants by sending them off for conscription. During the era of conscription (1797-1874), about 100,000 men were conscripted into the Tsarist army. The majority of them never returned to their native land.

In addition to conscription, peasants had to serve in militias during wars (1806-1807, 1812, 1854-1855), as well as fulfilling other duties such as accommodation, provision and transportation of troops.

Every year various **community duties** had to be fulfilled as well, for example, road maintenance and building communal granaries and schools. Road maintenance obligation usually involved fixing roads every spring, as each farm was given responsibility over a certain length.

Peasants also had to pay **church dues**, from which the maintenance of the entire church organisation was derived.

Peasant disturbances in South Estonia. The regulations of 1816 and 1819 hindered the development of the farm economy. The farmers lost their guarantee of permanent settlement in their farms, thus had little motivation to build new houses, cultivate the land, or improve the soil. The number of cottagers, who relegated themselves to a small cottage on the outskirts of a farm, increased. Such lifestyle provided a scantly living, but they were free from the burdens of farmers and duties to manors.

In 1840, a crop failure struck the land, followed by a famine. Rumours spread among the people, already driven to despair, that in Russia free land was being distributed to everyone who requested it. Hundreds of peasants flocked to Riga, the capital of the province, to "sign up." In Riga the peasants were treated well at first. Officials explained that there was no hope to get any land, and urged them to go home. However, as the peasants became more restless in the manors, the nobility once again called on the military for help.

The arrival of troops added fuel to the fire. A serious incident, the so-called **Pühajärve War**, took place in September 1841 at the manor of Pühajärve in Otepää. The peasants hindered the arrests of their comrades, who were deemed guilty of instigating unrest. Although the activities of peasants were limited to hiding in the woods and skirmishes around the manor armed only with clubs, they were severely punished: 30 peasants were sentenced to 500 lashes, while six were sent to labour camps in Siberia.

The interest in emigration continued in the years to follow. Shoemaker Gustav Jürgensohn from Võru announced that the new homeland would yield three crops a year, with the third batch so thick that it had to be cut like wood and straw could be used instead of firewood. The spreader of such rumours was deported to Siberia, but this aroused the population. Legislation prevented Estonians from settling in Russia. Some peasants managed to reach Pskov, though were later arrested and returned to Livonia. The peasants blamed their landlords for their failure, but believed that the state wanted to improve their situation.

From the 1840s, growing **potatoes** became common in peasant farms as well. Potato became one of Estonians' main dishes, which also put an end to frequent famines. However, there were a few years when both the normal harvest and the potato crop failed. At the same time, farms in South Estonia started to grow **flax** on a large scale.

*St George's Day
(O. Hoffmann).*

Conversion movement. The belief in the Tsar caused a mass conversion to Orthodoxy in South Estonia in the summer of 1845. The peasants believed that the adoption of the "Tsar's faith" would liberate them from labour dues and would grant them land and other benefits.

The movement soon spread with such speed that it caused anxiety in government circles. A six-month "time of consideration" was established for those willing to convert, which lowered the people's enthusiasm by some extent. The priest of Mustvee halted the flow of converts by announcing that he had run out of ink and the peasants must wait until more is brought from Riga. Although official statements pointed out that conversion would not result in economic benefits, the peasants did not want to abandon their dream so easily.

Within three years, over 60,000 Estonians converted to Orthodoxy. The percentage of converts varied throughout different parts of the country. While about ten per cent of peasants converted in the Võru region, over 30 per cent of peasants on Saaremaa did the same. In some communities and parishes (such as Tõstamaa, Muhu, and Pöide), as much as 70-80 per cent of the population converted to Orthodoxy. At the same time, the first Orthodox churches were built.

Most of the converts belonged to the poorer part of the population. They often became a joke for wealthier peasants. The latter laughed at the required cross around the neck: "What sort of a man are you now, you look like a dog with a bell around the neck!" New Christian names of Russian origin also aroused alienation: Juhan became Yefim, Toomas became Timofei, Villem became Vasili, Leenu became Yelena, etc. Orthodox customs like kissing the cross or worshipping icons with candles remained alien to most of the new converts. When they realised finally that they would not get any land, the disappointment was great and peasants wanted to return to Lutheranism. However, the government strictly opposed this. Some of the converts went back to the Lutheran Church secretly. Later history gave evidence that Orthodoxy could not really take root among the Estonian people.

29. Developments in Estonian Society in the Middle of the Nineteenth Century

New regulations for peasants. Economic difficulties and new peasant disturbances forced the nobility to revisit the question of the peasantry.

The more conservative part of the nobility considered it important to revert to the regulations of 1804. On one hand this would have meant the re-imposition of serfdom, which would guarantee manors with a sufficient workforce. On the other hand, this would have restored the hereditary right to farms, which would give a greater sense of stability to farmers. Baron Hamikar von **Fölkersahm** of Ruijēna, offered a more radical solution. His supporters saw a rapid transformation to a capitalist management system as the solution. Monetary rent had to be introduced and workers at the manor fields must be hired. The next step was to sell farms for perpetuity.

The new Livonian peasant regulations, published in 1849, reorganised the entire manor and farm economy. Farmers were relieved from work in manor fields and could now manage their own households with all their devotion. Farmers must now decide how to manage his farm effectively, learn to consider the price and demand at the market, and to handle money. All of this of course required enterprising spirit, activity and economic know-how. Some peasants were not willing to abandon statute labour since it was organised by the manor and did not require any initiative. However, the majority of peasants were willing to accept the new regulations. They began looking into ways to raise their incomes and adapted to market conditions. The **consolidation of peasants' land into lots** from disconnected plots helped enable a more effective use of land. Enterprising peasants also saved money and thought about purchasing their farms for perpetuity.

The transition to monetary rent and selling of farms also enabled the landlords to reorganise their establishments. Instead of statute labourers,

Hamilkar von Fölkersahm.

wage earners – **manor farmhands** – started to work the manor fields. This allowed the purchase of better machinery for agriculture. Distilleries and dairies in manors also got new equipment. This also enabled the improvement of the soil, fertilisation of fields, improvement of breeding, and even plant breeding.

Similar peasant regulations were adopted in **1856** in Estonia and in 1865 on Saaremaa.

In the 1860s, the reforms continued to be favourable for the peasantry. In 1865, the landlords were prohibited from punishing peasants. In 1868, the transition to monetary rent was completed as statute labour could no longer be exchanged for farmland rent. The community law of 1866 liberated the self-governance of peasants from landlord supervision. At this stage, Estonians could take their fate into their own hands in self-governance, as well as in economic life.

Selling land for perpetuity. The 1849 Livonian peasant regulation prescribed the way and conditions in detail for buying farms for perpetuity. It actually concerned the right to decide whether to sell the farms and to whom and at what price, of which the right belonged to the landlords. Farms could also be sold to peasants from elsewhere.

Although some farms had been sold for perpetuity earlier, a large-scale process started in the 1850s. In 1853, the landlord of **Abja** sold the farms of two villages to peasants for perpetuity. Within a couple of years, the selling of land spread over all of South Estonia, reaching its peask at the turn of the 1860-1870s.

The money for purchase came mostly from **flax growing**. While grain prices dropped in the middle of the nineteenth century, flax prices remained high. In some farms so much land was under flax that one even had to buy grain from the manor for personal needs. There were cases of orchards hacked down to cultivate flax.

One some well-off farmers were able to purchase their farms immediately. Usually only part of the sum was paid up-front, with the remainder paid back over decades as debt to the landlord. It was not rare for the purchase to be forfeited due to debts.

In North Estonia, the selling of land for perpetuity took place 15 to 20 years later than in South Estonia. It did not start on Saaremaa until the first decade of the twentieth century. **Potato growing** was a major source of income for North Estonian peasants.

Selling land for perpetuity signified a revolutionary change in the life of country folk. Estonians were no longer economically dependent on their landlords, and have become once again the full masters of their own land. Now peasants could build new houses or improve the soil with assurance. **Farmers' societies**, which introduced progressive farming among the peasantry, were founded all across Estonia.

Shipbuilding and seafaring. The second half of the nineteenth century signified a boom for Estonian shipping. The coast of **Häädemeeste**

The factory in Sindi (W.S. Stavenhagen).

The glass factory in Rõika (W.S. Stavenhagen).

in Pärnu region, situated in a large forest, became the main shipbuilding centre. Ships were also built on the northern coast, especially in **Lahemaa**.

Ships were used mostly for coastal shipping. They were used for carrying stones and firewood to Riga, and plaster to St Petersburg. The ships also sailed to Finland and Sweden. As most of the skippers of such ships had no special training and got their bearings by coastal signs rather than charts, they were called **wild captains**. The most famous wild captain was Enn Uuetoa from the island of Kihnu, called Kihnu Jõnn by the people.

Smuggling also brought good income. Peasants of the northern coastal area exchanged grain in Finland for salt that could be resold in Estonia or Russia with at least fourfold profit.

Trained sailors were needed for longer voyages. Navigation schools were founded in many places, the most famous being in **Ainaži** in 1864. Men who graduated from such schools sailed the oceans. In 1868, the "Matador" was the first Estonia ship that sailed to America.

Seafaring was a dangerous and hard job, but also brought wealth. The broadening of outlook in seeing strange and faraway countries offered by seafaring was even more important.

The Mahtra War. In both economic and social development, North Estonia and Saaremaa remained about **15-20 years** behind South Estonia. After the publication of the 1856 peasant regulation, peasant unrest increased there as well. The peasants who looked over the text mistakenly believed that additional labour was no longer compulsory. The peasants of Kurisoo and Anija manors in Harju region, who travelled to Tallinn to check the legislation, were publicly flogged at the Tallinn marketplace instead.

In the spring of **1858**, the peasants of some ten manors in Harju, Järva, and Virumaa regions refused to perform statue labour. Military units were summoned, and the peasants were punished by corporal punishment. On the morning of 2 June, about a thousand local peasants encircled the unit sent to the manor of Mahtra, parish of Juuru, demanding the soldiers leave immediately. The dispute soon turned into a bloody encounter. The killed and wounded from both sides were left at the battlefield of the **Mahtra War**. An officer of the Russian army was also killed in the battle. Rebellious peasants were court-martialled, with 40 peasants sentenced to corporal punishment. Two of them were sentenced to 1000 lashes, considered lethal. This was followed by exile for life in Siberia, including a lengthy stint at labour camps.

Emigration. The new passport regulation enforced in 1863 gave the peasantry full freedom of movement within the borders of the Russian Empire. This brought about extensive emigration from Estonia. The number of Estonians who left their native country reached tens of thousands. In the second half of the nineteenth century, **Estonian colonies** were established on the Volga River, in Crimea, in the Caucasus, and even on the Pacific coast. However, most emigrants settled in the immediate vicinity of Estonia. According to the 1897 census, some 64,000 Estonians lived in the province of St Petersburg (12,000 in the city itself), and 25,000 Estonians in the province of Pskov (which included the Pechory district).

One of the promoters of emigration, Juhan Leinberg (the so-called "prophet Maltsvet") gathered many people, mostly from the parish of Kuusalu, who hoped to settle in Crimea. They abandoned their farms and waited in vain for the "white ship" promised by Leinberg that would wait for them in Lasnamäe.

Many of those who left for the "promise land" returned as the real situation at the new location was not as fabulous as hoped. This reduced the interest in emigration significantly.

The development of industry and trade. Until the late 1860s, economic development in Estonia remained rather moderate. The peasants exhausted by statue labour did not have much to sell or buy. Most commodities, clothes and agricultural tools were home made. **Industry** took its rise from the wool mills in the first half of the nineteenth century. **Cloth factories** were founded in Narva, Sindi and Kärdla. Most of the raw material was bought from manors where fine-fleeced sheep were kept. The woollen cloth made in Estonia was of high quality and was valued.

The old post office at the Nun's Gate in Tallinn (E.H. Schlichting).

The **Kreenholm manufactory** founded in Narva in 1858 became the biggest industrial enterprise in Estonia. The raw material, cotton, was imported from America and Egypt by ships and the product – spun cotton – was sent mostly to Russia where cotton clothes were made. The location of the manufactory was chosen primarily because of the possibility to use the hydroelectricity generated from the falls of the Narva River. Until the last decade of the nineteenth century, **Narva** remained the most important industrial centre in Estonia.

Trade was lively at the seaports of Tallinn and Pärnu. The latter was most important in the flax trade. Most of the flax exported from Estonia was undressed. Although the percentage of Estonians among townspeople grew steadily, they usually were relegated to the more laborious and less profitable occupations.

Those Estonians who managed to become owners of shops or independent craftsmen were considered successful. At the same time, those Estonians who were better off tried to behave like Germans in every way and were ashamed of their origin. Such Estonians were called **wannabe Germans** (or "juniper Germans").

As the wealth of peasants grew, the economic development of the country received a new impetus. Farmers no longer wanted to walk in soft heel-less or birch-bark shoes, but wore boots. Light from a pine splinter or tallow candle was replaced by **oil lamp** bought in town. Gradually mass-produced goods started to replace home made cloth and folk costumes.

30. Spiritual Life in Estonia in the First Half of the Nineteenth Century

In the nineteenth century, Estonian culture was still divided into two parts: the Baltic-German **high culture** and **peasant culture** of the native Estonian people. Baltic-German cultural life was continuously connected with the spiritual trends and developments in western Europe (mostly Germany), which in turn influenced the culture of Estonians. In the nineteenth century, the traditional peasant culture started to disintegrate and the influence of European culture increased.

The reopening of Tartu University. During the Great Northern War, the possibility to attain higher education in Estonia was disrupted by nearly a century. Tsar Paul I, who was enthroned in 1796, decided to close the state borders firmly in order to prevent the "insurrection movement" of the French Revolution from spreading to the Empire. Starting from 1798, Russian subjects were no longer allowed to study in western institutions. As new universities were founded in Russia, Tartu University was reopened in **1802** at the start of the reign of Tsar Alexander I.

Like under Swedish rule, there were four faculties in the re-opened Tartu University: the faculties of Theology, Law, Medicine, and Philosophy. Most of the students came from the

A view of Tartu.

Baltic provinces. Foreigners and young men from Russia studied there as well. The languages of tuition at Tartu was German and Latin. Teachers from Germany brought with them the ideas of the Enlightenment, which were supported by the liberal-minded Alexander I. The close friendship of Georg Friedrich **Parrot**, the first rector of the university, with the Tsar guaranteed the university extensive autonomy and financial support. Within a short time the main building of the university, the observatory on Toome Hill, the anatomical laboratory and clinic were completed. A library was built on the ruins of the Dome Church. Dome Hill was also renovated.

Tartu University soon became a recognised centre of science and education in Europe. Astronomer Wilhelm **Struve**, physicist Moritz Hermann Jacobi, founder of embryology Karl Ernst **von Baer**, and other scientists of renown were active in Tartu. In 1828-1839, the **Professors' Institute** functioned at the University. More than 20 scholars who graduated from the Institute started to work as teachers in other universities of the Russian Empire.

Only a few Estonians are known to have studied at Tartu University in the first half of the nineteenth century, most of them Germanised.

Most of the **Baltic-German cultural life** concentrated around Tartu University. An art school was opened at the university, taught by Karl August Senff – a graphic artist and copper engraver from Dresden. The curriculum of the art school provided a good basis for further studies at major European art institutes. Aside from the University, the manor of Raadi, where the intellectual elite of the day gathered, also became a centre of fine arts.

In Tallinn, the Tallinn Museum Society and the Provincial Museum became centres of art from the middle of the century. Painter Gerhard Franz **von Kügelgen** from Rhineland was the best-know artist in Tallinn.

Various societies also played an important part of cultural life in the nineteenth century. Society movements included academic, scientific and agricultural societies as well as students' fraternities, choirs, clubs, charity organisations and funds. There were more than fifty different Baltic-German societies active in Estonia, which

Georg Friedrich Parrot.

contributed to the preservation of identity, as well as the economic and political control over the local population.

In the first half of the nineteenth century, the **Classicist** style, which was first featured in manor architecture (Saku, Aaspere, Raikküla), held prominence in Baltic-German **architecture**. Post offices and inns were also built in the Classicist style. In towns, building activities spread from the mediaeval town centres to suburbs. The architectural appearance of Tallinn was influenced by the fact that in 1857, the town was excluded from the list of fortifications and parks were created on several of the bastions. Wooden suburbs started to develop outside the park zone.

Educational conditions. The school reform carried out in Russian in the early nineteenth century established the basic four-level **comprehensive schooling**, comprised of the parish and county schools in districts, secondary school in provincial towns, and university throughout the Empire. The Baltic provinces and Finland formed one education district with Tartu University as the centre. In Tallinn and Tartu there were *gymnasia*, where pupils acquired extensive

Types of university students.

knowledge in ancient languages, literature and history. **County schools** were established in all towns and pupils were taught mathematics, natural science and geography in two to three years. **Elementary schools** formed the lowest level of town schools, where children were taught how to read, write, and do basic maths.

The road to education for Estonian peasants began at community schools, followed by **parish schools**. However, a regular network of schools developed only after the emancipation of serfs. As a result of the 1840s conversion movement, **Orthodox peasant schools** were founded in South Estonia. In North Estonia a stable network of schools developed only in the 1870s. Gaps in public education were compensated by Sunday and reformatory schools and with travelling teachers.

In 1828, a **training institute** for elementary school teachers was founded in Tartu to prepare teachers for public schools. It was the first educational institute of the kind in the Russian Empire. In the middle of the century, teachers for community schools were prepared by ten seminars. In Valga, a German training institute headed by Jānis **Cimze** prepared parish school teachers in Estonia and Livonia.

In the parish of Pilistvere, **compulsory school attendance** was established as early as 1854. In the 1870-1880s, this demand became normal throughout Estonia.

Thanks to public schools, almost all peasants were able to read and at least 30-40 per cent was able to write by the 1880s.

The Estonian written word. In the first half of the nineteenth century, the written word in the native language was characterised by the growth of secular literature. **Almanacs** had spread secular writings earlier, and in the middle of the nineteenth century some ten almanacs were published regularly. In 1806, the "Tarto maa rahwa Näddali-Leht" ("The Tartu District Weekly"), the first Estonian-language **newspaper** (in the Tartu dialect), was published. Otto Wilhelm **Masing** published "Maarahwa Näddala-Leht" ("Country Folks' Weekly") in 1821-1823 and 1825, and Friedrich Reinhold **Kreutzwald** edited the journal "Ma-ilm ja mõnda, mis seal sees leida on" ("The World and What Could be Found There") in 1848-49. Johann Voldemar **Jannsen** laid the foundations to the regular Estonian press when he becan to publish the weekly "Perno Postimees" ("Pärnu Courier") in 1857.

Adventurous stories and sentimental reading matter soon replaced the pious stories that dominated Estonian fiction in the early nineteenth century. The sentimental "Pious Jenowewa," translated by Kreutzwald, became especially popular among the people.

The Estonian written word favoured the establishment of the **standard language** in the second half of the nineteenth century. The services of Eduard **Ahrens**, pastor of Kuusalu, was especially remarkable. Ahrens took the North Estonian central dialect as the basis for the literary language and compiled a new grammar in 1843.

Estophiles and the first Estonian intellectuals. The growing interest in exotic and minority peoples in Europe launched the Estophile movement in Estonia. The **Estophiles** – Baltic Germans interested in Estonia – studied the Estonian language and culture, published fiction of considerable artistic level, newspapers, textbooks for schools, and founded various scientific societies. A lectureship of the Estonian language was founded at Tartu University. First-generation Estonian intellectuals, such as Kreutzwald, Dietrich Heinrich Jürgenson and Friedrich Robert Faehlmann, also participated in the Estophile activities of Baltic Germans. The role of **Faehlmann**, who gathered a group of Estonian students while studying in the Faculty of Medicine, was especially remarkable. On the initiative of Faehlmann, the **Estonian Learned Society** was founded in Tartu in 1838, which set "the promotion and knowledge of Estonia, its history and present day, language, literature, and the country inhabited by Estonians" as its aim. In 1842, the **Estonian Literary Society** was founded in Tallinn as another major Estophile organisation. The two organisations also supported financially and morally the publication of two masterpieces of Estonian national literature: an anthology of Estonian folk songs by Alexander Heinrich Neus (1850-1852) and the **nation epic** "Kalevipoeg" (1857-1861). The popular edition of the epic was published in 1863.

Some intellectuals of Estonian origin took positions in Russia. For example the painter Johann **Köler** and doctor Philipp **Karell**, who became the court physician of Tsar Nicholas I and Tsar Alexander II. They kept in touch with their native land and played a remarkable role in the Estonian national movement.

Besides the few Estonian top intellectuals, **public school teachers** formed the basic core of the developing national intelligentsia. They also became one of the main driving force of the national movement.

Church matters and religious movements. The **Lutheran Church**, which had preserved its earlier organisational form and wide autonomy,

A manor in the classicist style in Riispere.

remained an important moulder of spirituality in Estonian society in the first half of the nineteenth century. In 1832, the all-Russian law on Lutheranism was passed, abolishing the former privileged position of the Lutheran Church in Estonia and Livonia. Lutheranism was no longer the state religion in the Baltic region, but one of many religious sects permitted by the Tsarist government in the territory of the Empire. Orthodoxy, regarded as a means for Russification of the borderlands, remained the official **state religion**. By spreading the official state religion it was hoped to reduce local cultural and religious differences. Although the position of Orthodoxy strengthened remarkably as a result of the conversion movement, the "Tsar's faith" did not become predominant.

In the first half of the nineteenth century, the **Moravian movement** also underwent a new period of activity. The democratic atmosphere in the chapels and the steady organisation of the Moravian congregations, which saw no difference between classes or nationalities, made the movement quite popular among the peasantry.

There were about 150 chapels following the Moravian movement, with about 50,000 official members by the middle of the nineteenth century. In the second part of the century, the movement gradually faded away.

In the eastern part of Järva region and in Harju region, the so-called **Maltsvet movement**, led by Juhan **Leinberg**, started to spread in the 1850s. He was a wealthy farmer, merchant, and house owner who abandoned everything and started conducting prayer meetings. Juhan Leinberg's speech was brave and impressive. His sermons were mostly based on the Old Testament and he sought to save people from economic difficulties by religion. In the 1860s the Maltsvet movement was connected with the emigration movement.

The development of spiritual life in the first half of the nineteenth century, alongside economic progress, created favourable conditions for profound social reforms. These revolutionary changes were carried out through the Estonian national movement in the second half of the century.

VI The Era of National Awakening

31. The National Movement

In nineteenth century Europe, interest in nationalities and their cultural peculiarities was on the increase. Several nations went through processes of national awakening or the development of national self-consciousness. In Italy and in Germany, political union of the nations were sought, while other nationalities subjected by the great European powers Russia, Austria and Turkey, started to reclaim their ancient rights.

The consciousness of Estonian peasants, which had been evoked by their liberation from serfdom, grew considerably with the economic changes in the country in the middle of the nineteenth century, creating a favourable basis for national awakening. Estonians, who had only recently been freed from corvée, could not yet set statehood and independence as their goals. Instead, they claimed equal rights with other nationalities living in the territory of Estonia, first and foremost with the Baltic Germans.

Political conditions. The Slavophile movement, which was also gathering strength in Russia, increased tension in the Baltic region. Heated debate on the privileges of the Baltic nobility in the local and the Russian press was not reassuring for the Baltic Germans. Russian nationalists repeatedly expressed the opinion that the privileged position of the German nobility should be ended, the Baltic area should be assimilated into the Russian Empire, and a process of Russification of the nations should be pursued.

Carl Schirren, professor of history at Tartu University, waged a bold campaign for the privileges of the Baltic Germans. As a result of his pamphlet "Livländische Antwort" (The Livonian Response) he lost his university post and was forced to settle in Germany.

The threat of Russification forced the Germans to alter their attitude towards the native people. More attention was now paid to "Germanising" Estonians and Latvians. While at the beginning of the nineteenth century the nobility had opposed teaching German to the peasants, now it was actively promoted, with a call for uniting "into one Livonian nation."

At the same time Russian authorities tried to make allies of the Estonians, in an effort to replace the German supreme power with a Russian one. Under the slogan of "defending the rights of native people," they hoped to do away with the Germans and Russify the Estonians soon after.

The petition campaign. The peasant disturbances of the 1840s and 1850s had been based

Johann Köler

Johann Voldemar Jannsen

hopes were placed on Tsar **Alexander II** (who reigned from 1856 to 1881), who had liberated Russian peasants from serfdom.

In 1864 **Adam Peterson**, a farmer from Holstre (Paistu parish), together with **Johann Köler**, a successful Estonian artist living in St Petersburg, started a petition campaign in the hope of drawing the Tsar's attention to the problems of local peasants. In autumn a delegation of 23 people, headed by Peterson, was sent to St Petersburg. The petition the delegation took with them they asked for the establishment of fixed prices for land and rent, the abolition of corvée and corporal punishment, equality with other social groups and the use of the Estonian language instead of German in courts and public offices.

On 9 November **1864** the members of the delegation managed to meet the Tsar at Tsarskoye Selo. The reception was brief and seemingly went well. But from the Tsar's palace the delegation was sent directly to the Ministry of Internal Affairs where instead of being listened to they were interrogated. For initiating petitions that "included false information and were directed against the current regime," Adam Peterson was sentenced to a year in prison.

on the naive belief of Estonian peasants in the goodness of the Tsar, and this belief persisted during subsequent decades. Especially great

New law of parishes. One of the most essential laws for Estonians during the reign of Alexander II was the establishment of a new

Header of the first edition of "Perno Postimees"

The Väägvere brass band

regulation of parishes in **1866**, which liberated both parish government and the parish court from the control and supervision of local landlords. According to the new law, all farmers (including those renting a farm) and one-tenth of landless peasants would form a parish assembly. The assembly elected a **parish council**, executing supreme power in the parish, half of which had to consist of farmers and the second half of landless peasants (craftsmen, manor workers and farm hands, as well as adult children of farmers, who according to Estonian tradition, were expected to inherit their fathers' farms, but had not yet received ownership).

A parish was to have an independent budget, with the council dividing taxes and duties between the farms. Similarly the council had to define the expenditure, which included the maintenance expenses of the council building, as well as the roads and bridges, the teacher's wage, and relief to the parish's poor. On one hand the taxes could not be too high because the members of the parish council had to pay them too; on the other hand there was no sense in economising in areas concerning the interests of the parish.

The parish was lead by the **parish elder**, who bore the responsibility to see that legislation was followed and to guarantee order in the parish. He had a right to fine violators of public order or to arrest them for a couple of days.

The 1866 parish regulation laid the basis of "parish politics", opening a path for the Estonian people towards "big politics" later. Initially Estonians could not progress further than the parish level. The establishment of local government at the levels of *guberniyas* and counties remained in the hands of the nobility up to the end of the Russian era.

Johann Voldemar Jannsen. One of the central figures from the initial years of the national movement in Estonia was Johann Voldemar Jannsen (1819-1890), who came from the town of Vändra.

A miller's son, he spent his childhood in the family mill. There he learned the language of visitors and developed a good sense of humour. After finishing at the parish school, the young man continued his education with the local priest, Karl Körber. At the age of nineteen, Jannsen could write in German without making any errors, read fiction in German, and play the piano and organ well. Assisted by Körber, Jannsen became the priest of the church in Vändra.

One of Jannsen's greatest initiatives was to establish a newspaper which he edited himself. It took him ten years to receive permission for this, but in **1857** in Pärnu the weekly paper **"Perno Postimees"** (Pärnu Courier) started to appear.

Jannsen's goal was to develop the life of Estonians in a peaceful way, considering the conditions at the time. He hoped that everything the Estonian nation was able to achieve could remain in peaceful agreement with the Germans and the government. In his writings Jannsen encouraged Estonians to buy farms, gave efficient advice on how to run a farm and promoted education. His simple, figurative and idiomatic way of writing quickly made his newspaper popular, and "Perno Postimees" established the tradition of Estonian journalism.

Due to economic problems, Jannsen had to move to Tartu in 1864, where he established a new paper **"Eesti Postimees"** (Estonian Courier). Jannsen quickly became a popular figure in Tartu. 'Papa Jannsen' participated in every social event, as an initiator, promoter, leader or supporter. His daughter **Lydia Koidula** was of great help in his activities. On the initiative of the Jannsen family a singing and musical society named **"Vanemuine"** was established in 1865, which served as an example for many similar societies emerging in other Estonian towns: "Estonia" in Tallinn, "Koit" in Viljandi, "Kannel" in Võru and "Endla" in Pärnu.

The first national song festival. In connection with the approaching fiftieth anniversary of freedom, the "Vanemuine" society applied for a permission to organise a nation-wide song festival. Jannsen took responsibility for the preparatory work.

The tradition of song festivals came from Germany. In 1857, a day of singing by German choirs was held in Tallinn. There had also been singing days of Estonian choirs organised in Anseküla (on Saaremaa), Jõhvi, Laiuse and elsewhere. This time the plan was to summon Estonians from all over the country.

Preparation for the song festival required patience and constant work. Receiving permission to organise it took two years. The lean year and famine of 1868 did not help either. The leaders of the Estonians in St Petersburg, Johann Köler and Carl Robert Jakobson, argued against the song festival noting that to follow such tradition would be giving too much credit to German culture.

At the first national Estonian song festival, held on 18-20 June **1869** in Tartu, about a thousand singers and musicians gathered. Only male choirs performed as Jannsen considered inviting mixed choirs immoral and "extremely dangerous."

The song festival started with a procession and a festive service in St Mary's Church (Maarja kirik). The concert took place in the garden of the "Ressource" society (now the stadium of Tartu University). The conductors were Jannsen himself and a young Estonian composer, Aleksander Saebelmann-Kunileid. Patriotic speeches were made. A young theologian named Jakob Hurt delivered a speech before a large audience for the first time. In his speech he stressed the importance of education and implored the Estonian intelligentsia to remain loyal to their nation. The general elated mood at the festival was capped off by a dinner party in the garden of the "Vanemuine" society. The programme of the first song festival did not con-

Jakob Hurt

tain many Estonian songs as yet. Kunileid's songs "Mu isamaa on minu arm" (My Fatherland is My Love) and "Sind surmani" (Till Death) (words by Lydia Koidula), and also "Mu isamaa, mu õnn ja rõõm" (My Fatherland, My Joy and Happiness) – composed by the Finnish composer Pacius (words by Jannsen), which later became Estonian national anthem – were sung.

It is hard to overestimate the importance of the first national song festival. About twenty thousand people from different regions of Estonia gathered in Tartu. It was the first time when Estonians from all over the country were able to come together. The song festival increased the feeling of national unity of Estonians and gave strength and courage for the future.

Jakob Hurt. In the 1870s the nationalist movement reached a new level. All over the country national societies and organisations were established. Jakob Hurt (1839-1907) became an acknowledged leader of the movement.

Hurt was born in Himmaste near Põlva, the son of a parish schoolteacher. His father followed the Herrnhut movement and gave his children a strict religious upbringing. The young Jakob developed strict ethical principles as well as the habit and will to work hard. His road to education was smooth: first Põlva parish school, then Tartu county school, Tartu *Gymnasium* and the Faculty of Theology of Tartu University. The talented and hardworking youth received financial support from the inspector of schools, Carl. Oettel, whose temperamental daughter Eugenia he later married.

Simultaneously with his studies Hurt played an active part in the national movement. From there he developed a more profound interest in philology, especially in Estonian folklore. He took part in the work of the "Vanemuine" society, delivering reports on Estonian history and folklore. The speech Jakob Hurt gave in Helme in 1870 set a goal for Estonians **to become great in spirit.**

Jakob Hurt's activity was hindered by the lack of his own newspaper. His attempts to receive permission from the government to publish a newspaper failed. In these circumstances Hurt accepted Jannsen's offer to become an editor of the supplement of "Eesti Postimees." There Hurt published his account of Estonian history titled "Pildid isamaa sündinud asjust" (Pictures of Things that have Happened to our Fatherland) which was not well received in German circles. Jannsen was forced to dismiss Hurt. Thus Jakob Hurt joined one of the most radical personalities of the national awakening

Tarvastu students

Friedrich Reinhold Kreutzwald

period, Carl Robert Jakobson. They became good friends and partners in co-operation.

In 1872 Hurt obtained a post as a clergyman in Otepää, which noticeably improved his social status. From this point on he became the leader of the most important events of the national movement.

The committees of the Estonian Alexander School. Attaching the utmost value to education became the underlying principle of the Estonian national movement. At the beginning of the 1860s the teacher of the village school in Holstre (Paistu parish), **Jaan Adamson**, promoted the idea of establishing Estonian language schools that would meet the standards of county schools. As the government did not support the idea, these schools had to be established and maintained by the Estonian people. Since all the leading figures of national movement understood and appreciated the importance of education, they combined their efforts to realise the idea of the **Estonian Alexander School**. The

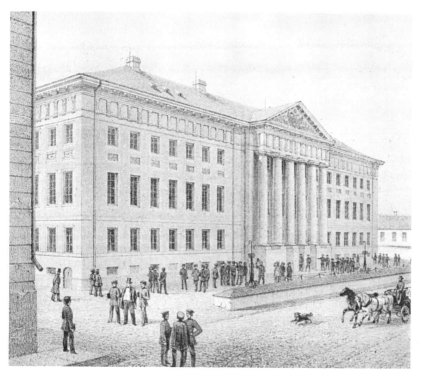

Tartu University in 1860.

school was named after Tsar Alexander I, who had given Estonians freedom.

The sums needed for opening and running the school had to be collected from donations. Committees for this purpose were established in almost every Estonian parish. In order to raise money, exhibitions and concerts were organised and plays were staged, which in turn enlivened social life in parishes. Each year a general meeting of the committees assembled and played the role of a national council. Issues topical for Estonia were discussed there, and the general committee and the president of the Estonian Alexander School were elected. The general committee established in 1871 included all the prominent public figures of Estonia: Jakub Hurt (president), Carl Robert Jakobson, Johann Voldemar Jannsen, Friedrich Reinhold Kreutzwald, Johann Köler and others. By 1874, enough money had been collected to buy a building for the school in Kaarlimõisa, near Põltsamaa.

Estonian Society of Literati. Another important nation-wide organisation was the Estonian Society of Literati, which was established in 1872 and consisted of educated Estonians, as well as some intelligent farmers. The main task of the society was to publish books, especially textbooks, in Estonian. The society also collected Estonian folklore and folk tales. An essential role was played by social events that took place twice a year.

Jakob Hurt, who was elected the first president of the Society, took an active part in every sphere of activity. Especially valuable was his contribution to the collecting and publishing of Estonian folklore.

The Society paid special attention to development and defence of the Estonian language. Thus Jakob Hurt stated, "We wish that the highest officials in this country – teachers, lawyers and civil servants – should learn the Estonian language and prove their knowledge of Estonian by passing an examination."

Following a decision of the Estonian Society of Literati, a new spelling system for the Estonian language was introduced in 1872 – and has been in use ever since.

Carl Robert Jakobson

Carl Robert Jakobson. The radical wing of the national movement was led by Carl Robert Jakobson (1841-1882).

Jakobson was born in Tartu. His spent his childhood in Torma, where his father worked as a parish clerk and schoolmaster. Although his father was a good friend of Jannsen and an active social figure, his mother brought up the son in German tradition. After graduating from Jānis Cimze's Teachers' Seminary in Valga, he tried to work as a schoolmaster in Torma but was forced to leave due to disputes with local noblemen. In 1863, he arrived in St Petersburg where he passed the chief-schoolmaster's examination and was hired as a private tutor to Olga Konstantinovna, the daughter of a grand duke, which guaranteed him a wealthy life.

The artist Johann Köler brought Jakobson into the national movement. In 1865, Jakobson's first letters were published in "Eesti Postimees," where he demanded improvements in the condition of schools, denounced the heavy load of religious education, and promoted temperance.

In 1868, Jakobson gave his first patriotic speech about the times of light, darkness and dawn, to the "Vanemuine" society. In his speech, he divided the history of the Estonian nation into three major periods: the golden period of ancient independence, the period of serfdom which lasted for several centuries under mainly German rulers, and the period of dawn when the people prepared for a rise to a new era of happiness, a period that would arrive when the Baltic Germans lose their power. The speech clearly expressed Jakobson's political orientation: "The mercy of our Tsar is the dawn which will expose all the deeds of the dark." This made Jakobson the Baltic Germans' most hated figure.

At the beginning of the 1870s Jakobson returned to Estonia, determined to become a farmer. He bought the Kurgja farm in Uus-Vändra and married a nineteen-year-old village beauty, a daughter of the Kirbla parish clerk named Julie Thal. Jakobson put a lot of energy in establishing a farm: he built a dam and a mill on the Pärnu River, and erected new farm buildings. As well as working his farm, Jakobson wrote more than twenty booklets about agriculture, paying special attention to questions of dairy cattle development. Jakobson was elected president of farmers' societies in Pärnu and Viljandi.

"**S**akala." After many attempts, Jakobson finally succeeded in receiving permission to establish his own newspaper. "Sakala," which started to appear in March **1878**, soon became the most popular Estonian paper. Nobody was as critical about matters in society as Jakobson.

He started a fierce campaign in his paper against the nobility and clergymen, demanding his rights and telling others to do the same. "I cannot understand," he wrote, "why we, Estonians, living in our own land, do not have the right to say a word in politics equal to that of the Germans, who moved here later." Jakobson had high hopes of support from the Russian government. He believed that the state would abolish the privileges of the German nobility and restore the rights of Estonians.

The Russian government met the numerous claims of the Baltic Germans and closed Jakobson's newspaper for a couple of months instead. Jakobson's attempt to get support from liberal circles in Russia also failed.

Jakobson's policy first and foremost relied on wealthy farmers. He did not pay any attention to the emerging petty bourgeoisie in towns. On the contrary, in his assessment on rise of social democracy in Europe, Jakobson stated, "A social democratic party is impossible in Estonia as we lack the city folk who would be the best material for this type of social movement..."

Jakobson's stubbornness and self-confidence caused disagreement between him and his followers.

A major split. In 1878, a serious disagreement arose between Hurt and Jakobson because of the latter's extremely critical articles against the Lutheran clergy, which included Hurt. In a public letter Hurt announced his plan to quit his position as a contributor to "Sakala." He wrote, "To my greatest dismay I have to see and read that you are doing the Christian Church an injustice. You tend to openly undermine religion and pull down the church walls." Hurt's position was weakened even further by conflicts with his Baltic German colleagues, who started to boycott him. In this situation, Hurt accepted an offer to become a priest of the Jaani congregation in St Petersburg and left Estonia in the autumn of 1880.

The old tensions between Jakobson and Jannsen also increased. Jannsen felt that he should not be considered old-fashioned only for the fact he did not want to "hit his head against the wall." A passionate public fight in the press, including accusations of selling out, was a cause of health problems for Jannsen in November 1880 that left him paralysed.

The quarrels did not take place only in the press, but also quickly reached the national organisations. Jakobson and his followers began to take over national societies Jannsen had led. In 1881, Jakobson was elected president of the Estonian Society of Literati, in place of Hurt who had resigned. This caused the resignation of Hurt's followers, who were the most educated members of the Society.

The national movement was influenced by the increase of unrest throughout the country. In 1881, Tsar Alexander II was assassinated. The national movement was blamed for several arson attacks in Tartu, and the German newspaper of St Petersburg demanded an end to the "wild and unrestrained agitation of Estonians that encourages dangerous passion."

In the early spring of 1882, Jakobson fell ill with pneumonia and died. The unexpected death of the 40-year-old leader caused deep national grief. On the day of his funeral, church bells tolled all over Estonia. In spite of the poor condition of the roads thousands of people gathered for his funeral in Kurgja.

Unfortunately even Jakobson's death was not able to settle the quarrels. In the general committee of the Estonian Alexander School, controversy arose between supporters of Hurt and Köler. Köler wanted to lend some of the money collected for establishing the Alexander School to Estonian expatriates in order to improve the quality of their life – to buy the Kuntaugan manor in Crimea. Jakob Hurt was against such aimless spending of the people's money. Hurt and his supporters were defeated, and Johann Köler was elected as the new president of the general committee of the Estonian Alexander School.

At this point, the national movement now had to face the start of Russification.

32. The Period of Russification

The accession to the throne by Alexander III in 1881 brought great changes to Estonia. Unlike his liberal father, the new Tsar was narrow-minded and reactionary. He tried to alleviate the growing discontent in the state by means of religion, patriotism and love of the Tsar, accompanied by Russification of the periphery.

The beginning of Russification in Estonia. Alexander III was the first Russian sovereign who did not confirm the privileges of the Baltic nobility. In answer to the complaints from the Baltic Germans that the authorities of the *guberniyas* were not able to restrain the national movement, Senator Nikolai Manassein arrived to inspect the Baltic *guberniyas* in 1882. The aim of **Manassein's inspection** was to collect data on the privileged position of the Baltic nobility. The Senator received about 50,000 letters from Estonians and Latvians complaining about the arrogant ways of the Baltic Germans and demanding an increase of their rights in their own countries. The material collected by Manassein was used by the government to carry out Russification.

The shortcomings found during the inspection gave a suitable excuse to start political rearrangements in the Baltics. In 1885, new governor-generals were appointed to the Baltic *guberniyas*: General Mikhail Zinoviev in Riga and Duke Sergei Shakhovskoi in Tallinn. Shakhovskoi saw his task as "joining the Estonians to the great family of Russians." Russians were appointed officials in place of Germans everywhere. They had no knowledge of local ways nor language. Instead of German, Russian became the official language. The opportunities for Estonians to have their say in the direction of their country decreased. Many parish executives, elected by the people, were dismissed due to insufficient knowledge of Russian. The peasant courts in the parishes were closed down. In the counties, the posts of commissars for peasant affairs were introduced. It was their responsibility to control the work of parish councils and courts, which essentially restricted the freedom of the parish executives.

August Kitzberg, a writer who worked as a community clerk in Pöögle (Karksi parish), described one of these commissars as follows: "I met the inspector at the entrance, wearing a black tailcoat appropriate for the situation. This was my first mistake. I should have been dressed like a barge haulier. And then there were my flowerbeds in front of the house. The commissar for peasant affairs was wearing a dirty shirt and mended trousers. Before he entered the house he sniffed three times and muttered the two words: "German influence!"" Thus management of public business passed into the hands of uneducated Russian officials who knew no languages other than Russian.

Reorganisation of education. The hardest blow from Russification was to the educational system of Estonia. In 1887, the Russian language became the compulsory language of tuition in all Estonian schools. In parish schools only religious study could be delivered in Estonian. According to new laws, other subjects had to be taught in the initial two years of schooling "in the language that would allow for the teaching of all subjects in Russian from the third year of study." Children were forbidden to speak Estonian even during the breaks. Teachers who did not know Russian well enough were dismissed. Due to insufficient knowledge of Russian, children had to learn everything taught to them by heart, which reduced their interest in school and education. The new Russia-oriented programmes discarded such subjects as Estonian history, national studies and Estonian literature. Russification increased illiteracy; of young men conscripted for north-east Estonia. In spite of the active propaganda, only one-fifth of the North Estonian population joined the Orthodox church.

Estonian society during Russification. Russification also caused setbacks in the cultural life of Estonia. The liveliness characteristic of the period of the national movement was replaced by anxiety and pessimism. The situation was complicated even further by the fact that the supporters of Jakobson, who had achieved a dominant position in the national movement, had expected support from the Russian government and were now extremely disappointed. Although the majority of societies continued to exist, their patriotic undertakings were replaced with entertainment.

In the programmes of singing and music societies, plays and comedies devoid of content appeared, such as "An Egg of the Turkish Horse or a Pumpkin Worth 15 Roubles or Foolishness Harms" or "The Devil and His Sooty Brother or a Moth in Hell." The titles speak for themselves. The activities of the Estonian Society of Literati also declined and in 1893, a government regulation finished its existence.

The decline was aggravated by the fact that there were several Estonians actively involved in Russification. Jakob Kõrv became the leader of the Russification process. He established the newspaper "Valgus" (The Light) in Tallinn in 1882. In order to get subscribers for his paper he informed against Jaak Järv, the editor of a popular newspaper "Virulane," which had remained true to national values, forcing Järv to leave Estonia. Intrigues, rumour-mongering and spying were characteristic of Russification. Also at the end of the 1880s, **Ado Grenzstein**, who had actively participated in the national movement, started to support Russification. He considered important the movement of Estonian people towards Russia. His newspaper "Olevik" (Present Day) tried to explain the material and cultural advantages Estonians could gain by becoming Russified. He defined the era of national awakening as a great error, campaigned against the song festivals, expressed his gratitude to the Tsarist government for closing down the Estonian Society of Literati and actively argued for Russification. Admitting that Latvians knew

Ado Grenzstein

military service in 1886, 98 per cent could read, but in 1901 it was only 80 per cent.

The Alexander School, for which Estonians had collected money and pursued, opened in 1888 as a Russian language school. The oldest school in Estonia – the Tallinn Dome School (toomkool) – was closed down due to Russification. In 1893, Tartu University, which had been renamed Yuriev University, introduced Russian as its language of tuition. All the German professors were forced to leave. The new lecturers that came from Russia could not preserve the high level of tuition for which the university had been famous.

Propagating Orthodoxy. As well as the rearrangement of education, there was an attempt to reform the religious beliefs of Estonians by spreading Orthodoxy in Estonia. Governor-general Shakhovskoi was actively engaged in this, building Orthodox churches all over the country. The biggest of all, the Orthodox cathedral, was built on Toompea in Tallinn close to the governor-general's residence. Shakhovskoi also established the Pühtitsa (Kuremäe) Nunnery in

Russian better than Estonians did, Grenzstein admonished Estonians to not lag behind their neighbours in this "useful field."

The only newspaper that tried to preserve the national spirit was "Postimees," edited by **Karl August Hermann** in Tartu. In 1891, it became the first daily newspaper published in Estonian. As a politician, Hermann remained rather conservative, avoiding conflicts with the authorities. Hermann's main achievement was to promote the cultural development of Estonians.

Of great importance for developing an Estonian intelligentsia was **Hugo Treffner's Private Gymnasium**, which was opened in Tartu in 1884. Although the restrictions of Russification were also applied to this school, the majority of Estonians entering Tartu University received their secondary education in Treffner's *Gymnasium.*

A new rise of the national movement. In spite of the harsh conditions, Estonian-minded activities continued throughout the period of Russification. Nationalist work was carried on in temperance societies that were established all over the country in the last decade of the century. An effort was made to preserve the spirit of national awakening by organising concerts and evenings of speeches, as well as staging plays. When Jakob Hurt started the campaign of collecting Estonian folklore in 1888, it found many active participants. In many places ways and opportunities were found to build clubhouses where local people could come together. Quite a number of the national leaders remained true to their ideals even in the harshest conditions and worked hard to keep hope alive in the people.

Villem Reiman (1861-1917) became the leader of the young generation fighting against Russification.

Reiman was born in Kõpu in Viljandi region as the son of a tenant farmer. He graduated from the Faculty of Theology at Tartu University and worked as a priest in Kolga-Jaani. His extraordinary capacity for work allowed him, in addition to serving his congregation, to develop the temperance movement throughout the country and to lay the foundation for scientific research into Estonian history and culture. Reiman was characterised by a strict sense of justice and honesty, adherence to peasant ideals, and serious religion and idealism. In a way he became a connecting link between Jakob Hurt and Jaan Tõnisson.

Great work on preserving national ideals was achieved by the **Estonian Students' Society**. The students who were inspired by the 1870 song festival started to meet regularly. At the beginning they read the national epic "Kalevipoeg" together but later these meetings laid the basis of a society consisting of young progressive Estonian-minded intelligentsia. In the situation where education had been provided in German and later in Russian, only educated people were accustomed to exchanging opinions and even thinking in a foreign language. One of the greatest achievements of the Estonian Students' Society was that they introduced the Estonian language as the language of communication among the intelligentsia. In June 1884, the blue, black and white flag of the Estonian Students' Society was consecrated in the Church of Otepää.

The Pechory region under Russian rule. The south-eastern periphery of Estonia – Pechory or Setu region – had been under Russian rule since the Middle Ages. Its difference from other regions of Estonia survived even af-

Villem Reiman

ter the Great Northern War, when the whole of Estonia became a part of the Russian Empire. There were no German nobles in that area. The people living there were members of the Orthodox Church even before Russification. In that region, which had been separated from the rest of Estonia by a state border and later the border of the *guberniya*, a unique culture had developed. It had preserved its uniqueness in spite of the Russian influence. It was Jakob Hurt who first paid attention to the uniqueness of the Setu folklore during his campaign of collecting folklore.

Pechory region remained untouched by the national movement. The first national societies appeared there only at the beginning of the twentieth century. Cultural backwardness was mainly caused by the poor condition of schools. Less than 20 per cent of the population were literate at the turn of the century.

As in other regions of Russia, the system of **rural community** had survived in that region. Farmers could not become the owners of their farms. This was the reason for lower living standards, which started to improve only in the days after Estonian independence. The central role in the spiritual and economic life of the region was played by the monastery established there in 1526. Until the Great Northern War, the monastery had had a military function as border fortification.

33. Economic Development from 1870 to 1914

The last quarter of the nineteenth century and the beginning of the twentieth century saw rapid expansion in the Estonian economy. During that period the economic preconditions for an independent state were formed.

Building railways. The Estonian economy was strongly influenced by the building of railways. In **1870** the first – **the Baltic railway** – was completed. It connected the port of Paldiski with Narva and St Petersburg via Tallinn. Soon the lines Tapa-Tartu-Valga-Riga and Valga-Võru-Pskov were opened. At the beginning of the new century, Haapsalu also gained a railway connection with Tallinn.

In addition to the broad-gauge railway, a private joint-stock company built narrow-gauge railway lines connecting Pärnu with Valga, Mõisaküla with Viljandi and Tallinn, Paide and Türi with Tamsalu. So all the towns of Estonia (except Kuressaare) had a railway connection.

The railways bound Estonia more tightly to the Russian capital and the inland *guberniyas,* as well as to Latvian areas. Thus favourable conditions for **exchange of goods** arose, especially for sending Estonian agricultural products to the market of St Petersburg. At the same time the proportion of goods arriving via the ports of Paldiski and Tallinn increased. The railway increased communication between different parts of Estonia and developed internal trade. The presence of the railway also gave rise to new industries and settlements.

Agricultural development. Estonia remained an agrarian country where two-thirds of the population were involved in agriculture.

The manor economy continued to dominate. At the beginning of the twentieth century almost half of the arable land belonged to the German barons. The manors developed into

Waiting for departure.

large economic enterprises producing for the needs of the market and using paid workers. The progressive manor owners boldly applied new technical methods in agriculture, which later gradually spread among the peasants.

The process of **buying land for perpetuity,** which had started in 1850, continued. In the last decades of the nineteenth century it was most evident in North Estonia, while at the beginning of the twentieth century it spread on Saaremaa. By 1916, four-fifths of arable land was freehold property. This did not necessarily mean the end of problems for the peasants, as the majority of the farms had been **bought on credit** and paying off debts took a large share of the income. Alongside the 52,000 freehold farms there were 23,000 rented farms for which the tenants paid rent to the landlords.

At the turn of the century, the development of farms was hindered by the fall in **grain prices**, due to which grain cultivation no longer produced the expected profit. As a result many freehold farms went bankrupt. The majority of the farms remained, looking for more profitable kinds of production – which appeared to be cattle breeding.

Dairy cattle rearing developed into the main branch of agricultural production. The availability of railway transport allowed the marketing of Estonian dairy products in St Petersburg at reasonable prices. Milk, cream, butter and cheese were all taken to Russia. This was profitable but demanded big preliminary investments connected with buying pedigree animals from abroad and establishing milk-processing enterprises. Therefore dairy cattle breeding remained mainly a part of the manor economy.

Beside dairy cattle, fattened pigs and beef cattle were also bred. For fattening the cattle, the residual products of the numerous distilleries proved useful.

The rise of livestock farming to the leading position forced the manor industries, as well as farms, to grow fodder grain, hay and potatoes instead of grain for bread.

Processing grain, 1912.

Cultivation continued to be **intensified**; new land was cleared for tillage, artificial fertilisers were introduced, and new modern agricultural machines were bought. Special attention was paid to plant breeding. Duke **Friedrich Georg Magnus von Berg** became famous for breeding a new winter rye called "Sangaste." The development of farming was promoted by spreading relevant knowledge among peasants. Farmers' societies took responsibility for this, regularly arranging agricultural exhibitions and hiring specially trained agricultural advisers and instructors on cattle breeding.

Social stratification progressed in the villages. Beside a few rich farm owners, the group of independent smallholder farmers started to dominate. The number of landless peasants and poor people increased. They lived by offering

A Tartu suburb, 1914.

labour. Farm hands, manor workers, servants and the poor constituted more than 60 per cent of the total number of peasants. They formed the bulk of the people who settled in towns, the Russian inland *guberniyas*, and abroad. By the start of the twentieth century the **shortage of land** had become the biggest problem of Estonian agriculture.

Development of industry. At the end of the nineteenth century a rapid growth of industry took place over the entire Russian Empire. Along with the development of the financial-commercial relationship, large investments in industry were made. In Estonia existing factories were extended and new establishments and industries were introduced.

The textile industry developed into a leading area of industry in Estonia. The Kreenholm Cotton Factory, which was established in Narva in 1857 and was continuously extended, became the biggest industrial establishment in Estonia; it had 5,000 workers in 1880. The Sindi and Keila textile mills underwent rapid development as well. In Tallinn the Baltic Cotton Mill was established.

The role of the **machine and metal industry** also grew considerably. A number of new plants were opened, the biggest being the Volta electrical machine factory, the Dvigatel carriage building plant, the metal industry of Franz Krull and the machine factory of Wiegand. Because of the policy of railway building, the Principal Railway Works was also established.

The third biggest area was the **paper industry**. In addition to the paper mills in Tallinn and Räpina, the biggest cellulose factory in the Russian Empire, the Waldhof, was built in Pärnu. Johanson's paper mill in Tallinn, as well as timber, cardboard and paper factories in Kohila and Türi, were added soon after. At the beginning of the century the paper mills of Estonia were responsible for 70 per cent of the paper production of the Russian Empire.

For a long time Narva had been the biggest industrial centre, but by the turn of the century **Tallinn** had occupied the first position. New enterprises were also established in other towns and in the country. In Kunda and in Aseri, cement works were built that produced one-tenth of the cement production of Russia. In the country numerous brickyards, lime kilns, wool, flour and sawmills were started. In manors the number of distilleries increased to 250.

The economic crisis in Russia in 1900-1903 reduced the pace of industrial development, but by the second decade of the century a rapid increase followed again. This was promoted by the **militarisation** of industry over the entire Empire. Preparations for war gave the reason for the establishment of more large industrial enterprises. In the years 1912-1914, three powerful naval shipyards were built in Tallinn: the Russian-Baltic, Bekker and Noblessner.

By the start of the First World War, Estonia had become one of **the most industrially developed areas** of the Empire. In 30 years the number of industrial workers had increased five-fold, from 10,000 in 1885 to 50,000 in 1916.

More than half the factories belonged to Russian business magnates; and a quarter of Estonian industry was controlled by German, French and English capital. Baltic Germans took third place, and only then came Estonian manufacturers. Although the number of Estonian industrialists grew constantly, they did not play a significant role in the total output of industrial production, as they mainly owned small enterprises and workshops.

The rapid development of industry was mainly aimed at the needs of the Empire and did not take Estonian needs and possibilities into account. Raw materials, equipment and workers had to be imported, whereas the production mainly went to Russia.

Trade. The building of the railways played an important role in the development of foreign and transit trade. Tallinn profited most from the increase of trade because of its port. Soon the role of the Estonian ports started to decline as the majority of Russian foreign trade was transferred to the Black Sea. Tallinn still remained an important **port of entry** where machines, chemical products and coal arrived for Russia, as well as for Estonia. Pärnu became an important **shipping port**, from where Estonian grain, flax and timber were shipped to western European markets.

Internal trade developed even more rapidly. Country people bought new agricultural equipment; manufactured clothes and footwear replaced the national costumes that had dominated before; and oil lamps, window glass and aniline dyes became popular articles of trade. The growth of the urban population meant there was a demand for foodstuffs and manufactured goods for tens of thousands of people.

Growth of towns. Industrial development and the social stratification of peasants caused rapid urbanisation. Whereas in 1862 the urban population of Estonia was about 64,000 people, in 1914 it passed the 250,000 mark, which was one-fifth of the total Estonian population. The biggest towns were Tallinn, Tartu, Narva, Pärnu and Valga.

The **national composition** of the urban population also changed; Estonians outnumbered other nationalities. At the beginning they constituted a lower social class, but gradually their economic condition improved. They built houses, opened workshops and grocery stores, and the number of Estonian officials and intelligentsia increased. Legally they still remained second-class citizens as the town governments consisted of Baltic Germans. The latter also influenced the look and attitudes of the towns: the German language and German customs dominated.

In addition to the twelve towns, several **settlements** developed in the vicinity of railway stations and industrial enterprises by the turn of the century, including Jõhvi, Otepää, Põltsamaa, Sindi, Tapa, Türi and Tõrva.

Co-operation. At the beginning of the twentieth century co-operative activities became popular. The main reason for this was the spread of dairy cattle breeding. In order to make more profit, peasants started to establish co-operative dairies which were responsible for processing and selling the milk and milk products. The first such dairy stated work in Restu-Antsla in 1898.

Different kinds of co-operatives became popular in Estonia. Consumer and economic co-operatives allowed their members to buy manufactured goods at a lower price, the members of machine co-operatives bought expensive agricultural machines jointly, while improvement co-operatives drained large swampy areas for cultivation.

An important development in the co-operative movement was the establishment of the **Estonian Loan and Savings Co-operative** by Jaan Tõnisson in Tartu in 1902. This can be considered as the first national bank in Estonia. From then on similar co-operatives were established all over Estonia and they made a considerable contribution to the development of the Estonian economy.

34. Political Development in Estonia at the Turn of the Century. The 1905 Revolution

In the middle of the 1890s the pressure of Russification began to weaken and the national movement came to life again. Whereas earlier the main supporters of national ideals had been the country intelligentsia and peasants, now the towns became the centres of the movement. Patriotic appeals and slogans demanding social freedom and political rights began to appear. The new rise of **the national movement** started in Tartu, led by Jaan Tõnisson.

The Tartu renaissance. In 1896 Karl-August Hermann, the editor of the first Estonian-language daily newspaper "Postimees," left his post. In order not to let business circles with little interest in the national question take over the newspaper, the leaders of the national movement – Villem Reimann, Oskar Kallas and Heinrich Koppel – bought **"Postimees"** and asked Jaan Tõnisson to become the paper's new editor.

Jaan Tõnisson (1868-1941?) was born in Viljandi region, in the family of a freehold farmer. He graduated from the Faculty of Law of Tartu University, was elected the head of the Estonian Students' Society, worked in the editorial office of "Postimees" and then went to work as a law officer in Russia. After returning to Tartu he joined nationalist members of the Estonian intelligentsia at "Postimees," including August Kitzberg, Karl-August Hindrey, Peeter Põld, Anton Jürgenstein and others.

Jaan Tõnisson gave the development of national self-consciousness top priority among his activities, and opposed both Russification and 'Germanisation'. He therefore had to conduct a media war against Ado Grenzstein, who preached Russification. In the struggle with "Postimees," Grenzstein remained alone and had to leave the country. Tõnisson's demand for Estonian language education created a conflict with those who supported the establishment of Russian state schools in Estonia.

Tõnisson's conflict with the Baltic Germans was aggravated by the fear of the latter of losing

Jaan Tõnisson

their power as Estonian national feelings kept growing. Tõnisson opposed the political and economic privileges of Baltic Germans and demanded equal rights for Estonians. When he was elected to the town council of Tartu in 1902, Tõnisson became an undesirable person for the town government – which consisted mainly of Baltic Germans.

In the general mood of those days, when Estonian intellectuals very often spoke German not only in social circles but also at home, the promotion of national self-esteem in "Postimees" had a refreshing effect. To set an example, Tõnisson and his supporters demonstratively spoke Estonian in public. The 'higher society' considered that to be a violation of the norms of proper behaviour, but soon using Estonian in public became quite common.

In the wider political arena – in respect of the Russian Empire, Europe and the world – the "Postimees" circles remained reserved. They considered over-ambitious behaviour dangerous for a little nation.

In the struggle where national ideals were of the highest importance, "Postimees" found support from Estonian intellectuals, prosperous farmers and the urban bourgeoisie. At the same time they forgot about the poorer classes – workers and landless peasants. They did not notice the social antagonism increasing the split in Estonian society. They looked at the Estonian nation as a homogeneous entity having joint interests. Tõnisson denied the class struggle, calling it a plant imported from abroad that could not become domesticated in Estonia. Overlooking that essential aspect gave rise to the development of the more **radical wing** of the national movement.

The **radicals of Tallinn.** In 1901, a competitor for "Postimees" started to appear in Tallinn in the form of the daily paper **"Teataja"** (Herald). This was founded and edited by Konstantin Päts.

Konstantin Päts (1874-1956) was born in Pärnu region, in the family of a farmer. He studied at a theological seminary, graduated from the Faculty of Law of Tartu University and was employed as a lawyer's assistant in Tallinn. He brought together young Estonian intellectuals at his newspaper, including the lawyers Jaan Teemant and Mihkel Pung, and the writers Eduard Vilde and Anton Hansen Tammsaare.

Unlike Tõnisson, the Tallinn nationalists considered the promotion of nationalist ideas as being of the same importance as economic and political struggle. They found that the national feelings of Estonians were feeble because of their harsh economic situation, therefore the economic situation of Estonians was the first thing to be improved. That, in turn, required the removal of the Baltic Germans from the Estonian economy and politics. In order to be successful it was necessary to take part in 'big politics'; in co-operation with the Russian democratic movement, improvement could be achieved through reforms throughout Russia.

It was by co-operation with Russians that the first serious victory was achieved, something the Tartu nationalists had not managed. The **1904 elections to the town council** of Tallinn were won by an Estonian-Russian coalition, which allowed them to replace the Germans in the town government. A good example had been set earlier, when in 1901 a coalition of Estonians and Latvians won elections in Valga.

The "Teataja" group did not deny the existence of social division and a class struggle in Estonia. They even considered that class struggle was necessary. That attitude was quite natural in the poorer area of northern Estonia and in industrial Tallinn. Therefore "Teataja" found supporters among Estonian intellectuals and the urban bourgeoisie, as well as the North Estonian peasants and industrial workers. Among the latter even more radical ideas soon began to spread.

Development of social democracy. Social Democratic ideas started to spread in Estonia at the end of the nineteenth century, disseminated mainly by intellectuals, including the lecturers

Konstantin Päts

of Tartu University. At first, the theoretical ideas did not find any application in practice.

The real activities were partly initiated by the policy of those in power in St Petersburg, who used to send socialists caught in the big centres of Russia to the quiet provinces for 'penance'. Thus a number of revolutionary workers arrived in Tallinn and rebellious students in Tartu. During the first years of the twentieth century support groups of the Russian Social Democratic Workers Party (RSDWP) emerged in all the bigger towns of Estonia – Tallinn, Tartu, Narva, Pärnu, Valga and elsewhere. The Social Democrats operated illegally. They organised secret meetings and distributed illegal leaflets and books, which added romanticism to the movement and brought many young people into the RSDWP. The Workers Party naturally found numerous supporters among workers.

The first Estonian socialists belonged to the RSDWPs, which operated on an international basis. In 1903, the development of Estonian social democracy started when the newspaper "Uudised" (News) first appeared in Tartu. Peeter Speek was one of the founders and editors of the paper, supported by Mihkel Martna and the brothers Gottlieb and Karl Ast. Many intellectuals contributed to the paper, for instance Eduard Vilde.

The groups gathering at the "Uudised" considered it necessary to replace the autocratic regime with a democratic republic, where all civil rights were respected. Unlike Russian socialists they also demanded respect for the rights of ethnic minorities. The fear of losing national identity did not allow them to join with the RSDWP. They found supporters among radically minded young people, intellectuals and workers.

Crisis in society. At the beginning of the twentieth century it became clear that the modernisation of Estonian society was hindered by the outdated political conditions. At a time when people had become aware of their national identity and their ability to act, power was still centralised in the hands of officials appointed by the absolute autocrat – the Russian Tsar. These were mainly people who were Russia-minded and spoke only Russian, kept their own interests in mind above all and followed orders blindly. They did not care about the welfare of the people. The local people had their say only at parish level.

In Estonia as elsewhere in the Empire, the principal **civil rights** were absent: freedom of speech, freedom of the press, religious liberty, freedom of association, etc. In the developed western European countries those rights were more or less guaranteed and certainly the more alert Estonians considered establishment of those rights essential.

There were great contradictions in the rural areas, where the supremacy of the Baltic German nobility had remained unchanged. The situation of landless peasants was especially difficult because they were also in conflict with Estonian freehold farmers.

In towns, **social differences** increased between the wealthy bourgeoisie and the factory workers. The long working day and low wages of the latter hardly allowed for a decent life. There was no chance to change anything because trade unions and strikes were forbidden.

Society badly needed profound reform. As the central government did not take any measures to improve the situation, a social explosion – a revolution – was inevitable. It was accelerated by the war against Japan in 1904-1905, in which Russia was defeated. Thousands of Estonians were recruited to take part in the war.

Outbreak of revolution. The news that troops in St Petersburg had opened fire on participants of a peaceful demonstration on 9 January 1905, whose aim had been to hand over a petition to the Tsar, triggered revolutionary events everywhere in Russia.

In Estonia, the first to react were the **workers** of Tallinn. They organised strikes, held meetings, demanded improvement of economic and political situation, and clashed with the police. From Tallinn the workers' movement spread to other towns, especially Narva. The **students** in Tartu joined the revolutionary movement. They disrupted their studies and joined the revolution of the students in Russia.

During spring and summer the movement kept spreading, gradually involving new layers of society. Following the example of the workers, farmhands also started strikes. They refused to work as long as their living conditions were not improved. There were some cases where manorial property was destroyed.

At the same time the struggle in the towns became more serious. **Strikes** took place more frequently (in Dvigatel alone there were 12 strikes in 1905) and violence was applied to the hated foremen and directors. The number of conflicts with police and troops increased. At a big midsummer meeting in Tallinn, speakers who had travelled from St Petersburg called the workers to start an armed struggle in order to overthrow the autocratic government.

The majority of the population held more conservative views. Therefore the most popular form of revolutionary movement was to draw up **petitions** to be handed over to the authorities.

Memoranda were also compiled by the Estonian national parties, which were still at the stage of formation. The "Postimees" group were campaigning for a general franchise and more extensive use of the Estonian language, as well as conservative land reform that would leave private ownership untouched. They stated that the changes had to be legal and warned against violence and the overwhelming enthusiasm for "Russian matters."

The intellectuals who had gathered at the "Teataja" demanded establishment of constitutional monarchy in Russia, civil rights, and reforms to local government, education, the church and the courts, which would give Estonians more opportunities for activity. "Teataja" was also used by Estonian social democrats to publish their appeals. In the eyes of the authorities, that turned Konstantin Päts into the leader of revolutionary movement.

The bloodshed of 16 October. A strike of Russian railwaymen that started in October and spread all over Russia was soon joined by the workers of Tallinn. Work stopped in factories, and businesses and workshops, schools and several public offices were closed. The demand by radical orators to take up arms was followed by massive burglaries in the gun shops of Tallinn. Some groups of workers did not miss the chance to break into liquor stores as well. The streets of the town filled up with crowds of **factory workers** who sang revolutionary songs and held meetings.

The Governor of Estonia was requested to free political prisoners and to withdraw the troops from the streets of Tallinn. To support these claims a mass meeting was convened at the New Market on 16 October. Although the Governor had not forbidden the meeting, a military unit opened fire on the people who had gathered. A total of 94 people were killed, and more than 200 wounded and injured.

The manifesto of 17 October. Under pressure from the increasing revolutionary movement, Tsar Nicholas II signed a manifesto on 17 October that promised to assemble the representative body of Russian people, the **Duma**, and to guarantee civil liberties including the right to establish political organisations.

Making use of the Tsar's concession, Jaan Tõnisson established the first legal party in Estonia – the **Estonian National Progressive Party** *(Eesti Rahvameelne Eduerakond)* – in November. This was a liberal-democratic reformist party, which on general questions shared the views of the Russian constitutional democrats and considered the most suitable form of government to be a constitutional parliamentary monarchy. For Estonia they claimed the right of national self-determination and an increase in the landed property of the peasants from state and church land. The party enjoyed its biggest influence in Tartu and southern Estonia.

The "Teataja" circle in Tallinn also attempted to create an Estonian party, but later development of events did not allow them to realise their idea. Estonian social democrats, lead by Peeter Speek and Gottlieb Ast, managed to found the **Estonian Social Democratic Workers Community** *(Eesti Sotsiaaldemokraatlik Tööliste Ühisus)*, which was based on national principles and did not find it necessary to belong to the RSDWP. In the future Russian Federal Republic they demanded autonomy for Estonia, with its own parliament and government. The influence and membership of the Estonian Social Democratic Workers Community increased rapidly.

The manifesto of 17 October also resulted in the first **trade unions of workers** founded in Tartu and Tallinn.

Meeting of people's representatives. Although the Tsar's manifesto met all the demands of the initial stage of the revolution, it soon appeared outdated as the concessions made did not pacify the masses excited by the revolutionary movement. The agitation of the social democrats for an armed struggle added fuel to the fire.

In order to soothe the explosive atmosphere and to work out firm principles, Jaan Tõnisson summoned a meeting in Tartu of representatives from all over Estonia at the end of November.

Counties, towns and different societies sent about 800 representatives to Tartu. At the beginning of the meeting it appeared that Jaan Teemant, a leader of the radicals of Tallinn, was preferred to Jaan Tõnisson as chairman, whereupon all of Tõnisson's supporters left the meeting. This **split** was never overcome. Two meetings took place simultaneously: the conservatives held a meeting chaired by Tõnisson in the "Bürgermusse" hall, while the radicals held their meeting chaired by Teemant in the assembly hall of the University.

The **conservatives** considered constitutional monarchy an acceptable form of government. They demanded a democratically elected parliament, uniting Estonia into one *guberniya*, restricting the privileges of the Baltic Germans, dividing state land between the people and supporting the purchase of farms for perpetuity.

The decisions of the meeting held in the University hall appeared much more **radical:** the current despotic government had to be overthrown and a democratic republic was to be established. The local government was to be taken over and the orders of the central powers were to be ignored. Taxes were not to be paid and Estonians were not to be recruited to the Tsar's army. In addition to the state land, the lands of the gentry and parsonages were to be distributed to people. In order to carry out the decisions, the people were to be armed.

Although the people approved the resolutions of both meetings, it was not quite clear how to carry them out. The representatives did not have any real power. Fantastic rumours started to spread among the people about the speedy arrival of freedom. It was said that the Swedish government would send warships to liberate their former subjects. According to other rumours, the Latvians were expected to come and release the Estonians with their army of 40,000 men.

Destroying manors by arson. The resolutions from the meeting of the people's representatives increased the revolutionary mood. In several places local governments were taken over. Thus the "Velise Republic" and the "Mõisaküla Republic" were proclaimed.

When, at the beginning of December, another **general strike** broke out in Tallinn, and authorities introduced stricter measures: meetings were forbidden, the leaders of the socialists and the workers' movement were arrested, and **martial law** was imposed in Tallinn and the Harju district. Instead of the expected abatement, this only increased unrest among the people.

On 12 December, about a hundred armed workers from Tallinn went to plunder manors. They called on local landless peasants to join them. The furniture of manor houses were smashed, valuable items were looted, and buildings were burnt down. The destruction mainly took place in North Estonia, especially in the Harju, Järva and Läänemaa districts, but also in Pärnu district. Altogether 160 estates were pillaged, 70 of them in Harju district. Some distilleries were also destroyed. No physical harm was done to the landlords.

Punishment troops. In order to end the disorder, the central administration sent additional troops to the Baltic *guberniyas*. Martial law was imposed in the whole country. A governor-general for the Baltic region was commissioned. Local administration, including justice, passed into the hands of the military.

In Estonia, punishment troops were led by the generals Bezobrasov and Orlov. They shot more than 300 people without any preliminary investigation or trial. The squad led by the squire von Sievers became notorious for executing 53 people in Viljandi alone.

In addition to those executed by the punishment troops on the spot, more than 500 people were sentenced to death by tribunals. The majority of them managed to hide themselves and the sentence was later overturned by the civil courts (for instance, the death sentence passed on Konstantin Päts was replaced by a year in prison). Hundreds of people were sent to penal colonies, imprisoned or exiled. Many received public corporal punishment.

The goal of the authorities was to return to the pre-revolutionary situation. The earlier concessions were cancelled, the parties, societies and workers' organisations were banned, and several newspapers were closed down. Many leading figures of the events of 1905 were forced to seek asylum abroad.

Political conditions after the revolution. The peak of the revolution had passed, but the following years were still quite restless. In the *guberniya* of Estonia alone **more than 2,000** different acts of resistance were recorded in 1906. It was only in 1908 that the authorities finally dared to suspend martial law in the Baltic countries. It was replaced by a slightly milder "reinforced surveillance," which actually did not restore normal political life. Strikes, opposition demonstrations and political meetings were forbidden. The media was carefully censored; for any seemingly disrespectful word towards the authorities a publication could be punished by closure. The trade unions, which had emerged during the revolution, as well as the majority of the political organisations, also remained illegal.

The only legal party in Estonia was the Estonian National Progressive Party, lead by Jaan Tõnisson, which had to follow strict prescribed restrictions. It was out of the question for the Tallinn groups to establish a new party. The Estonian Social Democratic Workers Community was totally paralysed, its leaders having emigrated or being in prison.

The **Bolsheviks**, who had formed a separate wing of the RSDWP, profited most from the repression of the Estonian socialists. *Bolsheviks* acted illegally, which made controlling them rather complicated and the "romanticism of the underground struggle" brought them many new recruits. The internationalist views of the *Bolsheviks* suited the Russian workers brought to live in Estonia. They were not interested in the nationalist endeavours of Estonian *Mensheviks*. A lot of Estonian workers also took the side of the *Bolsheviks*. In 1913, in Narva a Bolshevik newspaper "Kiir" started to appear, edited by the lawyer **Jaan Anvelt**.

The **Dumas.** Following the manifesto of 17 October of 1905, in Estonia, great expectations were put on the representative body of people – the Duma.

In the Duma, assembled in 1906, five representatives from Estonia were elected – four Estonians and one Russian, with the Baltic Germans not represented. This was a great victory in the circumstances. In general political issues the Estonian representatives supported the Russian constitutional democrats (KD, "Cadets"), while on national questions a coalition with the representatives of the ethnic minorities was formed.

The government did not take the Duma seriously from the very beginning; the first bill submitted to the parliament was an act about laundry at Tartu University. The Duma, which showed signs of opposition, was dissolved before it managed to start work.

The fate of the second Duma was no better – it was dissolved on 3 July 1907 and a more reactionary election law was adopted. According to this, three representatives of the Baltic Germans and only two Estonian representatives made it to the third and fourth Dumas. Bills submitted by the Estonian or Latvian representatives were not supported by the reactionary majority of the Duma and were turned down. Thus all hopes of reform via the parliamentary representative body failed.

The **Special Board** established by the governor-general of the Baltic region, to reduce social tension, did not do any better. Bills on land, county, church, law and school reforms submitted by the Baltic Germans did not meet even the humblest expectations of Estonians and in 1907 the Special Board was dissolved.

In these years Estonians were successful only at the level of **local government**. In addition to the town councils in Valga and Tallinn, the Baltic Germans were removed from the town governments of Võru, Haapsalu, Pärnu and Rakvere.

Punishment troops.

35. The First World War

The First World War, which broke out in July 1914, resulted in the defeat and dissolution of several European empires and the independence of small East European nations. The Finns, Estonians, Latvians, Lithuanians, Poles, Czechs and Slovaks achieved independent statehood. In spite of the final results, which favoured small nations, the World War represented a real ordeal for all states and nations participating in it and its negative consequences had an influence over many years.

General mood at the beginning of the war. Unlike the Russians, who shared an overwhelming mood of enthusiastic patriotism, Estonians did not have the slightest wish to fight for "religion, Tsar and fatherland."

There were no predictable final outcomes the war could bring which seemed favourable to Estonians. It was feared that a Russian victory would cause the rise of militant chauvinism and a new wave of Russification. A German victory would mean unlimited power for the Baltic Germans in Estonia. For the oppressed nations the only opportunities lay in the war dragging on and wearing out both sides. But at the beginning of the war the chances of this were not considered realistic.

It was necessary to be cautious with one's real thoughts – the press, as well as the Estonian representatives in the Duma, had to be seen to hold ultra-patriotic sentiments.

Reducing the influence of the Baltic Germans. When the war broke out the central government started to reduce the rights of the Baltic Germans. Organisations and newspapers sympathising with Berlin were closed down, many opposition figures were banished from the Baltic countries, the use of the German language was restricted and the influence of the Baltic Germans in state affairs decreased.

This now seemed to offer a chance for Estonians to occupy the higher posts in local governments that had been previously filled by Baltic Germans. Also, for the first time, the Germans offered some concessions to the local population in order to create a joint front against the general government. Thus a project was devised which envisaged the creation of a joint Estonian-German provincial council.

These hopes proved to be groundless: the coalition with Germans never happened as the majority of Estonians opposed this compromise. The central government did not trust Estonians to deal with local problems, and so Russian officials replaced German ones.

Activities on the people's own initiative. During the war the national movement became livelier again. This was initiated by the establishment of several war-related organisations and institutions.

In Tallinn and in Tartu, **war industry committees** started their activity. Their function was to deliver the orders for military goods to the Estonian enterprises. Beside Russians and Baltic Germans, Estonians also actively participated in them, thus receiving a chance for the first time to be involved in the management of the economy of their country.

The **Tallinn Committee of the League of Towns** became a gathering place for North Estonian nationalists. Formally this body had also been created to support the Russian army and to keep order on the home front. In practice, the more active nationalists met there to discuss topical issues, as well as the future of Estonia.

The largest organisation based on the self-initiative of the people became the **Northern Baltic Committee**, founded by Jaan Tõnisson. Departments of this organisation were based all over the country, and its central committee was located in Tartu. It united nationally-minded individuals. The task of the

Northern Baltic Committee was to take care of refugees arriving in Estonia, to provide the Russian army with food and to meet the economic needs of Estonia. In these areas the committee managed to achieve a lot. At the same time they kept propagating nationalist ideas.

Economic situation. The war had a harmful effect on agriculture. Some 30 per cent of the farmers and 45 per cent of manor workers were conscripted to the armed forces. This created a shortage of workforce and restricted production. The requisition of horses and a major part of the cattle and agricultural production for the needs of the army paralysed agriculture. It was impossible to buy new agricultural equipment and fertilisers, and ground and plant improvement and cattle breeding activities stopped. The decrease in agricultural production caused supply problems, which threatened to leave the bigger towns in a state of hunger.

Estonian **industry** had relied on imported raw materials before the war. Now the German navy had cut off trade in the Baltic Sea. The discontinuation of English coal imports caused irrecoverable damage. Due to the overloaded railways it was also more difficult to get raw materials from Russia. The majority of enterprises changed to **military production** – shells, cartridges, vehicles, uniforms, boots, etc. – creating a shortage of consumer goods. The equipment of the factories wore out, but it was impossible to renew it in wartime. The quality of the workforce decreased; skilled workers had been conscripted and farmers, adolescents and women replaced them. In 1916, only 51 per cent of factory workers were adult men.

Entrepreneurs, businessmen and farmers made huge profits from the increase in prices caused by the shortage of consumer goods and foodstuffs at the beginning of the war. Soon the increase in prices was accompanied by a decrease in the value of money and rapid **inflation,** which turned all savings into useless heaps of paper. The co-operative banks also suffered losses as there were no options for investment and they had to buy war bonds with some of their reserves.

Events of the war. Although the events of warfare did not directly concern Estonia, Russia's lack of success had an indirect influence. In 1915 German troops moved quickly eastwards, occupying Lithuania and part of Latvia. The front reached as far as the Daugava River, and battles took place near Riga.

Tens of thousands of **refugees** from Latvia arrived in Estonia, increasing the burden on the Estonian economy. The refugees needed to be accommodated, to receive food and other necessities, to find work, etc. The situation was especially complicated in South Estonia, where the majority of the refugees stayed.

In August 1915, **German warships** appeared in the coastal waters of Estonia. They sailed through the Straits of Irbe to the Gulf of Riga in order to destroy the Russian squadron located there. In the course of the operation

Mobilisation point in Viljandi region.

Kuressaare and Pärnu were fired upon, which caused the local authorities and population to fear a possible landing of German troops. In Pärnu, panicking people blew up the Waldhof paper mill that belonged to a German company. At the same time the inhabitants of Paldiski made their acquaintance with the new German air weapon – the Zeppelin airship. The bombs thrown from the Zeppelins did not do much damage, but they aggravated the fear spreading among the people.

The ruling circles considered **evacuating the Estonian population.** The nationalist circles opposed such plans. They informed people about the accompanying dangers and urged them to stay in their homeland. This created conflict with the Russian officials, who considered that such appeals undermined the ruling authorities.

Armed forces in Estonia. Before the war it had already been decided to turn Tallinn into a military base for the Russian Baltic fleet. During the war, extensive works were carried out to build a fortified naval base named after Peter the Great. The fortifications were situated on the islands in the Bay of Tallinn, on the coast, and as a semicircle around Tallinn. Tallinn was garrisoned with 30,000 infantrymen and 20,000 seamen.

Intensive **fortification works** were also carried out on the western coast and islands of Estonia. The fortified position of Muhu Strait was built. Tens of thousands of workers and soldiers were engaged with this work.

When the fighting reached the vicinity of Riga, Estonia found itself close to the front, an area where reserves were located and new units were assembled, supplied and trained. The biggest garrisons were situated in Narva, Tartu, Valga and Võru. At the beginning of 1917, the number of soldiers located in Estonia was more than 100,000.

Estonians in the armed forces. During the war about 100,000 Estonians were conscripted into the Russian army. About 10,000 were killed at the front, with many more injured. Many of the Estonian soldiers were taken prisoners of war and only managed to return home after the end of the war. This was the highest number of casualties the Estonian nation had ever suffered.

The majority of those conscripted were taken out of Estonia and scattered all over the huge front line. In military units that mainly consisted of Russians, Estonians were persecuted for their poor knowledge of the Russian language. In order to improve the conditions for the men and to be ready to offer better protection in case of a possible German invasion of Estonia, the idea developed in Estonia of establishing **national military units**. This idea was supported by figures from the more threatened northern areas, led by Villem Reimann and Jaan Tõnisson, while the Tallinn nationalist groups resisted it. The idea was sustained by the fact that national units established in Latvia contributed greatly to stopping the German army's offensive in 1915. But the plan of establishing national units in Estonia remained unrealised.

The crisis reaches its peak. By the end of 1916, due to the prolonged war, an exhausted Russia was on the verge of collapse.

The economy was ruined, and supplies of raw materials and fuel were about to run out. The disorganised transportation could not guarantee supply to businesses. There was a severe shortage of consumer goods. The shortage of foodstuffs threatened to leave towns in hunger. Inflation caused monetary problems.

The army was demoralised, the soldiers were weary of the war, and more than 1.5 million men had arbitrarily left the front. There was no sufficient supply of arms or equipment to form new military units.

The government was confused. The agreements concluded with other states did not allow it to abandon the war, but the worsening internal situation did not allow it to continue. Discreet attempts to find out about options of concluding a separate peace with Germany were met by resistance from the opposition. It initiated rumours about the need for a palace revolution replace the Tsar with Grand Duke Nicholas Nikolayevich, or a *putsch* to replace the monarchy with a democratic republic.

The weakening of Russia offered new chances for the **ethnic minorities.** The first to make use of the situation were the Poles, who declared a restoration of the independent Polish state on 5 November 1916. Similar ideas were held in Finland, as well as in the Baltic countries. All the necessary political, economic and cultural preconditions for independent statehood were now present in Estonia.

36. Cultural Development at the End of the Nineteenth and Beginning of the Twentieth Centuries

The rapid development of education and culture in the period under consideration gave rise to qualitative changes. Traditional Estonian popular culture, which had been influenced by German and Russian features, was about to develop into a national culture. It made bold attempts to contact the cultures of Western Europe.

Education. Thorough reorganisation of primary education started in the 1870s. Three-year **village school** attendance was made compulsory for everybody. Numerous new schools were established. The content of education was extended; writing, arithmetic and national studies became general subjects, which changed the nature of schooling that had previously been focused on teaching reading and writing. Those who wanted to continue their studies could choose between parish and county schools.

New teaching aids were introduced, such as geographical maps, globes, abacuses, blackboards, and harmoniums. The arrival in schools of textbooks written in Estonian played a major role. The school reading books compiled by Carl Robert Jakobson remained the basic textbooks for primary schools for years. The educational and professional preparation of teachers improved. Parish schoolteachers were trained at seminaries, the best known of which operated in Valga, headed by Jānis Cimze. Graduates from the parish schools became teachers in county schools.

More and more Estonians tried to continue their studies in order to acquire **secondary education**. In the 1870s new gymnasia (secondary schools) were established in Tallinn, Narva and Viljandi. The original three-year schools developed into eight-year educational establishments. In the 1880s a new type of school appeared – the seven-year scientific school, where more stress was laid on the natural sciences. Girls' gymnasia were also established.

The **reforms from Russification** represented a setback for education. Russian as the

Käsmu maritime academy.

compulsory language of tuition, textbooks that were not suitable for Estonian conditions, teachers who could speak no other languages beside Russian, and a boring system of study where everything had to be learnt by heart reduced the number of pupils and caused a slight reduction in literacy. However, the five-year state schools established in the country provided a more thorough education due to their longer study period.

In the 1890s, the promotion of education continued. The number of schools increased once more and for the first time total literacy was achieved among young people. According to the data of the 1897 census, the percentage of general literacy was higher than in any other Russian *guberniya*: 77.7 per cent.

In the period of revolution a demand for **vernacular schools** (teaching in the Estonian language) arose. In 1906, permission was granted to establish vernacular private schools. The Girls' Gymnasium of the Estonian Society of Youth Education in Tartu and similar establishments in Pärnu, Viljandi and Otepää started work.

The first **vocational schools** – schools of navigation in Heinaste, Narva and Paldiski and a railway polytechnic in Tallinn – had already been established in the 1870s. At the beginning of the new century the role of vocational education increased: business, commercial, sewing, agricultural and other schools were established.

It was also possible to acquire **higher education** in Estonia, provided by Tartu University, Tartu Veterinary Institute, Mikhail Rostovtsev's Private University in Tartu and Anton Jassinski's Higher Women's Courses in Tartu.

The proportion of Estonians among students increased. In 1914, more than 400 Estonians studied at Tartu University and about the same number at other universities in Russia and Europe. In addition to becoming priests, Estonians also became lawyers, engineers, doctors, linguists, and historians.

Science. Tartu University became the main centre of scientific research. Many internationally acknowledged scientists worked there. Initially they were only **Germans**: Carl Schmidt, one of the initiators of physical chemistry; Alexander Schmidt, a researcher in haematology; and Constantin Grewingk, a specialist in the geology and archaeology of the Baltic region.

Due to Russification many Germans left, leaving research at an ebb. It was only after the turn of the century that newly-acknowledged scientists rose among the Russian academic staff: Ivan Kondakov, the inventor of synthetic rubber; Vladimir Grabar, a specialist on international law; and Yevgeni Tarle, a researcher of the Napoleonic period. Alongside Russian academics some Baltic Germans were also active: Werner Zoege von Manteuffel became famous for the first successful heart surgery.

There were very few Estonians among university lecturers. Traditionally, lecturers on Estonian philology were Estonians. Among these, Mihkel Veske and Karl August Hermann had acquired doctorates in Leipzig, but they were not allowed to take a professorship. During the war years some more Estonians gained posts at the university: the theologian Johan Kõpp and the medics Aleksander Paldrok and Heinrich Koppel.

The university did not pay much attention to studies connected with the Estonian country and nation. Among research establishments located outside the university that developed that field, the most important are the Estonian Scholarly Society (Õpetatud Eesti Selts) and the Estonian Society of Literati.

The latter continued to collect folklore on the initiative of Jakob Hurt. After the Society of Literati was closed down, the collecting of folklore almost stopped, but the **Estonian Literary Society** *(Eesti Kirjanduse Selts)*, established in 1907, carried on the work. As well as collecting folklore they considered it their task to study the Estonian language, literature and history.

In the field of history, the **Estonian National Museum**, established in 1909 to commemorate Jakob Hurt, rose next to the Estonian Literary Society. The Museum collected artefacts of the Estonian people: everyday commodities, national costumes, ornaments, pieces of art; the archive and library of the Museum housed printed matter in Estonian and about Estonia.

Literature. The development of national literature started from nationalist-romantic patriotic lyrics written by Lydia Koidula, but also by

The Estonian National Museum in Raadi.

Mihkel Veskel, Ado Reinvald and Friedrich Kuhlbars. Almost simultaneously the first drama pieces in Estonian appeared. Lydia Koidula also pioneered that field, soon followed by Jakob Kunder.

Prose was initially of secondary importance. First Jakob Pärn and Lilli Suburg's stories were published, and in the 1880s the romantic-historical stories by Eduard Bornhöhe first appeared. His "Tasuja" (The Avenger) became vastly popular, which also led Jaak Järv and Andres Saal to write in the historic genre.

By the end of the nineteenth century, prose had become more popular than poetry, and romantic stories were replaced by **realistic** novels. The most outstanding novelist was **Eduard Vilde**, whose historical trilogy marked the peak of critical realism in Estonian literature. **Juhan Liiv** was the best-known poet of the period, while **August Kitzberg** became famous as a playwright.

The turning point for the literature came in 1905, when the first literary group **"Young Estonia"** (Noor-Eesti) made its appearance. This developed from a social-cultural circle of young people, where discussions about topical issues took place and members read their writings to each other. The leaders of the group were **Gustav Suits, Friedebert Tuglas** and **Juhan Aavik**. Their slogan "Let's be Estonians, but let's also become Europeans!" expressed the need to get rid of the one-sided Russian and German cultural influences and to find connections between Estonian national culture and that of western Europe.

Music. The national musical art started with choral songs, which were initiated by the song festivals and the large number of choirs. The first non-professional Estonian composers were graduates of the Jānis Cimze Seminary: Aleksander Saebelmann-Kunileid – two of whose songs were in the programme of the 1869 song festival – and his brother Friedrich August Saebelmann.

At the end of the century, professional composers educated in the conservatory started to influence musical life in Estonia. **Aleksander Läte** established the first symphony orchestra in Tartu in 1900. As well as composing, **Miina Härma** presented organ music and was an outstanding conductor. At the turn of the century the list was extended by the names of Artur Kapp, Mihkel Lüdig, Peeter Süda, Rudolf Tobias and others.

The **tradition of song festivals** continued. The number of participants increased. In addition to brass bands and male choirs, mixed choirs, female choirs and children's choirs, as well as string orchestras, joined the ranks of performers. The repertoire became more varied, and the proportion of original Estonian music increased.

Theatre. The birth date of the Estonian theatre was 24 June 1870, when the *première* of "Saaremaa onupoeg" (The Saaremaa Cousin) by Lydia Koidula took place at the "Vanemuine" society in Tartu. A year later the play was staged by the "Estonia" society in Tallinn, then by the "Ilmarine" society in Narva, the "Koit" society in Viljandi and the "Endla" society in Pärnu. Soon amateur theatres became popular all over Estonia. The plays were performed in larger farmhouses and in school buildings. As the actors were amateurs, the artistic level of the plays was not very high, and they mainly served the purpose of entertainment.

The greatest change took place in the "Vanemuine" society, the leadership of which was taken over by **August Wiera** in 1878. He formed a company with a stable membership, initiated weekly performances, and enriched the repertoire with western European classics. "Vanemuine" became a professional theatre in 1906 when **Karl Menning,** who had studied directing in Berlin, became the head of the company in a newly constructed building. The same year the "Estonia" in Tallinn became a professional theatre and some time later the "Endla" in Pärnu as well.

At the end of the century **film** made its way to Estonia. Initially there were short shows given by travelling cinemas. The first Estonian cinematographer was Johannes Pääsuke. He shot documentaries about Tartu and the Setu lands and made the first feature film "Karujaht Pärnumaal" (A Bear Hunt in Pärnu Region) before the First World War.

Fine arts. In the second half of the nineteenth century, Estonian fine arts were born. Among the first artists were painters Johann Köler, Karl Ludwig Maibach and Oskar Hoffman, and the sculptors August Weizenberg and Amandus Adamson.

Johann Köler laid the foundation of portrait and landscape painting, sometimes also using mythological subjects. In his paintings a realistic representation of nature and people was blended with romantic moods. The best known sculptures by Amandus Adamson were his marble portraits and antique figures based on Estonian mythology. Although Adamson was inspired by folklore, the greater part of his works depict realistic scenes of the life of people living by the sea. He was also interested in monuments; he created the "Russalka" (a memorial to a wrecked Russian warship) in Tallinn.

At the beginning of the twentieth century fine arts developed quickly in Estonia. A number of studio schools were established, art exhibitions were organised, and the **Estonian Art Society** *(Eesti Kunstiselts)* came into being. The range of themes handled increased, though landscape and still life were the most popular. The artists were also very interested in fashionable trends in art, such as post-impressionism, symbolism and others. The number of professional artists grew – including the painters Ants Laikmaa, Kristjan Raud, Konrad Mägi, and the sculptor Jaan Koort. The first Estonian architect was Georg Hellat, whose largest works were the building of the Estonian Students Society in Tartu and that of the "Endla" theatre in Pärnu.

Sport. The more systematic practice of athletics started at the turn of the century, when **sport societies** were founded in the larger towns. Initially the main field was cycling, but soon ballgames, athletics, water sports, boxing, wrestling and weightlifting became popular. The best-known sport societies were "Kalev" in Tallinn and "Taara" in Tartu.

Estonians achieved outstanding results in wrestling. **Georg Lurich,** Aleksander Aberg and Georg Hackenschmidt were famous not only in Russia, but also in all of Europe. Martin Klein brought the first Olympic medal to Estonia: a silver medal in Graeco-Roman wrestling won at the 1912 Olympics. In the Russian context, Estonians had good results in other fields as well. During the First World War, 16 out of the 29 Russian records for athletics were held by Estonians.

VII The Coming of Statehood (1917-1920)

37. An Autonomous Part of Democratic Russia

The February Revolution. The massive unrest which broke out in Petrograd (St Petersburg) in February 1917 grew into a revolution that resulted in Nicholas II giving up the throne and power passing into the hands of the Provisional Government. In the spring of 1917, Russia made an attempt at democratic reforms.

Vague rumours about what had taken place arrived in Estonia by the start of March. The focal point of events became **Tallinn**, where a large number of Russian workers lived and a garrison was situated. Unlike the 1905 Revolution, the February Revolution was dominated by the Russian language and Russian thought.

By **2 March**, sporadic strikes in the factories of Tallinn had developed into a general strike. About 20,000 people gathered at a meeting at the New Market, after which they joined the crews of warships stationed in the port of Tallinn. Carrying red flags and singing revolutionary songs, they marched to liberate political prisoners.

At the Paks Margareeta (Fat Margaret) tower, then used as a prison, the first casualties of the revolution occurred. The head of the prison and some guards were killed. The gates of the prison were opened, prisoners (criminal as well as political) were released, and the tower was set ablaze. After this event, other prisons in Tallinn were also ransacked.

Police stations and courts were also attacked. Their doors were broken down, windows were smashed, furniture and documents were thrown into the streets and stacked to form bonfires. The number of casualties grew during the day, and the soldiers of the garrison joined the sailors and workers after killing their much-despised officers.

It was a restless night in Tallinn. There were several fires, the sound of shooting could be heard, gangs of soldiers made noise in the streets and the newly-released criminals returned to their accustomed ways.

Similar events took place in all the towns of Estonia where there were many Russian workers or soldiers. In small rural towns and in the countryside it was silent, and most people only learned the fact that the revolution had taken place on 10 March, when a day of commemoration was held for the casualties of the revolution and the freedom fighters.

The disorder in the towns was put down relatively quickly. The Provisional Government of Russia recalled the Governors and appointed

Jaan Poska – Mayor of Tallinn, commissar of the Estonia guberniya

Demonstrations by Estonians in Petrograd (St Petersburg) on 26 March 1917

commissars of the *guberniyas* in their place. The Estonian lawyer **Jaan Poska** (1866-1920), Mayor of Tallinn, was appointed **Commissar of the Estonian *guberniya***. Elsewhere county commissars were appointed and a revolutionary militia began to operate.

During the period of the Revolution, **Soviets (Councils) of Workers' and Soldiers' Deputies** *(Tööliste ja Soldatite Saadikute Nõukogud)* sprang up, dominated by left-wing elements, and considering themselves self-styled revolutionary parliaments. The soviets continued after the appointment of the *guberniya* commissars but initially were not in opposition to the representatives of the government. The general mood appeared to have been calm.

Autonomy. The Estonian nationalist movement tried to find a suitable moment to introduce the reforms they saw as necessary. As the political climate was not yet ripe for claiming independence, they took as their aim the achievement of autonomy within the Russian state. This project was outlined at a meeting of nationalist or-ganisations in Tartu and presented to the Provisional Government for approval.

In Petrograd, the process became bogged down. The official pretext was that the question was of such great importance that it should be deferred until the assembly of the All-Russian Congress of Soviets. In order to push the process forward, Estonians used high-level personal contacts as well as a demonstration of Estonians in Petrograd on 26 March. Some 40,000 people took part in this demonstration, including 12,000 fully armed soldiers. The columns carried red revolutionary flags, but also blue, black and white national flags. The demonstrators" representatives demanded immediate passing of a law of autonomy.

At the **end of March** the Provisional Government issued a **decree on the interim structure of government of the Estonian *guberniya***. According to this, the Estonian *guberniya* (excluding Narva) and the northern part of the Livonian *guberniya* (excluding the Setu region) were united to form one new *guberniya*. This was to be governed by the commissar of the Provisional Government and his two deputies. To support them a **provincial council** *(Maapäev)* was to be elected.

Nationalist activities and the increase in tension. After the achievement of autonomy, the first task for the nationalists was to take over power. In both *guberniya* governments and their institutions, Russians were replaced by Estonians, and **Estonian** became the official language. Preparations were made for conversion to the Estonian language in education. This became the first source of conflict. The **Russian officials** who had been dismissed filed numerous complaints to the Provisional Government about the separatism shown by the Estonians, and demanded restoration of the previous order. These new problems created tension between Petrograd and Tallinn.

The second task for the new *guberniya* government was to normalise the overall situation as quickly as possible. This meant taking power into the hands of government officials and limiting the influence of the soviets. In response the soviets tried to undermine the trust of both the Provisional Government and the local people in the *guberniya* government and the Estonian officials. Tension was increased by Jaan Poska calling elections to the *Maapäev*, which the soviets claimed to be premature. The left-wing majority in the soviets was afraid that without pre-election propaganda they would be unable to achieve a majority in the *Maapäev*. The opposition became so strong that Poska was forced to leave Tallinn temporarily. The elections still took place on the intended date in May 1917.

The third source of tension arose from the **Russian soldiers**. The morale of the Russian army was in continuous decline, and the idea of creating **national army units** arose. Using the fact that two defence regiments were in the process of formation in Tallinn, the nationalists managed to get permission from the Provisional Government to recruit Estonians to form these units. The reaction of the Russian soldiers was stormy, convinced that the Estonians wanted to send them to the front while remaining in the rear themselves. Still supported by the Russian Provisional Government, the Estonians managed to form the **First Estonian Regiment** in Rakvere. This developed into a unit with nationalist ideals and a very strong sense of discipline, which supported the Estonian politicians in furthering their ambitions. Gradually the number of national army units increased.

Opposition to the Estonian nationalists was led by Estonian **Bolsheviks**, who considered the Russian revolution only a part of the world revolution, and thought that nationalist activities undermined revolutionary forces.

Political development in the summer of 1917. During the year, different political parties developed in Estonia. The Estonian National Progressive Party, founded in 1905 and led by Jaan Tõnisson, transformed itself into the **Estonian Democratic Party** *(Eesti Demokraatlik Erakond)*, which is backed by wealthy south Estonian farmers, members of the urban bourgeoisie, and the intelligentsia. The **Estonian Rural Peoples Union** *(Eesti Maarahva Liit)* brought together Estonian peasants, while the **Estonian Labour Party** *(Eesti Tööerakond)* united the urban middle classes and officials with a slightly left-wing viewpoint.

In addition to these, several socialist parties were active. The Menshevik wing of the RSDWP split from the main party to form the **Estonian Social Democratic Union** *(Eesti Sotsiaaldemokraatlik Ühendus)*, and the All-Russian Socialist Revolutionary Party spawned the **Estonian Socialist Revolutionary Party** *(Eesti Sotisialistide-Revolutsionääride Partei)*. The Bolshevik members of the RSDWP continued to be active. In the summer of 1917, they achieved outstanding success; by August the organisation, which in March had had 150 members, had become the largest Estonian political force with a membership of 7,000.

At the beginning of July the *Maapäev* assembled for the first time, and became the first Estonian national parliament. The *Maapäev* elected a government *(Maavalitsus)*, led by **Jaan Raamot** (later replaced by Konstantin Päts). So all the results possible under the framework of autonomy had been achieved. Two options existed: to be satisfied with these achievements, or to find ways of making further progress. At the **National Congress** in Tallinn, the leader of the

Estonian Labour Party, Jüri Vilms (1889-1918), set a new goal: to achieve statehood within a Russian federation of equal states.

Events of the First World War. The Provisional Government was unable to stop the collapse of governmental power and the Russian army. This was made worse by Bolshevik propaganda. Germany took advantage of this situation and forced Russia to conclude a separate peace treaty.

In August, the German army occupied Riga, and the Russian units that had lost the ability to fight retreated into Estonia. At the **end of September**, the war arrived in Estonian territory; the Germans landed on the island of Saaremaa, and by 8 October they had invaded all the western Estonian islands without resistance from the Russian army. In the fight for Muhu island, the First Estonian Regiment suffered extensive losses, with many taken as prisoners.

Russia's military failure was accompanied by a sharp increase in the popularity of the **Bolsheviks**. The soldiers based in Estonia easily accepted the slogan "Down with the War." The same slogan was supported by the workers, especially after the Provisional Government started to evacuate their industrial enterprises from Estonia in the fear of German invasion. This evacuation would have meant job losses for thousands of workers, and the only option to preserve their source of income appeared to be a rapid end to the war. At the same time, the Bolsheviks applied pressure to other socialist parties, claiming that their leaders were not interested in achieving peace. In the complex circumstances, this statement found believers, and many moderate socialists joined the Bolshevik cause.

By October there were 20,000 Bolsheviks in Estonia. They gained the leadership of the **Estonian Soviet Executive Committee** *(Eestimaa Nõukogude Täitevkomitee)*, which was formed to co-ordinate the activities of the socialist committees. They began preparations for the armed seizure of power, organising units of the Red Guard and hoping to make use of a demoralised Russian army.

The German military success made the question of Estonian **independence** topical once again. At the meeting of the *Maapäev* on 25 August, Jaan Tõnisson stated that, as the threat of German occupation had become almost a reality and there was no hope of help from the Russians, then it was time to take the question of Estonia into the world political arena. The meeting decided to send a delegation to western Europe, to raise the Estonian problem with politicians there and discover their attitudes towards the future of Estonia. A month later, the *Maapäev* decided to call elections to the Estonian Constituent Assembly *(Eesti Asutav Kogu)*, which would define the future status of the Estonian nation.

38. Independence

The October Revolution in Estonia. In order to take power, the Bolsheviks formed the **Estonian Revolutionary War Committee** *(Eestimaa Sõja-Revolutsioonikomitee; SRK)* in October 1917, headed by Ivan Rabchinski and Viktor Kingissepp.

On the evening of 23 October, the SRK sent its commissars to the military units, railway stations and public offices of Tallinn. Groups of Red Guards began to patrol the streets.

After receiving news of the successful revolution in Petrograd on 26 October, the SRK began the real seizure of state power. Meetings and demonstrations were organised in support of the Bolsheviks. On the same day, local SRKs seized power in Tartu and Narva. On 27 October, SRK deputies appeared in Toompea, and issued a document announcing the transfer of power from the *guberniya* commissar Jaan Poska to the vice-chairman of the SRK, Viktor Kingissepp.

Bolshevik reforms. Formally, the highest legislative institution in the *guberniya* was the SRK, but all important decrees and orders came from Petrograd. Executive power was exercised by the Estonian Soviet Executive Committee *(Eestimaa Nõukogude Täitevkomitee)*, headed by Jaan Anvelt.

In counties, towns and parishes, soviets of workers' deputies were elected which took power from the institutions of local government. The **elections** were not democratic – only proletarians (workers in industrial enterprises and estates, craftsmen, teachers and landless peasants) were allowed to vote. More well-off citizens were obliged to remain passive observers.

Although the Bolsheviks co-operated with left-wing Socialist Revolutionaries until January 1918, the new regime was into a dictatorship from the very beginning. When it appeared that the Bolsheviks would not achieve an absolute majority in the elections for the **Estonian Constituent Assembly** in January 1918, the elections were cancelled.

Civil rights were immediately limited. Political meetings were forbidden, several newspapers were closed down, and many leading nationalists were arrested. Citizens' freedom of

The Committee of National Salvation's secret location in Tallinn, on Tartu highway 11, in 1918

religion was not respected; the nationalised churches were turned into cultural centres, and religious education in schools was abolished.

Economic reforms were started by the nationalisation of banks, followed by industrial enterprises, big businesses, hotels and restaurants. Preparations were made for taking over private residences. Land was declared to be in state ownership, and estates were confiscated, but the land was not divided between the peasants. Rural estates were turned into large agricultural co-operatives, the leadership of which passed into the hands of committees of their former tenant labourers.

The national army units were becoming a problem for the Bolsheviks, as they represented a considerable military force that could not easily be disbanded. After the October Revolution, the Estonian regiments were combined into the Estonian Division, commanded by **Johan Laidoner** (1884-1953). It was not until January 1918 that the replacement of national units with Estonian Red Guards began.

The Bolsheviks' policies, which were accompanied by repression of political opponents, created unrest among the people, and the range and number of their supporters began to decline.

Preparations for independence. During the first weeks of Bolshevik power, the *Maapäev*, *Maavalitsus*, and local government institutions continued to operate. In November, the Estonian Soviet Executive Committee decided to dissolve the *Maapäev*, but the deputies did not follow these orders.

At the meeting of the *Maapäev* in the middle of November it was declared that the future state order of Estonia would be defined by the Estonian Constituent Assembly, and as long as this had not been convened, the only holder of supreme power in Estonia was the *Maapäev*. Therefore only decrees of the *Maapäev* had legislative power in Estonia. This decision effectively broke off the former connections with the Russian state.

On the same day the Bolsheviks used force to dissolve the *Maapäev*, but the deputies continued to meet illegally. At meetings held around the end of 1917, they reached the unanimous decision that as soon as Germany really occupied Estonia, Estonia had to be declared independent and recognition had to be asked from western countries.

In January 1918 the first real steps were taken in this direction. Contact was established with Russian political parties and with the Petrograd embassies of Great Britain, France and the USA. A foreign delegation was formed to promote Estonian aspirations in western Europe.

Germany launches an offensive. After the Bolshevik Revolution, the Baltic Germans became active. The Estonian nobility decided to split from Russia, and to ask for assistance from the German Kaiser. The Bolsheviks gained information about the secret plans of the Baltic Germans, and declared a **state of siege** in Estonia. All members of the nobility were declared outlaws, and a campaign to arrest and deport them began. The clergy and prominent nationalists were also arrested.

At the same time, peace negotiations in Brest between Soviet Russia and Germany and its allies broke off, and Germany started preparations for an offensive on the eastern front. A suitable pretext for this was found in the deportation of Baltic Germans from Estonia.

On 18 February [from this point on, all dates are given in the Gregorian calendar introduced in Estonia on 1 (14) February], the **general offensive of the German army** began. The Germans landed on the Estonian mainland near Lihula on 20 February from Saaremaa, and a day later at Haapsalu from Hiiumaa island. The units that began the offensive from Latvia marched into Valga on 22 February. A swift invasion followed. The Russian army had ceased to exist, and the Red Army, which was in the process of formation, was too weak to oppose the German forces.

The declaration of independence. The nationalist circles were aware of Germany's intentions, and understood the need to act quickly. On 19 February the **Committee of National Salvation** (Päästekomitee) was formed, with extraordinary powers, which comprised Konstantin Konik, Konstantin Päts and Jüri Vilms. A manifesto of independence was compiled, in which for the first time Estonia was named as an inde-

Manifest
kõigile Eestimaa rahwastele.

Eesti rahwas ei ole aastasadade jooksul kaotanud tungi iseseiswuse järele. Põlwest põlwe on temas kestnud salajane lootus, et hoolimata pimedast orjaööst ja wööraste rahwaste wägiwallawalitsusest weel kord Eestis aeg tuleb, mil „kõik pirrud kahel otsal lausa löökwad lõkendama" ja et „kord Kalew koju jõuab om'a lastel õnne taoma".

Nüüd on see aeg käes.

Ennekuulmata rahwaste heitlus on Wene tsaaririigi pehastanud alustoed põhjani purustanud. Üle Sarmatia lagendiku laiutab end häwitaw korralagedus, ähwardades oma alla matta kõiki rahwaid, kes endise Wene riigi piirides asuwad. Lääne poolt lähenewad Saksamaa wõidukad wäed, et Wenemaa pärandusest omale osa nõuda ja kõige pealt just Balti mere rannamaid oma alla wõtta.

Sel saatuslikul tunnil on Eesti Maapäew kui maa ja rahwa seaduslik esitaja, ühemeelsele otsusele jõudes rahwawalitsuse alusel seiswate Eesti politiliste parteidega ja organisatsioonidega, toetades rahwaste enesemääramise õiguse peale, tarwilikuks tunnistanud, Eesti maa ja rahwa saatuse määramiseks järgmisi otsustawaid sammme astuda:

Eestimaa
tema ajaloolistes ja etnografilistes piirides, kuulutatakse tänasest peale
iseseiswaks demokratlikfeks wabariigiks.

Iseseiswa Eesti wabariigi piiridesse kuuluwad: Harjumaa, Läänemaa, Järwamaa, Wirumaa ühes Narwa linna ja tema ümbruskonnaga, Tartumaa, Wõrumaa, Wiljandimaa ja Pärnumaa ühes Lääne mere saartega — Saare-, Hiiu- ja Muhum'aaga ja teistega, kus Eesti rahwas suures enamuses põliselt asumas. Wabariigi piiride lõpulik kindlaksmääramine Lätimaa ja Wene riigi piirjääretes maakohtades sünnib rahwahäältetomise teel, kui praegune ilmasõda lõppenud.

Eeltähendatud maakohtades on ainsamaks kõrgemaks ja korraldawaks wõimuks Eesti Maapäewa poolt loodud rahwawõim Eestimaa Päästmise Komitee näol.

Kõigi naabririikide ja rahwaste wastu tahab Eesti wabariik täielikku poliitilist erapooletust pidada, ja loodab ühtlasi kindlaste, et tema erapooletus nende poolt niisama ka täielikku erapooletusega wastatakse.

Eesti sõjawägi wähendatakse selle määrani, mis sisemise korra alalhoidmiseks tarwilik. Eesti sõjamehed, kes Wene wägedes teeniwad, kutsutakse koju ja demobiliseritakse.

Kuni Eesti Asutaw Kogu, kes üleüldise, otsekohese, salajase ja proportsionalse hääletamise põhjal kokku astub, maa walitsemise korra kõplikult kindlaks määrab, jääb kõik walitsemise ja seaduseandmise wõim Eesti Maapäewa ja selle poolt loodud Eesti Ajutise Walitsuse kätte, kes oma tegewuses järgmiste juhtmõtete järele peab käima:

1. Kõik Eesti wabariigi kodanikud, usu, rahwuse ja politilise ilmawaate peale waatamata, leiawad ühtlast kaitset wabariigi seaduste ja kohtute ees.

2. Wabariigi piirides elawatele rahwuslistele wähemustele, wenelastele, sakslastele, rootslastele, juutidele ja teistele kindlustatakse nende rahwuskulturlised autonomia õigused.

3. Kõik kodanikuwabadused, sõna-, trüki-, usu-, koosolekute-, ühisuste-, liitude- ja streikidewabadused, niisama ihiku ja koduhoide puutumatus peawad kogu Eesti riigi piirides määramata maksma seaduste alusel, mida walitsus wiibimata peab wälja töötama.

4. Ajutisele walitsusele tehtakse ülesandeks wiibimata kohtuasutusi sisse seada kodanikkude julgeoleku kaitseks. Kõik politilised wangid tulewad otsekohe wabastada.

5. Linna- ja maakonna- ja wallaoma-walitsuse asutused kutsutakse wiibimata oma wägiwaldselt katkestatud tööd jatkama.

6. Omawalitsuse all seisew rahwamilits tuleb awaliku korra alalhoidmiseks otsekohe ellusse kutsuda, niisama ka kodanikkude enesekaitse organisatsionid linnades ja maal.

7. Ajutisele walitsusele tehtakse ülesandeks wiibimata seaduste-eelnõu wälja töötada maaküsimuse, tööliseküsimuse, toitlusasjanduse ja rahaasjanduse küsimuste lahendamiseks alaliistel demokratlistel alustel.

Eestil Sa seisad lootusrikka tulewiku läwel, kus sa wabalt ja iseseiswalt oma saatust wõid määrata ja juhtida! Asu ehitama oma kodu, kus kord ja õigus walitseks, et olla määriliseks liikmeks kulturarahwaste peres! Kõik kodumaa pojad ja tütred, ühinegem kui üks mees kodumaa ehitamise pühas töös! Meie esiwanemate higi ja weri, mis selle maa eest walatud, nõuab seda, mele järeltulewad põlwed kohustawad meid selleks.

Su üle Jumal waiwagu
Ja wõtku rohkest õnnista,
Mis iial ette wõtad sa,
Mu kallis isamaa!

Elagu iseseis ew demokratline Eesti wabariik!

Elagu rahwaste rahu!

Eesti Maapäewa Wanemate Nõukogu.

24. weebr. 1918 a.

The manifesto proclaiming Estonia as an independent republic pendent democratic republic. The national military units received an order to maintain neutrality towards German forces.

On a local level, power was seized before the arrival of the Germans by national units, as well as by secretly-convened voluntary military groups known as **Omakaitse** (self-defence). The nationalists gained power in Haapsalu, Pärnu, Viljandi, Võru, Tartu, Paide, and other towns. On the evening of 23 February, the manifesto of independence was read in public for the first time, from the balcony of the "Endla" Theatre in Pärnu.

In Tallinn, the Bolsheviks boarded Russian warships anchored in the harbour on the evening of 23 February. The maintenance of order in Tallinn passed into the hands of the *Omakaitse*. On 24 February, the members of the Committee of National Salvation drove to Tallinn and based themselves at the building that later became the Estonian central bank. There they formed the Provisional Government of the Estonian Republic, with Konstantin Päts as prime minister. The manifesto of independence was proclaimed once again. The independent Estonian Republic was born.

The next morning was festive in Tallinn. Houses were adorned with national flags, church bells rang, and there were services in churches and celebratory meetings in schools. The last Russian warships left the port. But by the middle of the day, German units had already marched into the town. However, the events of 24 February still allowed Estonia to be considered as an independent state, though occupied by foreign forces.

The intervention of the German army continued until 3 March, and by then they had occupied the whole territory of Estonia, including Narva and Ivangorod. On the same day, the peace treaty of Brest was signed, and Soviet Russia gave up a large portion of the previous western territories of Russia. Formally, Estonia and Livonia remained under Russian power, but German military units were to be based there.

The German occupation. Power in Estonia passed to the German military command. Baltic Germans replaced Estonian mayors and county commissars. Estonian independence and the provisional government were not recognised. The activity of nationalist parties, as well as the or-

Jüri Vilms, a member of the Estonian Committee of National Salvation and deputy prime minister in the provisional government, killed on order of German military forces near Helsinki on 13 April 1918.

ganisation of political meetings and demonstrations, was forbidden, and the press was censored. The national military units and the *Omakaitse* were disbanded.

Several politicians were arrested and sent to prison camps, including Prime Minister Konstantin Päts. During the first days of occupation, more than 200 people were executed, the majority being Bolsheviks and members of the Red Guard, but with nationalists among them. In Helsinki, the Deputy Prime Minister Jüri Vilms and his companions were shot. The activities of the occupying powers were characterised with the words "keelan-käsen, poon ja lasen" (I forbid, order, hang and shoot).

The economic policy started to serve the needs of Germany. Everything possible was taken from Estonia: grain, potatoes, animal fodder, cattle, timber, raw materials, partly-finished goods, industrial products, factory equipment and so on. The majority of the industrial enterprises stopped work. Unemployment grew, living standards fell, and prices went up. Townspeople were supplied with ration cards, but the amounts they received were not sufficient on which to survive.

Cultural policy. The main aim of the cultural policy was to Germanise the local people. German became the official language, and education began to be converted to the German language. The historical contribution of Germans to the culture of the Baltic nations was emphasised.

The autocratic actions of the Germans caused opposition among Estonians. The provisional government, which had been removed from power, called for passive resistance to the occupiers, and the *Omakaitse* resumed activities illegally. The work of the foreign delegation proved successful: Estonian conditions and the autocratic regime of the occupying powers were brought to the attention of western Europe, and ***de facto*** **recognition** of the Estonian Republic was achieved from the governments of Great Britain and France.

At the same time the Baltic Germans were trying to establish a formally independent **Baltic Duchy** which would be tightly connected to Germany. In Estonia and Latvia, elections were held for a National Council (*Landesrat*), the main task of which would have been to ask assistance from the German Kaiser in establishing a duchy. In the *Landesrat*, 23 delegates represented Estonians and Latvians and 34 delegates represented Germans. Due to this proportion of power, the Baltic Germans managed to carry out their will at the meeting of *Landesrat* in Riga, in April despite protests by Estonian delegates.

The process of establishing a duchy became stuck because the ambitions of the Baltic Germans did not find wide support in Germany. The Brest peace treaty became another obstacle. According to this agreement, Estonia and Livonia still belonged to Russia. It was not until August 1918 in Berlin that the Russians were forced to give up their rights to the Baltic countries. In September, the Kaiser signed the act of recognition of independence of the Baltic countries and at the beginning of November the Baltic Duchy was officially proclaimed in Riga. But it was already too late.

The huge losses Germany suffered in autumn 1918 made continuation of the war impossible. At the beginning of November a revolution broke out, the Kaiser was dethroned and a socialist government took power. On 11 November 1918 the Compiègne Armistice was signed.

On 9 and 10 November, German soldiers and sailors based in Tallinn joined the strike. **On 11 November, the Estonian Provisional Government was reassembled**. The final seizure of power from the Germans took place on 21 November. The Estonian Republic, which had been proclaimed nine months previously, was restored.

39. The War of Independence

Preparations for war. Making use of the revolution that had broken out in Germany, the Russian government cancelled all the treaties it had concluded with the Germans and started preparations for restoring the previous borders of the Empire. Simultaneously they hoped to initiate revolutions in other European countries, which would provide armed assistance for the Red Army.

In November 1918, the Red Army concentrated considerable forces on the Estonian border. The invasion was to take place in two directions: from Narva towards Tallinn and from Pskov towards Võru and Valga.

The intervention about to begin was intended to be camouflaged as a **civil war**, using Estonian Bolsheviks who had escaped into Russia from the German occupation. The Estonian Provisional Revolutionary Committee *(Eestimaa Ajutine Revolutsioonikomitee)*, which had been formed in Petrograd, proclaimed itself the only legal institution of power in Estonia and called for restoration of Soviet power in Estonia. All Estonian communist rifle regiments fighting on the fronts in Russia were transferred to Narva. The basic forces of the Red Army on the Estonian border still consisted of Russian and Latvian units, altogether about 12,000 men.

They were opposed by German units, which were making preparations for returning home, and groups of the **Estonian Defence League** *(Eesti Kaitseliit)*, which had been formed from the outlawed *Omakaitse* units. The call by the Provisional Government of Estonia for volunteers to the **Estonian National Army** *(Eesti Rahvavägi)* brought together only a couple of thousand men. The compulsory mobilisation, which began at the beginning of December, could not provide quick results, as there was a shortage of everything: weapons, ammunition, uniforms, footwear, foodstuffs, and so on. Pleas for assistance to the governments of Finland and Great Britain, as well as negotiations with the leaders of the German occupation army and the Northern Corps of the Russian White Guard formed in Pskov, held out only vague hope.

Men from the Estonian cavalry in 1919.

The broad-gauged armoured train's artillery wagon "Tasuja" (The Avenger), in 1919.

The beginning of the War of Independence. The German army repulsed an attack on Narva by the Red Army on 22 November, but at the same time it hurried the Germans to leave Estonia. A couple of days later the Germans yielded Pskov to the Russians, increasing the threat to the southern border of Estonia.

The government sent all the forces at its command to Narva: officers, volunteers, even schoolboys from Tallinn, who were ready to sacrifice their lives for Estonia despite they having no military training.

On 28 November, the Estonian War of Independence began. Within several hours the Bolshevik attacks were successfully repulsed at Narva, but when the Germans started to leave their positions, the superior enemy forces forced the Estonian units to retreat. On the following day the Red Army marched into Narva.

In December 1918, the swift advance of the Red Army through Estonian territory continued. The Bolsheviks invaded one town after another: Jõhvi, Kunda, Rakvere, Tapa and Aegviidu in the north; Võru, Valga, Tartu, Tõrva and Mõisaküla in the south of Estonia. By the beginning of the new year, the front was dangerously close to Tallinn, Paide, Põltsamaa, Viljandi and Pärnu.

The **reasons for failure** of the Estonian National Army were due to the superior numbers of enemy forces, an insufficient amount of weapons and equipment, the absence of a rational system of leadership, and the low fighting morale of the men. The number of deserters was large, as people grew tired of fighting and they found it hard to believe that little Estonia could fight huge Russia.

Estonian Workers' Commune *(Eesti Töörahva Kommuun; ETK)*. After the seizure of Narva, the Estonian Bolsheviks stepped forward and formed the Estonian Workers' Commune, which developed into an autonomous unit within Soviet Russia.

Leadership on the territory of the ETK passed into the hands of the Commune Council, headed by **Jaan Anvelt**. The Council continued the policy the Bolsheviks had implemented before the German occupation. Once more large enterprises and banks were nationalised, while the estates, confiscated from their owners, were formed into agricultural co-operatives (communes). Political opposition was repressed: the number of those who lost their lives through the Red Terror was more than 500. The church and religious organisations were discredited.

The only country to recognise the independence of the ETK was Soviet Russia, as it gave them a chance to present the intervention as a civil war between the Estonian bourgeoisie and workers. In reality the ETK followed orders from Moscow and was not able to uphold its opinion even in minor disputes with the leadership of the Red Army.

A **turn in the War of Independence.** During the last days of 1918, the situation began to change. The advance of the Red Army slowed, and it seemed increasingly difficult for them to seize further towns. Counterattacks by the Estonian National Army were more and more successful, which considerably reduced the enemy's freedom of action. Especially successful were the **armoured trains** active on the Tallinn-Narva railway line. A landing by Estonian **naval forces** led by Johan Pitka in the rear of the Bolsheviks on the coast of the Gulf of Finland created panic amongst them.

The number of soldiers in the Estonian army grew, and at the beginning of January it reached 13,000.

The more the people understood about the goals of the Bolsheviks, the less they deserted from the National Army. Alongside the recruited units, **units of volunteers** were formed. Their fighting morale was higher and their action more effective. The most famous among them were the Kalevlaste unit, compiled of members of the Kalev Sport Society, the Kuperjanov Partisan Battalion, consisting of the members of Tartu *Kaitseliit*, the Scout Battalion formed in Viljandi district, and also the units formed of school pupils and the crews of the armoured trains.

Leadership of the army was reorganised. Initially, leaders of each military unit had acted according to their own discretion. Now they were subjected to the **commander-in-chief of the army**. Johan Laidoner became the commander-in-chief and Jaan Soots became his chief-of-staff. Although a guerrilla strategy was widely used in the War of Independence, the role of the centralised command grew gradually and made it possible to achieve more extensive military success.

The army's equipment also improved. They received horses, sledges, clothes and food as donations from people, but these were also commandeered. Weapons were received from abandoned stores, as well as from Finland and Britain.

The fighting morale was supported by the fact that Estonia did not face Soviet Russia alone, but could count on **foreign aid**. In December, a British naval squadron arrived in Tallinn, which prevented the Bolsheviks' plan to attack the Estonian capital from the sea. By the end of the year the first voluntary Finnish units arrived at the front. There were volunteers from Denmark and Sweden as well.

At the same time the condition of the Red Army deteriorated. The increasing distance from their bases slowed down the arrival of supplies. Soldiers who were constantly in action became tired. Recruits of nationalities other than Russian did not understand the aims of the war. General weariness of the war increased. The higher command of the Red Army considered the fate of Estonia settled and did not send any reinforcements.

A light artillery unit on the Viru front, autumn 1919.

L**iberation of Estonia.** On 6 January 1919, the counterattack of the Estonian army began. On its main line (Tallinn-Narva), armoured trains operated effectively. The resistance of the Bolsheviks was overcome. It took the Estonian army six days to move from Aegviidu to Rakvere, where they continued the advance. On 19 January, a unit that landed on the coast in Utria liberated **Narva**.

The armoured trains could not go further than Rakvere because of broken bridges, so they turned to the south. And in co-operation with the Kuperjanov Partisans, they liberated **Tartu** on 14 January.

After that, the advance on the southern front halted for some time, as the Red Army leadership sent Latvian communist units as reinforcements. In the process of fierce battles, Estonian units finally managed to liberate **Valga** and **Võru** on 1 February and **Pechory** three days later. The Estonian territory was cleared of enemy troops and the military activity moved onto Latvian and Russian areas.

L**ate winter battles on the southern front.** The military success of the Estonian army made the commanders of the Red Army reconsider their earlier views. In February, 75,000 to 80,000 soldiers were assembled to fight against Estonia. On the Pskov line an Estonian Red Army was formed, mainly consisting of Russian units, but with the aim of proving once more that the war was a civil war in its character. August Kork was appointed as chief of staff of this army.

The main battle activities, which started in February, took place on the southern front, as its length (300 kilometres) and landscape (rich in hills and lakes) did not allow organisation of an unbroken defence line. From February to May, the units of Red Army, which outnumbered the Estonian National Army, frequently broke through the defence line, giving rise to critical situations. The Bolsheviks managed temporarily to occupy Petseri, Vastseliina, Räpina, Ruhja, Heinaste. Their advance guard even succeeded in reaching as far as 1.5 kilometres from the railway station in Võru. In fierce battles on the **Vastseliina-Orava** and **Rõuge-Haanja** lines the speedy advance of the Red Army was stopped.

Chairman of the Constituent Assembly August Rei speaking at the Constituent Assembly's opening session on 23 April 1919.

By mid-May, the initiative had passed back into the hands of the Estonian army.

At the same time it was relatively calm on the Viru front. Estonian soldiers built fortifications on the line of the Narva River. Without clear-cut attack plans, the Bolsheviks destroyed a relatively large area of Narva with their artillery fire. The Joaoru (Juhkentali) quarter burnt down, and more than 2,000 people were left homeless.

O**rganising state affairs**. The most essential task for the Estonian Republic was to **improve the economic situation**. The country, devastated by war and revolutions, was on the verge of collapse. The supply of grain for food lasted only until the end of February. The bread ration

Captured Red Army soldiers, 1919.

was reduced to 140 grams per person per day. It was not until March that the situation began to improve, when the first grain shipment arrived from Britain. Estonia also received a loan from Finland. Several states opened credit lines for Estonia to import their goods.

Economic improvement and success on the front increased the reputation of the government, and provided a better ground to fight "local" **Bolsheviks**, who presented a serious danger. The activities of the Bolsheviks were co-ordinated by Viktor Kingissepp, who had remained in Estonia illegally. An attempt to organise a rebellion in Tallinn in the middle of December 1918, which would have enabled the Red Army to occupy the capital of Estonia, was discovered in time and eliminated. In spite of this, the Bolsheviks continued to propagate resistance.

The most tragic event was the **revolt in Saaremaa** in February 1919. The inhabitants of Saaremaa had already been cut off the mainland for a long period (since October 1917). The economic hardships they had to face therefore made them receptive to the Bolshevik propaganda, which told them the government was a tool in the hands of the Baltic Germans. The Bolsheviks managed to initiate a rebellion among the fresh recruits. The punitive detachment sent by the government to normalise the situation had to employ extremely repressive tactics.

After gaining victory over the Bolsheviks at the front as well as in the rear, the government found it necessary to call together the **Constituent Assembly**, which would finally determine the future development of Estonia. Elections to the first Estonian legislature took place at the beginning of April 1919. The people"s representatives assembled for their first meeting in the Estonia Concert Hall on 23 April.

In the elections, the left-wing parties were successful. The Estonian Social Democratic Workers' Party *(Eesti Sotsiaaldemokraatlik Tööliste Partei)* achieved the biggest representation. The left-wing Labour Party followed it. The People's Party *(Rahvaerakond)* also received many votes. The Rural Union *(Maaliit)*, headed by Konstantin Päts, suffered a serious defeat. A Socialist, **August Rei,** was elected chairman of the Constituent Assembly. The first government, replacing the provisional government, was formed by **Otto Strandman** from the Labour Party. The Constituent Assembly adopted a Declaration of Independence of Estonia and determined the transitional form of government. The next essential step was to prepare basic laws. The agrarian law was passed in October 1919. In the middle of July 1920, the Constituent Assembly adopted the Constitution of the Estonian Republic.

Great offensive of the Estonian army in May 1919. In order to ensure Estonian security, the army command decided to move military activity outside Estonian territory. This would give an opportunity to leave the fight against the Red Army to Russian, Ingrian and Latvian national units, and to withdraw the Estonian regiments to the borders of Estonia.

The first to advance was the **Russian Northern Corps**. Estonian units gave support in the form of landings on the coast. Due to the low fighting morale of the Red Army, the attack was surprisingly successful. Yamburg, Gdov and Volossovo were occupied. An Ingrian unit, which operated within the national corps temporarily, occupied a strong fort at Krasnaya Gorka. The artillery located there gave them an opportunity to fire at the naval base of Kronshtadt.

Thereafter, Estonian units launched an attack near Pskov. Taking advantage of the renegade units of the Estonian Communist Rifle Division, the Estonian army advanced quickly, forcing the Bolsheviks to cross the Velikaya River and occupying **Pskov**. The territories inhabited by Russians were given over to the administration of the Northern Corps, which became the major military force in the region.

On the southern front another successful operation was carried through. Its initial aim had been to occupy Valmiera and Alūksne. The breakthrough by the Estonian cavalry was more extensive than expected. Due to the retreat of the Red Army, the distance of the advance was 200 kilometres, from Võru to Jēkabpils. Thus the majority of Latvia was cleared of Bolsheviks.

The *Landeswehr* **war.** The Provisional Government of Latvia, headed by Kārlis Ulmanis, had serious difficulties in defending its independence. As the national rifle regiments formed earlier had joined the Bolsheviks, they had to ask for assistance from the Germans. Thus the main defenders of Latvia became the Baltic *Landeswehr,* which consisted of Baltic Germans and the Iron Division formed of German volunteers. Their activities were co-ordinated by German General **Rüdiger von der Goltz**. He had far-reaching plans supported by the Baltic Germans. In April, the Germans organised a *coup d'état* and replaced the Ulmanis government with a German-minded government led by Andrievs Niedra.

After occupying Riga, the Germans should have turned to the east to follow the retreating Bolsheviks, but instead they turned north and attacked the advance units of the Estonian National Army near Cēsis in the first days of June. The aim of the Germans was to subject as large an area of Latvia as possible to the Niedra government. The command of the Estonian Army had an agreement with the cabinet of Ulmanis and did not recognise the puppet government of Niedra. They demanded the withdrawal of the Germans.

The armed encounter that took place at the beginning of June grew into a serious **military conflict**. In a fierce battle near **Cēsis**, which lasted for four days, the National Army beat back the regiments of von der Goltz. The day of occupation of Cēsis, 23 June, has since been celebrated as Estonia's **Victory Day**.

The Germans were followed to Riga and it was only intervention by the western allies that kept Riga from being occupied by the Estonian army. The armistice, which was concluded, forced the Germans to abandon their plans. It also marked a victory by Estonians over their long-time occupiers. In Latvia, the government of Ulmanis returned to power.

Machine gunners firing at the enemy.

A **course towards peace.** In the summer of 1919, military activity continued outside the borders of Estonia. Its main burden was borne by the Russian White Guard. Unfortunately the leadership of the North-western Army (formerly the Northern Corps) was not able to get the support of civilians, which weakened its military force, and continuous Red Army attacks forced it to withdraw towards Estonia. To prevent the transfer of military activity into Estonia, more and more Estonian military units were committed to the battles on Russian territory. The majority of Estonian soldiers did not want to risk their lives in Russia, the more so since the leadership of the North-western Army did not hide their resentment of the independence of Estonia. They promised to destroy the "potato republic" as soon as the united and indivisible Russian Empire was restored.

At the same time, the government of Soviet Russia expressed their wish to end the war. The Estonian Workers' Commune Council was dissolved and the Estonian communist rifle regiments were taken to other fronts of the Russian civil war. In this way, Moscow admitted that the War of Independence was actually a war between two different countries – Estonia and Russia – and as such, unlike a civil war, could be finished by a mutual treaty of the states. At the end of August, a telegram arrived in Tallinn from the Russian People's Commissar for Foreign Affairs, Georgi Chicherin, offering to start peace talks.

The **peace talks, which took place in the middle of September in Pskov, ended without any results as the entente countries still** hoped to overthrow Soviet power and were not interested in small states leaving the war. Other small states, such as Finland, Latvia and Lithuania, did not join Estonia in its efforts, but Estonian politicians did not dare to conclude a separate peace with Russia.

The **Petrograd operation of the North-western Army.** In October, the North-western Army launched an wide-ranging offensive in order to occupy Petrograd. In spite of increasing tension with the Russian White Guard, Estonian military units supported the attack from the flanks. The Estonian Navy carried out several landings on the south

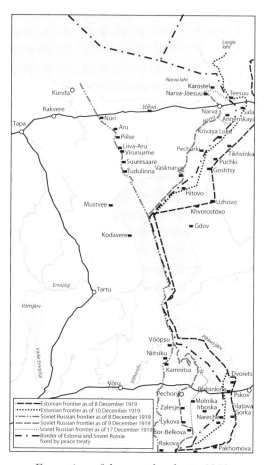

Formation of the state border in 1919.

coast of the Gulf of Finland, and its 2nd and 3rd Divisions were active on the fronts of Pskov and Pytalovo-Ostrov.

A counter-attack by the Red Army in the Pulkovo hills indicated the start of the defeat of the North-western Army. The demoralised Russian troops straggled to Estonia. The government decided to disarm the North-western Army. This relieved Estonia of an unpleasant ally, but also meant that Estonian military forces had to take over the defence of all the Estonian borders.

In October, an incident in Latvia demonstrated that the German threat had not left the Baltic countries entirely just yet. Under the leadership of **Pavel Bermondt-Avalov**, voluntary units consisting of Germans and Russians launched an offensive on Riga. They occupied

Region of activity in the War of Independence.

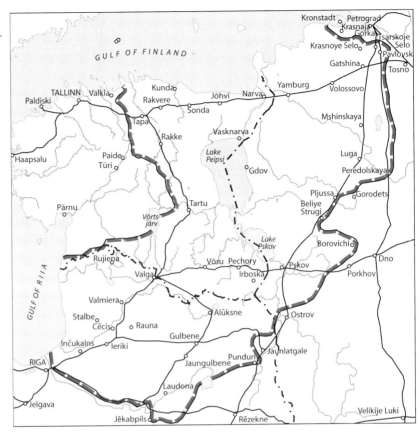

the south bank of the Daugava River. In this desperate situation, the Ulmanis government asked for Estonian help. Two armoured trains were sent to Riga and helped to eliminate the danger presented by Bermondt's units.

Defensive battles at Narva. By mid-November, the Red Army had reached the defences near Narva. In the battle for the positions, the Estonian army, which was in the minority and worse equipped, was forced to withdraw step by step. The Soviet Army headquarters had decided to occupy Narva at any cost and had assembled an army of 160,000 soldiers with more than 200 artillery pieces near Narva. The Estonian side also mobilised all its reserves and by the first days of December, the first Bolshevik attacks had been repelled.

At the beginning of December, **peace talks** began in Tartu. In order to support the claims of the Russian delegation, the Red Army began a new attack on Narva. By the middle of the month, the situation at **Krivasoo** and **Vääska** had become serious, because the Bolsheviks that had broken through the front were about to cut off the connecting routes between Narva and Tallinn and isolate the defenders of Narva from the rest of Estonia. By paying a high price in casualties, the Estonian army managed to eliminate the danger.

The Red Army made its last attempt to occupy Narva in the last days of December. On 31 December 1919, the exhausted regiments of the Red Army stopped fighting.

Tartu peace talks. After the Petrograd operation of the North-western Army had failed, the western countries began to lose their hope of overthrowing Soviet power in Russia. This fact was used by the Estonian government, which started preparations in November to continue peace talks with Moscow. The rapid conclusion

Head of the Estonian Republic's delegation to the peace talks, Jaan Poska, signing the Estonian-Russian Tartu Peace Treaty on 2 February 1920.

of peace was essential because of the economic condition of Estonia, as well as the military situation; the Red Army was once more about to attack the Estonian borders, while Estonians were exhausted by the war.

As the other Baltic states did not agree to start joint peace talks, Estonia decided to go for a separate peace. Russia accepted the Estonian proposal.

At the peace talks in Tartu, the Estonian delegation was headed by **Jaan Poska**, and the Russian side by Adolf Joffe. The first stage of the discussions (December 1919) aimed at agreeing an armistice. Besides ending military activity, this had to provide both sides with mutual recognition and define the future border line.

The discussions about the future border between the two countries were the most heated, as the Bolsheviks claimed the whole of the Pechory region and half of the Virumaa area (up to Kunda). The failure of Red Army attacks at Narva forced the Russian diplomats to yield, and on 31 December an armistice was signed which came into force on 3 January at 10.30 in the morning.

The peace talks continued in the new year. This time, several economic questions were under discussion, such as the mutual debts of Estonia and Russia, the Estonian share of the gold reserves of Russia, the fate of properties evacuated from Estonia to Russia, and so on. After a month of debate the Estonian delegation had achieved quite a lot. The Estonian financial debts to Russia were annulled. It was decided to pay Estonia a share of 15 million gold roubles from the Russian gold reserve. And the Bolsheviks promised to return to Estonia all the cultural treasures that had been removed to Russia, as well as to conclude favourable economic agreements with Estonia.

The peace treaty was signed on the first hour of **2 February 1920**. Estonia achieved a satisfactory border line. Soviet Russia declared that it would "definitely recognise the independence of Estonia and will give up forever every sovereign right Russia has ever had on the Estonian land and people...." All Estonians residing in Russia received the right to return to the homeland, and the Soviet government disbanded the Estonian communist military units, which had fought on the southern fronts of the Russian civil war.

The War of Independence, which had lasted for 402 days and had taken the lives of 3600 Estonians, had ended in a complete victory. It was only now that Estonians received an opportunity to begin building the Estonian Republic, which had been proclaimed two years before.

VIII The Estonian Republic (1920-1940)

40. The Economy in the 1920s

Basis for economic development. Estonia had been one of the best-developed regions of the Russian Empire. Due to its favourable location at the crossroads of Russia and Europe, new modern European production technologies, equipment and specialists arrived there first. The closeness of the huge Russian market allowed the development of extensive industrial and agricultural production.

At the same time, the situation of being **tightly bound to Russia** meant a dependence of the Estonian economy on the eastern market. The raw materials needed by large enterprises were imported from the east and the majority of their output went back there. The estate economy, which had become outdated from a world perspective long before, could survive in Estonia due to the indulgent eastern market consuming the timber, spirits and milk produced by the estates.

When Estonia became independent, its **role as a bridge** between Europe and Russia decreased, and the Russian market and sources of raw materials diminished. Economic indicators, which had been high in the context of Russia, were low when compared to European countries. Estonian production did not compete well with European goods.

Besides, as a **consequence of the wars and revolutions**, the local economy had become partly disabled. The evacuation and liquidation of industrial enterprises located in Estonia started in 1915. First they were taken to Russia, then in 1918 to Germany. The degeneration of agriculture was mainly caused by the fact that

The Estonian Agriculture and Industry Fair in Tallinn, 1920.

The Bank of Estonia's building in the Pechory region, built in 1928.

the men capable of work had been recruited and draught animals were requisitioned. The amount of arable land and the number of cattle had sharply decreased.

The **monetary system** had to be created from scratch. Several currencies were simultaneously in circulation in Estonia: Russian roubles, German marks, and Finnish marks. The Estonian mark, which had been introduced in 1919, was initially an unstable currency, and its reliability was undermined by continuing inflation.

During the War of Independence, Estonian incurred extensive foreign liabilities. The total sum Estonia owed to the United States of America, Great Britain, France and Finland was five billion Marks (the size of the state budget of 1920). The 15 million golden roubles received from Soviet Russia according to the Tartu Peace Treaty were not sufficient to cover the damage.

Economic rise at the beginning of the 1920s. The wartime decrease was followed by an extensive economic rise. At first, hopes were entertained of restoring the previous structure of the economy and developing ties with Russia. The latter seemed to be justified in the light of the political situation of 1920-22, when Estonia became the main economic channel between Europe and Soviet Russia. In these years, Estonia received extensive state orders form Russia.

The number of industrial enterprises grew rapidly, increasing from 2,900 in 1920 to 3,700 in 1924. Compared to the previous ones, these factories employed much smaller numbers of workers. The process was accelerated by the shortage of all sorts of goods on the Estonian market. Therefore a number of new factories were established in Estonia to meet the needs of the local population.

In order to establish enterprises, loans were used, preferably those given by the national financial establishment – **the Bank of Estonia *(Eesti Pank)*.** With expected profits in mind, everybody who expressed a wish to take out a loan received credit. By 1924, the Bank of Estonia had lent six billion marks. Often the authors of rather dubious business plans, or even swindlers, were granted a loan.

Soon it became clear that the great expectations of an industrial breakthrough in Estonia had been exaggerated. At the end of 1922, Soviet Russia closed its markets to Estonian goods and cancelled all earlier orders. Estonia was not able to sell its goods, which were produced using outdated equipment and technologies, to Western Europe. Products began to accumulate in stores, some factories were forced to restrict production, and some had to close down. The domestic market also proved to be too small, and many enterprises sharing a profile competed with each other to death.

In the second half of 1923, the economic situation became **critical** in Estonia. The Bank of Estonia had given more credit than it could afford and it appeared very difficult to reclaim the money from the debtors. In order to prevent major bankruptcies, the Bank of Estonia was forced to allow even more new credits. To create extra money, more notes were printed. The exchange rate of the mark, which by this time had stabilised, started to fall again. The government suggested the Bank of Estonia should utilise its gold reserves. By the start of 1924, out of the 15 million gold roubles received from Russia, only 2.5 million were left. It became clear that the economic policy adopted had brought the state to a dead end. The Estonian economy needed thorough reorganisation.

Land **reform.** In rural areas, one of the most radical agrarian reforms in Europe was in progress. According to the agrarian law passed by the Constituent Assembly on 10 October 1919, more than 1039 manors were nationalised, covering an area of 2.34 million hectares. The forests and swamps mainly remained state owned, while fields, grassland and pasture were given to new homestead farms.

In addition to the already existing 52,000 owned farms and 23,000 farms rented by the farmers (the latter were given to the ownership of the people who had rented them for years), 56,000 new **homestead farms were created**. This abolished the sharp social divisions in rural areas. An extensive class of propertied small-farmers appeared and the proportion of a paid workforce among the rural population decreased from 60 per cent to 17 per cent.

As well as the land, all agricultural equipment and livestock of the manors were nationalised. These were not sufficient, though, to supply all the new farmers, so they had to cope mainly on their own.

In rural areas new dwellings, stables and sheds were erected. In some places even whole new villages were built. The initial hardships were made easier to overcome by the very rich crop of 1921 and of course, by the realisation of the wish which had been living in the hearts of Estonians for centuries: to have their own land to farm. Even the initiators of the reform were surprised by its success. Initially they had been afraid that it would take more time and effort to bring the new farms into operation.

New **economic policy.** The reform of the economy started in the spring of 1924, when **Otto Strandman** took up the post of finance minister. The new economic policy introduced by him meant first and foremost bringing the external account of the country into balance. To achieve this, state expenditure was cut, imports were restricted, exports were increased, and obtaining loans was

The first electric train in the Nõmme suburb of Tallinn, 1924.

A farmhouse in Väike-Maarja, 1920.

made more complicated. In addition to these steps, the preferential development of industry was brought to an end. The most important branch of the economy became **agriculture**.

Although implementation of the new economic policy initially created complications, and the crisis appeared even to be aggravated, the chosen direction proved to be the right one. The second half of the decade could be considered as years of normal economic prosperity.

Agriculture. In the second half of the 1920s, the national interest in and support for agriculture grew. In order to support agriculture, the **Land Bank *(Maapank)*** was established, which mainly financed the creation of homestead farms. The number of livestock increased rapidly, surpassing the pre-war level by 1925. To be able to buy modern but expensive agricultural machinery, farmers created a huge number of **co-operative societies for sharing machinery**.

Restructuring of agricultural production took place. The leading position was still occupied by animal breeding, but beef cattle and fattened pigs, which had been taken to the market of St. Petersburg, were replaced by dairy cattle and bacon pigs. Estonian **butter** and **bacon** found a welcome niche on the markets of Great Britain and Germany from the mid-1920s.

In connection with the increasing importance of animal breeding, more attention was paid to growing fodder crops, and their acreage grew considerably. This was mainly done by restricting potato farming. There was no previous demand for spirits produced from potatoes. To some extent grain production also increased, but the majority of it was imported in the 1920s.

The shortcomings of agriculture were a considerable share of manual labour, a low level of mechanisation, and a shortage of pedigree animals and certified seed. Electrification had practically not reached the rural areas at this time. The large number of farms could also be considered a drawback, because it **split up landed property**. One-third of the farms were less than ten hectares in area and their owners had to look for extra income to allow their families to survive.

Industry. The large enterprises, which had been established to serve the interests of the Russian Empire and were not suitable for a small state like Estonia, were liquidated. Instead, new smaller enterprises and even new branches of industry were established. Factories relying on the raw materials found in Estonia were preferred.

Thus a native **fuel industry** developed, based on mining of indigenous oil shale. In addition, the peat industry was expanded and the two together enabled the end of the uneconomic destruction of forests and the extremely expensive import of coal.

The mining of oil shale also laid the foundations of the local **chemical industry**. At first, mainly oil was produced from the shale, but soon other products were added. Production of phosphorite increased. In Tallinn a galalith (a predecessor of plastic) factory was established, which was remarkable even in a European context.

Timber, which was plentiful in Estonia, was used by **timber industry** enterprises (sawmills, match factories, furniture works), as well as by **cellulose and paper mills**. To process agricultural products, numerous dairies, slaughterhouses and other food industry enterprises were established.

Many factories that had previously produced for the Russian market re-specialised on satisfying the needs of the **domestic market**. Thus engineering plants started to produce agricultural equipment, heating devices, furniture and road building machinery. Enterprises producing building materials supplied new building with bricks, cement, window glass and wooden constructions.

Compared to the Russian era, the level of industrial development remained somewhat lower in the 1920s. Several enterprises remained closed, and many worked at less than full capacity. This was because many enterprises could not find a market for their production. The quality and cost of the completed production did not allow successful competition in western Europe. **Unemployment** still remained a great social problem.

Monetary reform. In order to avoid the recurrence of the crisis that had devastated Estonia in 1923-24, monetary reform was carried out on the initiative of the finance minister Leo Sepp. Through the medium of the League of Nations, Estonia managed to get a foreign loan worth 28 million kroons from British banks. With the help of this money, the monetary and banking system of the Estonian Republic was rearranged. On 1 January 1928, a new unit of currency, the **kroon** (= 100 marks), went into circulation. It was pegged to the Swedish krona and guaranteed by a reserve. Simultaneously the Bank of Estonia stopped granting credits, and a new Bank for Long-term Loans was opened for that purpose.

41. Development of Domestic Policy in the 1920s

Political parties. Estonian parties cannot be considered according to the general definition, which says that a party is an organisation consisting of a more active part of a social group which aims to carry out a definite political programme. In Estonia, the parties were rather associations of people sharing views on some economic or socio-political matters. Often the policy documents of Estonian parties were rather indefinite, allowing no concrete conclusions on the political views of a given party.

The most right-wing was the **Farmers Party** *(Põllumeeste Kogu)*, which grew out of the Estonian Rural League, formed in 1917. This organisation, which initially had represented professional interests of rural people, gradually changed into a party of wealthy farmers and members of the urban bourgeoisie involved with agriculture. Its members shared an interest in promoting agriculture through the advancement of big farms. The leaders of the party were Konstantin Päts, Johan Laidoner, Jaan Teemant, and Jaan Hünerson.

The oldest of the parties was the **Estonian People's Party** *(Eesti Rahvaerakond)*, led by Jaan Tõnisson. It mainly united South Estonian national groups, including representatives of the

In the beginning of the 1920s, the facade of the Riigikogu *building was built in the inner courtyard of Toompea castle.*

intelligentsia, the urban bourgeoisie and peasants. It was a moderate liberal party, united by the idea of accentuating nationalism. Among the prominent members of the People's Party were such people as Jaan Poska, Jüri Jaakson, and Jakob Vestholm.

In 1919, a **Christian People's Party** *(Kristlik Rahvaerakond)* separated from the People's Party. This united a more clerical part of the population who were not satisfied with the weakening role of the church and the weakening of Christian morale. In the second half of the decade, the proportion of Christians decreased and soon the party became mainly the defender of the rights and property of congregations. This tendency was fostered by the leading position of clergymen (Johan Kõpp, Hugo Rahamägi, and Jaan Lattik) in the party.

In the centre of Estonian political life stood the **Estonian Labour Party** *(Eesti Tööerakond)*, the social basis of which consisted of representatives of the petty bourgeoisie: teachers, civil servants, artisans, shopkeepers, and small landlords. The aim of the party was to raise the living standards of the middle classes through social reforms. Among the leaders of the party were Otto Strandman, Ado Anderkopp, Juhan Kukk, and Ants Piip.

In 1923, a **Smallholders Association** *(Asunike Koondis)* separated from the Labour Party. It brought together smallholders, primarily the owners of homestead farms. The party came into being as a purely professional association. Its ideological basis developed from the view that the only source of wealth for a state is agriculture. From that basis the party demanded advanced development of agriculture, especially of smallholdings. The leaders of the Smallholders Association were Oskar Köster, Rudolf Penno, and Otto Tief.

On the left wing of the political spectrum stood the **Estonian Socialist Workers Party** *(Eesti Sotsialistlik Tööliste Partei)*. This was a social-reformist party, typical of Europe, which saw its goal as the establishment of socialism in a peaceful way. They aimed to achieve a majority in the elections to parliament. When in parliament, they wanted to pass laws on social reforms. A considerable proportion of the members of the Socialist Party were industrial workers. Representatives of the urban and rural poorer classes also belonged to the party. The Estonian Socialist Workers Party developed two wings: the right wing was represented by August Rei, Karl Ast, and Aleksander Oinas, while the left wing representatives were Mihkel Martna, Aleksander Jõeäär, and Erich Joonas.

The organisation uniting the Estonian Bolsheviks was the **Estonian Communist Party** *(Eestimaa Kommunistlik Partei)*, which had become formally independent in November 1920. In practice it was led from Moscow as a section of the Comintern. In Estonia its activity was forbidden, therefore its members operated illegally.

As well as the larger parties listed, **small groupings** were active at different periods, such as the Homeowners Association *(Majaomanike Liit)*, the Tenants Association *(Üürnike Liit)*, the Demobilised Soldiers Association *(Demobiliseeritud Sõjaväelaste Liit)*, and the National Liberal Party *(Rahvuslik Vabameelne Partei)*. Among these were also extreme left-wing parties, which dissolved and re-emerged from time to time, as well as parties representing the interests of ethnic minorities, such as the Baltic-German Party *(Baltisaksa Erakond)*, Russian National Association *(Vene Rahvuslik Liit)* and others. None of these played a significant role.

T**he first constitution.** Compiling the constitution of the Estonian Republic became the task of the Constituent Assembly as soon as it started to function. After a lengthy period of preparation the constitution was adopted on **15 June 1920.**

According to the constitution, supreme power in Estonia belonged to **the people**. People were given a chance to execute their power through parliamentary elections, popular initiatives and referenda. Referenda could be held on the adoption of all essential bills. Popular initiatives gave people a right to make their own proposals for improving legislation.

Legislative power was executed by the ***Riigikogu***, a unicameral parliament, and its 100 members were elected by the people every three years. The right to vote was generally granted to all men and women over the age 20 (several western European countries granted women the right to vote considerably later). Elections were organised by proportional representation, for which not single candidates but lists of members of different parties were voted.

Executive power was performed by the **government**, which was responsible to the *Riigikogu*. When parliament expressed a lack of confidence in the government, the latter had to step down. The government consisted of ministers and the ***Riigivanem*** (State Elder).

The *Riigivanem* fulfilled the tasks of a prime minister, to which were added some functions of a head of state, such as representing the state at various official events. The Constituent Assembly had considered establishing the post of a president of Estonia, who would be empowered to arbitrate disagreements between the *Riigikogu* and the government. The left-wing representatives turned down this suggestion for fear of concentrating too much power in the hands of one person. The *Riigivanem* could not play an arbitrating role, as he depended on the support of the parliament.

Local governments (county, town, settlement and parish councils and governments) were very independent in deciding local affairs.

The constitution established wide **civil rights**. The most essential of these was complete equality of the citizens before the law, regardless of their nationality, gender, religion, property status, and so on. The constitution also guaranteed the inviolability of personal liberty, the sanctity of the home, freedom of unions, meetings, conscience, religion and expression of personal ideas in words, as well as the right of private property and the freedom to strike. It should be noted that the constitutional rights did not extend over the whole territory of Estonia. In Tallinn, in frontier areas and around the railways a **state of emergency** was valid which allowed the restriction of several rights guaranteed by the constitution. The state of emergency had been intended to be temporary, but remained until 1934 when it was made nation-wide.

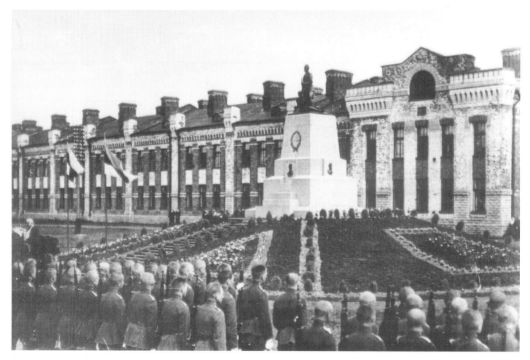

The 16 September 1928 unveiling of the memorial to cadets that perished on the 1 December 1924 Communist revolt.

Development of Domestic Policy in the 1920s

Arms used by the revolters.

How was Estonia governed? In 1920, the first *Riigikogu* was elected. By that time the left-wing euphoria was disappearing and the Socialists, who had dominated the Constituent Assembly, lost their leading position. The Farmers Party and centrist groupings increased their representation. This trend lasted for the whole decade.

Centrist parties received more than one-third of the votes, which were split between numerous small parties. The left-wing parties usually collected about 30 per cent of the votes, the lion's share of which received by the Social Democrats. Somewhat fewer votes (21-24 per cent) were received by the farmers parties.

The plethora of parties meant that none of them were able to form a strong government alone. The only type of government that could come under discussion was a **coalition government** that usually included at least three parties, but most likely four or five. In concluding coalition agreements temporary compromises were made, which often brought the parties to disagreements and cabinet crises.

In the years 1921 to 1931, Estonia had 11 cabinets. The average life span of a cabinet was about 11 months. Considering how young democracy in Estonia was, this was not a bad achievement. Even so, several changes of cabinet took place considering not the interests of the state as a whole, but those of a certain party who were interested in getting more power within the cabinet. This kind of action caused dissatisfaction with the parties among the people.

The struggle against enemies of the state. The greatest problem at the beginning of the decade was counter-activity to Estonian independence. The forces involved with this were the following: 1) Russian emigrants who dreamt of restoring the Russian Empire and denied the independence of all small nations; 2) The Baltic-German nobility who wanted their previous privileges and economic supremacy returned; 3) communists who were backed by the Comintern and the government of the Soviet Union.

It was the illegal activities of the **communists** that presented the greatest danger. The Estonian Communist Party acted according to commands arriving from Moscow and was supported by them. The programme of the Estonian Communist Party advocated the overthrow of the Estonian government, the establishment of Soviet power in Estonia, and joining the Soviet Union. At the beginning of the decade, local communists enjoyed great success on the basis of the post-war economic difficulties. The generally democratic slogans they used – pay rises, shortening of the working day, creating a system of pension and health insurance, cancelling the state of emergency – won support from the poorer layers of the population. Many communists made use of the lists of other parties to get into the *Riigikogu* and the councils of the bigger towns. This provided them with wider opportunities to spread their propaganda.

While in public the Communists claimed only the improvement of living standards of the working people, illegally the Estonian Communist Party prepared to take power. A revolt took place on **1 December 1924**. About 300 armed fighters attacked government offices, communication centres and military units in Tallinn. As the workers did not support the rioters and the soldiers remained loyal to the government, the *coup d'état* attempt was put down in a couple of hours. It happened so quickly that the revolters were not able to contact Moscow for help. Therefore the planned invasion of Estonia by the Red Army did not happen and the conspiracy was successfully crushed. It still claimed the lives of 21 innocent citizens and 20 revolters. The number of those executed by military tribunal was also large.

Increase in political stability. The revolt became a self-destructive act for the Estonian Communist Party, as people turned away from their violence. At the end of the decade the party had only about 300 members, half of whom were jailed.

The realisation of the danger from the communists made the parties assemble more tightly and temporarily forget their disagreements with each other. In order to fight the anti-state forces, a law of defence of the regime was adopted and the **Eesti Kaitseliit** (Estonian Defence League), a voluntary armed organisation of citizens, was restored. In order to involve ethnic minorities, a law of cultural autonomy was passed, which gave the representatives of other nationalities residing in Estonia rich opportunities to solve their ethnic-cultural problems. The international position of Estonia was strengthened by the decision to compensate the Baltic-German barons for their landed property that had been nationalised.

As a result of the above-mentioned steps and the overcoming of economic hardships, the domestic policy of Estonia stabilised considerably by the end of the decade. No further upheavals were anticipated.

In the 1920s, Estonia managed to get rid of the Russian economic inheritance and develop an economic structure meeting the needs of an independent state. Integration of the Estonian economy into the economic space of Europe began.

42. The Years of Depression

Economic crisis. The first manifestations of the world-wide Depression, which broke out at the end of 1929, reached Estonia the following year. In the conditions of a crisis of overproduction, competition on the world markets increased. There were more goods on offering than there were buyers and therefore prices fell. Although the quantity of Estonian exports even grew in the following years, the income received from them decreased considerably.

As the main Estonian export articles were foodstuffs, the crisis first affected **agriculture**. In addition to the fall in prices, European countries started to restrict the import of agricultural products and the market for Estonian goods became smaller. Due to surplus production, prices on the domestic market started to fall too. The income of the farmers sharply decreased, and many poorer farms went bankrupt. The same processes took place in **industry**. In addition to the marketing hardships and fall in prices, the domestic market declined rapidly, because the purchasing power of the people weakened. Many enterprises reduced production, shortened the working day or closed down

The balance of Estonian **foreign trade** became negative and the state budget went out of balance. Especially harsh was the influence of the British pound and, following its example, many other foreign currencies, including Swedish krona, gave up the gold standard. In the *Riigikogu*, fierce debates broke out about devaluation of the Estonian kroon. Due to ignorance, the opposition to devaluation lasted for a long time and preservation of the previous gold standard had a negative effect on the Estonian economy.

The living standards of the people worsened. The closure of enterprises brought with it extensive growth of **unemployment**. In order to prevent a social explosion, relief works were organised for the unemployed to erect various public buildings. The general cost of living went up, and the income of all classes of the population fell. This caused the growth of discontent, and people started to look for those who were guilty of causing the situation.

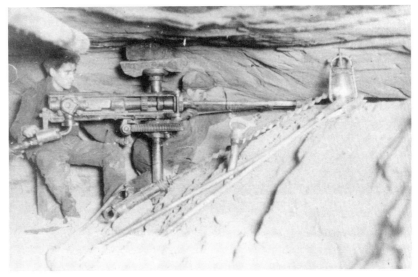

Drillers at work in a oil shale mine in Kohtla-Järve, 1930.

The co-operative meat market "Võhma Eksporttapamajad" in 1930.

Crisis of domestic policy. The blame for the poor living conditions was put upon the political parties.

More and more discussions were held on corruption among the parties, on placing party interests above national interests, on artificially bringing about and deliberately extending cabinet crises. The terms employed reflected the attitude of the people: "crisis making" (kriisitamine), "horse-trading" (lehmakauplemine), "having a finger in the state pie" (riigipiruka jagamine).

In 1931, an attempt was made to improve the situation by the **consolidation of parties**. In the conditions of economic crisis, where antagonism between town and country appeared very sharp, the Farmers Party and Smallholders Association merged in order to get an absolute majority in the new parliament. The example set by the farmers was followed by the centrist parties: the People's Party, Christian People's Party and Labour Party formed the National Centre Party *(Rahvuslik Keskerakond)*. The united farmers won the 1932 elections into the fifth *Riigikogu*, but their predominance was not absolute. Alongside them two larger groupings continued to operate: the centrists and the socialists. In order to form a government, a coalition was still needed.

A campaign for changing the constitution. Beside the multitude of parties, an inappropriate constitution was seen as a reason for all the trouble Estonia was going through. The representatives of the Farmers Party criticised the constitution extremely severely. They proposed a new constitution as early as the middle of the 1920s. They suggested the establishment of a post of president alongside the *Riigikogu* and the government, which would reduce the role of parliament in making important decisions on matters of state. They stated that the *Riigikogu* had accumulated too great a power in its hands, which was the reason why governments were not able to improve the situation in the country. It was believed that enforcing a presidential institution would bring Estonia out of the crisis, as the president would become a balancing power in conflicts between the government and the *Riigikogu*.

Freedom fighters. In 1929 the **Central League of Veterans of the Estonian War of Independence** (Eesti Vabadussõjalaste Keskliit) was founded from organisations of veterans of the War of Independence. Its initial aims were to improve the economic situation of its members, to record memories of the war and to preserve the spirit of the days of the struggle for independence. In the torment of crises besetting Estonia, the Veterans could not remain neutral, but became involved in the political struggle. At their second conference in 1931, they decided to exert pressure on the parliament and government to act on the suggestion concerning changing the constitution.

A year later, the Veterans decided to allow membership to people who had not fought in the War of Independence but supported their guiding ideas. From there on a stormy development of the League of Veterans of the Estonian War of Independence began, with an essential role played by their uncompromising fight against the parties.

The Veterans made use of the people's state of mind and criticised the politics of corruption. They demanded a reform of the governmental system of the country. In the conditions of severe economic recession their sentiments found widespread support from the people. The Association of Veterans became the biggest political organisation in Estonia. It had more members (over 20,000) than all the parties combined.

The general mood within the association became more and more radical. They considered the draft of the new constitution worked out by the parliament to be too moderate. They decided to compose their own project, which would give the future head of the state more extensive rights.

The formal head of the League of Veterans was retired General **Andres Larka**. The real leader of the association was actually by **Artur Sirk** (1900-1937).

While still a schoolboy, Artur Sirk had volunteered for the War of Independence, in which he was commissioned. After the war he graduated from the Faculty of Law at Tartu University and worked as a lawyer in Tallinn.

The movement of the Veterans has been characterised as an Estonian version of the movement propagating an authoritarian regime, typical in Europe between the two world wars (for example the Italian Fascist, Nazi, Latvia's Perkonkrusts (Fire Cross), and Finland's Lapua movements). Indeed, leader worship, the propagation of national integrity, and preference of professional associations to parties were typical of the movement of Veterans. It brought demagogic accusations and made promises. However, it did not blindly copy foreign models, but was rather a massive popular movement which had arisen from the complicated situation Estonia was in and which gathered its strength from the economic crisis.

The aggravation of the situation in the country. The crisis achieved its peak in the years 1932-33. In two years, Estonia had four cabinets. The life span of each one remained shorter than six months. The duration of Cabinet crises increased continuously. Amalgamation of the parties failed. Parties split again, and the Farmers Party and Smallholders Association were restored. Many deputies left the National Centre Party and the Estonian Socialist Workers Party and continued as independent members of parliament. As the result the fragmentation of the parliament increased.

In August 1932, the **first referendum** was carried out to adopt a draft constitution compiled by the *Riigikogu*. The proposal only just failed (334,000 "yes" votes and 345,000 "no"), because of the active counter-propaganda by the Socialists and Veterans.

The congress of the League of Veterans of the War of Independence in the Estonia concert hall.

Artur Sirk leading a march by the Veterans in the summer of 1932.

A couple of months later the Veterans submitted their proposal for a constitution to parliament. They demanded a referendum on their proposal. The parliament preferred its own failed version. They amended and improved it and put it to the vote for the second time. In conditions where the popularity of Veterans was growing increasingly and the crisis was deepening, the amended version of the constitution failed again in the **second referendum** in June 1933. The number of its supporters had more than halved.

Disagreements between different political forces increased. Several parties formed paramilitary security groups. The result was clashes at meetings, for which the Veterans and Socialists were especially notorious.

The government formed by Jaan Tõnisson in 1933 became extremely unpopular. One scandal was followed by another. Minor problems were frequently deliberately inflated, often these were false accusations from the opposition. Rumours spread about an approaching *coup d'état*.

In August the government had no option but to introduce **a state of national emergency**. The political freedom of the people was restricted and several organisations were disbanded, including the League of Veterans of the Estonian War of Independence. Due to the steps the government took, the situation seemingly calmed down a bit. In reality the authority of the government decreased even more and people's attitude to the measures taken was overtly disdainful.

P**reconditions for normalising the situation.** In October 1933, the time arrived to put the proposed constitution compiled by the Veterans to the vote. In the **third referendum** it achieved a clear victory, getting 417,000 affirmative and 157,000 negative votes.

Jaan Tõnisson's government resigned after it had cancelled the state of national emergency. A **transitional government** was formed of neutral specialists headed by Konstantin Päts.

In January 1934 the **new constitution** became valid.

According to the constitution, the power of the head of state had to be increased. It was not the position of a prime minister appointed by the parliament. The head of the state was now elected by popular vote for five years. The president was given powers to veto the laws passed by parliament and to dissolve parliament prior to the end of its term of office.

Legislative power still remained with the single-chamber *Riigikogu*. The term of office of parliament was extended, but the number of members was reduced. The government, which had executive power, had to have the confidence of both the president and the parliament.

In order to validate the constitution, parliamentary and presidential elections had to be held in April 1934. The following were put forward as presidential candidates: Johan Laidoner by the Smallholders Association, Konstantin Päts by the Farmers Party, August Rei by the Socialists and Andres Larka by the League of Estonian Veterans, which had reassembled after the state of national emergency was abolished.

At the elections to local governments, which took place at the end of the year, the Veterans were successful. Their representations were the biggest in several town councils. In rural areas they were outnumbered by the Farmers Party. The achievement gave enthusiasm to the Veterans, who set their goal as winning a majority in the *Riigikogu*.

The **election campaign** became very vigorous. There was not a single participant who would not throw mud at opponents. As this took place in the context of the pre-election propaganda campaign, it was believed that after the elections the situation would return to normal and the crisis would be overcome.

The **economic crisis** was about to settle. This was mainly due to the decision made by the Tõnisson government in summer 1933 to devalue the Estonian kroon by 35 per cent. This step, which was severely criticised by the opponents of Jaan Tõnisson, actually helped Estonia to overcome the economic crisis.

43. The Period of Silence

Coup d'état. The huge popularity of the League of Veterans allowed it to predict that it would win the parliamentary and presidential elections. To prevent the Veterans coming to power and gaining control, presidential candidates Konstantin Päts and Johan Laidoner decided to stage a *coup d'état*. On the afternoon of **12 March 1934**, the Military Academy and the Estonian Defence League took the centre of Tallinn and Toompea under their control and surrounded the buildings belonging to the Veterans. The officials of the political police carried out a thorough search and arrested everybody present. Simultaneously members of the League of Veterans were arrested all over the country. Altogether 400 people were jailed.

In the evening the government, following a request by Konstantin Päts, introduced **a state of national emergency** and appointed General Laidoner commander-in-chief. The new commander-in-chief disbanded the organisations of the Veterans and forbade political meetings and demonstrations.

The reason given for all these measures was the alleged violent plans of the Veterans to seize power. Another excuse was the "mental disease" of the Estonian people, caused by the propaganda of Veterans and not allowing the people to be considered the supreme power any more.

Subsequently, the elections were postponed until the end of the state of national emergency. The mandates of the Veterans in local governments were cancelled. Simultaneously a **purge** was carried out **in the state bureaucracy,** and the earlier attitude of the people to the Veterans became decisive. Beside the members of the League of Veterans, all people who were not personally acceptable to the new leaders were sacked. As parliament went into its summer holidays, all legislative power was concentrated in the hands of the government. To improve legislation, decrees of the head of the state were issued. The approval of parliament was not even asked for.

The period of silence begins. In the autumn of 1934, Konstantin Päts and Johan Laidoner started to reinforce their power. To start with, they appointed Karl Einbund as deputy prime minister and interior minister.

Leaders of the League of Veterans under arrest on 12 March 1934: Sergei Paul, Konstantin Hallik and Hjalmar Mäe.

Riigivanem *Konstantin Päts (centre) administering the oath of office to parliament members on 21 April 1938.*

Karl Einbund (1888-1942; from 1935 known as Kaarel Eenpalu) came from the Tartu region. He was a farmer's son. He graduated from the Faculty of Law of Tartu University, and participated as an officer in the First World War and in the War of Independence. Thereafter he repeatedly held the post of interior minister, and was also a *Riigivanem* and a speaker of the *Riigikogu*. Being a capable administrator, Einbund became the third key figure after Päts and Laidoner in defining the political direction of Estonia during the period of silence.

In September the state of national emergency was extended for one more year. This automatically postponed the presidential and parliamentary elections. When the **Riigikogu**, which reassembled in the autumn after their holidays, dared to criticise the steps taken by the government, the parliament sitting was cancelled by Einbund on 2 October. The members of parliament left for their homes in different parts of Estonia and were never allowed to assemble again. Officially the *Riigikogu* was not dissolved, it just remained in "silence."

In the spring of 1935, the activity of political parties was forbidden. Instead of them **the Fatherland Union** *(Isamaaliit)* was founded, which became the only party in Estonia and was directed by the government. Following the example of Italy, **corporations** were established, which had to unite all representatives of the same field of life and to mediate their thoughts and wishes to the government. Sixteen corporations were formed, including those for agricultural advisors, doctors and teachers, as well as landlords', domestic work and co-operative corporations.

State Assembly Speaker Jüri Uluots speaking on 11 October 1938.

Riigivanem *Konstantin Päts signing the decree promulgating the new constitution drafted by the National Assembly, 1 January 1938.*

Censorship was imposed, which meant the final shutting down of the opposition. Information approved by the government was distributed to the media by the **National Propaganda Service** *(Riiklik Propaganda Talitus)*. This also promoted so-called national integrity, organising various campaigns, such as translating foreign names into Estonian (before the campaign very many Estonians had German surnames and even first names), home embellishment, obtaining national flags, and so forth.

State control over different fields of life was established, such as trade union movement, youth organisations and local governments. By the end of 1935, the democratic order had been replaced by **authoritarian dictatorship.**

The fight against opposition. The core of the opposition was formed by members of the former Smallholders Association and National Centre Party. In addition, an opposition policy was followed by the left-wing Socialists (the right wing of the Estonian Socialist Workers Party co-operated with the government).

Any manifestation of life by the opposition was complicated. Political activity and formation of an organisation could not be even considered. The authorities closed down the smallholders newspaper "Maaleht" (Rural Daily). The centre of opposition in Tartu, the daily "Postimees," passed into the government's custody. The interior minister received power to restrict people's right of movement without judicial decision. Attempts were made to bribe opposition figures by offering them well-paid positions in public offices.

The opposition gathered new strength in summer 1935, when the **Veterans** were released. In court, nobody even tried to prove that the former accusations of planning a *coup d'état* were true. The leaders of the Veterans were put on probation for their activity that had endangered public order. The Veterans became very active. They openly criticised the unlawful activity of the government and demanded restoration of the democratic regime.

To be able to liquidate the Veterans movement, the political police staged an attempted *coup d'état*. On the night of **8 December 1935** the leaders of the Freedom Fighters were arrested at a meeting, which was claimed to have discussed plans for an armed uprising the following day. The trial that followed sentenced 133 people to jail for a total of 1,163 years. The people were told a story, which caused the Veterans to lose their popularity.

After the Veterans had been neutralised, the main centre of opposition was Tartu, which was the meeting place for the liberal intelligentsia. The **Tartu spirit** became a synonym for the fight against dictatorship. The efforts of the government to suffocate the opposition were not entirely fruitful.

The third constitution. At the beginning of 1936, Konstantin Päts announced that the time had arrived to return to normal, which required working out a new constitution. In February a referendum was held, in which the people gave the president the right to assemble a **National Assembly** *(Rahvuskogu)*, which would draft a new constitution. As the opposition boycotted the elections, the National Assembly, which assembled in February 1937, became a body loyal to the government. Therefore the constitution ratified on 1 January 1937 met all the expectations of Päts.

According to this constitution, the head of the Estonian republic was a **president** elected by popular vote for six years.

The *Riigikogu* was divided into two chambers. The 80 members of the lower chamber, or State Assembly *(Riigivolikogu)* were elected by popular vote. Of the 40 members of the higher chamber or State Council *(Riiginõukogu)*, some were elected by the corporations, some were members *ex officio*, and some were appointed by the president.

The **government** of the Republic, headed by a prime minister, was appointed by the president, based on his confidence in them. If the *Riigikogu* passed a vote of no confidence in the government, the president would have two options: either to replace the government or dissolve the parliament and announce early elections.

The people had lost their right of a popular initiative. The age limit for those entitled to vote was increased from 20 to 22 years of age. The proportional system of election was replaced by direct mandates. Civil rights were restricted. In spite of its seemingly democratic character, the constitution allowed a continuation of authoritarian government.

"Tractable democracy." The elections to the State Assembly were combined with the celebrations of the twentieth anniversary of the Estonian Republic. On the initiative of the Fatherland Union and National Propaganda Service, the Popular Front in Support of the Constitution *(Rahvarinne Põhiseaduse Toetuseks)* was founded. It put up 80 candidates loyal to the government, one candidate per constituency. Although the opposition was split and forced to be passive, its candidates received 238,000 votes against the 208,000 votes received by the Popular Front. But due to the principle of majority elections only 16 opposition candidates made it to the State Council.

As both chambers of parliament and the representatives of the local governments put up only one presidential candidate, the popular vote did not take place. In April 1938, Konstantin Päts was installed as **the first president** of the Estonian Republic. A couple of days later a new government took office. The prime minister was Kaarel Eenpalu, and Johan Laidoner was commander-in-chief.

As the head of the government, Kaarel Eenpalu began to carry out so-called "tractable democracy." The state of national emergency still existed, political organisations were forbidden, printed matter was still censored, and centralisation increased. There was an attempt to turn the *Riigikogu* into a formal legislative body. The parliament was allowed to work only on laws of secondary importance. The more essen-

General Johan Laidoner.

tial legislation was issued in the form of presidential decrees. Reversion from authoritarian dictatorship to democratic government did not seem possible in the near future.

The economy. In 1934, rapid economic development began in Estonia. Soon the pre-depression level was achieved and surpassed. This became possible owing to the favourable world economic situation.

Interference of the state in economic processes arose as a new phenomenon, characteristic of the period of silence. This was in the form of regulating the private economy through tax, price and credit policies. Several councils and institutes were established for registration of economic resources, research on natural resources, and modernising of production processes. The share of the state in the national economy grew, and state joint-stock companies contributed up to 25 per cent of Estonian industrial production.

Industry went through an especially rapid development. The number of industrial enterprises grew, and their equipment improved. The number of industrial workers rose to the First World War level, but this time it was not due to the huge military factories. Estonia was about to turn from an agrarian country into an **industrial country**.

In **agriculture** development was indicated by an increase in the area of arable land, wider use of soil improvement, fertilisation of the fields, an increase in the number of animals, breed improvement, and plant breeding. The **co-operative movement** played a continuously important role in rural areas. The number of co-operatives involved in all types of machinery, dairy products, potatoes, eggs, and dairy herd testing kept increasing. Electricity arrived in rural regions.

The main **foreign trade partners** were Great Britain and Germany, followed by considerably more minor partners in Finland, Sweden and Latvia. Among Estonian **exports**, agricultural production was in first place (butter, bacon, and eggs). Timber and industrial production (textile, paper, and shale oils) followed. Among the main **imports** were industrial equipment and chemical products, as well as raw materials (iron, coal, oil products, and cotton).

At the end of the 1930s, unemployment was eliminated. The income of the people increased and the cost of living decreased. Living standards in Estonia exceeded those of several southern and eastern European countries, including Latvia and Lithuania, but fell far behind the developed industrial countries. Estonia had completely integrated with the economic space of Europe and continued rapid development considering the means available to it.

44. Foreign Policy

The recognition of Estonia. The question of the future of Estonia arrived in the international arena at the beginning of 1918, in connection with the increase of the danger of German occupation and Estonian aspirations for independence. The *entente* countries, which were interested in a speedy defeat of Germany, were benevolent to the aspirations of Estonia. In May 1918, both the British and French governments recognised Estonia *de facto*.

The final resolution to the problems of Estonia came at the **Paris Peace Conference**. At this conference, which lasted from January 1919 until January 1920, the victorious great powers were busy working out peace terms most suitable to their own ambitions and did not pay much attention to the fate of the recently independent small nations. Estonia was supported to the extent necessary to ease the fight to overthrow the Bolsheviks. Legal recognition of the independence of Estonia was avoided.

By the summer of 1919 it had became clear that there was nothing Estonia could expect from Paris. The head of the Estonian delegation, Interior Minister Jaan Poska, suggested looking for new solutions. First, ending the war with Soviet Russia should come under discussion. This idea was realised by the **Tartu Peace Treaty** signed on 2 February 1920. In the international arena, the mutual recognition of Estonia and Soviet Russia did not change anything, as neither of the countries was recognised by other states.

Somewhat more importance could be laid on the recognition *de jure* by the Finnish Republic at the beginning of 1920. On the other hand, the first attempt by Estonia to become a full member of the League of Nations in September 1920 failed as the application was rejected.

A change in the policy of the western countries came when the Supreme Council of the *entente* countries recognised the Baltic countries in the second half of January 1921. This was followed by *de jure* recognition by the majority of European countries during the summer. In September 1921, Estonia, Latvia and Lithuania were admitted to the **League of Nations**. The

The arrival of delegations to Tallinn for the first conference of the foreign ministers of the Baltic states, held on 30 November- 2 December 1934.

Latvian President Kārlis Ulmanis receiving the heads of the delegation to the fifth conference of the foreign ministers of the Baltic states, held on 9-11 December 1936 (from the left, Friedrich Akel of Estonia, President Ulmanis, Stasys Lozoraitis of Lithuania, and Vilhelms Munters of Latvia).

last of the great powers to recognise Estonia was the United States of America in the summer of 1922.

E**stonia in jeopardy.** After September 1921, Estonia joined the international sphere of communication as an equal partner. From now on Estonia could start finding solutions to the problems its foreign policy faced. The most essential task was to ensure the security of the country, which arose from the dangerous geopolitical position of Estonia.

Out of all the countries that had once fought over Estonia, the only states to endanger Estonia at the beginning of the 1920s were Germany and Soviet Russia. The first of these was weakened by its defeat in the First World War, but several attempted *coups d'état* which took place in Germany at the beginning of the 1920s provided reminders of the danger. On the other hand, Soviet Russia was ready to destroy Estonian independence at the first suitable moment, whether under the slogan of world revolution or the restoration of empire.

Initially, Estonia saw the way out in a **normalisation of relationship** with Soviet Russia. Considering mainly international interests, huge storage facilities were built at the port of Tallinn to develop Russian transit trade. The eastern neighbour was also promised some economic advantages. To a certain extent Estonia was prepared to co-operate with Soviet Russia on an international scale. In 1922, the Baltic states presented to Moscow a joint proposal for a non-aggression pact. In spite of all the attempts at normalisation, the foreign policy of Soviet Russia did not encourage the Baltic states to believe they had sufficient security guarantees.

Support was simultaneously sought from the **Western great powers**. Since the days of the

War of Independence, people in Estonia had felt an attachment for Britain. Therefore great hopes were placed on London. No agreement was reached, because Britain had too little interest in far-away Estonia. After the attempted revolt of 1924, Estonian politicians finally understood that there was no sense waiting for actual help from Britain. Nevertheless, a certain attachment for that country remained.

Baltic alliance. At the beginning of the 1920s, great hopes were placed on a regional military-political defence alliance to guarantee independence. Co-operation between Finland, Estonia, Latvia, Lithuania and Poland had started in the days of war. By the summer of 1920, a proposal for a joint defence convention had been tabled. Its realisation was prevented by a military conflict between Lithuania and Poland. From then on joint activity of the five states became impossible.

Next an attempt was made to form an alliance of four states, excluding Lithuania. In 1922, a new draft agreement was worked out. This time a change in the foreign policy of Finland became an obstacle. Helsinki tried to approach the Scandinavian countries and keep its distance from the unstable Baltic region.

The only actual step to form a Baltic alliance was made at the end of 1923, when a **treaty of Estonian-Latvian defence alliance** was signed.

Simultaneously an agreement was reached about future economic co-operation and finally the border between the two countries, which had caused numerous conflicts, was defined. Yet the defence convention between two small countries did not essentially increase the security of either country.

In the following years the Baltic alliance remained on the agenda, but it was never actually founded.

League of Nations. In the middle of the 1920s, the danger of military conflicts in Europe decreased and the international status of small states, including Estonia, was consolidated. When the situation in Germany stabilised, the likelihood of reactionary revolutions declined, as well as the threat to the independence of Estonia. After the failure of the 1924 plot, Soviet Russia gave up organising conspiracies. At the end of the decade Estonia managed to conclude agreements about solving the border incidents and a trade agreement with its eastern neighbour. In 1932, after ten years of negotiations, a non-aggression pact was signed with Soviet Russia. It seemed to be possible to develop peaceful relations with the eastern neighbour after all.

At the same time the League of Nations strengthened. It had turned from the "political chat room" of great powers into an important fig-

The first tank in the Estonian National Army (English heavy tank MK-V) in Tallinn in 1920.

The submarine Kalev in 1937.

ure in world affairs. From the standpoint of small states, the conclusion of the Locarno agreements in 1925 was especially important. It demonstrated that the League of Nations could develop into an effective factor to guarantee security.

It can therefore be understood why, in this changed situation, Estonian politics relied on the League of Nations. Estonia actively participated in the work of the League of Nations, joining all the agreements and declarations, which seemed to reduce the danger of war. The plenary meetings of the League of Nations were used to introduce Estonia and establish contacts with the politics of other countries.

Simultaneously, **rapprochement between the neighbours** took place. This was conditioned by an increased interest in Estonia.

Especially noticeable was the growth of Swedish interest. At Tartu University, a chair of Swedish language and literature was endowed, Swedish businessmen invested in Estonia more boldly than before, and mutual state visits at the highest level took place. In 1928 the head of state Jaan Tõnisson paid a visit to Sweden and in 1929 King Gustav V of Sweden arrived on a return visit to Estonia and Latvia. Close contacts lasted until the 1934 *coup d'état*, after which democratic Sweden was not interested in communicating with an authoritarian regime.

The mutual interest between Estonia and Poland was expressed by the visit of the Estonian head of state Otto Strandman to Poland and the return visit of the President of Poland, Ignacy Mościski, to Estonia in 1930. The conflict between Poland and Lithuania remained an obstacle to the relationship between Estonia and Poland, because the rapprochement between the two countries was interpreted in Kaunas as a hostile act towards Lithuania.

The international situation grows more critical again. The crisis in international relations began with the **National Socialists** coming to power in Germany in 1933. The victory of the supporters of Hitler meant a new rise of aggressive tendencies in German policy. An open course was taken towards revising the peace treaty of Versailles and militarising the economy.

At the same time, the inability of the **League of Nations** to solve international problems became clear. The disarmament conference, which had been a long time in preparation, failed. **Japan** and **Germany** first left the disarmament conference and then renounced their membership of the League of Nations. The international organisation was also unable to solve several military conflicts in different regions of the world.

The Western great powers did not dare to apply decisive measures to tame the aggressors. Submissiveness only increased the ambitions of the latter. For Estonia, the **English-German Naval Pact** concluded in 1935 was not good news. It gave Germany the right to increase its navy. Arising from this pact it became clear that, in the event of war breaking out, Germany could block the Straits of Denmark, which would leave the Baltic Sea totally under the control of Germany and the Soviet Union.

Another sign of danger for Estonia was that **the Soviet Union became more active.** In the years 1934-35 Moscow proposed various projects aimed at tighter binding of the Baltic states to Moscow. In order to achieve this aim the threat of Germany was stressed, along with the importance of joining forces as a counterbalance. When the Eastern Pact, which should have guaranteed the security of the Baltic states at both their eastern and western borders, failed, because of the opposition of Germany, Moscow offered the Baltic countries an opportunity to conclude pacts of mutual assistance. The pacts would have given the Soviet Union the right to establish military bases in the Baltic states. In spite of the seemingly peaceful offer from its eastern neighbour, Estonia did not trust Moscow's proposal and rejected it.

Next, the Soviet Union started to promote the founding of the **Baltic Triple Alliance,** hoping to influence the foreign policy of Estonia and Latvia in a direction suitable to Moscow through Lithuania, which was rather friendly to the Soviet state. In September 1934, a co-operation agreement between Estonia, Latvia and Lithuania was signed. It foresaw close co-operation of the three states in the spheres of economy and culture, as well as regular meetings of the prime ministers to solve political problems. As to ensuring security, the agreement did not have any noteworthy importance. But the hopes of the Soviet Union failed, because the approach of the Baltic states to Moscow did not take place.

By the end of the 1930s, the Estonian situation had become unfavourable. The **danger from aggression** by both Germany and the Soviet Union increased, but there was no hope of help. The democratic western countries preferred a policy of appeasement towards the aggressors, the League of Nations was in a deep crisis, the formation of a strong military-political Baltic alliance had failed, and no foreign country was interested in Estonian independence to the extent of running the risk of war.

The only hope was to try to steer a middle course between the Soviet Union and Germany, in order to preserve independence. In 1938, Estonia, Latvia and Lithuania were declared **neutral**, following the example of the Scandinavian countries. This step had a mainly rhetorical value, as Estonia lacked the power to defend its neutrality in Europe, which became increasingly more difficult.

In these circumstances some circles, first and foremost the Estonian higher military officials, started **attempts to approach Germany.** But as the leaders of the state were not unanimous on questions of foreign policy, and Germany was not interested in Estonia as an equal partner, these attempts failed. When World War II began, Estonia appeared isolated and turned into an easy capture for stronger states.

45. Cultural Life

State cultural policy. The greatest achievement of the years of independence was in developing national culture, which flached European levels in development. This was the first time that Estonian culture had received attention and support from the state. The threat of losing the national culture through "Germanising" or "Russification" disappeared.

During the first years of independence it was hard to achieve a noticeable development of the culture due to the poor economic conditions. But in 1925, the **Cultural Fund** *(Kultuurkapital)* was founded.

The Cultural Fund became the main organisation funding culture in Estonia. The sums required were received from different taxes, and the income was divided between literature, music, fine arts, drama, the press, and sport. The decisions of the council of the fund about assistance, grants and prizes sometimes created bad feeling among cultural figures, but generally gave a chance to the outstanding creative people to live on their creative work, helping them to become professionals also in an economic sense.

The **professionalising** of culture was supported by reforming and extending the use of the Estonian language. This made education in the mother tongue available from primary school to university level. Preparation began of the Estonian top intelligentsia and specialists in all fields. The most talented ones received financial support from the state and when a need arose, were sent abroad to get further education.

The professionalisation processes were aided by founding **professional associations**. Among them the Estonian Writers Association *(Eesti Kirjanike Liit)*, Estonian Academic Society of Composers *(Eesti Akadeemiline Helikunstnike Selts)*, Central Union of Estonian Fine Artists *(Eesti Kujutavate Kunstnike Keskühing)*, Estonian Actors Association *(Eesti Näitlejate Liit)*, Estonian Engineers Union *(Eesti Inseneride Ühing)*, Estonian Teachers' Association *(Eesti Õpetajate Liit)* and other organisations were very active.

In the years of independence the number of **cultural contacts** with other countries increased and Estonian culture got rid of remaining German or Russian influences. Nordic, English and French cultural orientations became dominant. The Finno-Ugric kindred ties were strengthened. Simultaneously the achievements of Estonian culture were introduced more extensively. Exhibitions of Estonian art and performances by Estonian theatres and choirs were organised abroad.

Rapid modernisation of culture did not mean the decay of the **traditional popular culture**. It

The completion of the Tallinn Art Gallery in 1934.

Estonia's first art exhibition in Tallinn, 1919.

continued, became enriched and updated and achieved a new level. The participation of numerous members of the population in contributing to and creating culture remained active. In towns and rural areas, a tight network of cultural centres developed, and various societies, groups and choirs were active. Active publishing made books in Estonian available to everybody.

In the second half of the 1930s, some **negative phenomena** appeared in the cultural life of Estonia. Although the funding of culture improved, creative freedom became restricted. In the hope of economic prosperity several creative figures let themselves become involved in the propaganda of national integrity promoted by the state. Another part of the intelligentsia withdrew from active creative work, expressing silent protest against the signs of dictatorship. Although a general development of culture continued, the period of silence hindered its normal progress.

Education. The basis of organisation of education in Estonia was the principle of **comprehensive school**: the abundance of different types of schools was abolished and programmes of different school levels were co-ordinated. This allowed a transfer from a lower level of school to a higher one without additional tuition or examinations.

In the years 1920-34, the structure of the school system included two stages: a six-year primary school followed by a five-year *gymna-sium* (secondary school). Primary education was free of charge and compulsory for everybody. Secondary education was voluntary and chargeable. Tuition at both school stages was in the mother tongue, which guaranteed ethnic minorities **education in their native language.** The primary schools were all similar, but the secondary schools were often specialised, giving education in classical sciences or humanities, science, technology, commerce, home economy, or gardening.

In 1920, **compulsory primary education** was actually four years. Due to the economic hardships it was not possible to introduce full compulsory education, since there were not enough school buildings or teachers with sufficient preparation. Another obstacle was the lack of textbooks in the mother tongue. In time the situation improved, new schoolhouses were built, new modern textbooks were published, and in addition to the teachers' seminaries in Tartu and Rakvere, new seminaries were opened in Tallinn, Haapsalu and Võru. Transfer to the compulsory six-year primary education was possible in 1930.

But in the same year the first signs of economic depression made the government think of reducing the expense of the education system. Another problem requiring solution was the **overproduction of educated people**. As entrance to secondary schools was not limited, and only one-third of the graduates could continue their education at university, many young people with secondary education remained jobless. Their high level of education did not allow them to accept any job. This indicated a need to make the school system more flexible, and to increase the role of vocational education (professional training).

The 1934 **education reform** foresaw a transfer to four-year compulsory primary education, which would be followed by five years in an intermediary secondary school and then three years in *gymnasium*. The previous system was to be preserved temporarily only until the transfer was finished. The reform caused hard feelings among the population, because the length of free primary education, which was available for everybody, was reduced and the length of free-based schooling was extended. In order to reduce discontent, the six-year primary schools were not abolished. The problem that arose now was that the primary schools became a dead end; the graduates from six-year schools should have joined the course of secondary schools somewhere in the middle. New rearrangements were needed.

The second stage of school reform was carried out in 1937. In addition to the three stages of schooling, two directions became available. It was possible to choose between: (a) four-year primary school + five-year secondary school + three-year *gymnasium*; or (b) six-year primary school + three-year modern school + three-year *gymnasium*. The rights of graduates of both the secondary school and the modern school were equal (either of these was a stage of secondary education). The biggest difference between them was that in the secondary school, learning two foreign languages was compulsory, but in the modern school only one foreign language had to be learned.

The 1934/37 school reform gave secondary education in nine years. The *gymnasium* remained mainly for preparation of those who aimed to study at university. It enabled a reduction in the number of *gymnasia*. The options for specialisation were also reduced in the *gymnasia*, leaving a choice between two: humanities and science.

The school reform attached much more importance to **vocational education.** New vocational schools were opened, and their students were offered various advantages.

Whereas in the academic year 1924-25 there were 42 vocational schools in Estonia with 2,200 students, by the 1939-40 academic year the numbers were 177 and 13,000 respectively. At the same time, the number of secondary school and gymnasium students reduced from 18,700 to 16,700 respectively.

At the end of the 1930s, more attention was paid to improving the conditions of education. About 100 new schools were built and a number of old schoolhouses were renovated. But the negative tendencies characteristic of the period of silence also appeared in the field of education: school life became centralised and some activities were made compulsory.

From the concert garden of the Vanemuine Theatre, 1930.

Higher education. The foundations of Estonian-language higher education were laid when the War of Independence was still in progress. On 1 December 1919, the opening ceremony of **Tartu University** took place. In spite of the initial hardships, the university soon became a national establishment: tuition was carried out in Estonian, Estonians dominated among the teaching staff and students, and special attention was paid to national subjects. A huge contribution to the development of a national university was made by the curator Peeter Põld (1919-20) and rectors Heinrich Koppel (1920-28) and Johan Kõpp (1928-37).

In addition to the former faculties of theology, philosophy, medicine, law, mathematics and natural sciences, the faculties of economy, agriculture, and veterinary medicine became active in Tartu.

Initially students were accepted without entrance examinations, based on their certificates of secondary education. This took the number of the students to an unprecedented level: in 1928 there were 4,700 students. In the second half of 1930, selection of student candidates was introduced. This was partly caused by the fact that less than half of those who had entered the university made it to graduation. Due to the introduction of entrance examinations, the number of students fell to 2,800.

Technical higher education was offered by the **Tallinn Technical University,** which had developed from the Tallinn Polytechnic in 1938. This university had faculties of civil engineering and mechanics, chemistry and mining science.

Higher education in art could be acquired at the **Tartu Art School "Pallas,"** which was a private establishment, or at the **National Art School**, which was established in Tallinn in 1938.

Music specialists were also trained in Tallinn and Tartu. The **Tartu Music School** was private and the **Tallinn Conservatory** was a public institution. In 1938, the **National Drama School** was opened at the conservatory.

The **Military Academy** also provided higher education. It prepared leading staff officers.

Science. At the beginning of independence, the state of research in Estonia was rather sad. The majority of Russian and German scholars had left and the research societies they had headed were about to die out. The resources of Tartu University had mainly been taken to Russia. The young state did not have enough money to support science.

Nevertheless, the situation started to improve slowly. Tartu University became an essential centre of research. It included a number of research establishments, such as botanical gardens, a museum of zoology, an observatory, clinics of the faculty of medicine, and research institutes of the faculty of agriculture. The **research societies**, which traditionally belonged to the university, were restored: the Estonian Learned Society *(Õpetatud Eesti Selts)*, the Society of Nature Studies *(Loodusuurijate Selts)*, and the Estonian Doctors Society *(Eesti Arstide Selts)*. In addition to these, several similar new institutions were founded: the Academic Society of the Mother Tongue *(Akadeemiline Emakeele Selts)*, Academic Society of History *(Akadeemiline Ajaloo Selts)*, and Academic Agricultural Society *(Akadeemiline Põllumajanduslik Selts)*. The societies issued journals, yearbooks, and other scientific publications. International conferences were organised and those taking place abroad were attended.

In 1938, the **Estonian Academy of Sciences** was founded. Its tasks were to promote the sciences and to co-ordinate research. The period of activity of the Academy remained too short, however, to fulfil more essential goals.

Among the scientists of the Estonian Republic the following achieved **world-wide recognition**: astronomer Ernst Öpik, oil shale chemist Paul Kogerman, neurosurgeon Ludvig Puusepp, botanist Teodor Lippmaa, and economic geographer Edgar Kant.

The main attention during these years was turned to **national subjects**. The greatest achievements were made in studying the Estonian language, history, geography and botany.

As an innovator of the Estonian language, Johannes Aavik did very important work. Johannes-Voldemar Veski contributed to the orthology of the Estonian language and Andrus Saareste studied Estonian dialects. Outstanding researchers in comparitive Finno-Ugric languages were Julius Mark and Julius Mägiste. Folklore was studied by Oskar Loorits.

Historians reassessed the works of the Baltic German and Russian researchers, which had been meant to prove the positive role of Germany and Russia in the development of Estonia. History was also enriched by new original works. Two collections, each in three volumes, became unique proof of the work done by Estonian historians: "Eesti rahva ajalugu" (The History of Estonian People) and "Eesti ajalugu" (Estonian History). The best-known Estonian archaeologist was Harri Moora, while famous historians included Hans Kruus, Hendrik Sepp, and Peeter Tarvel.

As evidence of the maturity of Estonian science, the 8-volume **"Eesti Entsüklopeedia"** (Estonian Encyclopaedia) was published in the years 1932-37.

Literature. The period of stagnation which had started in the literary life of Estonia in the years of the First World War ended in 1917, when the **"Siuru"** group, a descendant of "Noor-Eesti," appeared on the scene, uniting such famous Estonian poets as Gustav Suits, Marie Under, Henrik Visnapuu, and Artur Adson.

In the first years of the 1920s, poetry dominated. The preferred literary tendency was still **neo-romanticism.**

In prose, the short forms prevailed, mainly short stories. The greatest masters of the genre were Friedebert Tuglas and August Gailit. Novels of the period worth mentioning included Anton Hansen Tammsaare's "Kõrboja peremees" (Master of Kõrboja) and Mait Metsanurk's "Taavet Soovere elu ja surm" (The Life and death of Taavet Soovere).

In the middle of the decade a break occurred in literature: neo-romanticism was replaced by **neo-realism.** Prose rose to the most important position, being mainly represented by the novel. Alongside the "village realism" of the earlier period (a trilogy by Albert Kivikas) "suburban realism" appeared, which was characterised by naturalism, as found in August Jakobson's "Vaeste patuste alev" (The Settlement of Poor Sinners). Neo-realism was presented in a wider context, using artistically more mature approaches, by Mait Metsanurk and also by Anton Hansen Tammsaare, whose great five-volume novel "Tõde ja õigus" (Truth and Justice) won widespread recognition. A noteworthy exception among the realists was August Gailit, whose novel "Toomas Nipernaadi" still belongs among the best neo-romantic works.

At the same period the success of original drama began. Hugo Raudsepp can be considered the founder of the genre. His plays "Sinimandria," "Mikumärdi" and "Vedelvorst" (Lazybones), which employed popular humour, won great popularity among the people.

In the middle of the 1930s, another break occurred in the literature of the independent period. Prose still remained in the first position, and the following years have even been consid-

Laureates of the literature awards from the Riigivanem, (from the left) Albert Kivikas, Johannes Semper, Friedebert Tuglas and Karl-August Hindrey.

The work of sculptor Amandus Adamson: a model of Germany"s liberation monument.

ered the peak of the Estonian novel, but circumstantial realism, which offered moderate artistic value, was replaced by **psychological realism**, which was artistically much more mature. Again Anton Hansen Tammsaare has to be mentioned for his works, along with Karl Ristikivi with his urban trilogy.

In connection with the propaganda of national integrity, characteristic of the period of silence, the **historic novel** achieved great popularity. It was successfully employed by the old masters Karl-August Hindrey and Mait Metsanurk, as well as by the newcomers August Mälk and Enn Kippel.

In poetry, beside the "Siuru" group a generation of young poets appeared who joined to form the **"Arbujad"** group, consisting of Heiti Talvik, Betti Alver, Kersti Merilaas, August Sang, Uku Masing, and Bernhard Kangro.

Fine arts. A very variegated scene could be found in this field in the 1920s. The former neo-romanticism was dropped, but there was no definite movement taking its place. The reason for this was the influence of very different schools on Estonian artists. The classical movements, such as impressionism and expressionism, were represented as well as the somewhat more extremist cubism and constructivism. The **grand old masters** of Estonian art – Ants Laikmaa, Kristjan Raud and Konrad Mägi –continued their activity. Alongside them a **young generation,** Nikolai Triik, Peet Aren, August Jansen, and Ado Vabbe, appeared.

Among **sculptors** Jaan Koort, who had won several prizes at art exhibitions in Paris, became famous. His most prominent works were portraits and animal figures. A while later, graduates from the "Pallas" art school, Anton Starkopf and Voldemar Mellik, joined the ranks of Estonian sculptors.

As the art public of those days could not afford big sculptures, the sculptors had to dedicate themselves to making small sculptures (busts, decorative pieces, and small figures). The exceptions were the monuments to the War of Independence. Their designs very often followed traditional patterns and therefore no outstanding sculptures were created.

At the turn of the decade the artistic life of Estonia settled. The previous multitude of movements disappeared and the stormy period of searching came to an end. **Neo-realism**, which was the ruling genre in France, became the major example in Estonia. Beside the artists mentioned earlier, Adamson-Eric, Aino Bach, Eduard Ole and Jaan Vahtra joined in. Eduard Viiralt became famous as a graphic artist.

Music. Relying on the earlier traditions, the musical life of Estonia developed speedily. In addition to the existing choirs and orchestras, new ones were formed, and the circle of people

Choir performing at the XI National Song Festival in Tallinn on 25 June 1938.

involved with music became larger. In order to promote musical life, several societies were founded, the most numerous of which became the **Estonian Singers' Association** *(Eesti Lauljate Liit)*, established in 1921, which included at least 1,000 local organisations.

The tradition of local days of music and national singing festivals had survived and even strengthened. National singing festivals took place every five years: 1923, 1928, 1933 and 1938. The last one, which was associated with the twentieth anniversary of the Estonian Republic, became especially powerful: 569 choirs with 17,500 singers participated, and the audience numbered 150,000.

Composers who had already become famous, such as Juhan Aavik, Heino Eller, Artur Kapp, Cyrillus Kreek, Mart Saar and Peeter Süda, continued to be active. Training of a **new generation** of composers could now take place in their homeland, in the higher music schools of Tartu and Tallinn. Among the graduates of these two schools were such famous Estonian composers as Evald Aav, Gustav Ernesaks, Eugen Kapp, Verner Nerep, Riho Päts, and Enn Võrk.

Original Estonian musical literature became more varied. In 1928, the first Estonian opera was staged, namely Evald Aav's "Vikerlased" (Vikings) Artur Kapp's Bible-inspired oratorio "Hiiob" (Job) and Cyrillius Kreek's "Requiem" became very famous. Several composers created symphonic music. Organ music was written by Peeter Süda. Numerous new solo and choral pieces were created.

In connection with the development of film, in the 1930s light music became popular. First it spread on gramophone records, but soon orchestras appeared which performed songs from popular films. In this genre Artur Rinne and Raimond Valgre started their music activity.

Theatre. In the theatre of the early 1920s a multitude of directions also appeared. The traditional methods of directing were abandoned, and bold experiments were carried out. At the beginning this kind of freshness was useful for the theatre, bringing plenty of people to watch the performances. When the general situation became more peaceful, the spirit of restlessness and search became more subdued as well. From the middle of the decade, **realism** became the predominant style of directing, pushing out former expressionistic ambitions. Nevertheless, the interim period had brought much refreshment into the theatrical life of Estonia, with new stage methods and directing patterns, and innovative designs.

In the period of independence, Tallinn became the main **centre** of theatre life in Estonia. There were three professional theatres there: the "Estonia," the Drama Theatre and the Workers Theatre. The "Estonia," which was headed by Karl

Jungholz and later by Hanno Kompus, was especially successful. In addition to drama and musicals, they also staged opera and ballet. The best actors of the "Estonia" were Paul and Netty Pinna, Hugo Laur, Erna Villmer, and Ants Lauter.

The **Drama Theatre** was born when the private theatre school of Paul Sepp joined the Travelling Theatre. The Drama Theatre paid special attention to staging Estonian original plays. As they did not have their own building (it was only in 1939 that they received the building of the former German Theatre of Tallinn), they toured over the whole country. The most famous of their actors were Liina Reimann, Aleksander Teetsov, Ruut Tarmo, and Mari Möldre.

The **Tallinn Workers Theatre** was founded in 1926 and its repertoire consisted mainly of plain popular plays. The director of the theatre was Priit Põldroos.

The theatre life of the provinces was much more moderate. The **"Vanemuine"** theatre in Tartu went through a crisis caused by the departure of Karl Menning. Therefore it could not achieve a level equal with "Estonia" or the Drama Theatre. Even more moderate were the professional theatres in Narva, Pärnu and Viljandi.

On the other hand, **amateur theatre** prospered especially in the provinces. In small towns, settlements and villages small troupes appeared, which were not afraid to stage even the most demanding repertoire. Of course it was done on an amateur level. Such amateurs were assisted by **Estonian Educational Association** *(Eesti Haridusliit)*, which sent their instructors and decorators to the spot, lent props and published plays.

In the years of independence, national film making also made great progress. About twenty or so feature films, which were made by local film companies, did not achieve a very high artistic value. On the other hand Estonian documentary films were highly successful. Documentaries were produced by "Estonia-Film" in the 1920s and by the "Estonian Cultural Film" *(Eesti Kultuurfilm)* in the following decade.

Physical culture and sport. Beside the existing sports societies and groups a large number of new ones appeared in the years of independence. All these soon joined into associations and in

Ida Urbel's figure dance team performing in Viljandi in 1931.

1922, the **Central Association of Estonian Sport** *(Eesti Spordi Keskliit)* was founded, which united all the associations. The best-known clubs were "Kalev" and "Sport" as well as the Tartu Academic Sport Club *(Tartu Akadeemilise Spordi Klubi)*. By 1940, the membership of sport societies had grown to 15,000. This large number of members allowed the arrangement of bigger festivals of sport to promote physical culture. This type of sports festival, the **Estonian Games** *(Eesti Mängud)*, took place in 1934 and 1939.

From 1920 onwards, Estonian sportsmen took part in the **Olympic Games**. The most successful were wrestlers and weight lifters. Especially popular was Kristjan Palusalu, who at the Berlin Olympic Games in 1936 won gold medals in both Graeco-Roman wrestling and free-style wrestling. Estonian sportsmen also won Olympic medals in the marathon, the decathlon and boxing.

Several **international matches** were organised in different sports. Mostly these were held with close neighbours, Finland, Latvia and Lithuania, but sometimes the competitors were rather exotic, for example, a football match against Turkey. After weightlifting and wrestling, football was the most popular field of sport. It was only at the end of the 1930s that more attention was turned also to light athletics, basketball, tennis, chess and shooting.

In chess, the world championship was achieved by Paul Keres. In shooting the Estonian team won the first prize in Helsinki in 1937 and repeated the achievement a year later in Luzern, thus proving their membership of the world's elite.

IX Estonia in World War II

46. The Period of Soviet Bases

The Molotov-Ribbentrop Pact. In 1939, tension in the world increased rapidly. Germany occupied Czechoslovakia and Memelland (Klaipéda region). Relations between Germany and Poland became strained. The western countries gave up their former policy of appeasement, and tried to conclude an alliance of Great Britain, France and the Soviet Union against Germany.

At tripartite talks in Moscow the Soviet Union suggested that they would only sign the treaty if they were given a free hand in the Baltic countries. The western countries were in no hurry to satisfy this desire. So in August, the Soviet Union turned to Germany instead.

On **23 August 1939**, the commissar for foreign affairs of the Soviet Union, Vyacheslav Molotov, and the minister for foreign affairs of Germany, Joachim von Ribbentrop, signed the Soviet-German **non-aggression pact** in Moscow. By a secret protocol of the pact Poland was divided between the two states and Finland, Estonia, Latvia and Bessarabia (and also, in a later supplement to the secret protocol, Lithuania) fell into the Soviet sphere of interest. For the right to start a war against Poland without any intrusion from the Soviet Union, Germany paid with the independence of the Baltic countries. Both sides of the pact were interested in acquiring new territories.

On 1 September 1939, Germany launched an offensive against Poland, which started **World War II**. In order to avoid getting drawn into the armed conflict, the Estonian government preserved its neutrality.

At first this policy proved successful and the war caused only economic restrictions due to supply problems; ration cards for petrol and sugar were introduced in Estonia. In diplomatic circles, ominous rumours spread about the Molotov-Ribbentrop Pact, but there was no precise information available about the essence of the treaty.

In the middle of September, the Polish submarine **"Orzel"** entered the port of Tallinn. In accordance with the law of neutrality, Estonia should have interned it. Due to the sympathy of

The conclusion of the Soviet-German friendship and border pact, 23 August 1939.

Foreign Minister Karl Selter departing Moscow on 25 September 1939.

Estonian soldiers for the Poles, this process dragged on. On 17 September, Russian troops crossed the eastern border of Poland and the following night the submarine escaped from Tallinn.

The leaders of the Soviet Union claimed the Estonian government had broken its neutrality by closing its eyes to the escape of the submarine. Soviet warships and planes repeatedly violated Estonian borders under the pretext of looking for the escaped submarine.

The treaty on bases. On 24 September, Vyacheslav Molotov put forward a proposal to the Estonian Foreign Minister Karl Selter to conclude **a pact of mutual assistance** between the two countries, according to which Soviet naval bases would be established on Estonian territory. In case of disagreement he threatened to use force.

On 25 and 26 September, the claims of Moscow were discussed by the Estonian government and commissions of parliament. At the same time planes of the powerful neighbour circled above Tallinn. On the Estonian borders the forces of the Red Army were assembled, outnumbering the Estonian army by some twenty or thirty times. The equipment of the Estonian army would have sufficed for only a couple of months and supplies would have been cut off. In addition, Estonia had fallen into **international isola-** **tion** and could only count on its own forces. In this situation the decision was taken to accept the requirements of the Soviet Union. A delegation was sent to Moscow, including the Foreign Minister Karl Selter, the Estonian Ambassador in Moscow August Rei, and professors Ants Piip and Jüri Uluots.

Vyacheslav Molotov announced that, as a Soviet vessel **"Metallist"** had meanwhile been sunk in Narva Bay, the Soviet government had been forced to decide to station 35,000 troops on Estonian soil to protect their naval bases (the Estonian army consisted of 15,000 men). After lengthy negotiations, all that the Estonian delegation achieved was a reduction in the initial number of troops. On **28 September 1939**, the pact of mutual assistance was signed.

According to this pact both countries had to avoid alliances directed against each other, and to provide mutual assistance in the case of attack or the danger of an attack. The Soviet Union promised to sell Estonia weapons on favourable terms, and Estonia allowed the Soviet Union naval bases on Saaremaa and Hiiumaa islands and near Paldiski. In a secret supplementary protocol, the number of forces was specified (25,000 men), the Soviet Union was given the right to use the port of Tallinn for a two-year period, and it was established that assistance would be provided only when the partner asked for it. Soviet leaders gave an oral assurance that the Soviet Union would respect Estonian sovereignty and would not intrude in the internal affairs of Estonia.

The march of the Red Army into Estonia. On 2 October, a Soviet military delegation arrived in Tallinn to specify the details of the locations of bases, as well as the process of the movement of troops into Estonia. In addition to the locations agreed to in Moscow, the representatives of the Red Army insisted on stationing troops inland. As a compromise, they received permission to station troops near Haapsalu and to build reserve airfields near Kuusiku and Kehtna.

On 18 October, the gates on the border were opened. By road and rail 25,000 soldiers of the Red Army, together with their technical equipment, spread over the territory of Estonia. The arrival of the troops, which took four days, caused some restrictions for local people, but no conflicts occurred.

Initially mutual relations remained cordial. The soldiers of the Red Army lived in closed territories, their movement was restricted and they were not allowed to communicate with Estonians. The Estonian side avoided any incidents. Minor conflicts, where they occurred from time to time, were quickly resolved.

Serious problems were faced by the people whose homes were on the territories of the bases. According to orders from the government they had to abandon their houses immediately.

Domestic policy in the era of bases. Due to the growing ambitions of Soviet Russia, the threat to the Estonian Republic could be sensed more clearly. The small clique in power since 1934 began to look for options for **increasing their number of supporters**. Kaarel Eenpalu, who had become fairly unpopular, resigned from the head of the government.

The formation of a new cabinet was entrusted to **Jüri Uluots**. He tried to involve opposition groups, from the Veterans to left-wing Socialists. The results were not promising. Only Ants Piip agreed to take the post of foreign minister. The steps taken by the new government confirmed that all hopes for the liberalisation of the situation had been premature: the state of national emergency remained, parties were forbidden, the press was subjected to censorship, and the *Riigikogu* discussed issues of secondary importance.

An essential event in the domestic life of Estonia was the **departure of the Baltic Germans**. On 7 October, the German government announced a decision to call to the homeland all Germans living in the Baltic countries, the Soviet Union and Italy, and ten days later the first ship

Departure of Baltic Germans.

full of Germans left the port of Tallinn. In seven months about 14,000 people left Estonia. As well as the Baltic Germans, many "Germanised" Estonians also resettled. The campaign strengthened rumours about "selling the Baltic countries" to the Soviet Union.

The continuing war in Europe increased economic problems in Estonia. The list of foodstuffs only available with ration cards lengthened. Prices of many consumer goods went up. Due to the decreasing options for export, the income of the state fell and unemployment increased.

These problems activated **left wing** forces, who began to establish contacts with the Red Army and the embassy of the Soviet Union. Communist activities were rejected by the Soviet Union, which as yet had a negative attitude to such undertakings in Estonia.

F**oreign policy in the era of bases.** After signing the treaty on bases, Estonian foreign policy became dependent on the Soviet Union. Although Moscow gave assurances that it would respect the independence of small states, it was clear that the fate of the Estonian Republic was in the hands of its eastern neighbour.

The war limited the chances of communication with **western countries**, more so since they actually lacked any interest or wish to negotiate over the fate of Estonia. The split was aggravated by the fact that the Estonian government gave the outside world inadequate and too little information about the real situation in Estonia.

Estonian co-operation with **Latvia and Lithuania** became more active. All three countries found themselves in a similar situation, having concluded a pact of mutual assistance with the Soviet Union.

The relations of Estonia with the **Soviet Union** became closer. In December 1939, General Johan Laidoner made a visit to Moscow where he was once more assured about the plans of the Soviet Union to develop friendly relations with Estonia. Several other delegations also paid visits to the Soviet Union. Economic relations between the two countries developed quickly.

The international situation of Estonia was complicated by the **Winter War**, which broke out at the end of November between Finland and the Soviet Union. The majority of Estonians secretly sympathised with the Finns and many young men illegally crossed the Gulf of Finland, in order to support their neighbours in their struggle. Officially neutrality was preserved. The Estonian delegation remained neutral even in the plenary assembly of the League of Nations, where a decision was made to exclude the Soviet Union from the world organisation. At the same time, Russian planes took off from the airfields located in Estonia to bomb Finnish towns. Estonia's mild attempts to protest did not receive any attention from Moscow.

The arrival of forces to Soviet bases in Estonia.

Occupation. In the spring of 1940, a favourable time arrived for the Soviet Union to do away with the sovereignty of the Baltic countries. According to a peace treaty concluded in March, Finland gave up any military resistance. In May, Germany started a decisive military action on the western front, occupying Denmark, Norway, the Netherlands, Belgium and invading France. In the middle of June, Paris was taken and on 22 June, France surrendered.

This was the period when **relations worsened** between Estonia and the Soviet Union. The number of soldiers in Soviet bases considerably exceeded the permitted limits. Moscow claimed an extension of the territories of the bases (the whole town of Paldiski was given up to the control of the Soviet navy). The Soviet press blamed the Baltic countries for violating the treaty of bases.

On 14 June 1940, Moscow delivered an **ultimatum** to Lithuania, demanding immediate replacement of the Lithuanian government and permission for the forces of the Red Army to enter Lithuanian territory.

On the same day, military **aggression** against Estonia began. The Soviet air force shot down a Finnish airliner that had taken off from Tallinn, the Soviet navy blockaded Estonian ports, and troops in the bases were put on a state of combat readiness. On 16 June, the ultimatum delivered to Lithuania was also presented to Estonia and Latvia. Eight hours were given to meet the demands. As there was no hope of military resistance, the government decided to yield.

On the early morning of 17 June, the forces of the Red Army crossed the Estonian border. Some 80,000 Soviet soldiers spread all over the country, all the bigger towns were garrisoned, and troops from the bases occupied Tallinn.

The occupation had actually already taken place when, on 17 June, General Laidoner signed the "**Narva decree**" at the railway station of Narva. According to this, control over all communications passed to the Red Army, political demonstrations and public meetings were prohibited, and civilians had to surrender their arms. The latter move was meant to disarm the *Kaitseliit* (Defence League). The brief period of independence of the Estonian Republic was replaced by occupation.

47. The First Soviet Year

The June rebellion. In order to co-ordinate forthcoming events, **Andrei Zhdanov,** a representative of the Soviet Union, arrived in Tallinn. Having established contact with local supporters of the Soviet Union, he assigned them to organise a demonstration on 21 June to support the demands of the Soviet ultimatum.

On 21 June, a couple of thousand people gathered in Freedom Square in Tallinn. They were factory workers, Russians from the Pechory region, and builders of the Soviet bases. The meeting demanded that the government, headed by Jüri Uluots, should resign (in reality the cabinet had already announced its resignation on 17 June) and a new cabinet should be formed. The whole event was supported by squads and armoured cars of the Red Army.

From Freedom Square, the demonstrators moved onto Toompea and thereafter to the Kadriorg Palace, where the president, who had come out to greet the people, was silenced by the whistles and noise of the crowd. Representatives of the demonstrators demanded replacement of the government. After their demands had been handed over, some less reasonable individuals, who had kept a distance from the organisers of the meeting, took the floor and started to call for revolution.

Next, some of the demonstrators moved to the Patarei Prison and released about twenty or thirty prisoners, among them some communists. Police departments, the castle of Toompea, government buildings, and the editorial offices of newspapers and radio were seized. The Estonian army, which had received orders not to intrude, was disarmed. The only resistance the rebels met was at the school on Raua street, where the communications battalion located there opened fire on them.

On the same day, meetings and demonstrations were organised all over Estonia, following directions from Tallinn. Nothing decisive was undertaken until news arrived from Tallinn.

New government. On the evening of 21 June, the new cabinet consisting of left-wing figures and opposition intellectuals was appointed. A doctor and poet, **Johannes Vares-Barbarus**, became the prime minister; a professor of history, Hans Kruus, was appointed deputy prime minis-

Johannes Vares-Barbarus

6 August in Moscow.

ter; and a writer, Johannes Semper, was appointed minister for education. Former members of the State Assembly were appointed ministers for agriculture, social and interior affairs. The cabinet did not contain any communists as yet.

The government's plan of activities, presented the following day, looked rather conventional: they promised to guarantee the rights of the people, increase material wealth, promote national culture, and develop normal relations with all countries. An oral promise was added, that Estonian independence and the system of government would stay the same, and that the land would remain in the hands of farmers and private property would not be nationalised. Those speaking were obviously unaware of the further intentions of the Soviet Union.

Directly after the June rebellion, the **purge in the state machinery** began. Higher officials of the ministries, the leadership of the army and police, and heads of county governments and town councils were replaced. In this way the key positions gradually went to **communists**.

Several organisations were closed down (*Isamaaliit, Kaitseliit*, and corporations). The leaders of societies of minor importance were replaced. The only legal political organisation became the Estonian Communist Party, which was still formally independent.

Incorporation. At the beginning of July, the *Riigikogu* was dissolved and early **elections** were announced. The new parliament was to consist of only one chamber, the State Assembly. In order to guarantee that the parliament would consist of people suitable to the Soviet Union, the **Association of Estonian Working People** (*Eesti Töötava Rahva Liit*) was established, which started an extensive campaign for its candidates. The election programmes of candidates in nationalist circles were prohibited.

In July, true Soviet "elections" took place in Estonia: there was only one candidate, voters were intimidated and votes were fabricated. The results were predictable: 92.9 per cent of the voters had voted for the candidates of Association of Estonian Working People. On 17 July, the results were officially announced and in the evening of the same day a big meeting was organised in Freedom Square in Tallinn, which proclaimed incorporation of Estonia into the Soviet Union.

At the first session of the State Assembly on 21 to 23 July, the real goals of the communists became clear. To start with, the Estonian Republic was renamed the **Estonian Soviet Socialist Republic**. A decision was made to apply for membership of the Soviet Union. The State Council began to work out the Constitution of the Estonian SSR and dismissed Konstantin Päts from the president's post (at the end of July he and his family were deported to the Soviet Union). The same session of the State Council decided to carry out land reform and to nationalise large enterprises and financial establishments.

The receivers of new land.

On 6 August 1940, the Supreme Council of the Soviet Union met the "request of Estonian people" and **incorporated** Estonia into the Soviet Union.

Reorganisation of the machinery of power. On 25 August 1940, the State Assembly adopted the Constitution of the Estonian SSR, which was based on the Constitution of the Soviet Union.

Legislative power was given to the **Supreme Soviet**, which was formed by renaming the State Assembly. This institution did not actually have real legislative power. The deputies just had to approve orders from Moscow. In order to manage the Supreme Soviet, the Presidium of the Supreme Soviet was formed. Johannes Vares-Barbarus was appointed chairman of the Presidium.

Executive power was held by the **Soviet of People's Commissars**, which consisted of 13 members. Their task was also to follow exactly the orders from Moscow. **Johannes Lauristin**, a communist, was appointed chairman of the Soviet.

The system of local government was also reorganised. Executive committees replaced town and county councils.

The constitution determined the leading role of the **communist party** in Estonian society. The Estonian Communist Party (ECP), which had formerly acted as an independent organisation, became part of the Russian Communist Bolshevik Party.

The membership of the ECP increased from 130 to 3,700 within a year. Part of the increase was due to the functionaries who had arrived from other regions of the Soviet Union, but the increase was also due to local people who supported the new regime. **Karl Säre** became the first secretary of the Estonian Communist Bolshevik Party, and the position of second secretary was held by an Estonian who had been living in Russia, Nikolai Karotamm. This system, where the leading post was occupied by an Estonian, backed by a Moscow emissary, became typical.

Next, Estonian legislation was replaced by the legislation of the Russian Soviet Federal Socialist Republic. It did not suit Estonian circumstances and therefore created a lot of problems. People's courts, typical of the Soviet court system, were established in Estonia. The Estonian police was replaced by the Workers and Peasants Militia. The Estonian army was reorganised into the 22nd Territorial Rifle Corps of the Red Army.

Economic reforms. The reorganisation of the economy started with **nationalisation**. Industrial enterprises, transport agencies, commercial companies, and financial establishments, as well as larger houses (almost half of all residential space) were nationalised. Only small trades and industrial businesses remained in private ownership.

The economy was subjected to **central administration.** In order to carry out the command economy, the compilation of economic plans was introduced, co-ordinated by the newly established State Planning Committee.

The **forced development of industry** on account of other branches of the economy began, which ignored Estonian potentials and needs. The extensive production process soon created the need to bring in a workforce from the Soviet Union.

In the course of **agrarian reform** a national land fund was established. This included land confiscated from the church, local government, and people who had left Estonia, as well as land taken from the big farms. A maximum size of farms was established, namely 30 hectares. As a result of redistribution of the land to peasants, unprofitable new small households appeared, which actually increased social antagonism.

As a first form of socialist **collective farming**, state farms were introduced in Estonia, based on reorganised manorial estates, and preparations for creating collective farms were also made. Centres were formed for lending machines and tractors, as well as horses. Nine collective farms were also established. Soviet authorities did not feel Estonia was ready for massive collectivisation yet. One precondition for successful formation of collective farms was to **impoverish the farmers**, using ridiculously low prices for compulsory state purchases.

The monetary reform carried out in November 1940, which replaced Estonian kroons with roubles at an exchange rate of 1 kroon to 1.25 roubles (the actual exchange rate should have been 1 kroon to 10 roubles), causing a sharp decline in **living standards**. It was followed by rapid rises in the prices of industrial goods and foodstuffs. Estonians became acquainted with another feature typical of the Soviet Union: a chronic shortage of goods.

Changes in culture. An immediate cultural revolution meeting Soviet standards was also carried out in Estonia.

The school programmes were improved, adding several compulsory subjects, such as Marxism-Leninism, the history of the Soviet Union, the constitution and the Russian language.

The majority of small magazines and newspapers were closed down. The numbers of copies of the few newspapers and magazines which were allowed to appear increased immensely. Soviet textbooks, translations of Soviet fiction, and socio-political literature, especially "The Brief Course on the History of the Soviet Communist Bolshevik Party" were published in great numbers.

The task assigned to the fine arts was to "get rid of the influences of the decadent art of deteriorating Europe" and to glorify Soviet power. The main "works of art" became propagandist posters and showy portraits of the heads of the Soviet state.

The repertoire of theatres, cinemas and concerts was replaced by work created by Soviet authors. The works of Estonian and foreign authors were allowed to be presented only to a limited extent.

Destruction of the earlier cultural values started: statues were demolished, some books were forbidden, amateur societies and groups were dissolved, and creative people who had fallen into disfavour were either entirely ignored or arrested and deported.

Repression. The first arrests had actually already taken place on 17 June, but after Estonia became incorporated and the People's Commissariat for Internal Affairs (NKVD) started to operate in Estonia, their scale became massive.

Up to the end of 1940, more than 1,000 people disappeared, including former political, military and police leaders of the country, businessmen, and representatives of the intelligentsia. They were convicted according to Soviet legislation for deeds committed in independent Estonia. The majority of them were sent to the prisons of the Soviet Union, and many were executed.

In 1941, the number of arrests became massive. People belonging to different layers of society were arrested, including workers and even Soviet activists. Nobody could be sure of tomorrow. Officially nothing was said about the arrests, which increased the fear even more.

The repressive policy culminated on 14 June 1941, when **mass deportation** took place simultaneously in all three Baltic countries. More than 10,000 people who were considered potentially dangerous were deported from Estonia. Adult men (who were in the minority) were announced as having been arrested and sent to prison camps, where the majority of them died. Their families were exiled. Nobody was actually prosecuted or sentenced.

48. The Theatre of War

Summer 1941. At the beginning of the war that had broken out between the Soviet Union and Germany on 22 June 1941, the Red Army withdrew in an unorganised way and in a hurry, suffering great losses. In two weeks, the Germans occupied Lithuania and Latvia and crossed the Estonian border at Ikla on **7 July**. Next day, without any resistance, the Red Army gave up Pärnu, Mõisaküla and Viljandi, a day later Valga and Võru, and on 10 July the southern part of Tartu.

Then the front stopped. As the German army command was aiming at occupying Leningrad, they sent only small forces into Estonia, which were not able to break the Red Army grouping located there. The German assault, heading from Pärnu towards Tallinn, was stopped at Märjamaa and driven back to Pärnu-Jaagupi. The troops heading from Viljandi to the north were stopped at a line of Vändra-Türi-Põltsamaa, and the Germans were also unable to continue the offensive in the Suur-Emajõgi area.

At the time when the front had stopped in the middle of Estonia, military conflicts became more frequent, with Estonians participating on both sides. The Soviet authorities organised **destroyer battalions** in order to carry out "scorched earth" tactics. When withdrawing, the destroyer battalions demolished industrial buildings, railways, and farms, and carried out raids and repression. As a result of their activity 2,000 civilians were killed. Beside communists and Soviet activists, workers and conscripts also belonged to the destroyer battalions.

The destroyer battalions were opposed by **forest brothers**. Already in the autumn of 1940, people had begun to hide themselves for fear of being arrested. A massive gathering of people in the forests started after the June mass deportation. Opportunities were sought to become armed and to exact revenge. The long-term goal was to liberate Estonia. In the first days of July, Soviet institutions, red activists and smaller

Karl Sigismund Litzmann (left) and Hjalmar Mäe (right).

units of the Red Army were attacked all over Estonia. Extensive encounters took place between the forest brothers and the destroyer battalions. The forest brothers occupied several parish administrative buildings. Local administrative units, which followed the pattern of the years of independence, started to operate. The forest brothers played an especially important role in the battle for Tartu. Unfortunately the activities of forest brothers were often accompanied by unjustified **terror**.

The standstill of the front forced the Germans to augment their forces. On 22 July, the German *Wehrmacht* launched an offensive from Põltsamaa in the direction of Mustvee and surrounded Red Army corps defending the Suur-Emajõgi area. Making use of the gap that appeared in the front, the Germans quickly advanced northwards. On 7 August, they reached the Gulf of Finland near Kunda. The troops turned east at Kunda, and ten days later occupied Narva.

The attention of the German headquarters was then directed towards **Tallinn**, which had become the main basis of the Soviet Navy in the Baltic Sea. After a battle from 20 to 28 August, the Red Army abandoned Tallinn. While leaving Tallinn, 53 of the 197 Soviet warships were sunk near the Cape of Juminda, either by hitting mines, being struck by torpedoes, or bombed.

In September and October, battles continued on the **western islands of Estonia**. Being cut off from their main forces, the units of Red Army could not put up prolonged resistance. The defenders of Saaremaa capitulated at the beginning of October. The Hiiumaa garrison managed to hold out until 21 October.

T**he German occupation.** In the summer of 1941, the majority of Estonians hoped to restore their independence with the help of Germans. It soon became clear, though, that the country had just exchanged its master, and sovereignty was out of the question.

Estonia was made a **general commissariat** subjected to the German Ministry of Eastern Regions. The highest representative of German interests in Estonia was Commissar-General Karl Sigismund Litzmann, who brought with him a number of arrogant German officials who did not know a word of Estonian.

Under the Commissar General, the **Estonian Local Government** was formed, consisting of Estonians but subjected to the orders of the occupation authorities. The Local Government was headed by the former propaganda leader of the Veterans, **Hjalmar Mäe**. Local administration was carried out by county, town and parish councils. Their leaders were not elected, but appointed, and in addition to the Local Government they were subject to the German regional commissars.

Massive **repression** continued. This started in the summer of 1941 with illegal forest brother actions, but became very widespread when the German Security Service was formed in Esto-

War refugees.

Tartu mayor K Keerdoja as the first to greet Harald Riipalu, the head of the battalion of the Estonian Legion in February 1944.

nia. Some 125,000 people were executed in the concentration camps of Estonia during the years of German occupation. The bulk of these were Soviet prisoners of war and Jews from Western Europe. There were about 4,000 to 5,000 Estonians among those killed. The people carrying out the repression were mainly Estonians.

The cultural policy, which forced "Germanisation" and National Socialism upon the Estonians, irritated people. The "Germanisation" appeared in a relatively moderate form, limited mainly to intensive teaching of the German language in schools. The main emphasis was laid on spreading **Nazi** ideology. Respective propagandist literature was published, cultural achievements of the "enemies" (Jews, French, English, and Russians) were not allowed to be even mentioned, part of Estonian cultural heritage was ignored, and the Nazi racial theory was promoted.

The first task of the Estonian **economy** became the supply of the German army and civilians. Meeting the needs of Estonia was considered a secondary task. However, the German authorities provided extensive material support for repairing the war damage. A large contribution to restoring the Estonian economy came from the **Estonian National Relief Committee**, whose main task was to take care of the families who had suffered in the war.

Building up **industry**, which had suffered through evacuations and war damage, began. Special attention was directed to the oil shale mining and chemical industry, which supplied the *Wehrmacht* with fuel. Mechanical engineering, textile, paper and cellulose industries were also developed.

In **agriculture**, each farm was appointed a compulsory sales target, which was not meant to corrupt the households, but to give the farmers an interest in extending production. This was even partially achieved. Although the area of arable land and crops was lower in 1944 than in the pre-war period, the number of domestic animals was greater.

The biggest disappointment was felt by those who hoped that the private property nationalised by the Soviet authorities would be **denationalised** by the Germans. The majority of industrial and commercial establishments were declared war trophies and were given to several German corporations having state monopolies. Even the process of returning residential houses was prolonged. Although the land reform was cancelled, the farmers did not become landowners but only land users.

General **living standards** decreased. The urban population had to face especially great difficulties, because the supply system in towns relied on ration cards. As the supplies received for the ration cards did not meet the needs of the people, a black market began to flourish. Many urban people travelled to rural areas in the hope of getting help from their relatives and acquain-

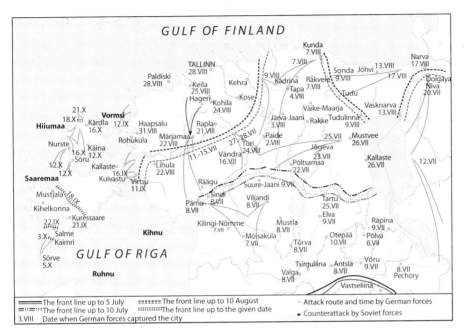

Hostilities in 1941.

tances living there. The situation was even worse for the supply of consumer goods.

Although the Estonians were disappointed in the Germans, no active **opposition movement** developed. The attempts of the communists to initiate a guerrilla war failed because of the lack of supporters. So only small sabotage groups of the Soviet intelligence forces operated in Estonia, but they were usually quickly liquidated.

The **nationalist forces** had no choice. Although they would rather have relied on the western countries, they did not consider it correct to undermine the military power of Germany. The defeat of the Germans would have meant the replacement of the German occupation of Estonia with a Russian one.

Estonians in the German army. The attitude of Estonians to the occupying authorities was expressed by the formation of Estonian military units within the German army. In 1941, voluntary battalions formed of forest brothers participated in action until Estonia was liberated. After that more than 40,000 men joined the *Omakaitse* (Self Defence), re-established by the German occupying authorities.

In place of the guerrilla units, in late summer voluntary **eastern and police battalions** began to be formed, which were used on Russian territory for action, suppression of the guerrilla movement and guard duty. These units included altogether 10,000 to 12,000 Estonians. As the occupation lasted, the number of volunteers began to decrease.

Recruitment to the **Estonian Legion** of the SS in 1942 almost failed. It took a lot of trouble to send the first unit – the "Narva" battalion – to the front. In the battles for Izyum, Kharkiv and Cherkassy the battalion demonstrated its capability, but suffered great losses. The whole Legion first went to the front at the end of 1943 near Nevel. In order to form the Legion, compulsory mobilisation of young men was carried out.

Mobilisations caused resentment among Estonians. They started to avoid military service. Some used fictitious medical certificates, some hid themselves, and some left Estonia. It became especially popular to flee to Finland to fight against the Red Army with the Finns. The Finnish **Infantry Regiment 200** (JR 200) was formed from more than 2,000 Estonian refugees, and took part in the battles to defend Karelia in the summer of 1944.

Estonians in the Soviet Union. In the summer of 1941, thousands of machinery, industrial raw materials and completed production, means of transport and cattle, as well as people, were

Hostilities in 1944.

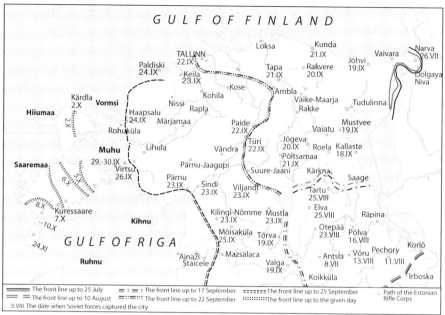

taken to Russia. About 25,000 Estonians were evacuated to the Soviet Union. In addition to the fleeing Soviet activists, among them there were many specialists and workers. Some 33,000 recruits were also transported to Russia.

Those evacuated were spread all over the Soviet Union. The greatest number of them were located at the Volga River, in the Urals and in western Siberia. Living conditions were harsh, and many of them lacked the necessary clothes and household goods. People were housed with the local population, whose accommodation was already overcrowded before. Initially they all worked in agriculture, but later specialists were employed in military factories, the railways and the navy.

The recruits were not sent into action but to **construction battalions**, which were prison camps by their nature, where people who had to survive in extremely hard conditions and were made to build factories or to cut timber. During the first winter almost one-third of those mobilised died of exhaustion.

Taking care of those evacuated and mobilised was the task of the Council of People's Commissaries of the Estonian SSR and the Central Committee of the Estonian Communist (Bolshevik) Party. The best they could do was to normalise the living conditions of those evacuated. A noteworthy achievement was the establishment of the **State Art Ensembles** in Yaroslavl.

These assembled the best figures of Estonian culture, who could otherwise have died due to the harsh living conditions. Among the creative people who belonged to the State Art Ensembles were the composers Eugen Kapp and Gustav Ernesaks, the actors Paul Pinna and Ants Lauter, the artists Adamson-Eric and Ferdi Sannamees, the writers Erni Hiir and Debora Vaarandi and many others who played a leading role in post-war Estonian cultural life.

The former officials of the Estonian SSR asked for the formation of Estonian units of the Red Army. They referred to the participation of Estonians in the Russian Civil War, as well as in the battles of the **22nd Territorial Rifle Corps** in the summer of 1941. The latter had been formed from the Estonian army, consisting of 7,000 Estonians. It was sent to fight the *Wehrmacht* in the region of Prokhov, Dno and Staraya Russa. Within three months, 2,000 men were killed or wounded and about 4,500 surrendered to the Germans, as they did not want to fight for Soviet power. In September, Estonians were taken from the front to work battalions behind the lines.

At the end of 1941, the governmental organisations of the Estonian SSR received permission to form national military units behind the lines of the Soviet Union. The formation of the **8th Estonian Rifle Corps** actually saved the lives of nu-

Ruins of the Türi Paper Factory.

merous Estonian men who had been sent to the work battalions. The Corps consisted of 27,000 people, 85 to 90 per cent of whom were Estonians. The latter included many Estonians who had been living in Soviet Russia. Beside the so-called "Soviet Estonians" (including the commander of the Corps, Lieutenant-General Lembit Pärn) several people among the leadership of the Corps had been higher officers in the Estonian Republic (such as the Chief of Staff of the Corps, Jaan Lukas).

The first battle of the Estonian Corps was fought in December 1942 and January 1943 at **Velikiye Luki**, where they participated in the destruction of the surrounded German garrison. Due to the unprofessional leadership of the units and poor organisation of intelligence and artillery support, the Corps suffered huge losses: three-quarters of its members were either killed or wounded. This also includes the 1,200 to 2,000 (the data varies according to different sources) who surrendered to the Germans.

After the seizure of Velikiye Luki the Corps was withdrawn from the front again for additional formation and training. They returned to the front in summer 1944 in Estonia.

The war returns to Estonia. As a result of the offensive launched by the Red Army in the middle of January 1944, the remnants of the beaten German forces withdrew to the western bank of the Narva River and Lake Peipsi. The soldiers of the Red Army, who moved closely behind the withdrawing Germans, established their first bases on the Narva River at the beginning of February.

As Estonia was a strategically important location, reinforcements were sent there by the Germans. All the Estonian police and eastern battalions, as well as the Estonian Legion, which was reorganised into the 20th Estonian SS Division, were assembled in Estonia.

On the last day of January the Estonian Local Government announced a **general mobilisation** into the German army. In the situation where Estonia was threatened by a new Soviet occupation, nationalist groups, headed by the last Prime Minister of the Estonian Republic Jüri Uluots, supported the mobilisation. In a couple of weeks, 38,000 men had been added to the 20,000 Estonians already serving in the German army. Six regiments of border guards were formed from the newly mobilised men.

In the middle of February, the **battles for Narva** started, which lasted until July. The situation was critical from the very beginning. The Red Army left its base located in the south of the town for the railway station of Auvere, thus cutting the railway connection between Narva and Tallinn. At the same time the troops of the Red Army landed in Mereküla. There was a danger that the German forces fighting near Narva would be surrounded. At a critical moment reinforcements arrived, the troops who had landed were beaten and the attack was stopped. Next the majority of bases on the western bank of the Narva River were destroyed. An outstanding role in these processes was played by Estonian soldiers.

As a reaction to the participation of Estonians in the battles, the Red Army carried out a number of **air raids** on Estonian towns. On 6 March, Narva was completely destroyed, on 7 March, Tapa suffered seriously and on 9 March, more than 250 planes bombed Tallinn for the whole night. More than 600 people were killed, about one-third of the residential area was destroyed, and 25,000 inhabitants of Tallinn lost their homes. The most damaging consequences were in the historic centre of the town, where the St Nicholas (Niguliste) Church and "Estonia" Theatre were destroyed. On 25 March Tartu was bombed and suffered serious damage.

In March and April, the battles for Narva continued. In spite of its predominance, the Red Army was incapable of seizing Narva, but the German-Estonian units also lacked the power to drive the enemy back on the opposite bank of the river. At the end of April a relative calm began in Narva for three months.

In summer, the situation became extremely unfavourable for the Germans. The western allies landed in Normandy, the Red Army launched a massive offensive in Belarus, and Finland was about to leave the war. At Narva, numerous Soviet reinforcement units arrived, while the Germans moved their units from there to more pressing points of the front. They were incapable of holding the former front line near Narva.

On 26 July, the Red Army seized Narva, but their offensive was stopped at about twenty kilometres from Narva, where in Vaivara, in the so-called Blue Hills (**Sinimäed**) the Germans had formed a new front line. Here the most violent battles ever held on Estonian territory took place, with the greatest number of victims. The attacking Soviet units suffered huge losses without achieving any success.

In August, the Soviet army command turned its attention **to the south of Estonia**. The offensive launched in the direction of Pärnu was stopped by the Germans at the Väike-Emajõgi River, but the *Wehrmacht* was incapable of defending **Tartu**. On 25 August, the Red Army seized Tartu and moved on to the north. At the end of the month, the Red Army was driven back to the opposite bank of the Emajõgi River, but the Germans did not manage to recapture Tartu. In these counter-attacks the former members of Infantry Regiment 200, who had returned from Finland, played an important role.

In the middle of September, the situation became critical for the Germans near Riga. If the assault forces of Red Army had reached the Baltic Sea they, would have cut off the German forces fighting in Estonia. In order to avoid this, the Germans decided to abandon Estonia and northern Latvia.

The advance of the Red Army in the area of **Väike-Emajõgi**, which had started in the middle of September, developed slowly, as keeping open the corridor between Lake Võrtsjärv and the sea was vital for the Germans.

The units of the Red Army that made an assault in the area of **Suur-Emajõgi** met little op-

Johan Pitka

position. The main attacking force in that front sector was the 8th Estonian Rifle Corps, which was faced by scattered and poorly armed Estonian units of the German army. During the first day, the Corps advanced 30 kilometres and soon cut off the withdrawal route of the Estonian units, which had fought in the battles in Sinimäed. The majority of these units were dispersed in the battles of Avinurme and Porkuni. After that the way to Tallinn was open.

An **attempt to restore independence.** During this period, general confusion reigned in Estonia: the roads were crammed with columns of soldiers and refugees, there was no objective overview of the situation, there was neither a defined front line nor a centralised command, and small scattered units acting on their own initiative tried to hinder the rapid advance of the Red Army.

In spite of all this, there were nationalist forces trying to restore Estonian independence. In the summer of 1944, the political groupings, which had since been of different opinions, gathered around the **National Committee of the Estonian Republic** (*Eesti Vabariigi Rahvuskomitee*). Otto Tief, a former politician in the independent republic who had close contacts with Jüri Uluots, was elected as chairman of the Committee. Through the mediation of the Estonian diplomats in Sweden, contact was established with the western countries. The members of the committee hoped that the history of 24 February 1918 would repeat itself, and between the departure of the Germans and arrival of the Red Army they would manage to declare a restored independent republic and form a provisional government.

On 18 September, Jüri Uluots, deputising for the president, appointed the government of the Estonian Republic, headed by Otto Tief and consisting of ten ministers. Colonel Jaan Maide was appointed as commander-in-chief of the armed forces. The "State Gazette" (*Riigi Teataja*) was published, and a state of neutrality in the war in progress was announced on the radio.

They tried to organise the defence of the capital city, making use of the men who had fought in the Infantry Regiment 200 in Finland and a military unit organised by **Johan Pitka**. The plan failed due to the small number of soldiers and the fact that the Germans were still in Tallinn. In some places clashes took place between Estonians and Germans, who blew up industrial premises. The national flag was raised at the top of the Pikk Hermann tower, but nothing more was achieved.

On the evening of 21 September, the government left Tallinn, hoping to escape to Sweden via the western area of Estonia. In reality, the majority of the members of the government fell in the hands of the Soviet security forces. Jüri Uluots, who was seriously ill at the time, managed to get to Stockholm, where he soon died.

On the morning of 22 September, the tanks of the Red Army entered **Tallinn** and by the afternoon the capital city of Estonia was in the hands of Soviet soldiers. One after another – Viljandi, Pärnu, Paldiski, Haapsalu and, as a last location on the mainland of Estonia, Mõisaküla – were seized by the Soviet army.

Without much delay, the Red Army also occupied Hiiumaa and Muhu islands, as well as the larger part of Saaremaa island, but they were brought to a halt at fortified positions on **Sõrve peninsula**. The battles in Sõrve were violent and had heavy casualties. It was not until 24 November that the Red Army was able to raise the red flag on the southern tip of the Sõrve peninsula.

Estonia in the final battles of World War II. Even before the total occupation of Estonia, the government of the Estonian SSR announced conscription to the Red Army. The 8th Estonian Rifle Corps was complemented with new men and sent to Latvia in 1945, where they participated in the offensive against a German grouping in **Couronia**. In fierce battles lasting for two weeks with heavy losses, only a little success was achieved.

In the winter of 1944-45, a new 20th Estonian Division was formed of the Estonians who had fought for Germany and left Estonia. At the end of January, it helped to hinder the Vistula-Oder offensive of the Red Army in the sector of **Opole**. When Germany capitulated, the majority of the Estonians were imprisoned by the Red Army in Czechoslovakia. A small number of Estonian soldiers were able to flee and join either the Americans or British.

Losses of war. In World War II, Estonia suffered huge losses. Narva was completely destroyed, and there was huge damage done in Tallinn and Tartu, as well as in several smaller towns. More than half the pre-war residential houses were destroyed. The percentage of damage in industry was 45 per cent, and in the oil shale mining region this figure was even bigger. The ports were destroyed, and 40 per cent of the railways were damaged. In agriculture the area of arable land and the number of cattle had decreased considerably, and crop production had dropped. The biggest loss of all was a **decrease of population** of about 200,000 people, which included about 80,000 who had fled to the west, 30,000 soldiers killed in battles, and tens of thousands of victims of terror. In spite of all the suffering and efforts of the Estonians, they were unable to restore the independence of the Estonian Republic.

X The Soviet Period. Restoration of the Estonian Republic

49. The Post-war Years of the Estonian SSR: Political Conditions and Mass Repression

In 1944, the Estonian SSR was again **incorporated** into the Soviet Union. Estonia once more became a union republic, wholly dependent on the central power. The official name for it was the Estonian Soviet Socialist Republic.

The Soviet Union of that time was politically organised as a **totalitarian state**. The political, economic, cultural and ideological conditions prevailing there defined the development of the post-war Estonia.

The Soviet structure of power. The restoration of Soviet power began immediately after the Red Army had invaded Estonia in the summer of 1944. The units of the Red Army were followed by **operative groups**, which had been formed behind the lines and charged with restoring Soviet power from place to place. The authoritative institutions of the Estonian SSR were first concentrated in Võru, as Tallinn was still in the hands of the Germans. In September and October 1944, they were transferred to Tallinn and the new power established its control all over the mainland of Estonia (the battles on the islands were still continuing).

The power structure of the Estonian SSR was analogous to that of the USSR, where the leading position was occupied by the **communist party**. The communist parties of the union republics were entirely subjected to Moscow and followed orders and instructions coming from there. At the end of the war the **Estonian Communist Party** (Estonian Communist (Bolshevik) Party, ECBP, until 1952) consisted mainly of party functionaries of different levels and officials of state institutions. At the beginning of 1945, the Party had 2,400 members. In the post-war years, the number of members began to increase rapidly. By 1951, the party already comprised 18,500 people, but still less than half of them were Estonians. The party activists had a comparatively low level of education. In towns, counties and parishes, party policy was carried out by local party committees and by the network of party organisations.

Since 1941 (when Karl Säre was imprisoned), the Party had been actually led by

One occupation replaced by another.

Nikolai Karotamm, who officially became the first secretary of the local Central Committee in the autumn of 1944.

Karotamm, who was born in 1901 in Pärnu, had left in 1925 for the Netherlands and had joined the party there. In 1926, he had travelled to Leningrad to take part in a congress of Esperanto experts and had stayed in the Soviet Union. In June 1940, he was sent to Estonia as an editor of the newspaper "Kommunist," and in September of that year he became a close assistant to Karl Säre, the second secretary of the ECBP.

The **government** of the Estonian SSR, which followed the policy of the central power of the USSR, consisted of people's commissariats until 1946 and of ministries and other central establishments after that. The chairman of the Soviet of Ministers of the ESSR (head of government) in the years 1944-1951 was a "June communist," **Arnold Veimer**. For a short period after the war, Estonia preserved its "own" army – the Estonian Rifle Corps.

The highest **legislative body** of the republic, the Supreme Soviet of the Estonian SSR and its Presidium, had no actual power. The elections of its new members in February 1947 were carried out formally, using the single candidate system. From 1940, the chairman of the Presidium of the Supreme Soviet of the ESSR was **Johannes Vares-Barbarus.** In 1946, he committed suicide. After his death, **Eduard Päll** (using the pseudonym Hugo Angervaks), an Estonian who came from Russia, became chairman of the Presidium.

The Estonian post-war party and government officials were mainly "June communists" – men who had served in the Rifle Corps, Estonians born in Russia, and foreigners. Moscow mainly supported the staff sent from there and placed increasing trust in them. The staff of local background was defeated in the internal power struggle and had to give up their positions in the hierarchy of the Estonian SSR by the beginning of the 1950s. This created the danger for Estonia of losing its "individuality" altogether in the conditions of the Stalinist regime taking over everywhere.

Territory and administrative division. Simultaneously with building the Soviet power structure, the former borders and traditional administrative division of Estonia were also changed.

In the years 1944-1945, **Estonian territory was reduced.** Three counties located on the eastern bank of the Narva River were joined to the Leningrad province. The majority of the Pechory region, including the town of Pechory, was joined to the newly created Pskov province. The former Pechory county was abolished and its territory which was not joined to Pskov province was joined to Võru county. Estonia had received the area joined to the provinces of Leningrad and Pskov (2,330 square kilometres or about 5 per cent of Estonian territory) as a result of the Tartu Peace Treaty in 1920, and 80 per cent of the population of the region were Russians.

Simultaneously with the reduction of Estonian territory, some of the Latvian territory was also cut off. As a result of this process, both formerly independent countries lost their **strategic border areas**. Further minor changes on the Estonian-Russian border areas took place in 1957.

When the Estonian SSR was restored, the existing administrative division was initially preserved. In 1945, Estonia consisted of 10 counties and 236 parishes. Later Hiiumaa (1946), Jõhvi and Jõgeva (1949) were established as separate counties. In the parishes, **rural councils** were formed, which became the primary organs of power. In 1950, parishes were abolished and rural councils became the only rural organs of power of the Soviet regime. In the autumn of the same year, **division of the country into districts** was carried out. The counties (13) were abolished and replaced by 39 rural districts. For a short period (1952-3) the Estonian SSR was divided into three provinces.

Armed resistance. The majority of Estonians had a negative attitude towards the re-established Soviet order for a long time. It was expressed in passive, as well as active resistance to the occupying regime. In the years 1944 to 1953, it occurred in the form of an armed struggle: the **forest brother movement**. At the same time, Estonians expected and hoped that the Western countries would like to restore Estonian independence and hinder the Soviet occupation in Eastern Europe.

The Post-war Years of the Estonian SSR: Political Conditions and Mass Repression

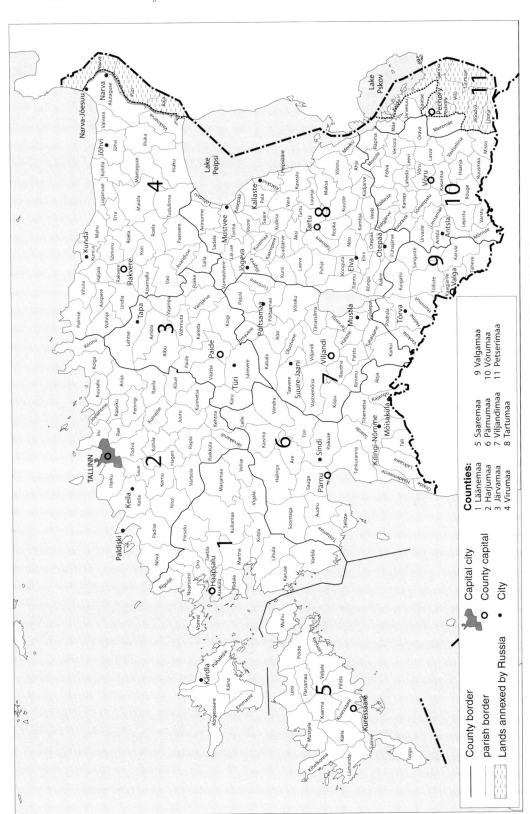

Changed administrative divisions in the Estonian SSR in 1944–45.

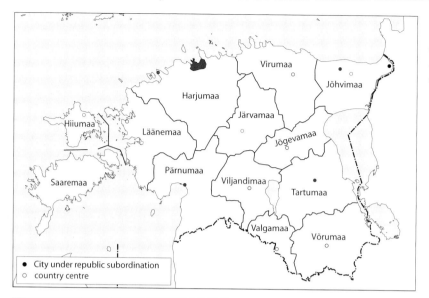

Administrative divisions before the abolition of counties...

...after the abolition of counties on 26 September 1950 and provincial borders 3 May 1952 to 25 April 1953.

In the final years of the war and after the war, there were many men in the forests who had served in the German army, had co-operated with the German occupying authorities, were hiding from conscription to the Red Army or were just trying to escape Soviet power. They formed the bulk of the members of the forest brothers. The total number of people in the forests reached 30,000 at different periods of time. There were about 10,000 active guerrilla fighters among them.

There were no national or rural resistance organisations in Estonia. The average number of members in the bigger groups was 50 to 60 men, but more often the groups consisted of five to ten people. There were representatives of different social classes among the forest brothers, varying from professional officers and wealthy farmers to poor peasants.

The forest brothers did not receive any foreign assistance, so they depended on support from local people, who supplied those in the forests with food, shelter when needed, and information. Resistance groups were located all over Estonia, the most active of them being in Pärnu, Viru and Võru counties. They attacked

Soviet security units and destroyer battalions, killed Soviet rural activists, and organised disruption of the railways. Simultaneously shops, dairies and even farms were robbed, which increased fear among rural people.

In order to fight the guerrillas, the Soviet authorities used regular army units and security forces, militia and local Soviet activists. This **"war after the war"** exacted a heavy toll on both sides. The resistance of the guerrillas was considerably weakened by the 1949 deportations. By the beginning of the 1950s, the occupying regime had managed to suppress the resistance movement. The years of forest brother fighting clearly demonstrated that Estonians **did not surrender without a fight**.

A few people remained in the forests for years. The last resistance fighter was captured in the forests of South Estonia in 1978.

T**he subjugation policy of the authorities.** The policy of enforcement of Soviet authority was varied and was directed towards different strata of population, aiming at subjecting the whole of society to its control. The policy was directed by the party apparatus and executed by the **security bodies**: the Ministry for Internal Affairs and the Ministry of Security.

Already in 1944, **massive arrests** were made of people who had actively supported the German occupation or been disloyal to Soviet order. They were sent to prisoners' and hard labour camps. In the years 1944 to 1954, the number of people repressed was about 30,000. Some people, trying to avoid arrest, escaped into the forests, thus adding to the numbers of forest brothers. In order to make people leave the forests, the authorities announced several amnesties and called on them to return to their everyday work. But it soon became clear that, in spite of the promises, several people who had left the forests were arrested. Therefore subsequent amnesties did not bring the expected results.

As well as direct physical repression, **intellectual violence** was applied. It was expressed by subjecting the intellectual life of society to the ideological dogmas of the ruling regime and levelling the pre-war cultural sphere (education, science, the arts, etc.). An excess of "red propaganda" accompanied it.

The post-war policy of violence achieved its peak in 1949, when **mass deportation** was carried out. On the night of 26 March, 20,722 people were deported to Siberia from Estonia. The majority of those deported were women and children, and they were mainly sent to the Krasnoyarsk territory and Novosibirsk province. The peak of the March deportation was directed towards the rural population (more than 90 per cent of those deported), to frighten them and thus achieve their "voluntary" joining of collective farms. Another goal was to reduce support to forest brothers. Those deported represented 2.5 per cent of the Estonians living in the territory of Estonia in March 1949. The present Viljandi, Valga and Pärnu counties suffered the biggest losses.

In 1950, a deportation was carried out in the territories of Pskov province, which had been taken from Estonia and Latvia in 1944-5. The total number of those deported was 1,400, mainly Estonians and Latvians.

S**talinist Despotism.** The central characteristic feature of the development of domestic policy of the Estonian SSR in the post-war years was the struggle against so-called **bourgeois nationalism**. This notion was introduced by Nikolai Karotamm in 1944, and the theoretical explanation of it was provided by Gustav Naan in his pamphlet "Reactionary Essence of the Ideology of Bourgeois Nationalists of Estonia" (1947).

Naan's views coincided with those of the "ideological fight" directed by **Andrei Zhdanov**, who was "so well known" to Estonians already. Naan stated that "bourgeois nationalists appear as deadly enemies of Estonian people" and that "the fight has not ended yet. The hostile elements have strengthened their struggle in anticipation of approaching death." It matched the Stalinist statement of the strengthening of class struggle in the process of development of socialism.

The first to receive the label of bourgeois nationalists were the members of the creative intelligentsia of the Estonian Republic. One of the chief organisers of this attack was Max

Laosson. At the same time, the **internal struggle** among the authorities of the Estonian SSR became more and more evident. The most serious was the conflict between the "June communists" and the Russian-born Estonians. The men in power, who had come from Russia could not help feeling that the top leaders of the ESSR, especially Karotamm and Arnold Veimer, were infected with bourgeois nationalism as well. Moscow shared this view and in 1949, a high-level Party commission was sent to control the situation in Estonia. Based on the commission's report, a separate decision was adopted in Moscow about mistakes and shortcomings in the work of the ECBP. In March 1950, the notorious **8th plenary session of the ECBP** assembled in Tallinn to discuss this decision and introduce measures to "improve" the situation.

The plenary accused the top leadership of the Estonian SSR of underestimating bourgeois nationalism, adopting an incorrect policy for collective farms, making inadequate choices of staff and many other faults. The organisers of the **massive accusations** were Moscow emissaries and their local henchmen. The 8th Plenary Session actually became their "moment of stardom." Karotamm was relieved of the post of party leader and **Johannes (Ivan) Käbin** was "elected" as First Secretary of the ECBP with Moscow's approval.

The Chairman of the Presidium of the Supreme Soviet of the ESSR, Eduard Päll, also lost his post, and was replaced by a popular writer of the time, August Jakobson.

Although Karotamm lost his position in the party hierarchy, he preserved his personal freedom. He became a researcher in the Academy of Sciences of the Soviet Union, then a Doctor of Economics and a professor. Karotamm died in 1969 in Moscow.

The immediate influence of the 8th Plenary Session was a thorough cleansing of the institutions of power in Estonia (from ministries to rural councils), the system of education, the cultural establishments and creative associations. In 1951, the Chairman of the Soviet of Ministers, Arnold Veimer, was replaced by **Aleksei Müürisepp**, who was more acceptable to Moscow. He held this post until 1961. Several leading politicians and "June communists" were arrested and sent to prison camps, and the minister for commerce August Hansen was shot.

The 8th Plenary of the ECBP was a **revolutionary event**, having far-reaching implications on the future development of Estonia. The Russian Estonians, together with Russian-speaking party activists, took power in the country. Fear and depression grew in society. The Stalinist ideology began to rule. Attacks on the national culture and national history increased.

50. The Post-war Years of the Estonian SSR: Enforced Industrialisation and Collectivisation

Sign for the "New Life" collective farm.

The economy of the Estonian Republic had been based on agriculture, relying on a farm economy, and industry relying on local resources and a local workforce. The destruction of the former economic system had already begun in the first year under Soviet rule (1940-41) and continued during the war. The economic model of a small state, which had developed during the years of independence, was finally destroyed in the post-war years when, simultaneously with restoration of Soviet power, a Stalinist economic policy was applied in the Estonian SSR. The characteristic features of this economic policy were forced industrialisation, forced collectivisation (introducing collective farms) and the development of a rigid planned economy in all spheres of life.

Forced industrialisation. The advanced development of heavy industry had been the cornerstone of the Soviet economy for years. A similar economic policy was forcibly introduced in the post-war Estonian SSR. The oil shale industry, mechanical engineering and light industry became the main areas developed in Estonia.

In June 1945, the Defence Committee of the Soviet Union adopted a decree according to which, in the oil shale area of the Viru county, the **oil shale industry** was to be expanded on a vast scale. During a five-year period, more than 40 per cent of all investment was to be made in this area of industry.

The Estonian SSR was actually turned into an economic backyard of Leningrad. The Viru county oil shale industry had to supply Leningrad with gas and to produce fuel for the Baltic Fleet. In 1948, in Kohtla-Järve, the first factory for oil shale gas was opened, using ineffective technology. At the same time, the gas pipeline to Leningrad was finished. It was only in 1952 that the gas pipeline from Kohtla-Järve to

The mechanisation of oil shale production using Soviet-style technology.

Tallinn was opened. In the oil shale area, new mines and settlements were constantly added. The centres of the region, **Kohtla-Järve** and **Sillamäe**, received town status. In Sillamäe, a secret factory for military production was built. The workforce for the factory was brought from the other regions of the Soviet Union. They arrived with their families. Sillamäe became a closed town (as did Paldiski), where "strangers" had no business.

Mechanical engineering and the metal industry were extended. Initially, former factory buildings were restored to produce equipment needed all over the Soviet Union. The industry of the Estonian SSR began to produce equipment for the oil shale and oil industry (boring machines, derricks, etc.), automatic equipment for making boilers, electric motors and other production. "Volta" became a big factory, which produced 10 per cent of all electric motors made in the Soviet Union.

The official reason given for the extensive development of **heavy industry** (first of all, the machine and metal industry) was the Estonian tradition of heavy industry and existence of trained staff. It resulted in the construction of huge factories in Estonia, which did not correspond to Estonian proportions. The raw materials for the factories were brought in and their production was taken out of Estonia.

The authorities of the Estonian SSR had no information about the production or number of workers of several factories. These factories ("Dvigatel" in Tallinn, "Baltiyets" in Narva and many others) belonged to the Complex of Military Production of the USSR and were subjected directly to respective departments in Moscow.

Beside heavy industry, **light industry** also developed rapidly in Estonia in the post-war years. The cotton mills in Tallinn and in Narva were restored and reconstructed. The staff for the factories was mainly brought from other regions of the USSR. The production of both the Baltic and Kreenholm factories was taken to the markets of the Soviet Union.

The restoration and industrialisation of the towns was accompanied by extensive **building**. This increased the production of building materials and demanded extra workers. Therefore the building industry became the main **cause of migration**, bringing a plentiful workforce to Estonia from other parts of the USSR during the whole period of Soviet rule.

In the process of industrialisation, **the private sector** finally disappeared from industry. In 1947, the last small enterprises in Estonia were nationalised.

Land reform. The first thorough Soviet reorganisation in agriculture was to carry through the land reform started in 1940 (and abolished during the German occupation). The Supreme Soviet of the ESSR adopted the necessary law in September 1944.

The Soviet land reform first meant **expropriation**, or nationalisation. In 1944-7, more than 927,000 hectares were expropriated in the Estonian SSR. From that state land fund, two-thirds were divided between new settlers, while one-third of the land remained in the state reserve.

Administrative division after the reorganisation of regions on 24 January 1959.

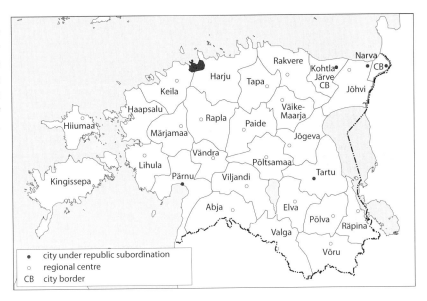

...After the reorganisation of regions on 14 April 1961 and 28 March 1962.

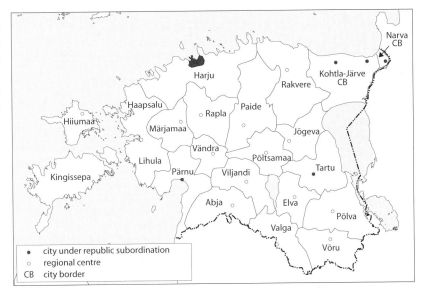

The post-war land reform defined the area of a farm as 30 hectares. Families who had co-operated with the German occupation authorities could not have more than five to six hectares of land. The majority of their property and livestock were also expropriated.

The land reform was generally finished by the spring of 1945. It was improved and modified further until the summer of 1947. By the end of the land reform, there were about **136,000 farms** in the territory of the Estonian SSR.

One-third of these were held by the new settlers and those who had received additional allotments, one-third were the farms reduced by the land reform and one-third were untouched by the reform.

The land reform did not improve social or economic conditions in rural areas, not to mention the relations between people. The households of the **new settlers** did not generally develop into viable farms. They were too small (less than 15 hectares on average). The level of

Tractor operators from the Võru tractor depot travelling for their spring-time work.

production technology was low and, even more essential, the new land owners were not ready to become masters of their farms. The expropriation of land often handicapped the farms that had been successful before. The free re-division of land increased tensions between people. Soviet authorities were pleased with the appearance of "class hostility" in rural areas, because that facilitated the way for later collectivisation of farms.

Farmers had several duties and obligations to the state. The most important of these was the obligation to sell agricultural products to the state. Farmers had to give an established amount of grain, potatoes, meat, eggs and other agricultural products to the state for a symbolic payment. Bigger farms had much greater duties than the small ones. In addition, farmers had defined labour duties (such as tree cutting in winter) and often they had to do urgent community jobs (such as repairing roads).

During the land reform, **state agricultural enterprises,** state farms and centres of agricultural equipment and tractors, as well as centres lending horses, began to be formed in the Estonian SSR. The latter were primarily meant to assist the new settlers. Their share of the total agricultural production and cultivation of land was rather modest.

Formation of collective farms. During the land reform, farmers received "acts of perpetual usage of the land." But by the end of 1946, the tendency was already beginning among the leaders of the ESSR to start the formation of collective farms, which rapidly accelerated due to pressure from Moscow.

In May 1947, the Central Committee of the Communist Party of the Soviet Union adopted a directive on the formation of collective farms in all three Baltic union republics. In the autumn of the same year, five collective farms were formed in the Estonian SSR, and according to the regulations of the Soviet Union, the process of defining *"kulak"* farmers began.

Farmers who had made use of wage workers and/or their own agricultural machines were considered *kulaks* – or "rich" farmers. Thus initially 2,700 farmers were labelled as *kulaks*. They had to pay a high agricultural tax and later the amount of production they had to sell to the state were increased. Then the tax load and compulsory selling norms for other farms were increased as well. The increase in tax pressure and extensive propaganda glorifying collective farms did not produce the expected results. The farmers did not "voluntarily" join into collective farms.

By the beginning of 1948, a tiny part (0.03 per cent) of Estonian farms had been collectivised. During 1948, the tax load and norms for the farms were increased again. The number of *kulak* households was also increased. This was done as part of the preparation for "liquidating *kulaks* as a class." The same method had been used for mass collectivisation in the Soviet Union at the beginning of the 1930s. Moscow did not accept the suggestion from the leaders of the Estonian SSR (primarily from Karotamm) to resettle the so-called *kulaks* within the boundaries of Estonia. The idea was also opposed by many local Stalinists.

The resistance of the farmers was broken by **deportations** in March 1949. As a result of the

March deportations, an atmosphere of fear was created which caused mass "voluntary" joining of collective farms. By the end of 1949, 65 per cent of farms had joined collectives. In the following years those farms that had not joined the collectives were made to do so, or to liquidate their households by an additional increase in the tax burden. Many farmers were forced to liquidate their households and leave for the towns. By the end of 1951, collectivisation in the Estonian SSR was complete. More than 95 per cent of all farms had been collectivised.

At the initial stage of collectivisation, a collective farm was formed in practically every village. In some cases, a collective farm connected two or three neighbouring villages. The formation of small collective farms was less painful for farmers since people living in the same village supported each other, and the elected leaders of the collective farms were the more active farmers from the same village and thus familiar to the people. The biggest drawback of small collective farms was that they were not economically viable. Therefore in 1950, a process started of uniting small collective farms into bigger ones. The collective leaders were also replaced. The loyalty of the new leaders to the Soviet regime was not sufficient for the effective running of the collective farms. It accelerated the decline of the collective farm system. By 1953, Estonian agriculture was in a worse state than after the German occupation in 1944.

According to official propaganda, all collective farmers were masters of the collective farms. The real situation proved different – they were just wage workers. Collective work soon changed the attitude of the farmers, who did not feel they were owners any more, and apathy became the dominant feeling in collective farms.

The centralised economy and its consequences. As a result of Socialist industrialisation and collectivisation, an economic policy was applied in Estonia which considered neither the local resources of raw materials and workforce, nor the historically developed traditions of production and needs. The economic life of the Estonian SSR was subjected to a **planned economy** at all levels. The plans for development (starting from the union republic and ending with a single farm) were all worked out at a higher level, in Moscow. The rigid form of planned economy excluded any social structure typical of the market economy and meant a transfer to a **centralised economy**. In turn, this brought far-reaching demographic and social consequences, which still are influencing life and development in Estonia.

The most essential **demographic consequence** of centralised economy was the influx of numerous **workers from other regions of the Soviet Union**. After the borders of Estonia were "rectified" by the Soviet Union, the Estonian SSR was initially a single-nation union republic, as the absolute majority of the population (854,000) were Estonians. The following years dramatically changed the situation. In the years 1945 to 1950, the population of Estonian SSR increased by 170,000 immigrants from other union republics. They arrived as a result of organised enrolment (especially to the building and oil shale industries), but also on their own initiative or at the

"Säde" collective farmers from Lihula parish transporting grain

invitation of relatives and acquaintances who had arrived earlier. The new settlers initially came from the north-western provinces of Russia. The majority of them were unskilled workers and former peasants. They brought with them different traditions, habits, attitudes and ways of life. The immigrants formed compact Russian-speaking settlements in Estonia.

The vast immigration reduced the **role of Estonians** among the population. According to the 1959 census, the Russian-speaking minority formed one-quarter of the population. The process of "internationalisation" of the Estonian population was meant to guarantee the merging of Estonians into the "brotherly family of the Soviet people."

As a result of the advanced development of industry, the towns kept growing and the majority of immigrants settled there. The formation of collective farms accelerated the migration of peasants into the towns.

In 1945, one-third of the population lived in towns. By 1953, the proportion was more than half. The material situation of the town dwellers was worse than in the rural areas after the war. In towns, ration cards were used to supply people with foodstuffs and industrial goods. Collectivisation ruined the majority of the rural population. In 1947, monetary reform was carried out, ration cards were abolished and the setting of prices was regulated. In conclusion, for a long time Soviet socialism did not guarantee a decent standard of living to either town dwellers or the rural population.

The extensive immigration raised the **language problem** (especially in the eastern part of Viru county and Tallinn), which was "solved" in favour of the Russian language. The language problem troubled not the immigrants, but mainly the native Estonians, because regions developed in Estonia where it was impossible to cope without a knowledge of Russian.

51. The Estonian SSR as an Exemplary Union Republic

The political conditions in Estonia in the 1950s were influenced by two essential events: firstly, Stalin's death in 1953, and second, the suppression of the uprising in Hungary by Soviet troops in 1956.

The death of Stalin was followed by the so-called **thaw period** in the Soviet Union. This made the liberalisation of social life possible in almost all spheres. This process also affected the Estonian SSR.

The suppression of the uprising in Hungary took away the last Estonian hopes of assistance from the West in order to free itself from the Soviet occupation. The liberalisation of political conditions, disappearance of the armed resistance struggle, recovery of the collective farm system and a slight improvement in the living standards of the people facilitated the process of **adjusting to the existing system**. The 1960s saw even bigger adjustment by the people.

In the all-Union perspective, the Estonian SSR became a kind of an **"exemplary union republic"**– a "showcase" of the huge empire. The Estonian SSR was headed by the First Secretary of the Central Committee of the ECP, Johannes Käbin (who was in office for 28 years in total).

Johannes Käbin and his team. Johannes Käbin, who led the Estonian SSR for many years, was born in 1905 in Kalvi parish of Viru county. In 1910, the Käbin family left Estonia for St Petersburg, and from there, moved to the Sussanino settlement near St Petersburg. There his *Komsomol* and Party career started. At the beginning of the 1930s, he was sent to do Party work in Siberia and then to study in Moscow. Later he worked as a lecturer on Marxism-Leninism in an institute in Moscow. It is noteworthy that the "great purge" in the Soviet Union of the second half of the 1930s did not concern him, although the majority of communists who were Estonians were repressed. In February 1941, Käbin returned to Estonia to work in the party apparatus. Karotamm and Käbin had contacts only at an official level. In 1948, Käbin became the Secretary of Ideology of the ECP. Although he was not a supporter of Karotamm, he did not appear to be one of those preparing the notorious 8th Plenary Session, either.

In March 1950, Käbin became "the first man" of the Estonian SSR, being approved by Moscow. This was the period when Stalinism enjoyed its zenith in the Soviet Union. Without any doubt, Käbin was more obedient to Moscow's orders than Karotamm had been. However, he did not prove to be a passionate Stalinist, nor a man to carry out extreme Russification in the Estonian SSR, as local Stalinists who had supported him had hoped. Käbin

Johannes Käbin

did not accept their brisk but careless policy, and did not support the idea of carrying out new deportations in the Estonian SSR. The fiercest of the Stalinists were those who soon lost their posts among the leadership of the ESSR instead.

During his period in power, he carried out a moderate **policy of "tacking"** – trying to be sufficiently Moscow-minded, but at the same time to consider the "characteristic" features of Estonia. He was able to adjust himself to the political conditions of Stalinism, the thaw period and stagnation, and to preserve his post.

Käbin developed good contacts with Nikita Khrushchev, who took notice of dissent. This enabled the Estonian SSR to achieve certain economic advantages and helped to avoid some of the extreme experiments of the Khrushchev period. At the invitation of Käbin, Khrushchev paid an unofficial visit to Estonia in 1954. In Käbin''s period of office, the obligatory shipments of Estonian agricultural production into the central stock of the Soviet Union were moderate. Generally the principle was that the needs of the Estonian SSR were catered for first, and the rest of the production was sent to supply the Soviet Union. Therefore, the supply of foodstuffs was sufficient in the Estonian SSR during the 1960s and at the beginning of the following decade. The situation started to change during the period of office of Leonid Brezhnev, when compulsory shipments to the stock of the Soviet Union increased considerably.

In carrying out his policy, Käbin mainly relied on "moderate" Estonians born in Russia. During his office, Aleksei Müürisepp (1951-61) and Valter Klauson (1961-84) were chairmen of the Council of Ministers. After August Jakobson, the post of Chairman of the Presidium of Supreme Council was also held by Estonians born in Russia, Johan Eichfeld (1958-61), Aleksei Müürisepp (1961-70) and Artur Vader (1970-78).

Partial amends for injustice. An essential feature of the internal policy of the thaw period, which followed Stalin's death, was a partial making amends for the violence carried out – a **rehabilitation** at the local, as well as all-Union level.

In the Estonian SSR, the rehabilitation primarily meant restoring the honourable name of people who had been labelled bourgeois nationalists. The process was initially very wary, and became somewhat quicker only after the 20th Congress of the Communist Party of the Soviet Union in 1956, where Khrushchev denounced the personality cult of Stalin in his report. Rehabilitation in the Estonian SSR mainly concerned numerous groups of educated people, who received the opportunity to return from "mental exile" to active creative work. But many creative people were no longer able to create anything. There was also no official disapproval of the policy of violence, only the mention of some "minor mistakes" in the activity of the ECP. This was connected with the fact that Käbin and many "party soldiers" who had come to power with him still held posts where they could shape the political life of the Estonian SSR. Only the fiercest Stalinists had been removed from the leadership of the Estonian SSR. Therefore the "thaw" in the political atmosphere of the Estonian SSR was very careful and moderate in its extent.

On the all-Union scale, the death of Stalin stopped the action of the machine of violence. Next came the **acquittal of those repressed** and their release from prisons, from the GULAG camps, and from exile. More than 30,000 people, who had been deported or arrested, returned to Estonia. But the return to their home country did not mean full rehabilitation. Those repressed did not get back their property and many of them were not allowed to return to their native place.

Secret organisations of young people. In the 1950s, the opposition movement changed its character. The struggle by forest brothers was replaced by the activity of a few small illegal youth groups.

The secret organisations of young people (there were more than 30 in total) emerged mainly as a form of protest against compromise and acceptance of the Soviet system. The secret organisations of the period were characterised by strict discipline, constitutions, hand-written leaflets, oaths and the collection of weapons. The forest brothers movement, and literature and memories of the period of independence served as examples.

One of these secret organisations was the **Association of Estonian Nationalists** *(Eesti Rahvuslaste Liit)*. One of the leading politicians of present-day Estonia, Enn Tarto, was a member of this organisation.

The illegal youth organisations were not widely supported. The regime in power, or rather its security service, stifled the youth movement at the beginning of the 1960s, using extensive repression, as well as preventive actions. At the end of the decade, the illegal youth protest revived to a certain extent. Some groups did not follow the example of the independence period, but the idea that "the enemy of my enemy is my friend." These were **pro-fascist** groupings, whose members idealised fascist ideology, regimes and external attributes. It was easy for the security forces, even from a propagandist perspective, to do away with such single small organisations. Liquidation of the pro-fascist youth groups finished the illegal youth movement in the Estonian SSR.

Recovery of agriculture. By the beginning of the 1950s, the agriculture of the Soviet Union was totally corrupted. This caused the leaders of the state, who took office after Stalin's death, to rectify the former agricultural policy. This had a positive influence on development of the collective farm system in the Estonian SSR. In 1953, the compulsory sales norms for agricultural production were decreased, prices were raised, and the tax burden on farmers' households was reduced. In 1954, collective farmers began to receive pay for their work in the Estonian SSR, part of which was in cash. At the end of the 1950s, this arrangement became general and the compulsory sales norms of agricultural production for private households were abolished. The centres of agricultural equipment and tractors were liquidated and their machines and equipment were sold to collective farms. This helped to make more efficient use of agricultural machinery. The changes gave rural people more freedom to decide their own affairs and facilitated the **recovery of agriculture** from the ruin of the period after collectivisation. The following years also saw improvement of professional training of the leading staff of collective and state farms. An important role was played in the process by the Estonian Academy of Agriculture, which was established in 1951, as well as development of the network of agricultural vocational schools.

The restoration of agriculture was a difficult process. The grain production of the 1950s was at the level of the last quarter of the previous century, and it was not until the end of the following

A lot of resources were expended on developing rural centres.

decade that it reached its pre-war level. The same situation applied to milk production. The production of meat achieved the pre-war level slightly earlier. The "experiments" of Khrushchev paralysed the development of agriculture: among these were the vernalisation (cooling) of seeds, compulsory growing of corn, the square-cluster method of potato raising and others.

The second half of the 1960s witnessed the beginning of extensive **specialisation of agriculture**. The collective farms specialised in the production of a certain agricultural product. The first to be transferred to an industrial basis was poultry breeding, then dairy cattle breeding and then pig breeding.

The 1970s saw the formation of large collective farms and agricultural enterprises. Initially the combining of smaller collective farms into large ones had a positive effect, as economic indicators improved, and in rural centres new administrative, culture, service and shopping centres were built. The living conditions and standards of rural people improved considerably. But the negative consequences of such megalomania did not take long to appear. The over-exertion ruined the historically developed structure of settlements, exhausted the fertile soil and aggravated environmental conditions.

Expansion of industrialisation. In the 1950s, an extensive development of industry to meet the needs of the great state continued in the Estonian SSR. Beside the oil shale industry, increasing attention was attached to developing mechanical engineering, metalworking, the textile industry, and fishing.

The oil shale industry received the directive of producing fuel and energy to meet all-Union needs. This meant that increasingly larger amounts of valuable oil shale were mined to fire power stations and to produce gas. Two new power stations (the Baltic and Estonian power stations) were put into operation. They were switched into the energy system of the north-western Soviet Union. More than half of the energy produced was sent out of the Estonian SSR, mainly to the Leningrad and Pskov provinces and to Riga. The price for this exported electricity was lower than it was paid for inside the Estonian SSR. Using oil shale in the chemical industry was not considered worthy of attention.

At the end of the 1950s, extensive development of **equipment manufacturing** and **industrial fishing** began. The Estonian SSR received a large ocean fishing fleet, and maintenance bases and necessary coastal services were established.

The growth of industry caused an increase in **industrial and civil construction**. In the 1960s, several former large building material enterprises (for example, the cement factory "Punane Kunda") were restored and new ones were established (in Narva and Ahtme). In Tallinn and Tartu, building material plants were founded.

The development of industry still followed the **extensive** pattern, which meant that additional production units (new mines, establishments, etc.) were created and the workforce for them was brought from other regions of the Soviet Union. In the 1950s, the influx of foreign workers was smaller than in the immediate post-war years, but during the following decade immigration grew considerably again. The direct result of the extensive development of industry in the Estonian SSR was that the

The Baltic combined heat and power plant – built by Komsomol members from all over the Soviet Union

proportion of workers among the population grew, reaching 60 per cent by 1970. The arrival of numerous workers of foreign descent in Estonia decreased the proportion of Estonians among the population and accelerated urbanisation.

Public officials of the Estonian SSR had practically no say in development of the industrial policy of the union republic, because the majority of the enterprises were subjected directly to the all-Union ministries. During the period of the **Soviets of National Economy** (1957-65), economic administration became more flexible, as the majority of industry was subjected to the control of the union republics. These were years of economic growth in the Estonian SSR.

The 1965 economic reform abolished the Soviets of National Economy, and gradually the centralised economy was restored. Its internal resources, though, were finally exhausted in the 1970s.

Contact with the Western world. During the reign of Stalin, the entire Soviet empire was isolated from the rest of the world by the "iron curtain." Therefore it was also difficult in the Estonian SSR to receive truthful information about events happening in the world. Some of the main channels of information of this period were **foreign radio stations,** some of which soon started to transmit broadcasts in Estonian. The first of these was the Voice of America, which started its activity in 1951 in New York.

This was an official channel of information from the United States of America. The information connected with Estonia (primarily information about the life and activities of Estonian immigrants in America) could not exceed 15 per cent of the broadcast time. In the years 1953 to 1958, Estonian language broadcasts were also transmitted from Munich. Simultaneously, other radio stations, directed towards Eastern European countries and the Soviet Union and financed by the USA, were active in Munich. These were Radio Free Europe and Radio Liberty. Radio Liberty did not initially transmit broadcasts to the former Baltic states. In 1970, a Baltic section was formed at Radio Liberty, which also began to broadcast in the Estonian language. In 1983, that section was made independent and a year later was amalgamated with Radio Free Europe.

The aims of the Estonian language broadcasts of the foreign radio stations were to transmit uncensored information about events in the world, and to give news, commentary, analyses and reports of events taking place in the USSR and the Estonian SSR. The radio stations had unrestricted access to the international media, news agencies and press of the world. Feedback from the home country was usually small, so they had to guess what subjects and themes could interest people in Estonia. In spite of the fact that the transmissions were constantly disrupted, the broadcasts of the foreign radio stations were an essential source of information in the Estonian SSR and they helped to preserve mental opposition to the reigning regime.

During Khrushchev's thaw period, **direct contacts** with the outside world began to be gradually restored. Researchers in the Estonian SSR started to study "fashionable" sciences (psychology, sociology, cybernetics, etc.) and some of them managed to participate in international symposia. In Estonia, the Western youth movement of the 1960s – jazz and rock music (such as The Beatles), the hippie movement, and modern art trends (abstractionism, etc.) – found followers.

An important "window to the West" for Estonians was neighbouring **Finland**. The broadcasts of Finnish Television could be seen in the north of Estonia and the sea connection on the Tallinn-Helsinki route, which was opened in 1965, brought a relatively large number of foreign tourists into the Estonian SSR, which was rather unusual at the time. They were the first to introduce Western consumer culture and consumer goods into Estonia.

For the rest of the Soviet Union, Estonia became a kind of a "Western oasis" – the Soviet-West (*Sovetski Zapad*). The external "westernisation" of the Estonian SSR was mainly expressed by "gaining" material well-being (the so-called "trafficker" of consumer goods became the key-word of the period). This lured many people from other regions of the Soviet Union to move to Estonia. The living standards and level of consumption in the Estonian SSR indeed surpassed the average indicators of the Soviet Union. The drawback of this was that the younger and mid-

"We are the children of Lenin, we are the children of Stalin ..."

dle-aged generations adjusted fairly well to the Soviet system.

The "**golden sixties.**" At the beginning of the 1960s, the cultural life of the Estonian SSR became more animated and a new generation of educated people came into creative activity. Political conditions were also liberalised considerably. The changes, which had started in Moscow, reached Estonia after a delay, but were more extensive and longer lasting. The disappearance of the atmosphere of fear and physical violence of the Stalin era brought an elementary **personal liberty** to society, which in its turn made people more optimistic about the future. The **openness** of society increased, along with a **self-realisation** of people in all spheres of life, including political life. In the "golden sixties" a multifaceted generation of so-called **national communists** developed, who were convinced that the existing political regime could be modified to make it more humane, democratic and fit for decent living. They relied on the principle that "socialism in itself is the only true system, but it has been violated," meaning mainly the reign of Stalin and everything connected to it.

The 1960s were characterised by an increase in **the activity of young people**. New forms of youth organisations appeared, such as the Estonian Students' Brigades *(Eesti Üliõpilaste Ehitusmalev)* and Estonian Pupils' Brigades *(Eesti Õpilasmalev)*. Political activity of the students found its expression through *Komsomol* organisations.

The *Komsomol* had been turned into a mass youth organisation, in which participation was almost universal. Students tried to democratise the *Komsomol* organisation and change it to a real student self-government, which would solve everyday problems of young people. They tried to avoid open discussions of questions of power and ideology and turn more attention to national culture. They hoped to improve the situation of the Estonian people, and that of themselves, by internal reorganisation of the existing regime according to their vision. They called on young people to join the Party, to make a career and to take the leading positions in the Party. The **culmination** of this particular ***Komsomol* organisation** was in the years 1967-8 at Tartu University.

At the same time, an adjustment and accommodation with the liberalised conditions continued in Estonia and a general atmosphere of "it is possible to live this way too" spread.

While in the 1950s the ECP had been clearly an executor of foreign power in Estonia, and had been joined only by those aiming to make a career, the following decade witnessed an increase in the proportion of Estonians (about 52 per cent) who were Party members. Thus Estonians had a bigger opportunity to speak up when matters important for them were discussed by those in power in the Estonian SSR. The class of the **political elite**, who were Estonians by nationality, increased. This was a group of people in the Estonian SSR who lived on the advantages provided to the *nomenklatura*.

In October 1964, Khrushchev was overthrown in Moscow and replaced by Leonid Brezhnev, which indicated the beginning of a policy of "tightening the screws" in the Soviet empire. In the Estonian SSR, the thaw period actually continued until 1968, when Soviet tanks put an end to the attempts to build "socialism with a human face" in Czechoslovakia. That also broke the hopes of the Estonian national communists of reforming the Soviet regime from the inside. The suppression of the "Prague Spring" also indicated a turn in the Estonian SSR.

Administrative steps were taken to "calm down" the centre of free thinking: Tartu University. The leaders of the *Komsomol* organisation there were replaced, as well as the rector, the scientist Feodor Klement, whose post was given to a loyal guardian of ideology, Arnold Koop. Some time later, the laboratory of sociology of the university, which had dealt with the problems of society, was dissolved. Ideological oppression increased and censorship strengthened in society.

A slow but continuous stagnation of power began, which did not accept the ideals of the "golden sixties." Many representatives of that generation found self-realisation in literature, research, arts, and other spheres of life. But there were some that gave up their former principles and started to serve the reigning regime loyally.

Democratic movements. Suppression of the activity of the secret youth organisations did not entirely disrupt the opposition movement in Estonia. From the second half of the 1960s, the former illegal youth movement was replaced by **democratic movements**, which were ideologically and politically more supported, but various in their forms.

At this time, simultaneously with the reactionary attacks, a considerable **dissident** movement arose, directed against the ruling regime. Different movements directed against the regime, which had emerged in the Estonian SSR, tried to establish contact with the dissidents throughout the Soviet Union and to be aware of events happening in the world. The democratic movements did not involve only Estonians, but also other nationalities living in Estonia. Their common aim was the democratisation of the USSR. Thus the main emphasis was not on nationality, but on democracy. While earlier opposition movements had been mainly Estonia-centred, now the fact was considered that no nation enslaved could achieve independence when fighting alone. The conclusion was drawn that the independence of Estonia was also an international issue. The activity of the organisations of Estonians abroad made a big contribution to spreading information about the Baltic issue in the international arena.

In 1972, the **Estonian National Front** *(Eesti Rahvuslik Rinne)* and the **Estonian Democratic Association** *(Eesti Demokraatlik Liit)* composed a letter to the General Assembly of the United Nations, claiming restoration of the independence of Estonia, acceptance of Estonia as a member of UN, withdrawal of the Soviet army from Estonia, and so on. The appeal did not actually arrive in the West until 1974. The Western countries did not react to it (as they had not to several others of the kind), but such applications still had an indirect influence. Thus the striving of Estonians towards democratic ideals was demonstrated to the world and Estonians abroad were given an impulse to act more rapidly.

The Baltic émigrés co-operated to establish a common organisation in the 1960s (Baltic Appeal to the United Nations, BATUN), which began to apply for fulfilment of the memorandum sent to the United Nations. The activity of BATUN contributed to the process whereby Western countries did not accept the occupation of the Baltic countries, even in the conditions of détente at the beginning of the 1970s.

Success in easing the tension was achieved in 1975, when in Helsinki, the Final Act of the Conference on Security and Co-operation in Europe (CSCE) was signed. As the USSR also signed the Act, it was hoped that Moscow would follow human rights more consistently. This also encouraged the dissidents of the Soviet Union, who formed so-called **Helsinki groups** in many places, to monitor how human rights were followed in the Soviet empire.

In the Estonian SSR, the democratic movements had been suppressed before the Helsinki Final Act was signed. No separate Helsinki group was established, although attempts were made towards it.

52. The Estonian SSR in the New Era of Russification

In the 1970s, the official national policy of the Soviet Union centred on the idea that the people living on the territory of the Soviet Union would fuse into one **Soviet** people – *homo soveticus*. In the majority of the union republics of the Soviet Union, including the Estonian SSR, a systematic execution of that policy meant **Russification** in its essence.

Beginning of Russification. The leaders of the Estonian SSR did not seem to Moscow to be the right people to carry out the new national policy. In 1978, Johannes Käbin was moved from the post of Party leader to that of Chairman of the Supreme Soviet of the Estonian SSR. Thus Käbin was moved aside from the "big policy" of the Estonian SSR. Käbin supported the candidacy of **Vaino Väljas** for the post of First Secretary of Party, but Moscow did not find a candidate of local descent acceptable. They appointed the Siberian-born **Karl Vaino,** who was practically unable to speak Estonian but was firmly loyal to Moscow, as First Secretary of the Central Committee of the ECP.

Vaino was born in Tomsk, Russia in 1923. In 1947, he was sent to the Estonian SSR as a Party functionary. He was an obedient *apparatchik*, who worked as Secretary for Industry of the Central Committee of the ECP for many years before his "lucky break" arrived. After Vaino had taken office, several national communists were forced to leave the leadership of the Estonian SSR. Vaino Väljas was sent into "political exile" by being appointed as Soviet ambassador to Venezuela.

The change of those in power in the summer of 1978 facilitated the start of the campaign of Russification in the Estonian SSR.

In December 1978, the Central Committee of the ECP adopted a confidential resolution on "the further improvement of acquisition and teaching of the Russian language," which relied on a corresponding all-Union regulation. The resolution attached extraordinary ideological and political importance to the learning and teaching of the Russian language. An active propaganda campaign began on the usefulness of knowing Russian. The main slogan of the campaign was **bilingualism**: only a person who speaks their mother tongue and the "language of international communication" (read: Russian) deserves to be considered fully valuable. The rather questionable principle followed was "when a person speaks two languages, he/she becomes a double person." A primary aim was to increase the role of the Russian language in education. In newspapers, a purposeful campaign was carried on for bilingual kindergartens and schools and partial transfer to Russian-language tuition at the universities. In 1976, an order had already been established that scientific dissertations had to be written (and defended) in the Russian language.

In reality, this policy aimed at **one-sided bilingualism**, as the Estonians had to acquire the Russian language, whereas representatives of other nationalities living in Estonia did not have a similar obligation to learn Estonian.

The limitless glorification of the Russian language reached its peak in 1980, when the "language of international communication" began to be taught in kindergartens and the first year of primary school, and the quotas for entrance to university departments delivering lectures in Russian were increased.

Youth unrest and the "Letter of 40." The pressure of Russification strengthened the feeling that the national culture was in danger. This in its turn gave rise to dissatisfaction in society, which found its expression in **youth unrest** that took place in the autumn of 1980. The appointment of Elsa Grechkina as Minister for Education played a significant role in initiating a spontaneous wave of protest among pupils and students, because she was thought to be a supporter of Russification.

Karl Vaino on hay.

In September 1980, a student demonstration was induced by the authorities' dispersal of a football match between television and radio staff at Kadriorg stadium, and the concert (by the punk group Propeller) that was supposed to follow the match. In response, the young people who had gathered to watch the match and concert went on a spontaneous protest march. The militia started to arrest the participants. Later many of those who had been arrested were expelled from their schools. This gave rise to extensive solidarity protests in schools, leading to street unrest in Tallinn on 1 October. The militia and security forces were mobilised to "normalise" the situation in the town. Later the authorities attempted to label the participants of the street unrest as "hooligans."

The youth unrest activated a **mood of protest among the intelligentsia**. In October-November 1980, a group of intellectuals composed an "open letter from the Estonian SSR," which was addressed to the editorial offices of the central papers of the USSR and the ESSR ("Pravda," "Rahva Hääl," and "Sovietskaya Estoniya"). The letter was signed by 40 well-known Estonian intellectuals (Jaan Kaplinski, Marju Lauristin, Paul-Eerik Rummo, and others), who hoped to direct the attention of those in power to problems and negative processes in society, such as the question of language, increasing immigration, and failures in youth policy. The letter was a sort of attempt to "humanise" the existing regime.

As a result, the authorities directed their efforts not towards easing the tension in society, but towards eliminating those who had composed the letter from social life. They were either dismissed from work or prohibited from performing in public.

The "Letter of 40" found wide support among the people. Hand-written copies of it were illegally passed from hand to hand, and the mood of protest among the people increased. Publishing the letter abroad attracted the attention of the outer world to Estonia (as the yachting events of the 1980 Moscow Olympic Games, which took place in Tallinn, had also done). In any event, the policy of further Russification became somewhat milder in the Estonian SSR.

Open resistance movement. In the middle of the 1970s, attempts to form a central organisation of dissidents in Estonia, or in any other Baltic countries, failed due to their low number of supporters and effective preventive action by the KGB. But activities against the existing regime became much more widespread in this period. The main forms of activity were open letters and applications to the authorities, international organisations, and governments of foreign countries. One direction followed was to find out about violations of human rights, to obtain documentary evidence and publicise it, and also to pass true information about the real situation in the Estonian SSR to émigré organisations.

At the end of the 1970s, the first real contacts were established between the organisations of Estonian émigrés and the dissidents in Estonia. The basis of these contacts was laid by the **Centre for Assisting Imprisoned Dissidents of Estonia** *(Eesti Vangistatud Vabadusvõitlejate Abistamiskeskus)*, founded in Stockholm in 1978. The organisation also had committees in Canada, the USA and Australia.

In 1978, an **underground publication** "Additions to the Free Dissemination of Thought and News in Estonia" *(Lisandusi mõtete ja uudiste vabale levikule Eestis)* started to appear in the Estonian SSR, bringing together all the important applications, memoranda, surveys of political trials, and more. It also included articles about Estonian history and political overviews of neighbouring countries (especially Latvia, Lithuania and Poland).

One form of resistance was the reproduction and distribution of original or officially forbidden written works. Many participants in the resistance movement made what were called one-man-application-protests, which exposed the real nature of the regime in power. Collective memoranda proved more influential.

In 1979, a group of Estonian, Latvian and Lithuanian dissidents (45 people altogether) composed an open letter to the governments of the Soviet Union, the German Federal Republic, the German Democratic Republic, and other countries, as well as to the Secretary-General of the UN, Kurt Waldheim. The letter was timed for the fortieth anniversary of the notorious Molotov-Ribbentrop Pact, and it demanded the disclosure and invalidation of the secret protocols of the Pact as well as the abolition of all its consequences. This common letter by the Baltic dissidents became known as the **Baltic Appeal**. On the basis of this, the European Parliament adopted a resolution in 1983 demanding restoration of independence of the Baltic states. The Baltic Appeal was followed by several other appeals to the public of the world and to the neighbouring states.

When the resistance movement came out into the open, the **repressive policy** of the authorities increased. The most active dissidents were arrested, political trials were arranged and they were sent to prison camps.

A member of academic staff of Tartu University, **Jüri Kukk**, was tried for his anti-Soviet way of thinking. He died in a prison camp in Russia in 1981. The last person to be sent to a restricted-regime prison camp was **Enn Tarto**. This ended the open resistance movement in Estonia.

The regime in power had seemingly eliminated the resistance movement. In fact, the relative silence that followed was a period of preparation for the resistance of 1987, which grew into a general resistance in 1988.

An **economic cul-de-sac.** In the 1970s, the resources for extensive development of industry and agriculture ran out in the Soviet Union. The Soviet economic model continued to exist first and foremost on account of the dollars received for oil. Although the economic figures of the Estonian SSR surpassed the average level of the Soviet Union, the drop was felt there as well.

During Karl Vaino's years of office, the development of **agriculture** had been subjected to the all-Union nourishment programme. This meant increasing the "contribution" of the Estonian SSR of meat and dairy products to the all-Union fund. Based on imported grain, pig

Estonia's contribution to the progress of the USSR.

breeding was extensively developed in Estonia. In order to receive grain imports, the New Port was built in Tallinn. At the same time, local consumption decreased, as the choice of goods in the shops became smaller and smaller. Due to constant shortages of consumer goods the **crisis of foodstuffs** increased.

In industry, the situation where local economic policy was shaped by the all-Union services, based on their interests, continued to exist.

By the end of the 1970s, the administration of industry of the Estonian SSR was subjected to 19 all-Union ministries and organisations, as well as to 23 union republic or local ministries. By the 1980s, more than 90 per cent of industry was subjected to **all-Union** institutions. A significant proportion of industrial production of the Estonian SSR was of military importance. The technological backwardness of industry, compared to comparable industries in the Western countries, increased.

One of the characteristics of the economic cul-de-sac was the growth of a **shadow economy**, which became a regular feature of everyday life. As there was a shortage of everything, only those having "the right acquaintances" could lead a normal life.

Accumulation of social problems. The onslaught of the new wave of Russification and the continuing extensive economic policy increased social and political as well as ideological problems in society. From the point of view of the native people, the most negative consequence was a further increase in tension in the **demographic situation**.

The extensive development of industry had increased the **influx of immigrants**, which gradually reduced the proportion of Estonians among the population of the Estonian SSR, as well as overpopulating the towns. By the 1980s, Estonians formed less than 65 per cent of the population. The urban population formed 70 per cent of the total population of Estonia.

The increase in the proportion of immigrants strained relations between the native people and the newcomers. The official "policy" of providing people with flats to live in added even more tension. The majority of the newcomers quickly received new convenient flats, with central heating and hot and cold running water, in new dwelling areas of the towns. For Estonians, this extended the time they had to wait to get a new flat. Some regions of Estonia, especially the big industrial towns in the eastern part of Viru county, became completely Russian-speaking as a result of this **settlement policy** and the few remaining Estonians left the towns.

As compared with the earlier period, the distance from which people settled in Estonia became increasingly greater. Initially the workforce had been brought in from the neighbouring regions of Russia (e.g. the Pskov province), but in the 1980s the immigrants came from the furthest areas of the Soviet empire.

The policy facilitating immigration was backed by the all-Union ministries and industrial enterprises subjected to them, as they constantly needed additional workforce. Workers were "looked for" in different regions of the Soviet Union and those who agreed to move to Estonia were promised better work and living conditions. This kind of migration policy suited people who felt at home anywhere and considered better consumer conditions to be the most important factor. This was the overwhelming mentality among the newcomers.

In spite of the active **re-nationalisation policy**, the native people did not mingle with the immigrants. The newcomers have also not become fused with Estonians. The majority of immigrants have preserved their language and traditions. This was fostered by the duplicated system of education, beginning with kindergartens and finishing with university education, in which it was possible to learn either in Estonian or in Russian.

The extensive development of industry, which did not take into account the natural resources of Estonia, caused a considerable worsening of the **ecological situation.** Alongside the colonial economy, a second cause of pollution was the Soviet Army and its military bases.

The lack of hope and prospects for the future deepened **social pessimism** in society, which was expressed by an increased consumption of alcohol and a growth in the number of suicides. In addition to these, the Afghanistan war (1979-89) claimed the lives or health of numerous Estonian young men.

53. Basic Features of Cultural Life in the Estonian SSR

World War II and the restoration of the Soviet regime in 1944 tore Estonian culture into two pieces, between local and émigré culture. Nevertheless, although many creative people left Estonia as refugees, the survival of Estonian culture was decided in Estonia, where the majority of Estonians had stayed. Their vitality and resistance guaranteed the continuation of Estonian culture during the Soviet years.

The **essence of the Soviet cultural policy.** The aim of the official cultural policy of the Estonian SSR was to introduce a culture that would be "Socialist in essence and national in form." Therefore the attitude of the new authorities to the cultural inheritance of Estonians strictly followed class principles. This put intellectual life in Estonia under **ideological pressure**, which was more or less depending on political conditions of the period. The intellectual pressure of the last years of Stalin's rule was especially depressing. This pressure increased again in the Brezhnev years, especially in the second half of the 1970s. The years in between, during the so-called "thaw," were marked by much more liberal conditions in the intellectual life of the whole Soviet Union and also of the Estonian SSR. Even so, in spite of the relative liberality or strictness of the regime in power, censorship never disappeared in Soviet society. While carrying out continuous control of the intellect, it had to restrict the spread of free thought in society. To guarantee "social peace" in society, the security forces (KGB) played an important role.

Political and economic isolation had a negative effect on intellectual life in the Estonian SSR. The isolation was accompanied by an extensive (but fortunately not total) **blocking of information** about intellectual development and trends in the West. This meant a **forced orientation** towards Russian culture, which was especially strong at the end of the 1940s and beginning of the 1950s.

Part of Soviet cultural policy constituted the **selective destruction** of the intellectual heritage created by preceding generations. Thus in the post-war years, extensive cleansing of the "inheritance of bourgeois society" from libraries was carried out. During this process a considerable quantity of periodicals and fiction of the years of independence were destroyed. Only some files of newspapers and magazines and single copies of books were preserved. All the inadvisable units of writing were secured in special collections, and in order to use them written permission had to be sought from the authorities.

All these processes were accompanied by extensive **propaganda** aimed to assist in subjecting the sphere of intellectual life to the control of the ruling regime.

New generation of intellectuals. In the final years of World War II, many Estonian intellectuals fled to the West in fear of the Soviet order.

According to estimates, 120 writers and artists, 40 journalists, 120 scientists, 500 doctors and more than 500 engineers and technicians left Estonia. The **intellectual heritage they created in exile** is astonishingly rich (especially in literature) and forms an organic part of Estonian cultural history. But the majority of Estonians could not share that inheritance during the Soviet years.

The intellectuals representing the "old school" (the period of independence) who remained in Estonia were subjected to **ideological terror**, which meant restricting or eliminating their freedom of creation for decades. The political distrust of the Estonian intelligentsia culminated in the period following the 8th Plenary Session of the Central Committee of the EC(b)P (1950), and formed part of the struggle against the so-called bourgeois nationalism. The scientists, writers and other creative intellectuals who had been active in the period of independence faced the danger of becoming carriers of "bourgeois influences" and therefore enemies of Soviet culture. They were told by the authorities to reassess (read: disown) their earlier creations. Criticism, self-criticism and firm following of Soviet realism in their further work were expected from them. This was accompanied by the marginalisation of creative associations, and dismissal or arrest of those who were "insubordinate." Extensive campaigns of exposing bourgeois nationalists were also carried out in research establishments and institutions of higher education.

In the middle of the 1950s, intellectual suppression abated to a certain extent. This gave the intellectuals of the older generation an opportunity to return to their creative work. The partial **self-restoration** of national culture began, in which an increasingly important role was played by the **intellectuals of the new generation**. They filled the empty space created by the war and the terror policy, thus restoring the continuity of professional Estonian culture. The final breakthrough of the new generation took place in the **1960s**.

The cultural renovation of this period was characterised by a noticeably more liberal creative atmosphere, subjective and innovative concepts of form, and new values and ideals. The young generation of writers, artists and critics tried to find a positive programme to survive in the "enriching" conditions of the Soviet order.

Consumption of culture and mass media. The war and the following years of intellectual suppression dealt a serious blow to high-level professional culture. As for **popular culture**, Estonians were as active as ever at organising their cultural life.

The most expressive output of **cultural activity** was in **amateur activities**; the tradition of amateur orchestras, choirs and drama societies, which had been active in the years of independence, was continued. In the post-war years, folk dance became especially popular. The **tradition of song festivals** was also restored, and the song festival of 1947 became a great national event. Despite the flying of red flags, the song festivals became a unique nationally-biased mass event during the Soviet years.

In the second half of the 1950s, amateur activity began to retreat in the face of high-level **professional culture**. On one hand, this was caused by the arrival of a new generation of creative intelligentsia in cultural life, but on the other hand several social processes played an important role, such as urbanisation, an increase in the level of general education of the population, and a growth in economic living standards. The role of the **mass media** (printed media, radio and television) in the cultural life of the Estonian SSR increased gradually.

The broadcast time of **Estonian Radio** *(Eesti Raadio)* increased. In 1967, in addition to the first station, the "Vikerraadio" and "Stereoraadio" stations began to broadcast. In 1985, the total broadcast time of Estonian Radio was 35 hours per day. In 1955, **Estonian Television** *(Eesti Televisioon)* transmitted its first broadcasts. However, television sets did not become part of the everyday part of Estonians until much later.

The Song Festivals took place with red flags flying.

In the 1970s, the changeover to colour TV took place. The **printed media** were divided into republic-wide and town and district newspapers, magazines and administrative publications. All the mass media were subjected to censorship. Although the mass media appeared to be ideological supporters of the reigning regime, as well as disseminators of official propaganda, their influence was not restricted to this. The printed media, radio and television made a welcome contribution to Estonian intellectual life, distributing news from Estonia and elsewhere (mainly from the Soviet Union), educating people and acting as mediators of culture.

The traditional **fondness of reading** of Estonians, as well as the relatively low prices of books, increased the home libraries of the Estonian people. The "Loomingu Raamatukogu" publisher played an important role in bringing world literature to the Estonian readership.

From the 1960s onwards, the consumption of culture at home was characterised by the increasing **use of technology**: more and more stereos, TV sets and tape recorders were bought for home use. The number of visits to theatres, cinemas, museums and exhibitions increased rapidly. The consumption of culture in the north of Estonia became influenced by Finnish TV, which facilitated the cult of a Western life style.

The development of a general pattern of cultural consumption similar to that of developed countries caused a gradual disappearance of **rural culture**. The urban way of life spread among rural settlements, and many small village schools and clubs were closed down, while libraries were closed. The "urbanisation" of the consumption of culture in rural areas caused a decrease in popular culture, which became restricted to the fields of the song festivals, folk dance and choral singing.

The role of the church in society. In the years of the Estonian SSR, the formal freedom of religion was preserved, but in everyday life many direct and indirect restrictions were made on religious folk and congregations. The buildings and property of the churches were nationalised and the congregations had to pay a high rent for them. As the Faculty of Theology of Tartu University was abolished, the training of priests became concentrated in Tallinn in the **Institute of Religious Science** *(Usuteaduste Instituut)* at the Tallinn Consistory. Due to the conditions imposed, tuition was mainly carried out in the form of distance education.

It was attempted to reduce the influence of the church in society by **atheistic** propaganda and by introducing several **secular traditions**. In order to replace the religious tradition of confirmation, the summer days of youth were introduced. Religious commemoration events in cemeteries were replaced by secular ones. However, church funerals remained comparatively widespread even in the days of Soviet rule. The goal of the atheistic propaganda was to develop a hostile or at least indifferent attitude towards the church and religion in society. With the younger generations this policy was quite successful.

By the 1960s, the church had lost its traditional role of maintaining morale and balance in the everyday routine of Estonians. But in spite of the repression and propaganda, the church remained practically the only public institution in the Estonian SSR that was not entirely subjected to the control of the regime in power. Therefore, the church had a role of an **intellectual opposition** in Soviet society.

Education. In the post-war years the educational system typical of the years of independence was finally abolished in Estonia.

The **school system** was based on the pattern used in other union republics of the Soviet Union. In teaching and education, the principles of Soviet pedagogy were applied. The training programmes were thoroughly revised. Humanities subjects and their teachers were subjected to strong ideological pressure. Alongside courses on the history of the world and that of Estonia, a thorough course on the history of the Soviet Union was introduced.

The main features of the Marxist approach to Estonian history included the class struggle and friendship between the Russian and Estonian nations. Teachers were strongly affected by the exposure of bourgeois nationalists, and many teachers who had worked during the years of the independent Estonian Republic were dismissed. This caused a fall in the quality of tuition.

The fortieth anniversary of Tartu University under Soviet rule.

In the Estonian SSR, a seven-year, and after 1959, eight-year compulsory education was established. In the 1970s, secondary education was made compulsory. After finishing the eighth year, pupils had to continue their education in either secondary or vocational schools. The latter provided secondary education in addition to the vocational education.

Making secondary education compulsory essentially devalued the education provided, as graduation certificates were also awarded to pupils who did not deserve them. Schools were given compulsory percentages of academic achievement, which meant that less talented pupils were allowed to pass. This became morally devastating for both pupils and teachers. Various campaigns (closing down rural schools, transition to a system of subject boards, etc.), which were carried out without being thoroughly considered or well planned, had a negative effect on education.

The Sovietisation of **higher education** was mainly expressed by replacing the subject system with a course system, which essentially restricted the freedom of movement and independence of students. In 1950, the higher art school "Pallas" in Tartu was closed down and the Estonian State Art Institute *(Eesti Riiklik Kunstiinstituut)* was opened in Tallinn. In addition, the following higher education establishments were active in Tallinn: the Polytechnic Institute *(Polütehniline Instituut)*, the State Conservatory *(Riiklik Konservatoorium)* and, from 1952, the Pedagogical Institute *(Pedagoogiline Instituut)*. In Tartu, the University continued to operate, its official name now being Tartu State University (Tartu Riiklik Ülikool). In 1951, the Estonian Agricultural Academy *(Eesti Põllumajanduse Akadeemia)* was opened in Tartu. The most important of the higher educational establishments was still Tartu University, which partially managed to preserve its academic way of thinking and life.

Culture of resistance. The events of 1968 in Czechoslovakia put an abrupt end to the period of relative liberalism in the Soviet Union. A **reactionary fallback** could be clearly felt in domestic policy, as well as in the sphere of intellectual life in the Estonian SSR. In cultural life, the atmosphere of optimism of the 1960s was replaced by moods of pessimism and indifference. In the conditions of increasing Russification, the administration of cultural life, propaganda of bilingualism and censorship grew. Connections with Western cultural areas became extremely restricted. The slogan of ideological struggle became common again. All these negative tendencies appeared especially clearly at the end of the 1970s, when **Karl Vaino** became head of the power structure of the Estonian SSR.

At the same time, the stuffy atmosphere of the 1970s was the period at which a peculiar **culture of resistance**, which relied on the nationally-minded intelligentsia, appeared. While the post-war ideological pressure had made many intellectuals accept the general ideology, the wave of Russification of the 1970s caused a considerable increase in protest against the regime in power. A good example of this was the "Letter of 40" in 1980. The absence of a future perspective, characteristic of this period, made people look backwards in time, to find support from history to survive in the present.

In the second half of the 1980s, the majority of the creative intelligentsia of Estonia, making use of the options offered by "*perestroika*," actively joined **the process of democratisation and restoration of independence.**

54. Restoration of the Independent Estonian Republic

By 1985, the international and economic cul-de-sac of the Soviet Union were obvious. Therefore reformation and restructuring of the Soviet system was inevitable. The huge state needed a reformer, who would take the empire out of its crisis and simultaneously preserve the basis of the existing political regime. In March 1985, **Mikhail Gorbachev**, who came to power after the end of the rule of a peculiar gerontocracy (Leonid Brezhnev, Yuri Andropov, Konstantin Chernenko), became that reformer.

Gorbachev initiated a reorganisation that was much more thorough than any other reforms in the recent past of the Soviet Union. The cornerstone of the ***perestroika*** **policy** was the principle that all reforms had to take place in the framework of Socialist choice. In the end the main aim of *perestroika*, which was to get the ruling regime out of the crisis by improving and reforming it, failed. Instead of preserving the empire, the policy of *perestroika* led to the break-up of the Soviet Union in 1991 and abandonment of socialism as a model for society.

To sum up, *perestroika* meant a demolition which led to the disappearance of the Soviet empire and the break-up of the so-called Soviet world (at least in Europe) as a whole. In its turn this gave a historic chance to small nations to restore their independence.

New period of awakening. The leadership of the Estonian SSR, headed by Karl Vaino, was convinced that the innovation initiated by Moscow would soon die away and the life would continue in the old way. These hopes failed.

In the Estonian SSR, the stuffy atmosphere of stagnation started to break up at the end of 1986, when plans by Moscow (supported by the leaders of the Estonian SSR) to open extensive new phosphorite mines in Estonia (at Kabala-Toolse) became public. The plans caused active protest in Estonian society, which in the spring of 1987 grew into an extensive **phosphorite campaign** that gradually became more political in nature. The campaign gave the Estonian people the chance to experience the

Mikhail Gorbachev and his wife at a collective farm in Paide region on 9 May.

A meeting organised by the Estonian Group for Publicising the Molotov-Ribbentrop Pact (MRP-AEG) in Hirvepark.

power of unity for the first time. As a consequence of the protest, the preparatory works for opening the new mine had to be stopped.

In the middle of August 1987, a group of dissidents laid the foundation for purely political developments. They established the **Estonian Group for Publicising the Molotov-Ribbentrop Pact** *(Molotov-Ribbentropi Pakti Avalikustamise Eesti Grupp)*. The group organised a political meeting in **Hirvepark** in Tallinn on 23 August, where the 1939 secret agreement between Hitler and Stalin and its tragic consequences for the Baltic nations were openly discussed. Although official propaganda attempted to disparage the Hirvepark event in every possible way, the meeting became an important signpost for further **organisation and politicisation** of society. This process included several developments.

At the end of 1987, the first mass organisation relying on the people's initiative and democratic principles, the **Estonian Heritage Society** *(Eesti Muinsuskaitse Selts* – EMS) was established. At the beginning of the following year, a call was made for forming the first political party, the **Estonian National Independence Party** *(Eesti Rahvusliku Sõltumatuse Partei* – ERSP). The party was formed in August of the same year. The EMS and ERSP attached great importance to bringing **historically important dates** into the consciousness of the Estonian people. In February 1988, they organised widespread celebrations of the anniversaries of the Tartu Peace Treaty (2 February) and the Estonian Republic (24 February). A month later, the tragic events of the March deportation of 1949 were commemorated.

The growth of political activity and emergence of different popular organisations came as a surprise to the political leaders of the Estonian SSR. Their reaction to these processes was to use the old, "well-tried" methods. The demonstration, which took place in Tartu on 2 February, was opposed by units of the militia equipped with plastic shields and bloodhounds. Luckily, no more serious clash between the demonstrators and the militia took place. By 24 February, the authorities had already adopted a more flexible approach. They had understood that they were unable to "discipline" the people with force.

April 1988 became revolutionary for Estonian society in several ways. At the beginning of April, the **joint plenary session of creative associations** took place, indicating the fact that the creative intelligentsia had actively joined the process of change in society. The plenary session gave much attention to the situation of national culture, a number of demands were made to the central powers, and dissatisfaction was expressed at the activities of the authorities of the Estonian SSR (especially those of Karl Vaino and the Chairman of the Soviet of Ministers of the ESSR, Bruno Saul). These demands received nation-wide support.

In the middle of April, an appeal was made on the popular TV programme *Mõtleme veel...* (Let's think about it...) for the formation of an **Estonian Popular Front to Support Perestroika** *(Eestimaa Rahvarinne Perestroika Toetuseks – Rahvarinne)*. The idea was widely supported by people, and in a short period, the Popular Front became the most numerous mass organisation in Estonia. In the middle of April, during a heritage day in Tartu, the blue, black and white **national flag** made its first appearance in public.

The singing revolution. Criticism of the leadership of the Estonian SSR became more and more open. Karl Vaino, who was opposed even by members of the higher leadership of the ECP, did not want to take voluntary leave. This caused a **power crisis**, which became especially obvious in June 1988. This was made even clearer by the fact that a political mass meeting at the Tallinn Song Festival Grounds, organised by the Popular Front, was approaching and there was a fear that the authorities would not be able to control the development of events. In this situation, Moscow finally understood the necessity of replacing the leading figure in the Estonian SSR. On 16 June, Karl Vaino was dismissed from the post of First Secretary of the Central Committee of the ECP. In his place, the candidature of **Vaino Väljas** was suggested. He had been hurriedly recalled from his diplomatic post in Latin America. The change of leadership temporarily alleviated the tension in society.

The demonstration called by the Popular Front at the Song Festival Grounds on 17 June was meant to apply pressure to the authorities. The 150,000 participants, carrying blue, black and white national flags, were triumphant. The political demands presented to the authorities were clear. They had to stand up for the rights of Estonia in Moscow. A week later, according to a decision of the Supreme Soviet of the Estonian SSR, the blue, black and white flag became once again the national flag of Estonia.

Simultaneously, the restoration of the **awareness of history** was continued. An important role in this process was played by the press and television media, which enjoyed a decrease in the pressure of censorship.

The ECP tried to keep up with events and, after its leadership had been replaced, began to support the idea of self-financing of the Estonian SSR, the national flag and the need to proclaim the Estonian language as the official language in Estonia. But the leaders of the ECP were always a step behind events and therefore were not able to direct their development.

Meeting of the Intermovement in Red Riflemen Square.

The tidal wave of the national movement culminated in September 1988 with the mass event **"Eestimaa Laul"** (Estonian Song), organised by the Popular Front. This became a national demonstration of an unusual extent, in which at least 300,000 people participated. Alongside slogans calling for democratisation of the existing society, the idea of restoration of the independence of Estonia was expressed in public.

To oppose rise in nationalism, the **forces supporting the empire** also became organised in 1988. In the summer, the heads of factories of all-Union importance initiated the formation of the **International Movement of the Workers of the Estonian SSR** *(Eesti NSV Töötajate Internatsionaalne Liikumine – Interliikumine)*, and in the autumn they also established the **Joint Soviet of Workers Collectives** *(Töökollektiivide Ühendnõukogu* – TKÜN). The supporters of these two organisations considered Estonia an inseparable part of the Soviet empire. The laws on language and citizenship that were being drafted, received powerful criticism from them.

By the autumn of 1988, distinctive features of the political landscape had developed clearly in the Estonian SSR. The general picture was as follows. The nationalist forces (ERSP, EMS and others) had adopted the idea of **restoration of independence**, which was opposed by the idea of *status quo*, that nothing should be changed in the empire, of the empire's supporters (*Interliikumine*, TKÜN). The National Front, which held its founding conference in the autumn of 1988, as well as the national communists in the ECP, supported the idea of concluding an **agreement of federation** with Moscow which would give Estonia a "confederate status" within the Soviet Union. Strong opposition to this idea from Moscow, as well as developments in the domestic policy of the Estonian SSR, made the political leaders of Estonia give up the idea of federation and begin the process of restoration of the independence of Estonia. This idea was finally formulated by the spring of 1990.

Declaration of independence. In the initial years of *perestroika*, the relationship between the Estonian SSR and the central power of the USSR remained practically unchangeable. Estonia had to continue as part of a great power with the rights of "a fraternal union republic." With the increase of democratisation in society, the idea of a **confederate relationship** became popular by 1988, which would have given Estonia greater independence of decision as a federal republic within the Soviet Union. The new status would have to be fixed by an **agreement of federation**. Moscow found this idea unacceptable, because it endangered the idea of integrity of the empire.

In an attempt to maintain control over the growing nationalist movements in the union republics, the authorities of the Soviet Union took the direction of improving the constitution of the USSR in the spirit of *perestroika*. Several union republics, Estonia included, saw danger for the process of democratisation in this development. The open discussion of improvements to the constitution divided Estonian society into two distinct wings – the nationalists and the supporters of the empire. Opposition also increased in the administrative structures of the Estonian SSR, including the ECP.

The "constitutional crisis" found its logical solution in the extraordinary session of the Supreme Soviet of the Estonian SSR on 16 November 1988, which adopted the **declaration of sovereignty** and amendments to the constitution of the Estonian SSR. The declaration of sovereignty stated the supremacy of the legislation of the Estonian SSR over the laws and regulations of the authorities of the USSR. Relations between the central power of the Soviet Union and the union republic had to be based on the agreement of federation. Thus for the first time in the history of Soviet power the question of Estonian **statehood,** although in a restricted form, was raised publicly and officially. The decision of 16 November 1988 turned the problem of Estonia into an object of international policy. The negative reaction from Moscow did not succeed in stopping the development of subsequent events, but rather had the opposite effect.

The movement of the Committees of Citizens. In 1989, the political disagreements became even more distinct. The domestic policy of the Estonian SSR developed through confrontations and even some serious crises. Its development was

The Baltic human chain.

characterised by strengthening of the nationalist wing, weakening of the power positions of the ECP in competition with the National Front, and activation of the forces supporting the empire.

In January 1989, the **language law** was adopted, which gave the Estonian language the status of the official language. Shortly afterwards, 24 February was declared as **independence day**.

On the evening before the independence day, the flag of the Estonian SSR was lowered from the Pikk Hermann tower in Tallinn, and at dawn on 24 February, the tricolour was hoisted. These steps met with strong protest from the supporters of the empire. They demanded that the north-east of Estonia should be changed into an "autonomous province," formed strike committees and strengthened the Moscow-minded propaganda among the Russian-speaking population.

In the first months of 1989, nationalist forces organised themselves more clearly. On independence day, the movement of the Committees of Citizens *(kodanike komiteed)* was started, which became very popular. The aim of this political movement was to restore Estonian independence relying on legal continuity. In order to achieve this, the citizens of the Estonian Republic were to be registered according to the law of citizenship of the former independent Estonian Republic. The registered citizens had to elect a representative organ – the **Congress of Estonia** *(Eesti Kongress)*.

In February 1990, elections to the Congress of Estonia took place. More than 520,000 registered citizens and more than 34,000 applicants for citizenship voted. Neither the Popular Front nor the ECP recognised the movement of the Committees of Citizens. Later their attitude changed slightly, but they still rejected the movement. It was not until just before the elections that their attitude changed completely. For this reason the membership of the Congress of Estonians was formed of representatives of different political groups. Émigré Estonians also took part in the elections.

In March 1990, the first session of the Congress of Estonia took place. The schedule of activities adopted there foresaw the opening of negotiations with the Western countries and the Soviet Union in order to achieve the end of occupation and restoration of independence. As an executive organ of the Congress of Estonia, the **Estonian Committee** *(Eesti Komitee)* was elected, which had 78 members and was chaired by **Tunne Kelam.**

Also in March 1990, the **20th Congress of the ECP**, the biggest political change, took place. The Party had split in two: the independent ECP, consisting of the national communists, and the Moscow-minded Estonian organisation of the Communist Party of the Soviet Union. This concluded the long process of peaceful decline of the "old power" and did away with the final considerable internal obstacle to the way of restoration of independence.

In March 1990, elections to the Supreme Soviet of the Estonian SSR were also organised. These were the first more or less democratic elections in a period of fifty years, in which all the most important political forces participated. **Arnold Rüütel**, who had been chairman of the previous Presidium of the Supreme Soviet of the ESSR since 1983, was elected as chairman of the new Supreme Soviet. The government of the ESSR headed by **Indrek Toome** (in office 1988-1990) left office and **Edgar Savisaar** was appointed by the Supreme Soviet as the new head of the government. The smooth co-operation, which had been hoped for between the Estonian Committee, the Supreme Soviet and the government, did not come to pass.

Relations with the central powers, the period of transition. Since 1989, one of the most topical themes in relations with the central powers had been giving a legal assessment of the Molotov-Ribbentrop Pact (MRP). The Supreme Soviet of the Estonian SSR of the time condemned the MRP. The Estonian delegates succeeded in including the question of the MRP on the agenda of the supreme organ of power of the *perestroika* period, the Congress of the People's Representatives of the Soviet Union. In order to consider the question, a special committee was formed, but giving legal assessment of the secret agreement between Hitler and Stalin dragged on in Moscow. On the anniversary of the MRP on 23 August 1989, the popular fronts of the Baltic countries organised a unique protest action: an unbroken human chain was formed reaching from Vilnius to Tallinn.

The length of the Baltic chain was 600 kilometres and about 2 million people participated in it. They claimed freedom for the Baltic countries. The action of the Baltic chain essentially contributed to the world-wide recognition of the problems of Estonia, Latvia and Lithuania.

In Moscow, the joint event of the Baltic nations was labelled as an action promoting nationalist hysterics. At the end of 1989, the Congress of the People's Representatives of the Soviet Union finally admitted the existence of the secret protocols of the MRP and declared them unlawful. This created a basis for subsequent developments.

The Supreme Soviet, which had been elected in the early spring, adopted a decision about the statehood of Estonia on 30 March 1990, which proclaimed a **period of transition** that would end when independence was restored. In May the same year, the name of the Estonian Republic was restored, public use of the symbols of the Estonian SSR (anthem, flag and coat of arms)

Lenin in departure in front of the Communist Party headquarters in Tallinn.

Tension on Toompea in August of 1991.

was forbidden, and it was stated that only laws adopted in Estonia were valid.

These acts activated the forces supporting the empire in Moscow as well as in Estonia. At the all-Union level, Estonia was threatened with an economic blockade and introduction of a state of emergency. Local "Internationalists" organised a noisy meeting in Toompea on 15 May 1990, and even attempted to invade the Toompea Palace (the site of the government and the Supreme Soviet). Shortly afterwards, **strikes** began in the factories of all-Union importance. The economic and political pressure of the central power on Estonia and the other Baltic countries increased. Moscow's aim was to make the Baltic countries accept the agreement of federation (which the authorities in Moscow now supported), to tie them to the Soviet Union again. **In January 1991**, the supporters of the empire attempted to "discipline" the Baltic countries by using military force. Several civilian targets were attacked, first in Vilnius and then in Riga. The attacks resulted in **casualties**. In Estonia neither public military encounters nor casualties occurred.

In January 1991, the rest of the world and the democratic forces in Russia increased their support for the Baltic nations. Moscow kept up the hope that the Soviet Union would stay intact. They even arranged a referendum to that effect.

The Baltic countries carried out an **anticipatory referendum** in March 1991.

In Estonia, the question "are you for the restoration of independence and sovereignty of the Estonian Republic?" was answered positively by 77.8 per cent of the people voting. Even about one-third of the Russian-speaking population supported the independence of Estonia. The results of the referendum prevented any negotiations with the central powers on the agreement of federation. The negotiations could take place only on one question, which was **restoration of the independence of Estonia.**

Estonian programme of independent economy. After Gorbachev had taken office, some economic innovations began in the Soviet Union. In 1987, an extensive plan of economic reform was made public, which aimed at thorough improvement of the Socialist planned economy. The result of the economic innovations was **a reformed planned economy**: the extent of centralisation of the economy was reduced, the independence of business establishments was increased, and foreign trade and the system of payment were liberalised. But the reform did not bring about a revolutionary change in economic life.

In the Estonian SSR, the economy was reformed according to the Soviet pattern. But the peculiarity of the process here was that a **concept of an independent Estonian economy** *(Isemajandava Eesti kontseptsioon)* was worked out.

The concept was based on the article "Proposition: Introducing an Independent Economy in the Estonian SSR" *(Ettepanek: kogu Eesti NSV täielikule isemajandamisele)* by Siim Kallas, Tiit Made, Edgar Savisaar and Mikk Titma, published in the newspaper "Edasi" on 26 September 1987. The essence of the concept was economic separation of the Estonian SSR from the all-Union economic complex. In order to achieve that goal, the Estonian economy had to be subject to local administration, a local budget had to be introduced, and a transfer to goods-for-money or market relationships had to be carried out, including the introduction of a local currency.

The administration of the Estonian SSR of the time had a negative attitude towards the concept, but among the population the idea found unprecedented support and some research establishments started relevant studies. By 1989, **an extensive plan for economic reform** was drafted, which served as a basis for the law on "Fundamentals of the independent economy of Estonia," which was adopted (after nation-wide discussions) in May 1989. At this time, the planned economy was improved on a local level, that is in the Estonian SSR, adopting laws on prices, businesses, farms, banks, and so forth.

This process laid the foundation for continuing economic reforms in the future. The central power of the Soviet Union agreed to give way to a certain extent and at the end of 1989, a law was adopted by the Supreme Soviet of the Soviet Union on the economic independence of the Baltic countries.

The economic programme of the Savisaar cabinet was actually an improved version of the concept of an independent economy. In the process of applying it, prices were gradually liberated; the budget of the Estonian SSR was separated from that of the USSR; and the existing monetary system was reformed (on 1 January 1990 the Bank of Estonia was restored).

These economic reforms were mainly aimed at **breaking down the system of a centralised economy**, which was unavoidably accompanied by economic decline and imbalance. In the economy, in spite of the **growth of private sector**, state regulation existed. The essence of the change was that in the heyday of the planned economy state monopolies existed, but now businesses had taken control. The goal of the establishments was to make as great a profit as possible. This caused a rise of prices.

Therefore inflation was continuously high from the autumn of 1990. This forced people to make use their money and they started to buy supplies for the future, which brought more money into circulation from their bank ac-

Dangers of independence.

counts. Special coupons were introduced granting the right to buy a certain rationed amount of goods. Long queues in the shops became a regular feature of the everyday routine, as well as unpaid salaries and pensions.

Restoration of sovereignty. The internal crisis of the Soviet Union culminated in the attempted *coup d'état* by the reactionary forces in August 1991. A State of Emergency was declared over the whole territory of the Soviet Union, and government of the state passed into the hands of the State Committee of the State of Emergency. The aim of the *coup d'état* was to preserve the integrity of the Soviet Union.

The government and the Supreme Soviet of the Estonian Republic declared the orders of the State Committee of State of Emergency illegal. The attempted *coup d'état* ruled out negotiations with the central powers and provided Estonia (and other union republics of the Soviet Union) a historic chance to restore its sovereignty. By agreement between different political groups, in the late hours of 20 August, the Supreme Soviet of the Estonian Republic adopted the "Decision on National Independence of Estonia," which restored sovereignty *de jure* as well as *de facto*. International recognition was requested for the restored sovereignty. In order to work out the constitution of the Estonian Republic, a Constitutional Assembly was formed, comprising an equal number of members of the Supreme Soviet and the Congress of Estonia.

On 21 August, the attempted *coup d'état* failed in Moscow. This was accompanied by normalisation of the situation in Estonia. The restored independence received international recognition in a couple of weeks. On 6 September 1991, the State Soviet of the USSR recognised the total independence of the Baltic states and formed a delegation for negotiations with the Estonian Republic. On 17 September 1991, Estonia and the other Baltic states were accepted into the United Nations. The Estonian Republic appeared on the map of the world as an independent and sovereign state once again.

55. The Estonian Republic in the years 1991 to 1997

Building a constitutional state. After restoration of sovereignty the process of building a constitutional governmental power began. The draft of the new constitution was compiled by the Constitutional Assembly by the end of 1991, and a nation-wide discussion of the draft took place. By a referendum on 28 June 1992, the constitution was accepted and it came into force on 3 July 1992.

Simultaneously, preparations took place for elections to the *Riigikogu* (Parliament) and for a state president, on the basis of the election law adopted in April 1992. Political groups also started to organise for the elections to be held on 20 September 1992. By the summer of 1992, coalitions had been formed and their preferences for presidential candidates had become clear: Arnold Rüütel (Coalition Party), Lennart Meri (Pro Patria), Rein Taagepera (National Front) and Lagle Parek (Estonian National Independence Party).

In the first round of the presidential elections, none of the candidates received more than half of the votes. Therefore the *Riigikogu* had to choose as president one of the two candidates who had received the majority of the votes – either Rüütel with 195,743 votes, or Meri with 138,317 votes. On 5 October 1992, the *Riigikogu* elected Lennart Meri as President of the newly independent Estonian Republic.

In the elections to the *Riigikogu*, eight coalitions, five parties, 39 associations and 25 individual candidates participated. About 67 per cent of the citizens entitled to vote took part in the elections. Representatives of nine coalitions or parties were elected. Pro Patria *(Isamaa)*, which had the biggest representation in *Riigikogu*, formed the government in coalition with the Estonian National Independence Party (ESRP) and the Moderates *(Mõõdukad)* coalition. The leader of Pro Patria, Mart Laar, became the head of government.

After the elections to the *Riigikogu*, the Congress of Estonia and the Estonian government-in-exile were dissolved. At the end of 1992, the *Riigikogu* appointed Rait Maruste as chairman of the Supreme Court, and at the beginning of the following year, Eerik-Juhan Truuväli was named legal chancellor. On 27 May 1993, the Supreme Court held its first session in Tartu. Thus the basic foundations of statehood had been laid by spring 1993: legislative power (the *Riigikogu*), executive power (the government), and judicial authority (the Supreme Court).

Transition to a market economy. The restoration of independence created the political and economic preconditions for the transition to a

Lennart Meri, the first president of Estonia after the restoration of independence.

market economy. The monetary reform carried out in the summer of 1992 became the foundation of economic reform. The Estonian *kroon* (EEK) was tied to the German *Deutschmark* (DEM) at the ratio of 1 DEM = 8 EEK. Monetary reform gave Estonia a chance to leave the "rouble zone" and focus its economic policy on Estonian needs. In a couple of months, a balance was achieved in the domestic economy and inflation slowed down.

The Estonian economy became open to the West, and economic integration of Estonia into Europe is a process which cannot be reversed. On 1 January 1995, a free trade agreement between Estonia and the European Union became effective. Today, more than 60 per cent of the Estonian economy is linked to member states of the EU. In addition, Estonia has concluded agreements on free trade with several other countries (Norway, Latvia, Lithuania, the Czech Republic, and others).

In the process of transition to a market economy, important roles have been played by privatisation, development of banking, property reform, and restructuring Soviet agriculture on the basis of the private farm system. All these processes, especially reorganisation of agriculture, have developed with difficulty and have met with setbacks.

Development of the legislative environment, promoting enterprise and keeping the state budget in balance have facilitated better arrangement of economic life. In the years 1992 to 1995, on average 12,000 to 14,000 new businesses were opened. The growth of the role of small business, the private sector and foreign investment has been a characteristic feature of development.

Withdrawal of foreign military units. For the consolidation of independence, it was vital that the occupying army should leave Estonia and its military bases (including the naval bases in Tallinn and Paldiski) needed to be closed. In September 1992, there were about 40,000 soldiers of the Russian army on Estonian territory. About 2 per cent of the territory of the state were in the possession of foreign military forces, on which 570 military units of various sizes and functions were located.

International organisations and the public supported the idea that foreign forces had to be withdrawn from Estonia. In November 1992, the General Assembly of the UN adopted a resolution on withdrawal of foreign forces from the Baltic countries. The issue of removing the military forces was one of the main questions of the negotiations between Estonia and Russia. Russia tried to link the withdrawal of its military forces to a demand for changing Estonian domestic legislation (including the law of citizenship), and later for compensation to be paid to Russia. A breakthrough in the negotiations was only achieved in July 1994 at the meeting of the presidents Boris Yeltsin and Lennart Meri in Moscow, which took place due to the support of the western countries. At their meeting, the heads of state signed agreements on withdrawing the military forces from Estonia and giving social guarantees to those retired from military service.

According to these agreements (the "July agreements"), the Russian military left Estonia on 31 August 1994. The Estonian Republic provided army pensioners who stayed in Estonia with an option to apply for a residence permit. A separate agreement was concluded about abolishing the Paldiski training centre and dismantling the nuclear reactors. These tasks were completed by 31 September 1995 according to the agreement.

The agreements were approved on an international level and strengthened the international position of Estonia. Within Estonia, they caused sharp political debates.

From the point of view of the development of Estonian statehood, the withdrawal of the military served as an end point in the process of regaining independence.

Development of statehood 1993-1997. According to the constitution adopted in 1992, Estonia is a democratic parliamentary republic, where the supreme power of state is vested in the people. The development of legislative and executive power has indeed progressed in the framework of the constitution. According to the law on parties of 1994 a multiparty system has developed. The government (prime minister, twelve ministers and two ministers without portfolio) acts according to the law of the government of the Republic adopted in 1995.

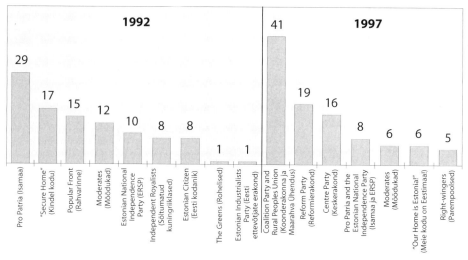

Results from the Riigikogu elections.

In March 1995, elections to the *Riigikogu* took place, in which seven coalitions, nine parties and twelve individual candidates participated. About 68.9 per cent of the citizens eligible to vote took part. The majority of votes were received by the Coalition Party *(Koonderakond)* and the Rural Peoples Union *(Maarahva Ühendus)*, which altogether gained 41 seats.

Presidential elections were held in 1996. According to the constitution, the president had to be elected by a two-thirds majority in the *Riigikogu*. The different political groupings nominated two candidates: Lennart Meri and Arnold Rüütel. But at the elections, which took place in the *Riigikogu* on 27-28 August 1996, neither candidate received the required majority, thus the president had to be elected by an electoral college, which assembled on 20 September 1996. Beside the members of the *Riigikogu*, the electoral college included representatives of all local councils. The electoral college nominated three more candidates: Tunne Kelam, Siiri Oviir and Enn Tõugu, though none of the three made it to the final round of the election. On 20 September, the electoral college elected Lennart Meri as President of the Estonian Republic with 196 votes. Arnold Rüütel received 126 votes.

The legal system of Estonia has been built on the basis of the principle of legal continuity, following the example of the legislation of the member countries of the European Union. The main legislation regulating the function of the state and its economy has been adopted. The Estonian legal system is related to the continental legal systems and is based on Roman law. The Estonian court system has three stages: county and city courts, circuit courts and the Supreme Court. The court system relies on the law of courts and the law of the status of a judge, adopted in 1991. Judges are appointed for life.

In the newly independent Estonia, two local government elections have taken place (in 1993 and 1996) according to the law of elections to local governments. In working out the respective legislation, the European Charter of Local Government has been used. Non-citizens can participate in local government elections.

Human rights in Estonia. The legislation of the Estonian Republic does not allow discrimination against people on the basis of their nationality, race, sex, profession, financial or social status, religion, or cultural background. Everyone has the right to preserve his or her ethnic or religious identity. The law of cultural autonomy, adopted in 1993, grants ethnic minorities (with at least 3,000 members) with the rights to unite and form institutions of self-government prescribed by legislation in order to preserve their identity based on culture, religion or language. In addition to the governmental bodies, non-governmental organisations deal with the problems of human rights. The most important of these are the Estonian Institute of Human Rights and the Presidential Roundtable.

The Estonian Republic has joined several international agreements on human rights. Estonia has signed the European Convention on Human Rights and has accepted the principles of the documents of the Organisation of Security and Co-operation in Europe (OSCE) adopted in Helsinki, Vienna, Madrid and Copenhagen. On 22 March 1996, the *Riigikogu* ratified the European Convention on Human Rights.

The people who came to Estonia after World War II posed a serious problem. The law of citizenship adopted in 1995 regulates the relationship of non-citizens with the Estonian Republic.

Various missions (OSCE, UN, the Council of Europe) and international institutes that have studied the state of human rights in Estonia, have not found any considerable violations.

Between the East and West. The international policy of the Estonian Republic is clearly directed to the West, in order to become as closely involved as possible with Europe and not to be tied to the East – to Russia – again. Due to the geopolitical location of Estonia, the most secure guarantees to its sovereignty would lie in joining the Northern Atlantic Treaty Organisation (NATO) and the European Union.

The process of integration towards that end has developed favourably due to the stability of domestic policy and successful economic policy. On 14 May 1994, Estonia was accepted as a full member of the Council of Europe. Simultaneously, preparations began to join the European Union. On 9 May 1994, Estonia became an associate member of the European Union.

Estonian co-operation with NATO has also been successful and on 3 February 1994, Estonia became a member of Partnership for Peace (PFP). Estonia is also an associate partner of the Western European Union (WEU). Co-operation on defence with NATO and neutral countries has essentially strengthened the Estonian defence forces and thus gradually creates the practical preconditions for joining the defence structures of Western Europe.

In the foreign policy of the Estonian Republic, a central place is occupied by the Nordic countries and the other Baltic States: Latvia and Lithuania. Co-operation with the other Baltic countries mainly takes place through the framework of two organisations, the Baltic Council of Ministers and the Baltic Assembly. On 13 September 1993, a free trade agreement between the Baltic countries was signed in Tallinn. The three Baltic states are also joined into a joint visa zone. There is close co-operation between the defence forces, police and border guards. In September 1994, an agreement on forming a joint Baltic peacekeeping battalion (BALTBAT) was signed. Estonia actively participates in the work of the Council of Baltic Sea States (CBSS), to facilitate the stability of economic and political development in Baltic region.

The relationship with Russia has developed in conditions of mutual opposition. The concepts of close foreign countries and defence of the foreign policy of Russia are hostile to Estonia. On political grounds Russia has also given up economic co-operation. Various political forces in Russia have not lost hope of restoring their former empire.

Relations between Estonia and Russia are made more complicated by the problem of the border, because initially Estonia proceeded on the basis of the border fixed by the Tartu Peace Treaty of 1920. The Russian side did not accept this. In February 1993, Russia adopted as its official borders the former borders of the Russian Soviet Federal Socialist Republic with the other union republics of the USSR. On 18 June 1994, president Yeltsin issued a decree on unilateral designation of the frontier with Estonia. Further negotiations did not bring any concrete results. At the end of 1996, the Estonian delegation gave up the claim to mention the Tartu Peace Treaty in the Estonian-Russian border agreement, which meant giving up the disputed areas as well. In spite of this, Russia has not agreed to sign the border agreement.

Estonian co-operation with other members of the Commonwealth of Independent States (CIS) has been more successful than with Russia. In August 1993, Estonia opened its embassy in Kiev and has developed mutually beneficial contacts with Ukraine. Estonia has received support in its opposition to Russian claims and assisted Ukraine in integrating into Europe, as well as advising on economic reforms in Ukraine.

56. Estonians in the World

Before World War II, the number of Estonians in the world was estimated at about 1,175,000 people. About 15 per cent of Estonians lived outside the borders of Estonia, mainly in the Soviet Union. World War II made fundamental changes to the number and location of Estonians in the world. The total number decreased by about 9 per cent during the war. At the same time, the proportion of Estonians living abroad grew to 17 per cent. After the war, the Estonian nation could be divided into three: Estonians living in Estonia, émigré Estonians living in the West, and Estonians living in the Soviet Union.

Development of émigré Estonian communities. The movement of Estonians to the West started at the turn of the nineteenth and twentieth centuries. At that time, some of the Estonians who had settled in Russia resettled, mainly to the United States of America and Canada. During the period of the Estonian Republic, Estonians left their home country for all parts of the world, but the number of emigrants was limited compared to the number of Estonians living in Russia. The numerous community of Estonian émigrés came into being during World War II, and the primary reason for this was **political**; thousands of people (not just those who had co-operated with the Germans) fled the country because of fear of the Soviet occupation. Many Estonians also remained in the West as former prisoners of war or having been deported to German labour camps during the war. The majority of these people – **refugees** – had assem-

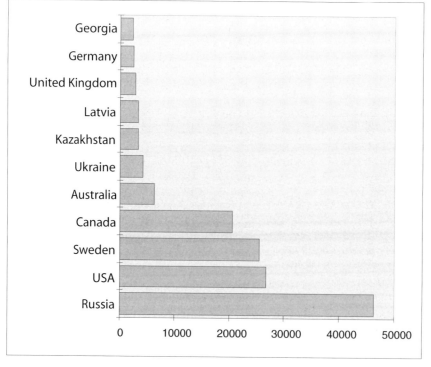

The main countries in which Estonians living abroad are located.

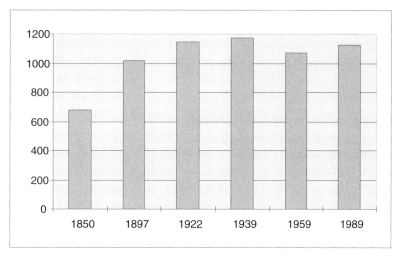

The change in numbers of Estonians in the world (thousand individuals).

bled in Sweden and other countries of Western Europe. From there they were sent to camps for **displaced persons** (DP camps).

The Soviet Union considered that all refugees "belonged" to them, as it had occupied their home country and incorporated it. Therefore they sent their representatives to the camps of displaced people to conduct active propaganda that the refugees should voluntarily return to Estonia. Simultaneously, the Soviet Union applied pressure to the governments of several countries, to make them co-operate in the returning of refugees to their home country whether they wanted to return or not.

Some states yielded to pressure from the USSR. In October 1945, the Swedish parliament decided to repatriate 167 Baltic refugees, among them about ten Estonians. That day has since been known as a dark day in Swedish history. About 15,000 Estonians returned to Estonia voluntarily or were **repatriated** by the spring of 1946, mainly from the areas of Europe controlled by the Soviet Union.

All in all, about **65,000 Estonians** stayed in the Western countries. The majority settled in Sweden and Germany, with smaller numbers in Austria, Denmark, Belgium, and France. The situation of the Estonians in Sweden (about 20,000 people) was taken under control by the Swedish government and their integration into society was relatively painless. The refugees who had stayed in other countries began to resettle, through the mediation of the International Refugee Organisation (IRO).

In the years 1947 to 1953, more than 27,000 Estonians found a new home country for themselves, with the assistance of the IRO. The majority of them (more than 40 per cent) went to the United States of America, but also to Australia, Canada, Great Britain and Sweden. A fairly large colony of Estonians remained in Germany, and small numbers settled in many other countries.

By the beginning of the 1950s, the process of refugee resettlement had slowed down. At that time the largest number of Estonians lived in Sweden (20,000), Canada (19,000), the USA (16,000), the Federal Republic of Germany (4,000) and Australia (6,500). The most important centres of Estonian émigrés were **Toronto, New York, Stockholm** and **Sydney.**

Activity of the expatriate communities. The most important output of the expatriate society was **political activity**, which relied on various expatriate organisations.

Initially, Sweden became an important centre of the political life of émigré Estonians, because the majority of the leading politicians of the Estonian Republic who had managed to flee their home country had settled there. It was in Sweden that the first émigré organisations were founded – the Estonian Committee *(Eesti Komitee)* in 1944, and Estonian National Fund *(Eesti Rahvusfond)* in 1945. After this, the **Estonian National Council** *(Eesti Rahvusnõukogu* - ERN) was established as a co-operative body of Estonian political parties. The supporters of the

ERN formed a **government-in-exile** in 1954, headed by the eldest active member of the constitutional government of the Estonian Republic (the "Otto Tief government"), **August Rei.**

Unfortunately this government was not accepted by the **Consulate General** of the Estonian Republic in New York, which considered itself the essential representative of the Estonian state abroad. This view was shared by the most important organisations of émigré Estonians in North America, the Estonian National Committee in the United States (*Eesti Rahvuskomitee Ühendriikides* – ERKÜ) and the Estonian Central Council (*Eesti Kesknõukogu* – EKN), which functioned as the representative body of Estonians in Canada. Those groups formed the **Estonian World Council** (*Ülemaailmne Eesti Kesknõukogu* – ÜEKN) as a counterbalance to the government-in-exile. The supporters of the ÜEKN in Sweden established the Estonian Mission in Sweden (*Rootsi Eestlaste Esindus* – REE).

In simplified terms, these groups were supporters of the policies of Konstantin Päts. In opposition to this, the Swedish émigré community (the ERN and government-in-exile) had adopted political ideas from the period before 1934.

An important feature of the domestic policy of the émigré society were **the émigré Estonian newspapers**: "*Vaba Eesti Sõna*" (Free Estonian Word, from ÜEKN, ERKÜ) published in New York, "*Meie Elu*" (Our Life, from EKN) published in Toronto and "*Teataja*" (The Gazette, from ERN) published in Stockholm. In addition to these, a neutral "*Vaba Eestlane*" (The Free Estonian) was published in Toronto.

In spite of the **differences of opinion** between the émigré organisations and their leaders, the main result of their activities was that the majority of Western countries did not recognise the annexation of the Estonian Republic by the Soviet Union *de jure*. The country that came closest to recognition was Sweden. An effective campaign to gain support in the Western countries for non-recognition of the Soviet occupation was also carried out by joint organisations of expatriates of all three Baltic states (BATUN, etc.).

Political disagreements did not hinder active **cultural activity** of the émigré Estonian community, which had already begun in the refugee camps. In co-operation with Latvians and Lithuanians, the **Baltic University** (active in 1945-49) in Hamburg and the Baltic Institute in Bonn were organised. Active literary, dramatic and artistic activities had also begun in the refugee camps.

Lively cultural activity continued after the refugees had resettled to their new home countries. It found expression in the scout movement, amateur dramatic and artistic groups, student societies and corporations. From 1967, the so-called "forest universities" were organised, where university lecturers would deliver lectures. In 1972, the first **world gathering of free Estonians** (ESTO) took place in Toronto. In several countries, **Estonian Houses** acted as

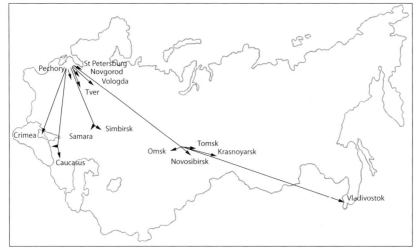

Main routes of Estonian emigration in 1858-1918.

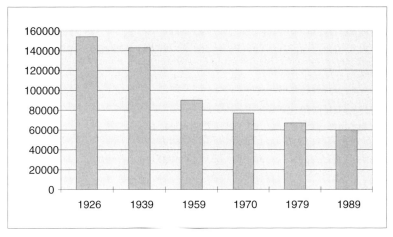

The change in number of Estonians according to Soviet censuses that live outside the Baltic countries.

centres of Estonian culture. **Estonian** *émigré* **literature** has been a unique cultural phenomenon: Estonian domestic literature achieved a level equal to it only in the 1960s.

In conclusion, the émigré Estonian society guaranteed continuity and development of Estonian national culture abroad. Beside political and cultural activities, the émigré Estonians succeeded in managing their everyday lives.

Relations between émigré and local Estonians. Contacts between the émigré and local Estonians were few and random in character during the "cold war" period that followed World War II. The Estonian SSR was closed behind the "iron curtain" together with the whole of the Soviet empire. It was only after the death of Stalin that the "iron curtain" began to be lifted slightly.

In the 1950s, contacts between émigré and Estonia began to be restored gradually and cautiously. They were mainly **personal contacts**, which in the prevailing conditions meant correspondence and rare visits to the home country. Contacts were possible only in one direction – from abroad to Estonia. No official contacts were established in this period.

Private contacts with the home country induced contradictory feelings in the expatriate circles. The groupings that considered any communication with Estonia inadvisable, because they saw it as an implied recognition of the Soviet occupation, were relatively strong.

Alongside personal contacts, **cultural contacts** acquired increasing importance in the 1960s and were even extended in the following decade. The Soviet leadership tried to make use of these contacts, hoping to demonstrate to the world how "liberal" the ruling regime was. In the Estonian SSR, official propaganda was increased to entice the émigré Estonians into returning to their home country. Propagandist literature was sent to foreign countries and a newspaper directed towards expatriate Estonians, *Kodumaa* (Homeland), was published. The propaganda was co-ordinated by the **Committee for Developing Cultural Contacts with Émigré Estonians** (*Väliseestlastega Kultuurisidemete Arendamise Komitee* – VEKSA), established in 1960. Although formally VEKSA was a public organisation, its activity was controlled by the KGB.

For home-based Estonians, an important role was played by **scientific contacts**, which initially were restricted to correspondence between scientists, exchange of publications, and so forth. From the 1970s onwards, home-based Estonians were invited to deliver papers at scientific conferences abroad. From the side of the Estonian SSR, these contacts were mainly mediated by VEKSA, which had to guarantee the loyalty of the scientists travelling abroad, as well as feedback from them. After returning home everybody had to write a report about their visit.

The **new attack of Russification** made the rare contacts between émigré and local Estonians even more random. Official propaganda also became increasingly aggressive. As a result of the growing ideological pressure several creative people left Estonia.

Relations between émigré and local Estonians began to be restored in the second half of the 1980s and broke free of all restrictions when sovereignty was restored in 1991.

Estonians in Russia. The mass exodus of Estonians to Russia began in the middle of the nineteenth century. By the end of the **mass exodus** (1858–1918) Estonian settlements had been established in many regions of Russia. In 1917, more than 200,000 Estonians, about one-sixth of the total number of Estonians in the world, lived in the territory of Russia.

After that, the number of Estonians in Russia began to decrease quickly. This was because of the enforced collectivisation carried out in the Soviet Union in the 1920s, mass repression, prohibition of education in the mother tongue, and later on, the events of war. Thus during World War II, the majority of Estonians living on the Russian shore of Lake Peipsi were repatriated by the German occupation authorities.

In the post-war years, a large number of Estonians resettled from Russia to Estonia. This movement was especially extensive in the second half of the 1940s and in the 1950s. Altogether about 70,000 people returned to Estonia in the post-war years.

The Estonians in Russia served as a convenient "staff reserve" for the Soviet authorities. They were in the majority in the leadership of the Estonian SSR until the middle of the 1980s. At the same time, some Estonians moved from Estonia to other regions of the Soviet Union, being represented almost in all union republics of the former USSR. This movement was not very numerous. Some Estonians still live there.

Estonians today. According to the census of 1989, there were 963,281 Estonians in Estonia. At more or less the same time, there were about 150,000 Estonians in other regions of the world, forming 13 per cent of the total number of Estonians. Of Estonians abroad, about 86,000 lived in the Western countries and about 63,000 in other union republics of the Soviet Union, which still existed at that time. The collapse of the Soviet Union in 1991 scattered Estonians to the new states which emerged from the ruins of the former USSR. The war in the Caucasus has endangered the lives of Estonians living there. Therefore many Estonians have returned as refugees from Georgia and other countries of the region.

Today, the biggest Estonian émigré community is located in Russia, where more than 45,000 people of Estonian descent live. Other numerous communities are located in the United States of America (26,700), Sweden (25,500) and Canada (20,500). About 80 per cent of émigré Estonians live in these four counties. There are 27 or 28 countries in the world where the Estonian population consists of at least a hundred people.

It is difficult for Estonians living abroad for a long period to preserve their ethnic identity. The émigré Estonians in Western countries, as well as those in Russia, are gradually **assimilating** into their surrounding environment. An example is given by the gradual decrease in the usage of Estonian as a language of communication among people of Estonian descent. Today about half the people of Estonian descent living abroad speak Estonian.

Oskar Kallas has said: "The trunk and the branches have been created to live together, otherwise the strength from the roots cannot reach the branches and they are left without the nourishing juices in spring. It is for only a limited time that the branch which has been cut off is able to exist on its nutritive supplies, but then it dries off, disappears." The strength of the roots of Estonians today is the independent Estonian state.

Chronology

Chronology

~9000 (or 7500) BC		The oldest known traces of human settlement in Estonia: the Pulli settlement near Sindi, on the bank of the Pärnu River.
~4000 (or 2500) BC		Arrival of the comb-pottery culture tribes; the Finns of the Baltic Sea region are considered to be their direct descendants.
~3000 (or 2200) BC		Arrival of the boat-axe culture tribes on Estonian territory, also marking the beginning of early husbandry and land cultivation in the region.
~1500 BC		Beginning of the Bronze Age in Estonia. General lack of metals in the area causes tools and objects to also be made of bone and stone.
~500		Beginning of the Iron Age in Estonia.
600 AD		Military expedition by Swedish King Ingvar to Estonia.
1030		Yaroslav the Wise of Kiev conquers Tartu, putting Tartu under Slav rule for the next 31 years.
1187		Estonians conquer Sweden's important trade centre, Sigtuna.
1202		**The Order of the Sword Brethren is established in Riga.**
1208		German looting raids in Ugandi give way to the Ancient Fight for Freedom.
1210		Estonian victory in the Battle of Ümera (Jumara).
1217	February	Estonian victory over the Germans in the Battle of Otepää.
	21 September	The Battle of St Matthew's Day.
1219	June	Danish military lands at Tallinn.
1220		Swedes attempting to invade Läänemaa turn back.
1223		Estonians manage to free themselves of foreign rule for brief interim. Only Tallinn is left under Danish rule.
1224	**August**	**The fall of Tartu marks the return of foreign rule across mainland Estonia.**
1227	**February**	**Defeat on Saaremaa marks the end of Estonia's Ancient Fight for Freedom.**
1236		Lithuanians crush the Sword Brethren in the Battle of Saule. What remains of the Order is united with the Teutonic Order, thereby forming its Livonian branch (called Livonian Order).

1238		The Stensby Agreement puts Tallinn, Rävala, Harjumaa and Virumaa under Danish rule; Sakala, Järvamaa, Mõhu, Nurmekund and parts of Vaiga given to the Livonian Order. The Tartu Diocese keeps Ugandi, Jogentagana and parts of Vaiga. Most of Läänemaa and the islands remain under the Saaremaa-Läänemaa Diocese.
1242		**The Battle of Lake Peipus on ice; the border between East and West (between the Order and Russia) remains intact for centuries.**
1248		Tallinn receives its town rights.
1343	**23 April**	**The St George's Day Uprising breaks out in Harjumaa.**
	4 May	Estonian "kings" killed in Paide.
	14 May	Estonians suffer great losses in battle with the Order.
	24 July	Beginning of the uprising on Saaremaa.
1345	Winter	Suppression of the people of Saaremaa marks the end of St George's Day Uprising.
1346		**Danish King sells North Estonia to the Livonian Order.**
1404		Tallinn's Town Hall is completed.
1421		The fist diet is held in Livonia.
1492		Russians build the Ivangorod Fortress on the eastern bank of the Narva River.
1502		Livonian Order Master Wolter von Plettenberg's victory in the Battle of Lake Smolino puts a stop to Moscow's westward expansion to the Baltics for some time.
1523		**Beginning of the Reformation in Estonia.**
1524	14 September	Pro-reformation city residents attack Catholic churches and cloisters.
1525		**The first known book to be printed in the Estonian language published in Lübeck.**
1558	22 January	Russian troops invade Tartu Diocese, marking the beginning of the Livonian War.
	19 July	Russians conquer Tartu.
1560	2 August	The Battle of Hoomuli – the Livonian Order's final field battle.
	20 August	Viljandi (the Order's strongest fortress in Estonia) falls to the Russians.
	October	Uprising by Estonians in Läänemaa.
1561	28 November	The Livonian Order capitulate to the King Sigismund II August of Poland; this marks the end of Old Livonia's mediaeval political structure.
1577		Having conquered nearly all of Estonia, Russians attempt to take Tallinn but no to avail. Counterattacks by Poland and Sweden nullify Russia's previous victories.
1578		First publication of Balthasar Russow's chronicles.

1583		Sweden and Russia sign an armistice at the Plyusa River. Russia had also signed a peace treaty with Poland in the previous year. The Livonian War comes to an end. Sweden is left with North Estonia, Poland takes South Estonia, and Denmark gains the island of Saaremaa.
		Jesuit college is established in Tartu.
1600-25		Victory in conflict between Sweden and Poland (vying for rule of the Baltics) goes to Sweden.
1625		The fall of Tartu to the Swedes puts an end to Polish rule of South Estonia.
1629		**A truce signed at Altmark establishes Swedish rule across mainland Estonia.**
1632		Tartu University is founded.
1645		Denmark loses Saaremaa to Sweden under the Brömsebro Peace Treaty.
1656		Russian troops attack Livonia, conquering Tartu and gaining control over much of Eastern Estonia.
1661		Peace between Russia and Sweden concluded at Kärde. The Russians are forced to give up the conquered territories and return to Russia.
1671		The policing order by Governor-general Clas Tott results in the beginning of legalised serfdom of peasants in Estonia. Serfdom in Livonia had started decades earlier.
1680		**Swedish *Rikstag* passes decision regarding widespread reduction in the Baltics.**
1684		Bengt Gottfried Forselius heads seminary for school teachers in Tartu.
1694		Swedish authorities limit powers of Livonia's local government. The system of rural advisors is broken down.
1695-97		Mass starvation. Nearly one of five Estonians dies of starvation.
1700	12 September	Russians assemble to take Narva.
	19 November	**Swedish troops led by Karl XII crush troops outside of Narva.**
1704	14 July	Russia gains control of Tartu.
1708		Some residents of Tartu deported to Russia, town fortresses completely destroyed by the Russians.
1710	29 September	Having gained control of Tallinn, Russia succeeds in taking over all of Estonia.
1721		**Under the Uusikaupunki Peace Treaty, Sweden gives Estonia and Livonia to Russia. The Baltic provinces maintain local governments, the so-called special Baltic order.**
1739		The Rosen Declaration takes away every last right of the Estonian peasantry.

1739		Translated by Anton Thor Helle, the Holy Bible is published entirely in the Estonian language for the first time.
1740-43		The Moravian Movement achieves its highpoint in Estonia.
1765		The Livonian diet is forced to take the first steps toward improving the situation of the peasantry.
1783		Regency system puts significant limits on the nobles and local governments.
1784	4 July	The "Orchard War" in Räpina.
1797		Estonians taken as conscripts into Russian military service.
1802		First publication of *"Iggaüks"* (regulations for the peasantry), marking the beginning of agriculture reform in the Baltic provinces.
1802		**University is re-opened in Tartu.**
1804		Laws on the peasantry in Estonia and Livonia put taxes on peasants and limit property rights. Village courts are established. Taxes in Livonia are calculated according to each farm's potential capacity and the registry of socage holdings and taxes imposed on them is taken into use.
1805	2 October	Major uprising of peasants in Kose-Uuemõisa, Harju region.
1807		Recruitment of peasants into the rural militia.
1816	**23 May**	**Estonian peasants freed of serfdom.**
1819	26 March	Livonian peasants freed of serfdom.
1838		Society of Educated Estonia established in Tartu.
1841	7 September	The "Pühajärve War" in Otepää.
1845		Livonian peasants active in their acceptance of the Russian Orthodox Church.
1849		Livonia's new agrarian reform law opens the way for monetary rent and complete property ownership rights.
1853		The Abja manor marks the beginning of wider farmstead ownership across Estonia.
1856		**New agrarian reform law passed in Estonia.**
1857		Publication of the newspaper "Perno Postimees" begins in Pärnu.
		Kreenholm Manufacturing starts operations in Narva.
1858	**2 June**	**The Mahtra War.**
1862		Publication of the popular edition of *"Kalevipoeg."*
1864	9 November	Rural people from Mulgimaa district present a petition to the Tsar, applying for extension of the rights of Estonians.
1865		Founding of the *"Vanemuine"* song and drama society, Tartu.
1866		**New law of parishes lays firm foundation for the self-government of rural people.**

1868		Abolition of *corvée* or serfdom.
1869	**18-20 June**	**First Estonian Song Festival, Tartu.**
1870		Completion of St Petersburg – Paldiski railway, the first in Estonia.
1872		Founding of the Estonian Society of Literati.
1878		The newspaper *"Sakala"* begins publication, Viljandi.
1882		Death of Carl Robert Jakobson.
1884		**Consecration of the blue, white and black flag of the Estonian Students Society, Otepää church.**
1887		In the course of Russification, Russian becomes the compulsory language of tuition in all Estonian schools.
1889		Reform of rural institutions severely restricts the rights of parish self-government. Russian is introduced as the official working language.
1896		Jaan Tõnisson is invited to become editor of the newspaper *"Postimees,"* Tartu.
1901		The newspaper *"Teataja"* begins publication, Tallinn.
1904		Estonians, in coalition with Russians, win the elections to the town council of Tallinn. Konstantin Päts becomes deputy mayor.
1905		The cultural movement "Noor-Eesti" (Young Estonia) comes to public attention.
	16 October	Troops fire on a public demonstration in Tallinn.
	27 November	**Meeting of the peoples' representatives of Russia, in Tartu.**
	December	Arson attacks on manor houses and action by punishment troops in Estonia.
1906		*"Vanemuine"* and *"Estonia"* become the first professional theatres in Estonia.
1909		Founding of the Estonian Folk Museum.
1914		Outbreak of the First World War.
1915		German warships appear in Estonian coastal waters. In the resulting panic the Waldhof cellulose factory in Pärnu is blown up.
1917	**2 March**	**Beginning of the February Revolution in Tallinn.**
	6 March	Commissar Jaan Poska of the *guberniya* takes office in Tallinn as representative of the Provisional Government of Russia.
	30 March	Provisional Government issues a decree on interim arrangements for the government of Estonia, which unites the majority of Estonian territory into one *guberniya* with extended rights to autonomy.
	27 October	**Bolsheviks seize power from the commissar.**
	15 November	The *Maapäev* (provisional parliament) declares itself the supreme power in Estonia.

1918	**24 February**	**Declaration of independence of the Estonian Republic, Tallinn.**
	1 March	German capture of Narva completes foreign occupation of all Estonian territory.
	11 November	Estonian Provisional Government seizes power from the leadership of the German occupation army.
	28 November	**Red Army attack on Narva marks the start of the Estonian War of Independence.**
1919	23 April	Estonian Constituent Assembly meets in Tallinn.
	23 June	*Landeswehr* (German army) troops defeated near Cēsis, Latvia.
	10 October	Constituent Assembly adopts Land Law.
1920	**2 February**	**Peace treaty with Russia signed in Tartu.**
	15 June	Constituent Assembly adopts the constitution of the Estonian Republic.
1924	1 December	Attempted communist *coup d'état* suppressed in Tallinn.
1926		Publication of first volume of Anton-Hansen Tammsaare's *Tõde ja õigus (Truth and Justice)*.
1934	12 March	Konstantin Päts and Johan Laidoner overthrow the government and introduce an authoritarian style of government.
	2 October	*Riigikogu* (parliament) dissolved and the "period of silence" begins.
1938	24 April	Päts elected as first President of the Estonian Republic.
1939	28 September	Treaty of Bases signed with Soviet Union.
1940	**17 June**	**Estonia occupied by the Red Army.**
	21 June	Soviet Union appoints new government of Estonia.
1941	14 June	Mass deportations from the Baltic countries.
	22 June	Outbreak of war between Germany and the Soviet Union.
	28 August	German Army occupies Tallinn.
1944	31 January	Estonian Local Government announces conscription to the German Army.
	9 March	Soviet Air Force bombs Tallinn.
	18 September	Jüri Uluots appoints the government of the Estonian Republic.
	24 November	**Whole territory of Estonia under the control of the Red Army.**
1944-45		The Pechory region and the area east of the Narva River incorporated into the Russian SFSR.
1944-47		**Post-war land reform carried out.**
1945		Beginning of extensive industrialisation.
1947	May	Decision made in Moscow to start collectivisation of agriculture in the Baltic union republics.
		First collective farms formed in Estonia.

1949	**25 March**	**Mass deportations.**
	Spring	Enforced collectivisation of agriculture completed in Estonia.
1950	**21-26 March**	**8th Plenary Session of the Central Committee of the Estonian Communist Party, followed by the major period of Stalinism in Estonia.**
		Deportations from the Pechory region.
		Counties (*maakond*) replaced by administrative districts.
1951		Founding of the Estonian Academy of Agriculture.
		"Voice of America" radio station begins Estonian language broadcasts.
1952		Founding of the Tallinn Pedagogical Institute.
1952-53		Estonian SSR divided into Tallinn, Tartu and Pärnu *oblasts*.
1954		**Formation of "government in exile."**
1955		First transmission of Estonian Television.
1957-65		Period of Soviets of National Economy in Estonian SSR.
1959		Transfer to eight-year compulsory education begins.
1965		Regular ferry service begins between Tallinn and Helsinki.
1967		Beginning of "forest universities" in Estonian expatriate communities.
1967-68		**Peak period of "*komsomol* opposition" in Tartu.**
1970		"Radio Liberty" begins Estonian language broadcasts.
1972	July	First "world gathering of free Estonians" (ESTO) in Toronto.
1978	July	Karl Vaino appointed as First Secretary of the Central Committee of the ECP. Party policy on national and language issues becomes more rigid.
1978-82		New period of Russification.
1979		"Baltic Appeal."
1979-89		Afghanistan War.
1980	July	Moscow Olympic Games sailing regatta, Tallinn.
	Autumn	Sporadic youth unrest in Tallinn.
		"Letter of 40."
1981		Death of Jüri Kukk in prison camp.
1986-87		**Phosphorite campaign indicates beginning of national reawakening.**
1987	23 August	Political demonstration held in Hirvepark, Tallinn.
	26 September	"*Edasi*" newspaper publishes idea of independent Estonian economy.
	12 December	Founding of Estonian Heritage Society.
	14 December	Secret decision by the Politburo of the Soviet Communist Party on outbreaks of nationalism in the Baltic union republics.

1988	February	Commemoration of Tartu Peace Treaty and anniversary of the Estonian Republic.
	1-2 April	Joint plenary meeting of the creative associations of Estonia, awakening the conscience of the intelligentsia.
		Formation of the Popular Front begins.
		Blue, black and white flag shown in public during Heritage Day in Tartu.
	June	**Karl Vaino forced to leave office, mass meeting of Popular Front at Song Festival Grounds, Tallinn.**
	July	International Movement of the Workers of the Estonian SSR formed as a counterbalance to the Popular Front.
	9-11 September	9th Plenary session of the Central Committee of the ECP, at which the Party leadership supports the people's aspirations for the first time.
	11 September	Mass event "*Eestimaa Laul*" organised by the Popular Front at the Song Festival Grounds.
	1-2 October	1st Congress of the Estonian Popular Front.
	16 November	**Adoption of Declaration of Sovereignty in Estonia begins the process of decomposition of the Soviet Union.**
1989	24 February	Blue, white and black flag raised on Pikk Hermann tower, Tallinn.
		Beginning of movement of Committees of Citizens.
	23 August	**Baltic Chain.**
	27 August	Central Committee of the Soviet Communist Party publishes statement on "the Situation in the Soviet Baltic Union Republics."
	November	Supreme Soviet of the USSR adopts a decision on transfer to independent economies in Estonia, Latvia and Lithuania.
	24 December	Supreme Soviet of the USSR recognises the existence of the secret protocols of the Molotov-Ribbentrop pact and declares them invalid.
1990	24 February	Elections to the Congress of Estonia.
	11-12 March	Congress of Estonia assembles for the first time.
	18 March	Multi-candidate elections to the Supreme Soviet of the Estonian SSR.
	23-25 March	Split of the Estonian Communist Party at its 20th Congress. Reform Communists decide to form an independent ECP.
	30 March	**Supreme Soviet of the Estonian SSR adopts a decision on "National Status of Estonia" which declares a transition period.**
	8 May	The name "Estonian Republic" is adopted instead of "Estonian SSR."
	15 May	Demonstration by supporters of the empire in Toompea, Tallinn.

	7 August	Supreme Soviet of the Estonian SSR adopts a law on the Estonian national flag and coat of arms.
1991	January	**Acts of violence by the Soviet Union in the Baltic countries.**
	3 March	Referendum on restoration of sovereignty and independence of Estonia.
	17 March	Baltic countries boycott the All-Union referendum.
	12 June	Supreme Soviet of the Estonian Republic adopts a law on the foundations of private property reform.
	19-21 August	Attempted *coup d'état* in Moscow.
	20 August	**Independent Estonian Republic restored.**
	6 September	Soviet Union recognises the independence of the Estonian Republic.
	17 September	Estonian Republic admitted to United Nations.
1992	20 June	Estonia introduces its own currency.
	28 June	**Following a referendum the constitution of the Estonian Republic is adopted.**
	20 September	**Elections for President and members of the *Riigikogu*.**
	5 October	Riigikogu begins its work. In the second round of elections in the *Riigikogu* Lennart Meri is elected President.
1993	13 May	Estonian Republic is accepted as a full member of the Council of Europe.
	17 October	Local government elections.
1994	26 July	Estonian-Russian summit meeting, Moscow.
	31 August	**Withdrawal of foreign military forces from Estonia completed.**
1995	5 March	*Riigikogu* elections.